BEYOND THE COAL RUSH

Climate change makes fossil fuels unburnable, yet global coal production has almost doubled over the last twenty years. This book explores how the world can stop mining coal – the most prolific source of greenhouse gas emissions. It documents efforts at halting coal production, focussing specifically on how campaigners are trying to stop coal mining in India, Germany and Australia. Through in-depth comparative ethnography, it shows how local people are fighting to save their homes, livelihoods and environments, creating new constituencies and alliances for the transition from fossil fuels. The book relates these struggles to conflicts between global climate policy and the national coal–industrial complex. With coal's meaning transformed from an important asset to a threat, and the coal industry declining, it charts reasons for continuing coal dependence, and how this can be overcome. It will provide a source of inspiration for energy transition for researchers in environment, sustainability and politics, as well as policymakers.

BEYOND THE COAL RUSH

A Turning Point for Global Energy and Climate Policy?

JAMES GOODMAN
(University of Technology Sydney)

LINDA CONNOR
(The University of Sydney)

DEVLEENA GHOSH
(University of Technology Sydney)

KANCHI KOHLI
(Centre for Policy Research)

JONATHAN PAUL MARSHALL
(University of Technology Sydney)

MANJU MENON
(Centre for Policy Research)

KATJA MUELLER
(Martin-Luther-University, Halle-Wittenberg)

TOM MORTON
(University of Technology Sydney)

REBECCA PEARSE
(The Australian National University)

STUART ROSEWARNE
(The University of Sydney)

CAMBRIDGE
UNIVERSITY PRESS

CAMBRIDGE
UNIVERSITY PRESS

University Printing House, Cambridge CB2 8BS, United Kingdom

One Liberty Plaza, 20th Floor, New York, NY 10006, USA

477 Williamstown Road, Port Melbourne, VIC 3207, Australia

314–321, 3rd Floor, Plot 3, Splendor Forum, Jasola District Centre, New Delhi – 110025, India

79 Anson Road, #06–04/06, Singapore 079906

Cambridge University Press is part of the University of Cambridge.

It furthers the University's mission by disseminating knowledge in the pursuit of education, learning, and research at the highest international levels of excellence.

www.cambridge.org
Information on this title: www.cambridge.org/9781108479820
DOI: 10.1017/9781108786805

First published 2020

A catalogue record for this publication is available from the British Library.

Library of Congress Cataloging-in-Publication Data
Names: Goodman, James, 1965– author.
Title: Beyond the coal rush : a turning point for global energy and climate policy? / James Goodman, University of Technology Sydney [and ten others].
Description: Cambridge, United Kingdom ; New York, NY : Cambridge University Press, 2020. | Includes bibliographical references and index.
Identifiers: LCCN 2020009073 (print) | LCCN 2020009074 (ebook) | ISBN 9781108479820 (hardback) | ISBN 9781108786805 (epub)
Subjects: LCSH: Coal trade–India. | Coal trade–Germany. | Coal trade–Australia. | Coal–Environmental aspects. | Coal–Public opinion.
Classification: LCC HD9540.5 .G63 2020 (print) | LCC HD9540.5 (ebook) | DDC 338.2/724–dc23
LC record available at https://lccn.loc.gov/2020009073
LC ebook record available at https://lccn.loc.gov/2020009074

ISBN 978-1-108-47982-0 Hardback

Contents

Figures

Tables

About the Authors

James Goodman (convening author) is a professor of political sociology and director of the Climate Justice Research Centre at the University of Technology Sydney. He researches global politics, socio-cultural change and climate justice. He has co-authored five books, including *Justice Globalism* (Sage 2013) and *Climate Upsurge: An Ethnography of Climate Movement Politics* (Routledge 2014), and has co-edited seven volumes.

Linda Connor is emeritus professor of anthropology at the University of Sydney and is a Fellow of the Academy of Social Sciences in Australia. She has conducted long-term ethnographic research into coal mining and climate change in rural and regional Australia. Publications include *Climate Change and Anthropos* (Earthscan, 2016) and *Environmental Change and the World's Futures* (Routledge 2016).

Devleena Ghosh is professor of social and political sciences at the University of Technology Sydney. She publishes in colonial, global and environmental history and has co-authored and co-edited several books, including *Colonialism and Modernity* (Allen & Unwin 2007), *Cultures of Trade: Indian Ocean Exchanges* (Scholars Press 2007) and *Teacher for Justice: Lucy Woodcock's Transnational Life* (ANU Press 2019).

Kanchi Kohli is a senior researcher at the Centre for Policy Research, New Delhi. She researches environment law, industrialisation and environment justice. She regularly writes for *Economic and Political Weekly* and has several academic publications, including the co-edited book *Business Interests and the Environmental Crisis* (SAGE-India 2016).

Jonathan Paul Marshall is a research fellow in social and political sciences at the University of Technology Sydney, where he researches the problems of energy transition. Publications include *Living on Cybermind* (Peter Land 2007), the co-authored book *Disorder and The Disinformation Society* (Routledge 2015) and several coedited volumes, including *Environmental Change and the World's Futures* (Routledge 2016).

Manju Menon is a senior fellow at the Centre for Policy Research, New Delhi. She collaborates with community organisations, regional and global networks working on decentralised resource governance, and environmental compliance of industry and energy projects. She has published popular articles and papers on the environment, law and development for over two decades.

Katja Mueller is a researcher in anthropology at Martin Luther University Halle-Wittenberg where she also coordinates the Center for Interdisciplinary Area Studies. She is linked to the University of Technology Sydney for her research in energy, mining and the environment and is affiliated with University College London for her work on digital museums.

Tom Morton is an associate professor of journalism at the University of Technology Sydney. His research focusses on environmental journalism and the communication of climate change. He is an award-winning radio journalist, and his work has been internationally recognised. He recently produced 'Beyond the Coal Rush' for ABC Radio National's *Science Show*.

Rebecca Pearse is a lecturer in sociology at the Australian National University. Her research has focussed on climate and energy policy, and on gender, social movements and climate politics. She is author of *Pricing Carbon in Australia* (Routledge 2017) and co-author of *Gender: In World Perspective* (Polity Press 2015) and *Climate Action Upsurge* (Routledge 2014).

Stuart Rosewarne is an honorary associate professor in political economy at the University of Sydney and focusses on environmental and ecological economics, socialist ecology and the political economy of gender. He has published critical analyses of capital accumulation, coal and climate policy in various journals and is a co-author of *Climate Action Upsurge* (Routledge 2014).

Foreword

Coal made the modern world, yet coal is also the key driver of climate change, the greatest ecological disruption to the planet we have known. This book seeks to explain why coal production has expanded despite the urgent reality of climate change, and highlights the pressures and possibilities for a world 'beyond coal'. The book is especially timely as it comes at a crucial historical juncture for coal. In 2017, twenty countries announced the creation of the Powering Past Coal Alliance, which commits them to phasing out coal for power generation by 2030. Major multilateral and financial institutions such as the World Bank and Lloyd's of London will no longer fund coal projects or are actively divesting from coal. In 2011, the International Energy Agency stated that coal consumption had to start declining from 2020 to preserve any chance of climate stability. And in 2019, the UN announced there could be no new coal-fired power stations.

Despite this international consensus, coal remains dominant for most industrial and industrialising countries. In many countries coal mining is integral to the national development project and has produced a highly durable coal–industrial complex. In some contexts advocacy for coal against renewable energy has become a vote winner and a central stake in national politics. Australian aspirations to become a fossil fuel 'energy superpower' directly mirror Canada's fossil fuel export policy under the conservatives. US President Donald Trump's defence of 'beautiful clean coal' in his 2018 State of the Union Address echoed Australia's former Prime Minister Tony Abbott who in 2014 claimed 'coal is good for humanity'. The political disruption is a sign of deep crisis for coal, and of a painful passage ahead for a new era in energy production.

Deeper understanding of this contest over the global future of coal, at this juncture, is urgently needed. The cultural meaning of coal is undergoing a dramatic transformation, and we need to understand the problems and possibilities this offers. The book offers a unique and original approach to these issues. In an interdisciplinary collaboration, it brings together anthropology, political economy and sociology to analyse the 'coal rush' and its aftermath. It reports on ethnographic research conducted in the central Indian state of Chhattisgarh, in Lusatia (Lausitz) in eastern Germany and on the Liverpool Plains in southeast Australia, where local people are fighting to prevent the construction of new coal mines. It tracks the emergence of a post-war 'coal–industrial complex' in the three countries, how it delivered a coal boom in the 2000s exactly at the time when global climate policy was gaining momentum, and then more recently how it has unravelled with the rapid shift into a new and rapidly intensifying state-renewables nexus.

As such, the book offers a unique combination of comparative multi-sited ethnographic study integrated with the political economy and sociology of coal-based energy. The book bridges the gap between climate policy and social action at local, national and transnational levels. The use of a comparative model uniquely captures a range of divergent but also parallel dynamics, allowing for common lessons and insights. The ethnographic investigations, paired with analysis of related political economy and policy conditions, offer a window onto the socio-ecological relations that are reshaping the future of coal. The multi-scale and comparative scope of this book reflects the logic of the coal conundrum, and breaks new ground in this increasingly crucial field.

Dipesh Chakrabarty
University of Chicago
Ortwin Renn
Institute for Advanced Sustainability Studies, Potsdam

Acknowledgements

The authors would like to thank all the research participants who shared their time with us for this book. We are very grateful for their many insights into the process of contesting proposed coal mines. We also would like to thank the additional researchers, interpreters, transcribers, photographers and journalists, as well as the administrative workers at our institutions who helped us to establish and complete the research project on which this book is based. We would also like to thank our respective universities and other institutions that have supported us in undertaking the project. Thanks are also due to the Australian Research Council, which supported the project between 2014 and 2017 through a Discovery Project, 'The Coal Rush and Beyond: Climate Change, Coal Reliance and Contested Futures'. This book would not have been possible without the commitment of this Australian governmental agency to exploring key challenges that face societies, not least among them the challenge of climate change and decarbonisation. Finally, we would like to thank Cambridge University Press and their staff: it has been a great pleasure to work with them to bring this book to fruition.

Introduction

The burning of coal has powered the modern world. Western industrial capitalism was founded on coal, and coal industries became a symbol of human progress. The invention of coal-fired steam traction, what Andreas Malm (2016) describes as an 'earth-shattering exploit', was critical to industrial capitalism. Energy from coal enabled the creation of the factory system in Britain, 'irreversibly changing the scale, nature and location of industrial enterprise' (Freese 2005: 67). Factories and railways driven by steam engines spread first across Europe and then the United States. As William Jasper Nicolls wrote in 1898, in his *Coal Catechism*, 'With Coal, we have light, strength, power, wealth, and civilisation; without Coal we have darkness, weakness, poverty, and barbarism' (Nichols 1906: 6–7). Coal remains the fuel of choice for high-income countries, and subsequently has fuelled successive waves of industrial development, most recently in China and India. Today, coal-fired power accounts for about 38 per cent of global electricity (IEA 2018b).

Coal is also a key driver of climate change. Coal is especially rich in carbon: when black coal is burnt, it produces almost three times its weight in carbon dioxide (EIA 2019). Atmospheric chemist Paul Crutzen and biologist Eugene Stoermer (2000) famously dated the beginning of the proposed new geological epoch, the 'Anthropocene', from the invention of the Watt/Boulton coal-fired steam engine in 1784. There are many other theories about the duration, onset and causes of the Anthropocene, but dependence on coal is a common feature. Coal currently accounts for almost half of global fuel-based emissions, and 80 per cent of the world's remaining coal reserves need to remain unburnt if the world is to meet the climate targets agreed at the 2015 United Nations (UN) Paris summit (McGlade and Ekins 2015). Yet, during the first decade of the twenty-first century, under the UN's Kyoto Protocol, world coal production almost doubled. While countries in high-income countries failed to reduce coal dependence, China, India and other industrialising countries embraced coal-fired power as the foundation for economic development and poverty reduction (IEA 2017). In an interview for this book, India's former Environment Minister, Jairem Ramesh, claimed this to be an inescapable necessity:

> Right now we are 1.25 billion and we'll be 1.7 billion by the year 2050. Given our demographic pressures, given the fact that we have to grow at about 7.5% to 8% per year, India will need to at least double its coal consumption in the next 15 years. There's no escaping that. That's what I call the cruel coal conundrum as far as India is concerned. Even with the most optimistic of assumptions on solar and wind and nuclear and hydropower, 55% of our electricity would still come from coal. I don't see India getting out of this trap of increasing coal consumption. I don't like it but it's a reality.
>
> *(Interview, Ramesh 2016)*

This book confronts the global coal conundrum. We seek to explain why coal production has expanded in the context of climate change and highlight the pressures and possibilities for a world 'beyond coal'. We link local struggles over coal mining in India, Germany and Australia with the national and global politics of climate policy. Each of these struggles has lasted a decade or more, dividing communities and creating a pervasive sense of uncertainty and insecurity. While these localised wars of attrition are fought out, an important shift in coal's status has been underway, reflecting the advancing climate crisis and the related global and national climate policy commitments. Coal is now a risky asset, and its future is under question at multiple levels.

Certainly, from 2012, the coal rush of the early twentieth century appeared to be slowing: coal prices plummeted, and it looked like a structural shift to renewable power was underway, especially in China. In its 2015 *World Energy Outlook*, the International Energy Agency (2015: 25) predicted 'turbulent times ahead' for coal, a 'reversal of fortune' in the face of growing reliance on renewable energy. Global coal production had peaked in 2013 and began to fall in 2014; there was a slight recovery in 2017 and 2018, but not to 2013 levels (IEA 2018b). At the same time, a new 'comprehensive' climate agreement, embodied in the goals agreed by 195 countries at the 2015 Paris Climate Summit, was creating new uncertainty for coal advocates and investors. Efforts at rehabilitation, through the rhetoric of 'clean coal', promoted for instance by the US Trump administration in its only public event at the 2017 UN climate talks in Bonn, have been widely challenged (Harvey 2017).

The coal mines we focus on in this book were first proposed at the height of the 'coal rush'. They were developed by some of the largest mining and energy conglomerates in the world – India's Adani corporation in Chhattisgarh, central India; BHP Billiton, based in the UK and Australia and the Chinese state-owned Shenhua Group on Australia's Liverpool Plains; and the Swedish state-owned company Vattenfall in Lusatia, Eastern Germany. All these projects were strongly supported by respective government authorities but were heavily contested and delayed (and, in the BHP and Vattenfall cases, halted).

Whether or not they have been successful, one key effect of these local struggles, and many others like them, is to expose what Barbara Freese (2005: 166) calls the 'invisible power' of coal. Freese notes that coal mines and coal-fired power stations tend to be located far from major cities and population centres, making it difficult to expose the connections between electricity use, the burning of coal and its contribution to climate change. The varying forms of activism and protest we describe seek to make the power of coal visible in the public sphere (DeLuca and Peeples 2002).

Actions such as the *Ende Gelände* (End Coal) protests in Germany in May 2016, which involved coordinated acts of civil disobedience at the Schwarze Pumpe coal-fired power plant and Welzow-Süd open-cut brown coal (lignite) mine in Lusatia, directly highlighted coal's continuing role in the German energy mix, and its contribution to climate change. The Ende Gelände protests were themselves part of a coordinated series of protests in the United Kingdom, the United States, Turkey, Brazil and Australia, carried out under the banner organised by Break Free from Fossil Fuels (Breakfree 2016). In Australia there is a parallel emergence of grassroots social movements challenging coal and coal seam gas, often through direct civil disobedience. The anti-coal campaigns have created new political alliances between farmers, environmentalists and Indigenous peoples, targeting fossil fuels, and in some places forcing a corporate and government retreat (Baer and Burgmann 2012). In India, plans to expand domestic coal production have been frustrated by large-scale corruption scandals and local opposition from coal-affected communities, especially Indigenous *Adivasi* communities, in alliance with national forest rights advocates and an emerging climate action movement (Thaker and Leiserowitz 2014).

Such forms of activism expose the institutionalised power of coal industries. As Freese and others (Chubb 2014; Kemfert 2017; Schneider et al. 2016) have documented, until relatively recently the coal industry and its associated lobby groups have been able to operate behind the scenes, employing strategies of 'corporate ventriloquism' to influence government policy. Instead of debating climate action and the abstracted notion of carbon emissions, from the late 2000s the climate movement increasingly focussed on climate justice and on targetting fossil fuel. There has been a central focus on halting 'unburnable fuel', recognising that 'the only feasible means' of doing this is to leave the fuel in the ground (Princen, Manno and Martin 2015). On the ground, new political constituencies and alliances have been mobilised against coal mines and the wider coal industry, and these together have contributed substantially to exposing the entrenched power and influence of the coal lobby.

In this book we compare the proposed mines across very different countries – India, an industrialising country seeking to drive high levels of economic growth and extend energy access; Australia, a high-income settler society traditionally dependent on primary industries and mineral exports, including coal; and Germany, a high-income post-industrial society with an explicit commitment to 'energy transition'. All three countries are representative democracies and the proposed new coal mines have generated extensive opposition and debate at both regional and national levels about whether the mining should go ahead. In each country we find that policies on energy and coal are, or have been, central to national development ideology. We find that contestation over the proposed coal mines resonates across multiple levels of political life and is producing the possibility for major transformations in energy systems and in associated social relations and power structures. A series of potential strategies emerge from the three contexts – strategies that have enabled new political leverage against coal mining. As argued later in the book, these centre on the re-evaluation of development and offer the possibility of a shared repertoire for overcoming coal in the era of climate change.

The Coal Conundrum: Coal vs Climate

Global climate policy, as noted, coincides with the coal boom. Since the 1990s growing coal consumption has driven rising greenhouse gas emissions. Unlike oil, which has become harder to extract, coal remains plentiful and relatively accessible (WCA 2019). About 2 billion tonnes of coal was mined annually in the 1950s, climbing to 3 billion per year by the end of the 1960s, and 4.5 billion by the end of the 1990s; since then production has almost doubled, to 8 billion tonnes (IEA 2017; IEA 2018b). Coal-fired electricity contributes about half of all fuel-based emissions and a third of all anthropogenic CO_2 emissions: it is the 'single largest source of global temperature increase', accounting for about 0.3 DegC of the current 1 DegC of global warming (IEA 2018a: 7). It is also recognised that coal drives global emissions growth: in 2017, coal-fired power accounted for 85 per cent of the 1.7 per cent increase in emissions for that year (IEA 2018a).

Since 2010, there has been growing recognition that coal is the chief barrier to global emissions reduction and needs to be the main target for climate policy. In 2011, the IEA stated that climate stability 'requires coal consumption to peak well before 2020 and then decline' (IEA 2011: 5). The following year the IEA stated that keeping global warming below a target of 2°C would mean burning 'no more than one-third of proven reserves of fossil fuels' (IEA 2012b: 3). In 2014, reflecting this, the IPCC called for the phase-out of all 'fossil fuel power generation' by 2100 that did not sequester its emissions (IPCC 2014: 19). Also in 2014, and quite remarkably, the IPCC stated with 'high confidence' that 'the increased use of coal has reversed the long-standing trend of gradual decarbonisation' (IPCC 2014: 5). As detailed in Chapter 1, since the 2015 Paris Agreement, the end-game for coal has moved even closer, with the United Nations stating unequivocally in 2019 that no new coal-fired power stations could be opened after 2020.

The challenges that we confront in this book could not be starker or more urgent. Climate change is already having a direct impact on ecology and livelihood across the globe, most directly on low-income climate-vulnerable countries, but also elsewhere. If emissions are unchecked, such impacts will intensify. But critically, as now recognised by numerous climate and energy agencies, preventing future impacts hinges on the capacity to link climate change with the burning of coal as the principal source of fossil fuel emissions. One key means of achieving this, as argued in this book, is to focus in the first instance on stopping the extraction of coal, at source.

Mediating between climate concerns and anti-coal struggles has become critical. In many instances, including the three cases examined here, opposition to new coal mines is only in part driven by climate concerns. Immediate local impacts often play a more important role. Coal extraction, both underground and open-cut, devastates local environments, not only through landform change but also through the blasting of bedrock, the release of toxic gases and particulates, damage to aquifers and waterways, including contamination and wastage, and biodiversity loss (Armstrong 2015; Morrice and Colagiuri 2013). Mines also disrupt rural community life and livelihood, and displace existing economies (McManus and Connor 2013). Concerns for the loss of community well-being, including Indigenous culture, livelihood, health and local ecosystems are generally at the forefront of anti-mining campaigns.

While participants in local struggles can at times forge links with the emerging global climate movement, and these alliances can become important moments in the developing coal-climate public discourse, they are not always at the core of what is driving local opposition (Brown and Spiegel 2017). Local opponents can be indifferent or actively opposed to climate concerns for many reasons, including a perception that climate is not necessarily relevant, a fear of alienating public support or a reluctance to engage with the science.

Yet, as revealed in these case studies, climate change has a crucial reframing effect on coal mining, and hence on the political space that is available for campaigns against new coal mines. Local people may or may not link their struggle against a coal mine to climate change, but their capacity to politicise proposed mines and gain traction for their claims beyond the locality can sometimes hinge on climate change discourses and wider climate policy. An important focus for this book is on how these local priorities can become inter-meshed with global climate concerns, enabling a new politicisation of coal mining, and with it wider energy policy. It was this nexus between coal and climate, and its articulation across society, which initially attracted our attention to this topic as researchers. In these 'turbulent times', as the IEA put it, new constituencies for climate action appeared to be emerging from contestations over coal.

With growing anti-mining struggles, across multiple levels, powerful conflicts can emerge over society's systemic dependence on fossil fuels. Anti-coal alliances are confronted by a backlash in favour of 'fossil capital', and may become more engaged with coal-dependent communities, for instance through agendas for 'just transition'. By the same token, coal advocates may develop a more sophisticated pro-mining stance that recognises climate change. The one forces changes in the other, reshaping the social and political field as part of a wider socio-ecological dialectic (Moore 2015). Two dominant narratives especially come to play an important role in this struggle. The first stresses the need for an immediate transition from fossil fuels, approximating to a 'decarbonise now' position. The second broadly accepts climate science and the need to move beyond fossil fuels but stresses the costs of transition and disputes the necessity for rapid change, voicing a broad 'decarbonise later' approach that offers ideological cover for inaction, on a 'business-as-usual' trajectory.

Proponents of the need for immediate action cite the growing embrace of wind and solar energy, the lower cost of renewable energy, the decline of jobs in coal extraction, the growth of employment in renewables, and continuing improvements in renewable technology (see Teske 2019). They argue the barriers to transition are surmountable, through varying degrees of government intervention and socio-technical innovation. Advocates for this narrative point to forecasts from authorities such as the IEA, and decisions by major banks and multilateral institutions to divest from fossil fuels.

This position was encapsulated in a 2015 public statement from the Governor of the Bank of England, Mark Carney, to Lloyd's of London, in which he stated that the vast majority of oil, gas and coal resources are becoming stranded assets. This, he stated, would affect 'one third of global equity and fixed income assets' and posed a 'potentially huge' risk to insurers. On the other hand, Carney argued, 'financing the de-carbonisation of our economy is a major opportunity', bringing with it a 'sweeping reallocation of resources and a technological revolution' (Carney 2015: 17). In this narrative, history is no longer on the side of fossil fuels, but has already moved towards a global energy transition.

The alternative narrative frames coal as a transitional fuel that is necessary to maintain energy security and secure economic growth, offering a stable foundation while decarbonisation through renewables is achieved. From this perspective some industrialising countries, notably India, have sought to invoke a 'moral case for coal' (Lahiri-Dutt 2017), which has been eagerly embraced by bodies such as the World Coal Association and echoed by coal-exporting countries such as Australia (Aston 2015). Here, globally unequal responsibility for climate change, as expressed in the UN recognition of 'common but differentiated responsibilities', provides a licence (ironically) for expanded coal exports to India from Australia. Setting aside the question of whether development rights are in any way served by increased coal dependency, the intent is to discount the development impacts of current and accelerating climate change, and to retain primacy for coal. Advocates of this position will generally claim to accept climate science, and insist they are not climate sceptics, but stress that the uncertain timetable of climate change allows for both the recognition of anthropogenic climate change and the continued pursuit of fossil fuels. To bolster this 'decarbonise later' position, advocates often celebrate the role of coal, and, as discussed in Chapter 1, mobilise deliberately provocative and populist arguments against renewable energy (see Lockwood 2018).

These ideological dynamics are vitally important. As demonstrated most clearly in the Australian case, but also in the United States and Canada, climate science can become a political football. Climate and energy policies can become a tool for political advancement, for would-be party leaders to wedge rivals in leadership struggles within political parties, as well as between parties. Both pro-coal and pro-renewables constituencies can then be mobilised in elections.

In this collision, climate change and the fossil fuels that drive it become highly politicised. As climate is transformed by fossil fuels, so the social response to climate change transforms the meaning of fossil fuels. More simply, as coal burning changes the climate, climate change alters the meaning of coal. The two are locked into a dialectic of human agency in ecological transformation. The question of how to then enable new socio-ecological relations, beyond fossil capital, becomes the key political issue, and one that only intensifies over time. In the context of an advancing climate crisis that is (more than) bearing out the predictions of climate science, measures that seem adequate today can become obsolete and ineffective by tomorrow. Within five years a call for coal phase-out by 2100 becomes a call for an end to new coal-fired power by 2020. The twin trajectories of extractivism and developmentalism enter a zone of extraordinary 'turbulence' where the legitimacy of continuing coal extraction is questioned both at the grassroots level, as our case studies document, and at the commanding heights of liberal capitalism itself.

Themes and Structure of the Inquiry

The book centres on three lengthy in-depth ethnographic investigations, in Chapters 2–4, of contestation over proposals for new or extended coal mines.

These mine proposals relate directly to state policy, and Chapters 5–7 focus on struggles at the national level between coal-focused energy policy and emerging climate policy. The book's closing chapter draws lessons from the comparisons, and discusses concrete strategies for superseding coal reliance.

The ethnographic investigations centre on regions that possess rich coal deposits: Lausitz and Chhattisgarh are already defined as coal-mining regions, and a low mountain range separates the Liverpool Plains from the intensively mined Hunter Valley. In all three cases the locality is to be sacrificed for coal, ostensibly in the 'national interest'.

In Chhattisgarh, villagers and forest dwellers are being displaced from their traditional lands in the name of energy access and national development, though the coal is to fuel a private industrial conglomerate and urban middle-class households. In Lausitz, villagers are being relocated and farming lands destroyed, paradoxically to secure reliable energy supplies to complement Germany's renewable revolution. In Australia, some of the country's best arable lands and associated water supplies are threatened by proposed mines, one of which will produce coal for power plants in China at a time when Chinese policy is to reduce coal dependence. In fighting against these mines, local people frame their struggles primarily in terms of livelihood and living environments, though, as noted, there are times when this leads them to forge links with the emerging global movements for more effective climate action.

We chose these countries because they evidence very different relationships to coal and development. Germany is a high-income early industrialiser, positioning itself as a world leader in emissions reduction and the phase-out of coal-fired energy through the so-called *Energiewende* (energy transformation). It aims to have 80 per cent of the share of gross electricity consumption supplied by renewables by 2050 and reduce emissions by 80 per cent on 1990 figures (FMEAE 2015). However, German attempts to simultaneously phase out nuclear energy may have inadvertently contributed to an increase in the mining and burning of lignite, the most polluting form of coal (Morris and Pehnt 2015; Renn and Marshall 2016). India is industrialising on the basis of a rapid expansion in coal-fired power. It has a relatively very low level of emissions per capita (1.8 tonnes), yet is the fourth-highest global emitter after China, the United States and the European Union (EU) (EDGAR 2016a, 2016b).

Australia, in contrast, is a developed extractivist economy, and its government is set on expanding its ability to provide the world with coal. Sporadic efforts to reduce dependence on domestic coal-fired energy are more than offset by increased fossil fuel exports, especially coal. Huge new mines are under review by state and federal bodies, and are likely to go ahead. Australia also records amongst the highest per capita greenhouse emissions of any country (17.3 tonnes per head), even before emissions from coal exports are counted (EDGAR 2016a). In all three cases developmental commitments to subsidising and supporting coal are embedded in state processes, ostensibly to generate employment and economic growth while enhancing energy security.

In this book we interpret contestations over coal as contests over national developmentalism, and as posing questions about the meaning and value of coal as a commodity. Struggles over developmentalism, we argue, are centred on cultural struggles over specific narratives and scripts of prosperity and security. The narratives of developmentalism rarely consider community or environmental costs and often reflect the interests of the corporate sector and dominant state-defined concepts of national security. Some become sacrificed for the (alleged) good of all. Resulting conflicts over the narration of development are crucial to legitimation and, as we discuss in Chapter 1, become central to struggles for and against coal mining.

Narratives of development are intertwined with narratives of coal, as a 'resource' to be exploited. Hence opposition to coal mining becomes a contest over development and the assumed socio-cultural value that coal offers. Culture, state and economy in this respect are intimately enmeshed. To describe this we develop the concept of a 'coal–industrial complex', of coal embedded in the exercise of state power. In this we borrow from the idea of the military-industrial complex, first identified by US president and former US army general Dwight Eisenhower, who in 1961 warned of the need to 'guard against the acquisition of unwarranted influence, whether sought or unsought, by the military–industrial complex' (in his farewell to the nation; Eisenhower 1961). In Chapter 5 we outline a similar capture of state power by the coal sector; in Chapters 6 and 7 we detail how it has come into direct contradiction with climate policy, been undermined by anti-coal struggles, and put under serious challenge.

As noted, alternatives to coal are mobilised in the move to renewable energy, which already can offer lower-cost forms of appropriating energy in the form of hydro, wind and solar power (Teske 2019). As a result, the influence of coal interests, and their leverage over state institutions, is much more visible. Mobilising against the transition to renewables is an immediately political matter, which sees the coal sector exposed as never before. In this context, the required transition induces a political crisis at the heart of state power (Goodman and Morton 2014). Because of its public character, state power is never monolithic, or entirely coherent, and is always subject to challenge and change, and not least in relation to the power of the fossil fuel sector (O'Connor 1998). With coal mining refigured as a threat to national well-being, and dominant interests fractured between an increasingly isolated fossil fuel bloc and the rest, substantial possibilities for change have begun to emerge. These possibilities are a key focus for the book.

Book Contents

The book begins with a conceptual overview and then presents three in-depth ethnographic investigations into local responses to the proposed new coal mines in India, Australia and Germany. Each place is linked to international and national policy frames and is influenced by corporate advocacy and civil society contestation. The factors that determine whether these mines go ahead vary across different geographic and political scales, and involve a variety of participants and institutions. Building on the ethnographic chapters, the book then develops an extended account of the rise and incipient demise of the coal–industrial complex in the three countries and internationally, highlighting new conceptions of development under climate change. The idea of 'development' is by definition a process of transition from one condition to another, and in this section we document how the temporal shift analysed in the case studies is part of a wider processes of encountering and apprehending the climate crisis and its implications for the continued extraction and burning of coal.

Chapter 1 introduces the book's main theme, namely the growing global contest over the future of coal. Three main aspects are identified: the changing world-historical status of coal as the fuel of development; the shifting significance of the coal commodity in economic growth and accumulation; and coal's now widely recognised impact as a central driver of climate change and ecological exhaustion. These themes, and how they inter-mesh to generate growing instability for the commodity, are elaborated throughout the book.

Chapter 2 investigates the proposal for a new thermal coal mine in Chhattisgarh, Central India. The mine would destroy forested lands and displace a large number of villages populated by Indian Indigenous *Adivasi* people. The national and regional governments strongly favour expanded coal extraction as a source of revenue and influence. Within civil society there is strong village-level opposition to the mine, with concerns centred on land and livelihood. Villages opposing the mine find allies at the regional level and are able to disrupt regional politics; they also are able to make legal claims at the national level, and link with some national and international NGOs.

Chapter 3 is focussed on the local conditions for neighbouring 'greenfield' coal mines in Australia proposed by two of the world's largest mining companies, UK-based BHP Billiton and China-based Shenhua Corporation. The coal projects are to be situated on highly productive agricultural land in the Liverpool Plains in NSW. In directly counterposing local large-scale agro-industry against transnational mining giants, the proposed mines have been highly controversial. Local opposition is grounded in the landowning classes and Indigenous people who are the Traditional Owners of the land. The developmental myths of both agricultural reliance and sovereign nationhood are challenged by the mine's approval, disrupting established political alignments.

Chapter 4 focusses on proposed lignite mines for Lusatia, a region of Eastern Germany on the Polish border. The mines aimed to extend existing concessions, supplying coal for nearby power generators, and threatened to destroy local villages. The chapter shows how local opponents mobilised to establish scripts of home or 'Heimat' against the mining, linking local belonging with concerns about impacts on livelihood, the environment and climate change. The direct contradiction between Germany's post-industrial 'green economy' and its determination to expand emissions-intensive lignite is particularly powerful, not least as it destabilises technocratic authority.

In Chapter 5 we chart the post-1945 history of energy policy in the three countries, focussing on the consolidation of a national 'coal–industrial complex'. This chapter maps national policy across the three countries as coal extraction expanded through the second half of the twentieth century. The national state was a key agent in this process, whether through private mining companies (Australia, West Germany) or via nationalised coal industries (East Germany, India post-1973). The state-led push for coal was a key aspect of the post–World War II boom and, as we outline, was later accelerated during the Oil Crisis of the 1970s, which, with the advent of neoliberalism, reasserted scripts of coal as the fossil fuel of choice into the 1980s.

In Chapter 6 we investigate the contradiction between expanded coal use and the climate policy regimes that emerged after the adoption of the UN Framework Convention on Climate Change (UNFCCC) in 1992, and the subsequent Kyoto Protocol. During this period coal mines and coal-fired power remained 'locked in' as the key foundation for energy security and economic growth. Struggles over climate policy in support of renewable energy did secure some changes, especially in Germany, but overall there was a steep increase in aggregate emissions from the coal sector. During this period, 'business as usual' entrenched the primacy of coal: international agencies such as the IEA predicted that climate policy would fail and coal would remain dominant. Yet coal was now in direct collision with climate stability, and this was profoundly disruptive of coal's hegemony.

In Chapter 7 we take the historical analysis into the present day and chart a significant unravelling in the coal–industrial complex. Investor uncertainty about the future viability of energy installations has shifted into a dramatic (and long-awaited) process of capital flight from coal to renewables. Perhaps most revealing, the coal sector itself has begun hedging its losses by investing in renewables. The chapter discusses the reasons for this shift. The Paris Agreement's 2050 deadline for 'net-zero carbon', which, at the time of writing in 2019, was well within the investor horizon for coal-fired power plants, has imposed a growing perception of risk associated with coal facilities. It has also precipitated an unexpected realignment of low-income economies to seek new industrial strategies linked to the renewables sectors, creating a new state-renewables nexus to rival coal.

The concluding chapter, Chapter 8, brings together the three local studies and national-level analysis to develop a series of comparative themes and strategic lessons from the study. We outline parallel shifts across the three case-study countries. In Germany, the 2019 Coal Commission has created a plan for the closure of coal mining and coal-fired power by 2038. Also in 2019 India's new Energy Transitions Commission mapped virtually zero growth for coal in India, predicting the major generators would abandon new coal-fired plants and embrace renewables. In Australia, a decision of the NSW Land and Environment court has created a significant precedent in acknowledging that approval for coal mining has to take account of resulting coal emissions (NSW Land and Environment Court 2019).

In each country, we find that coal's legitimacy crisis has created sharp contradictions in wider society and within state institutions, and that local contests over new mines are contributing to the wider devaluing of coal. Coal's value to 'development' reflects its cultural narration as a valuable commodity and a source of energy. In concluding, we chart the way these narratives are contested, and are changing, and in particular how anti-coal groups have gained strategic traction in the context of growing contradictions in national climate and energy policy. In this we return to the book's initial provocation, expressed in the coal conundrum of increased coal extraction coupled with climate instability, arguing the conundrum is on the way to being resolved, for a post-coal future.

1

The Global Contest over Coal and Development

By 2018, a global confrontation had opened up between anti-coal and pro-coal forces. The conflict saw those arguing for the phase-out of coal-fired power posed18 against coal advocates who in some contexts had found new rhetorical fervour and new allies in coal-dependent communities. The confrontation quickly became an ideological contest of advocates of a coal phase-out, often aligned with technocratic globalism, against coal populism, often (but not always) linked with nationalist and conservative forces. In several key national contexts, the support for coal gained political traction, with climate policy reimagined as an illegitimate imposition by global elites, threatening both national development and the survival of bedrock communities. The contest was played out with the most intensity in high-income, still heavily coal-dependent countries, especially the United States, Canada and Australia, but also European countries, including Germany.

For climate policy advocates, the end of coal was in sight. The IPCC special report on achieving the 1.5°C target, published in 2018, stated that the Paris target required the effective end of coal fired power generation by 2050 (excepting possible plants with 'Carbon Capture and Storage' [CCS] technology). Global reliance on coal-fired power for electricity would have to fall from 32 per cent in 2020 to less than 1 per cent in 2050 (IPCC 2018: 134). The IPCC stated this would entail a halt in the construction of coal-fired power stations not equipped with CCS by 2030 (IPCC 2018: 154).

In the same year, the UN Environment Program's annual Emissions Gap Report issued the sobering message that national emissions reduction commitments needed to increase fivefold to meet the 1.5°C target, and threefold to meet the 2°C target. Significantly, the report unequivocally identified coal-fired power as the key problem for climate policy and 'the most important cause of carbon lock-in today': coal-fired power stations under construction would have an operating life of at least thirty years and would likely push the world beyond the 2°C maximum increase (UNEP 2018: 22).

The logic of this 'lock-in' has pushed the 2050 Paris target of net zero emissions backwards, not just to 2030, but to the present day. Announcing an urgent UN Climate Action Summit for September 2019, the UN Secretary-General Antonio Guterres issued the following tweet:

> Here are 4 shifts @UN chief @AntonioGuterres wants us to focus on: 1. Tax pollution, not people 2. No subsidies for fossil fuels 3. No new coal plants by 2020 4. Focus on a green economy.
>
> *(UN 2019)*

The third 'Shift' was detailed as follows:

> Coal-based power is key according to UN-environment's 2018 Emissions Gap Report . . . if all coal power plants currently under construction go into operation and run until the end of their technical lifetime, emissions will increase by another 150 giga tonnes, jeopardizing our ability to limit global warming by 2°C as agreed upon in the 2015 Paris Agreement.
>
> *(UN 2019)*

On the other side of the coin, and in lock-step with the growing disruption in the coal industry, coal populism has also gained momentum. The coal industry itself has been a key player, along with other fossil fuel corporates, in sponsoring attempts at agenda-setting by think-tanks, faux community organisations and various front groups, as well as through direct sponsorship of coal-friendly politicians (Dunlap and McCright 2011; Plehwe 2014).

In the United States, the 2016 contest for the presidency brought the issue of transition from coal into sharp focus. In the United States (and elsewhere, including Australia), partisan polarisation on energy policy and reliance on fossil fuels is closely linked to a scepticism if not rejection of climate science (Fraune and Knodt 2018). In the United States, the Republican Party has consistently rejected global climate policy-making, exiting from the Kyoto Protocol in 2001 under President George H. W. Bush and then from the Paris Agreement in 2017 under President Trump.

With Trump, coal became an explicit focus, and in large part this appears to have been driven by the desire to recruit key disillusioned working-class constituencies. At the core of right-wing populism, and a key source of its strength, is an ostensible rejection of political elites in favour of an established cultural echelon, deemed to be the legitimate expression of the 'nation'. The capacity to mobilise a working-class segment is especially important (Abraham 2019). In this context climate policy and the threat to phase out the coal industry offered a ready-made opportunity for right-wing political forces, and this is evident across a number of countries, including Germany and Australia, but also, and perhaps most especially in the United States (Lockwood 2018).

Coal has been in decline in the United States since the mid-2000s. Coal-fired power supplied half of the country's electricity in 2004 but fell to less than a third by 2018. This was principally due to a shift to natural gas–fired power and renewable technologies, along with local campaigns against pollution from coal-fired plants, rather than climate policy per se (Gruenspecht 2019). President Barak Obama's 2015 Clean Power Plan would have required power plants to reduce greenhouse gas emissions by a third on 2005 levels, but this was halted by the Supreme Court in 2016 (Aldy 2017). During the 2016 presidential election campaign, Donald Trump promised to 'end the war on coal' and restore coal jobs; for instance, in a speech to Appalachian miners he praised 'great clean coal' and declared he would 'get those miners back to work', his campaign posters announcing 'Trump Digs Coal' (Brown and Sovacool 2017). The clear intention was to sway voters in otherwise Democratic Party–held districts in coal-mining states such as Wyoming, Pennsylvania, West Virginia and Ohio (see Faber et al. 2017).

Once in power, President Trump replaced the Federal Clean Power regulations with his own 'Affordable Clean Energy Rule', which sought a 1.5 per cent emissions reduction target, to be achieved by 2030 (Milman 2018). He also sought to remove other regulatory impediments to the expansion of coal mining, though many were delayed in the courts, and related proposals to subsidise coal-fired power were rejected by the Federal Energy Regulatory Commission. With the continued structural shift to natural gas and renewables, there was little impact on the still shrinking coal industry (Selby 2019). Two years into the presidency, investors in the United States had abandoned coal and were flocking to renewables; even investment in natural gas was in decline. As Bloomberg (2019) put it, 'Trump likes fossil fuels but investors don't.'

The important lesson of coal populism is that the climate crisis and associated social transformations offer rich pickings for politicians able to capitalise on disillusion with political elites in coal-reliant contexts. The same lessons were being learnt in Australia, for instance, where the far-right One Nation party gained ground in coal regions in the 2018 election (and in response the Labor Party came more strongly behind export coal). Likewise in Germany, the far-right Alternative for Germany had made headway in similar contexts where coal-mining communities could be mobilised against established climate and energy policy in the name of their own livelihood and legitimacy (Abraham 2019).

A sharp political collision had emerged between an elite consensus that climate policy required the dismantling of the global coal industry and increasingly strident far-right political forces linked to marginalised coal-dependent communities. The collision is not arbitrary or contingent but expresses deep-seated contradictions between climate stability and fossil fuel dependency. As we outline, the presumed nexus between coal-fired power and development is under challenge, and in the process, established political blocs and interests are being disrupted, with far-reaching results.

This chapter explores how the idea of national development became intertwined with the growth in coal-fired power, and how this may be unravelling under advancing climate change, posing new questions of transition and decarbonisation. Across the book we address the question of coal through the lens of developmentalism, as an ideology that applies equally to high- and low-income countries, and which translates the meanings associated with the coal commodity into national energy and climate policy. This chapter charts some of the broader themes for this study, particularly in relation to the dynamics of coal and development.

The first section of the chapter sketches the coal–development nexus, and its emergence and growth through the dynamics of national rivalry. Coal-based developmentalism generates a 'coal–industrial complex', as discussed in Chapter 5, expressed in the persistence of state policies that advance coal interests in the face of climate change. The second section focusses on the contradictions of the coal commodity as the entrenched developmentalist project comes under challenge from climate policy. Increasingly, we argue, the social value and meaning of coal are being transformed. The third part of the chapter discusses dynamics for a transition from coal, focussing on the narratives and scripts that may emerge as the coal industry is increasingly contested. As noted, a global official consensus has emerged that coal-fired power needs to be superseded by renewable energy. The debate then turns on the question of when and how that transition will occur. As a whole, the book shows how this plays out on the ground in coal narratives, and the associated scripts of everyday developmentalism that emerge in the context of a still-expanding coal industry.

The Coal–Development Nexus

'Development' has been a central concept in politics from the late nineteenth century onwards. It is intimately intertwined with the kinds of understandings, organisations and practices that have produced our current world climate crisis. Since the late eighteenth century, the modern world has been built around technological systems that utilise fossil fuels, and in particular, coal. Coal liberated economic processes from the constraints of human, animal, wind and water-based power (Malm 2016). This 'liberation' did not occur easily and involved political struggle. For example, the use of the steam-powered Cotton Jenny in factories only displaced hand looms and a class of independent weavers with the intervention of the state against the Luddite resistance (Sale 1996). The use of steam energy not only gave competitive advantage but was also encouraged by state authorities, and it was hard to profit and expand in a craft without using it. Steam became necessary, and industrialism was born.

The use of coal for steam power freed energy from the restraints of place, so that factories did not have to be near, or share, a natural power source. Factories could be concentrated in cities, while coal-powered railways and steam shipping enabled speedy, reliable and far-flung supply chains. Coal-fired steam and then electrical energy, together with coking coal for steel production, helped enable the continuing development of the modern industrial state, fuelling industrial technology, world trade, colonialism, modern weaponry and warfare. Coal was also instrumental in the rise of the labour movement, which, as Mitchell (2011) notes, was to a significant extent founded in the coalfields and went on to advance democratic transformations and social welfare policies. Coal and coal-powered technology, as such, are structured into the production of the social system that we know as contemporary capitalism.

Ideologies of Development

The race to industrialise, initiated in Western Europe and replicated globally, was reflected in the emerging global ideologies of development. With its roots in mercantile capitalism, where European powers competed to dominate trade routes, industrial developmentalism centred on state strategies designed to marshal resources and mobilise the country in the drive for industrial power. In the context of British imperialism, the imperative to industrialise was directly related to national security concerns and the desire to project both economic and military power. Germany under Bismarck and Japan under the Meiji challenged the liberal empire and are good examples of competitive developmentalism at work. The Japan case is especially remarkable, in delivering military victory against China (1894–1895) and Russia (1904–1905) less than fifty years after the industrialisation drive was initiated. Japan demonstrated that developmentalism could produce independence from Western colonialism, giving a clear signal to the new wave of anti-colonial independence movements.

In the following century, national development emerged as a global norm. The science of 'development studies' emerged to define and contest orthodoxies, from 'modernisation' theory to dependency theory, and developmentalism became structured into competitive relations within a globalised states system. As a self-conscious ideology of statecraft, developmentalism became integral to the emergence and extension of the capitalist world system. Wallerstein divides this history into three overlapping phases. The first is colonial imperialist competition during the nineteenth century, in which conquered areas were integrated into the colonial economy, in competition with other colonial societies. The second is a wave of modernisation in the post–World War II era, in which development through colonial independence was embedded in competition between capitalism and communism. As we discuss in Chapter 5, during this period coal was rehabilitated as a primary source of energy security, especially after the oil crisis of the 1970s. Third, from the 1980s there was a dramatic shift to neoliberal developmentalism, which intensified with the collapse of Soviet communism and the advent of corporate globalism (Wallerstein 2005). In this period there was a rapid increase in coal use, especially centred on the newly industrialising countries of East Asia, first with Japan and the 'Tiger Economies', then with China, and latterly India. At the same time, neoliberal development ideology was increasingly exposed as serving dominant corporate interests, leading to an intensified global assertion of 'alternative development' models, for example as expressed in the emergent 'global justice' movement.

To this schema can be added a fourth stage, of growing awareness of climate change and ecological crisis. Awareness of the growing costs of fossil fuel–based development, in terms of climate change, overlaps with the growing assertion of 'alternative development' in the 1980s and later, 'post-development' approaches which identified development as an ideological concept expressing the dominance of high-income countries. With climate change, development is no longer simply a matter for 'developing countries', but is also defined as a problem for the high-income 'developed' world. The clear need for a new development trajectory, beyond fossil fuels, for rich as well as poor countries, now challenges the existing model.

There is a collision between the causes and consequences of developmentalism. National development projects that still prioritise fossil fuels are in direct collision with an emergent 'reflexive development' that requires attention to globalised side effects (Peiterse 1998). Increasingly, as climate change negates development gains worldwide, the side effect is in danger of becoming the main effect. The collision is not just semantic – it involves a clash of interests between an entrenched coal industry and an emergent renewable sector supported by a popular desire to address climate change. As such, the clash is structural, implicating state legitimacy and forcing ever-more vociferous assertion of the existing fossil fuel–based model (as exemplified in attempts at quashing anti-coal protests, and also in the rhetorical support for the coal industry from conservative political leaders, especially US President Donald Trump).

Indeed, it is remarkable the extent to which coal-based developmentalism is so forcefully embraced, across a diversity of social systems (Tyfield 2014). Energy systems link directly to accumulation and cohere what Wallerstein characterises as the capitalist world system. Coal's value relates to its biophysical properties as a source of energy and the associated technologies designed to harness it; it also relates to narratives and scripts of development. Industrialism is wedded to coal, and the ubiquity of development-through-coal reflects this. In the Soviet Union, for instance, coal was central both for advancing the state communist political project and for guaranteeing security in competition with the West. Lenin stated that without coal, 'the large-scale industry of all countries would collapse, fall to pieces and revert to primitive barbarity' (1920b). Lenin posited a strong link between political power and electric power, famously declaring 'communism is Soviet power plus the electrification of the whole country, since industry cannot be developed without electrification' (and this meant through coal) (1920a). Celebration of the coal miner as revolutionary hero was, as noted in Chapter 4, rarely out of the picture.

The competitive pressure between national economies, and wider inter-state insecurity and rivalry, puts the state into the prime position. Throughout it, the state assumes the leading role in seeking to establish and secure energy supplies and define a mandate for fossil fuel–powered technology. Reflecting this, the national state almost universally asserts its rights over coal deposits, positioning coal as a resource to be extracted, backed by the threat or use of force. While the institutional organisation of this process has varied, the state is always vital. In this sense, coal dependence is always as much a political as an economic phenomenon.

Competitive Developmentalism

Developmentalism operates as a competitive set of relations. In the context of the Cold War and the revolt of the colonies of the Soviet- and US-centred blocs promoted contending models for 'development', what Hirschman called 'mono-economies' (Hirschman 1981; Norgaard 1994). The implementation of a material 'infrastructure' of electricity, coal and steel (and occasionally hydro power) was characteristic, as reflected in the normalising term 'modernisation'. Development became a key stake in Cold War rivalry, and after. William Rostow's (1960) famous modernisation text, 'The Stages of Economic Growth', subtitled 'A Non-Communist Manifesto', laid great emphasis on removing internal barriers to development. Critics such as Samir Amin (1977) opposed the 'extroversion' of society to meet external needs, and instead focussed on meeting local needs for 'autocentric' development.

In the 1970s, a range of more authoritarian anti-communist and Western-orientated states, mainly in East and South-East Asia, began defining a 'catalytic' role for what became recognised as the 'developmental state' (Berger 2004). This developmentalist model, led by the bloc of 'Newly Industrialising Counties' into the 1980s, was inspired in part by the active role of the state in post-war Japan. The approach broke the mould of dependency relations and, most significantly, prefaced the large-scale industrial transformation of China, and then India, into the 2000s.

India, Australia and Germany were part of the post-war development dynamic. India emerged from independence in 1949 with a post-colonial developmentalist project centred on the newly democratised state. The development planning cycle centred on the development of heavy industry driven by coal, assumed as the precondition for prosperity. Australia's history as a commodity-producing colony translated into post-war dependence on agriculture and then mineral exports. Australia became strongly aligned with the United States as a mixed, state-organised economy with a growing role for transnationally owned corporate conglomerates, especially in the mining industry. The defeat of fascism saw Germany divided between East and West, with development in both driven by coal production. Coal and steel production in the Federal Republic of Germany (FRG) was integrated into the emerging European Community as an insurance against future conflict; in the German Democratic Republic (GDR), coal production was integrated into the Soviet-led COMECON.

Post–Cold War, developmentalism became closely tied to neoliberalism, expressed in the US-IMF-WB 'Washington Consensus' (Williamson 2003). In this regime, notwithstanding market rhetoric, the state took on a more active role in promoting business interests through privatisation, tax cuts and subsidies for powerful players (Duménil & Lévy 2004, 2013; Hildyard 2016). Neoliberalism made developmentalism almost entirely about capitalism, and its main effect was to create a wave of commodification, across public services, natural resources, social or leisure time and everyday life, enabling what Harvey (2005) called a process of appropriation, or 'accumulation by dispossession'. Crucially, for our purposes, the drive for cheap energy was greatly accelerated. Global economic power became increasingly concentrated, with transnational corporations becoming even more dominant, including those in the mining, transport, marketing and combustion of coal. With the subsequent coal boom, as outlined in Chapter 6, this process was intensified.

Across this recent history the dominant ideas of development have been heavily contested. Whether during the Cold War or after, the destructive consequences of mainstream development have consistently been challenged. The enforcement of neoliberal precepts, first with national-level structural adjustment in the 1980s, imposed by the IMF, and then, after the Cold War, with new 'constitutional' provisions at an international level, such as through the World Trade Organisation (WTO), became a lightning rod for discontent (Ostry et al. 2016). A powerful wave of counter-movements emerged, centred on 'human' and 'sustainable' development and a myriad of 'alternative development' models. The imposition of what Friedman (2000) glowingly called the 'golden straitjacket', not just for debt-ridden 'developing countries' but also for high-income economies, created new political forces across the North–South divide. Globalised neoliberalism, or 'market globalism', was increasingly targeted by advocates for 'justice globalism', North and South (Steger et al. 2013).

With the global model exposed and politicised through the 1990s and 2000s, multilateral institutions such as the WTO were in large part stalled, forcing a shift into bilateral and unilateral initiatives. The pattern was paralleled in global climate policy regimes, as the 'global justice' movements of the 1990s and early 2000s quickly developed a focus on 'climate justice' (Goodman 2009; see Jafry 2014). The role of climate policy in neoliberalising and displacing emissions reduction, via carbon trading and carbon credits, was a particular focus. The subsequent shift from global agreement-making to Intended Nationally Determined Contributions (INDCs), under the 2015 Paris Agreement, saw these debates moving into the domestic arena and playing out much more directly in national energy policy, including policy on coal.

The decades-long politicisation of 'development', and with it 'climate action', is critical to the shift in the status of coal. Coal, as noted, is embedded in concepts of development, both for early industrialisers and current industrialisers. 'Global justice' and 'climate justice' politicised and globalised debates about 'development' as a problem both for high-income and low-income countries, creating common agendas and themes across otherwise radically different contexts. The articulation of post-coal alternatives in this respect is intimately linked with critiques of mainstream development, and with ideas of 'alternative development'. Here, an intense debate opens up between models of ecological modernisation and the green economy, linked with a transition to renewable energy, and models of 'post-growth' and 'living well', as forms of 'post-developmentalism' (Salleh and Goodman 2013).

Coal and the Contradictions of Developmentalism

Capitalist development has centred on coal as a key means of appropriating energy (Malm 2016). Individual capitalists require continuously expanding profit to amelioratate economic and social crises. One key means to achieve this is through spatial expansion, such as through empire, to capture markets and expropriate resources, an argument that originates with Hobson (1902) and Lenin (1916). Another is to accelerate throughput, as with financial circulation, or to deepen the commodification of daily life and ecology. Hence, what Marx called 'primitive accumulation', where relatively powerless people are stripped of land, independence and sometimes their lives, is an ongoing and necessary part of capitalist activity. Luxemburg (1951: 467) emphasises the resulting paradox, where capitalism 'tends to engulf the entire globe . . . tolerating no rival', yet at the same time 'is unable to exist by itself [and] needs other economic systems as a medium and soil'.

The vital point is that capitalism needs non-capitalistic areas of life and economy to survive, yet always extends the frontiers of commodification, thus undermining the conditions of its own existence. The thesis known as the 'capitalisation of nature' (O'Connor 1992, 1994a) elucidates this point by arguing that capitalists inevitably attempt to subsume the 'natural' world into their way of operating by making it equivalent to capital, owned as capitalist property, and subjected to capitalist precepts. This logic of commensurability, as discussed across Chapters 2–4, is replicated in efforts to 'offset' lost ecological values or indigenous 'heritage' due to coal mining, or to compensate displaced peoples with new homes and forms of livelihood. The intrinsic value of ecology, as having irreplaceable value, resists commensuration, as does the intrinsic value of culture and society.

In a similar mode, David Harvey argues that capitalism attempts to resolve its inner crises by geographical expansion and restructuring. Material structures later become obsolete, or unworkable, leaving behind waste, devastation and unemployment. Production of destruction is, again, a vital part of the system of production. Harvey (2004) calls this process 'the spatial fix'. Like Luxemburg, he recognises that primitive accumulation continues through 'accumulation by dispossession' in which social commons and other aspects of material or social life outside capitalism are taken over and turned into private property. Accumulation by dispossession usually occurs with the aid of the state, which protects business, controls people and intensifies capitalistic property relations, while presenting this as developmental prosperity.

As climate stability deteriorates, the self-destructive process of appropriating fossil fuels is being challenged by its own conequences. If climate change demonstrates anything, it is that ecology and society are inseparable (see Moore 2016): it is no longer possible to assume that ecology can be destroyed for prosperity. In this context, the legitimacy of fossil fuel–based developmentalism faces a serious and growing challenge.

Climate and Developmentalism

Clearly, developmentalism continues to offer political leverage, both for post-colonial elites and for their counterparts in the high-income post-industrial world, and it remains the key mechanism through which North–South power relations are played out. This is evidenced in the developmentalist focus of the G20, the WTO and, most notably, the UNFCCC. In re-engineering the global climate crisis, the UNFCCC entrenched Third Worldism in an unholy alliance with neoliberalism. The Kyoto Protocol simultaneously exempted newly industrialised countries from emissions reduction requirements, while allowing industrialised countries to commodify and displace carbon credits on a grand scale (Bryant 2016; Steger et al.

2013). As such, the UNFCCC attempted to force climate crisis into the pre-existing ideological frame, as an instance of 'path dependence'.

Climate change and climate policy reflect global power inequalities and rivalries, and in many respects magnify them. It is a commonplace that the overwhelming majority of people who will be affected by climate change in the next fifty years live in the Global South, and that these societies bear negligible historic responsibility for the crisis, have minimal capacity to adapt to its impacts and have little influence over policy debates about how to address it (Parks and Roberts 2008). Industrial expansion in countries such as India and China creates a new international division of labour and a new displacement of emissions-intensive industrial activity. As these countries become the new workshops of the world, they become directly responsible for the bulk of current increases in greenhouse gas emissions. Yet the resulting global flows of embodied carbon, in the form of manufactured goods, from South to North challenge the spatial fix of national carbon accounting (Weibe and Yamano 2016).

National climate policy, based on national carbon accounting, becomes a means for governments to force climate crisis into the developmentalist consensus, making it a stake in battles for advantage in global negotiations. The early industrialisers, with historic responsibility for climate change, are ranged against late industrialisers responsible for the bulk of current emissions. As the two blocs wage their distributional wars, vying for global competitiveness, global emissions continue to rise (Ritchie and Roser 2019). Here, posturing over the allocation of emissions responsibility can distract from the broader existential challenge posed by climate instability. In this context the justice claims pursued by small island states facing collapse collide with elite coal-based developmentalism, wherever it manifests (Harlan et al. 2015). As discussed in Chapter 7, there is some evidence that this important recognition of the immediate domestic effects of climate change is starting to impinge on national energy policy.

Contradictions of the Coal Commodity

Coal is made into a resource through a regime of technical, economic and political systems. It is not inherently a 'fuel to be used'. Some societies have used it only occasionally for fuel, some have ignored it and others have turned it into jewellery (Freese 2005). The state plays the central role in advancing claims over coal as a fuel, in approving exploration and extraction, through a process of capitalisation. Capitalisation 'encloses' what is held in common, allowing it to be treated as a 'resource' or 'asset' and transformed into property (see O'Connor 1998). Property excludes others from potential 'ownership' and encloses people and ecologies, including land, water, power systems and transport. Given the interest of the state in maintaining cheap energy production, coal may become an asset of a state-owned company, fuelling public power stations, for instance, and in this case its value may lie in its reliability and its strategic worth, rather than in monetary worth per se (Thurber and Morse 2015). The same may be true for a vertically integrated conglomerate, where coal supply from its mines to its furnaces may be relatively insulated from coal's market price.

Regardless of how insulated, the social value of coal, as with all commodities, is unstable and changeable. Whether produced for sale or for state-owned or private conglomerates, commodities express the social conditions of their production. Under capitalism, all commodities are in some sense contradictory, in terms of profiting owners as against producers, and in terms of appropriating ecologies (Burkett and Foster 2006). A key aspect of coal's problem for capitalism is that ecology cannot be entirely subsumed into the process of accumulation. Ecology's biophysical autonomy means, as Engels argued, that each 'victory [over nature] takes its revenge on us' (Engels 1975: 460). Reflecting this, contemporary development creates maldistribution, and forms of socio-ecological 'dumping', as well as producing wealth and prosperity (for some). The value of commodities reflects power relations (Nitzan and Bichler 2009) and wider socio-ecological narratives. As social relations, commodities express the conditions of their production, and this can change over time. Coal, arguably, is becoming especially contradictory as a marker of national development, but also as a marker of resource dependence and ecological degradation.

The unequal distribution of impacts and benefits is central. Developmentalism can be said to be 'sacrificial' of both people and ecology, making them 'obstacles' to be removed or improved (Barton 2007; Hirschman 1965). In this respect it forcibly sets terms for how 'the poor' or less powerful have to live (Escobar 2012; Kothari et al. 2019). Coal-based development imposes a wide range of adverse local effects. Linked to these effects, the legitimacy of state authority can be undermined as mine approvals are corrupted or discredited. With the capture of state governance structures and the co-optation of key civil society institutions, those benefitting from coal are empowered and those bearing its costs are marginalised. These aspects of the 'coal curse' are compounded by the climate change impacts of coal extraction and burning, which, again, have uneven and unequal effects (Goodman 2008). These sacrifices made for coal can create deep antagonisms in the social fabric, producing protests, counter-movements and alternative models that define, articulate and pursue post-coal futures.

Post-coal Transitions?

The contradictions of the coal commodity will not automatically transform its meaning and decarbonise development. There is no 'scientific' ecologism:

anti-extractivism is socially driven. The key question then is whether there is sufficient social and political pressure to force transition. As demonstrated in the cases discussed in this book, any serious attempt at transitioning away from coal reliance is likely to produce a major clash of social forces. Social forces and state priorities shape the development of energy technology, including alternatives to fossil fuels (Feenberg 2002, 2010). Coal mining and coal-fired power have their own momentum, as a legacy system, with considerable 'sunk capital', locked in for decades to come. There is much to lose in the fossil fuel economy, across policy-making agencies, coal-dependent communities and corporate fossil fuel investors. In this context the need to transition to a post-coal future may be publicly acknowledged, but in practice deferred to some stage in the relatively distant future, safely beyond the coal industry's investment horizon. In this context timing becomes key.

The process of a commodity becoming a 'non-good', or (on the other hand) of being re-commodified, is an inherent part of capitalism. Goods go out of fashion, or their value becomes obsolete as new products become available (Packard 1960). Innovations occur which completely supersede old products, and there is no reason to assume that coal's status as a good is unshakeable; it could become marked as 'old-fashioned', dirty, polluting or redundant, or the technological system it sustains could be modified or superseded through a transition to renewable or other systems. Certainly, under climate change, coal's existence as property and a resource has become inherently political. In contrast with the recent past, coal is no longer unquestioned, and its existence as a commodity increasingly depends on cultural repertoires of persuasion and normative scripts, as well as on forms of political mobilisation and social action marshalled by coal advocates.

These contending meanings of commodities are constituted by a range of narratives. Past political action has reframed once-valued goods as socially harmful, although with the ever-present possibility they may return into use. Examples of some successful transformations in some parts of the world include slaves, ivory, uranium, chloro-fluorocarbons and asbestos (Bettany and Kerrane 2011; Bond 2011; Goodman and Rosewarne 2015; Jingjing et al. 2008; Muecke 2013). Social groups tend to be aligned with one or another meaning, reflecting their stake in the commodity or position in the commodity chain. But no commodity can have a 'settled' meaning where all narratives converge. As noted, there are always contending meanings and potential instabilities in the commodity form. The key question is whether these conflicting narratives disrupt the viability of commodification. Certainly, coal has recently become a 'contested commodity', but it is still not clear whether that is sufficient to force its demise as a dominant energy source.

Contested Coal Narratives

In this book we use a 'narratives of coal' approach to map how the value and meaning of coal may be changing. We investigate coal as a contested commodity, asking what is required to enable transition to a post-coal future. Coal is endowed with a range of social, political and cultural meanings that have developed over time, from the birth of industrial modernity to the late twentieth century, and, as noted, are deeply intertwined with narratives of developmentalism. These narratives are increasingly contested as they collide with organised opposition to coal extraction and the material reality of climate change.

A dominant normalising narrative of coal centres on its socio-technical role in the industrial process, as a ready source of intense heat and a central aspect of industrialism. This narrative has its roots in the nineteenth century, when writers like Ralph Waldo Emerson celebrated coal as a commodity with extraordinary, almost supernatural powers:

> Every basket is power and civilization. For coal is a portable climate. It carries the heat of the tropics to Labrador and the polar circle; and it is the means of transporting itself whithersoever it is wanted. Watt and Stephenson whispered in the ear of mankind their secret, that a half-ounce of coal will draw two tons a mile, and coal carries coal, by rail and by boat, to make Canada as warm as Calcutta; and with its comfort brings its industrial power.
>
> *(1875, quoted in Freese 2005)*

Already, at the height of the industrial revolution, coal was not simply a fuel or a commodity; its praises were sung by a chorus of enthusiastic writers, scientists, businessmen and theologians, for whom it represented 'humanity's triumph over nature – the foundation of civilization itself' (Freese 2005: 10).

Claims for coal and prosperity are still routinely invoked. Governments in industrialising low-income countries, and the exporters that ship coal to them, including Australia, have as noted recently developed a 'moral case for coal' as a means of extending energy access and reducing poverty (Lahiri-Dutt 2017). Often, though, these claims are questioned, as coal-fired power is 'captured' for powerful industrial conglomerates and does not reach impoverished communities, who, even if they were connected, could not afford to pay for the power; the advent of low-cost household renewables now offers the required alternative to coal-prosperity claims (Talukdar 2017).

Socio-cultural narratives for coal extraction are invoked, and likewise can be disrupted. Coal mining has played an important role in histories of working-class and community solidarity. Coal companies recruit mining unions to support coal jobs, and invest in 'Community Social Responsibility' (CSR) to bolster this legitimacy. This can be upturned when mining companies abuse their workers, or when coal-affected communities mobilise against the local health and environmental effects of the coal industry. A third important narrative relates to the state, where coal is defined as a strategic asset, and positioned in competition with other states and their contending energy sources. Such concerns may play a key role in the development of the coal–industrial complex, underpinning extraction. Set against this, we may see the emergence of an 'energy–environment' complex, where the state seeks a transition to a 'new developmentalism', centred on more sustainable energy supplies, by capitalising and monetising wind and solar power (Dent 2014).

Finally, coal is deeply embedded in ecological narratives. Until recently, the ecological impact of coal was primarily defined in terms of mining and particulate pollution (smog). These impacts were initially urban and then, with the relocation of power stations away from the cities, became more concentrated in coal regions, with the consent of affected communities close to coal mines and coal-fired power plants managed through various forms of local coal-based development, employment, amelioration, compensation and relocation (Della Bosca and Gillespie 2018). With the emergence of climate change as the potentially dominant ecological narrative of the early twenty-first century, these local impacts are overshadowed by the impact of the commodity itself, as a global hazard. This poses new incommensurable challenges, which must be denied, displaced or delayed if the industry is to survive.

We see the clash between these sets of narratives, and others, as producing new initiatives and meanings. As noted, coal is positioned at the intersection of two overarching and countervailing claims – one contending that history is moving towards a global 'energy transition' and is no longer on the side of fossil fuels, the other stressing the intractability of the 'coal conundrum' and framing coal as necessary to maintain energy security and expand access to electricity for the poor, at least while the transition to renewables is progressed.

The nature of this encounter is critical. Some counter-narratives can be accommodated relatively easily within the pro-coal script. There may be some reform in the extractivist model to encompass concerns, rendering impacts commensurable with expanded coal mining. This may entail a package of job creation, community relocation, cultural compensation, offets, rehabilitation, recultivation and various other environmental safeguards – on water use, for instance. These measures may be opposed by more incommensurable demands, for indigenous culture, local community survival, existing livelihood structures and local ecological conservation. Climate impacts can likewise be hard to accommodate: coal mining companies simply deny responsibility for the emissions produced by the coal that they dig up, though this argument is becoming increasingly difficult to maintain (see Chapter 3). Coal-fired power plants meanwhile claim they use efficient 'ultra-supercritical' technology (so-called 'clean coal'), and that at some time in the future they will be able to store emissions underground via CCS (though at present with little success). The industry has long claimed a capacity to overcome its own emissions, and this has been re-invoked in recent years in response to growing public disquiet, for instance by the World Coal Association (2019).

As illustrated in Chapters 2–4, the various narratives, and whether they are reconcilable or irreconcilable, are vitally important in shaping the course of struggles beyond coal. Persistent counter-narratives can escape the confines of the locality and become articulated into wider social fields, driven by climate concerns. As the climate crisis intensifies, the battle for the legitimacy of coal is cascading across multiple sites – in civil society between pro-coal and anti-coal NGOs, in the business sector between coal corporates and the renewable sector, and in the public sector between agencies managing energy and those responsible for climate policy. As discussed in Chapters 6 and 7, these fields of conflict are highly dynamic, with cross-cutting impacts, as, for instance, developments in the business of renewable energy shift the debate in governmental and NGO contexts.

A wider ideological conflict overlays these articulations as climate policy becomes a stake in rivalry between political parties, whether in a bidding war for 'green energy' or the reverse – a race to the bottom to support the threatened coal industry. Maintaining the coal system depends on maintaining a stable narrative for the coal commodity, and this rests on the continued capacity to marginalise threats. This task is becoming more difficult, as reflected in growing coercion on the ground against anti-coal groups and, as noted, the growing resort to overblown pro-coal national rhetoric.

In the chapters that follow we seek to map these contending meanings and thereby map the social construction of coal as a commodity, and how it is changing, identifying players and their narratives and positioning them in the field of contending accounts. In doing so we make a methodological distinction between the overarching narratives of coal and the concept of more immediate scripts, which may be broadly defined as how narratives are embodied, enacted or played out in everyday life, in the concrete context of local struggles. In this we draw on Vanclay and Endicott's definition of a script as a 'culturally shared expression, story or common line of argument, or an expected unfolding of events, that . . . provides a rationale or justification for a particular issue or course of action' (2011: 257). Reflecting this, they identify four types of script: a socially perceived routine; a frequently cited catch-phrase, metaphor or allegory; a mini-story, narrative or parable; and a commonly used line of argument (Vanclay and Endicott 2011: 257).

In each of our three case studies, we find opponents and proponents of the expansion of coal mining invoking a range of scripts to position themselves and advance their interests. In this we follow the work of Connor (a coauthor for this book) and McManus, drawing on their research into the expansion of coal mining in the Upper Hunter region in rural New South Wales. Usefully, they also developed the notion of scripts as 'ways of speaking in everyday life that are shared among specific cultural groups, expressing taken for-granted knowledge and values, and thereby demonstrating and affirming personal identity and group solidarity' (McManus and Connor 2013: 166). These scripts are not necessarily discrete, but may overlap and interweave; in some cases, different 'readings' of the same script can be mobilised by both opponents and proponents of new coal mining. At the same time, scripts enacted in everyday life, in local struggles, draw on, and intersect with, the larger cultural and political narratives of coal and development.

This approach, centred on contending narratives and how they play out in everyday scripts, enables us to move between different levels of analysis, and to make connections between local, national and transnational political contexts, and between coal's contested meanings in local communities and its place in global commodity chains. The relationship between these different levels of analysis is dynamic: global narratives of coal may shape the understandings and motivations of local actors, and local contests may also affect the larger 'narratives of coal' in the context of climate change. We characterise the key social antagonisms that arise from coal's contradictory logic, and look to ways for advancing, transforming or overcoming one narrative in relation to another.

The analysis examines the politics of embedded climate action, and in doing so reverses the idea of climate action based on solidarity with the 'suffering of the distant strangers' (Arnold 2012: 15). It is not the suffering of the distant climate change victim that motivates the communities in Lusatia, Chhattisgarh and the Liverpool Plains in their struggle against coal, but the protection of their own lands and livelihoods, their homes, forests, fields, heritage and biodiverse environments. As we show for climate movements in Germany, India and Australia, at least, these communities are becoming the locus of climate action – in concrete terms by keeping coal in the ground, and at a symbolic level. Importantly, this local focus is immediately global, as a way for citizens concerned about climate change to make real their solidarity for 'distant strangers'. Narratives specific to the particular local context come into play – forest rights in Chhattisgarh, food security on the Liverpool Plains, home or 'Heimat' in Lusatia – but these become articulated and sometimes interwoven with the overarching narrative of climate change.

The focus on narratives of coal and climate change is central to our analysis. Such narratives have the power to influence policy, public opinion and business decisions – and the actions (or inactions) of citizens and civil society. But they alone are not decisive. A narrative alone cannot stop a bulldozer. Throughout the book, our consideration of the narratives of coal is anchored in an analysis of coal's function as a commodity, a pillar of the extractivist state and the foundation of differing forms of developmentalist ideology. Our approach offers an appraisal of how current tendencies can point to future directions for ending coal reliance and building a constituency for global climate action.

2

India

Coercion, Impunity and the Fight for *Adivasi* Rights in Chhattisgarh

It is a hot and dusty day in Salhi. It is strange to think that we are in Kipling land. Mowgli, Baloo, Bagheera and Sher Khan lived within these forests. Even Kipling, that Orientalist writer par excellence, recognised the ancient history of the *Adivasi* Gond inhabitants of Chhattisgarh and their ownership of the land. State control of these spaces, after Indian independence, continued the history of *Adivasi* marginalisation, with the continued advocacy of scientific forestry, the intensive cultivation of commercial timber and other forest products, the mapping of forest resources and a crackdown on shifting agriculture.

We meet the villagers in the main hall of the Salhi, a long whitewashed mudbrick structure, open to the elements on three sides and sporadically painted with the powerful motifs of Gond art. There is a little misunderstanding in the beginning. As visitors from the city, we are given chairs along with the men; the Gond women sit on the ground. We try to negotiate this; two of us women researchers sit on the ground with the women, while one of us seeks the chair due to arthritis. In the distance, we see a crocodile of women wending their way past us. They are engaged in boundary mapping required for any claims they might make under the Forest Rights Act, a complicated process. The villagers have never previously had to codify their rights to village land. The Forest Rights Act confers many rights on *Adivasis*, but it also illuminates their changing relationship with the modern Indian state. Legal rights have to be written, on *pattas*, or ownership certificates. There must be material archives, not just those of memory or oral history.

The fieldwork for this chapter was carried out over three years from 2014 to 2016, and was aimed at understanding the nexus between coal and the environment in the state of Chhattisgarh in the framework of expanding coal mining. Our research focussed on three villages in the district of Sarguja, two of which – Salhi and Ghatbarra – were particularly affected by the Parsa East Kete Basan (PEKB) mine and its extensions, and the third – Madanpur – was the site of protest movements against this expansion. Our participant observation involved attending village meetings and conducting fifteen to twenty semi-structured interviews with villagers, NGO workers, lawyers and journalists. This information was enriched with another fifteen interviews held elsewhere, including with a judge of the Delhi High Court, an advocate who litigated against the Coal Concession Allocation case in the Supreme Court, a former Minister of Environment in the government that established the National Green Tribunal and the Forest Rights Act, and other NGO workers, activists, lawyers and academics. Throughout this process, we sought to understand the complex, sometimes contradictory motivations and actions of the various stakeholders, some of whom, initially, were not opposed to the mines. We paid attention to the ways in which narratives of the events were shaped by the changes caused by the acceleration of mining activities. We also sourced pro-mine narratives from mining companies, government and pro-coal sources.

Our method of work was necessarily different from the other case studies in this book. State surveillance in the area is very high; there are arbitrary arrests of protesters, and any long-term or sustained presence of 'strangers', academics or researchers would have been difficult for local people to accommodate (Ghosh 2018). Consequently, our trips were necessarily short in actual duration but usually planned around particularly important events. During these trips, we focussed intensely on the ways in which the villagers in this area used legal and democratic processes to assert their rights and their connections to global environmental movements.

In this chapter, we examine the experience of contestation over new coal mines in Chattisgarh from several perspectives. Since it is important to grasp the historical context of these contestations, we provide some historical background to the region and the mining struggles within it. Also, it is crucial to understand the legal and regulatory frameworks within which coal mining proceeds in India, as it demonstrates the ease with which permissions for coal mines can be granted as well as the constitutional and other legal remedies available to protestors. Accordingly, the chapter continues with an overview of the intricate complex of laws and regulations that govern coal mining, and the responses available to – and exercised by – those affected by these activities. We then give a detailed account of our research encounters in the villages affected by proposed mining, before discussing contestations over development between villagers and the authorities, and how these are played out in on the ground struggles and ecological impacts in Sarguja. Finally, we explore common themes across these experiences, concentrating on three aspects: temporal dynamics of delaying projects, alliance-building and mobilisation, and articulation with climate concerns.

Chattisgarh As a Mining Area

The resistance movements to coal mining in this region have a long history, going back to the carving-out of Chhattisgarh into a separate state from the huge state of Madhya Pradesh in 2000. Nine years later, the issues over land, livelihood and resources became so fraught that, according to Alok Shukla of the NGO *Jana Abhivyakti*, in early 2010, trade unions, community groups and other progressive political parties formed an alliance called the Chhattisgarh Bachao Andolan (Save Chhattisgarh Movement), of which he is co-convenor. *Adivasis* (the Indigenous people of these areas) draw inspiration for their protests from their special status in the Indian constitution; their autonomy and dignity, as set out in Article 21 and under Schedules V and VI, are often seen as the core of *Adivasi* rights. The struggle around their right to '*jal, jangal, jameen*' or 'water, forests, land' as opposed to the developmental goals of coal power are also, therefore, a test of the resilience of the Indian constitution and its guarantees for the protection of minorities. *Adivasi* rights also interrogate the emergence of new development possibilities for India in the context of climate crisis.

The nexus between *Adivasi* peoples and resource exploitation is inscribed into the jurisdictional landscape of central India. For more than a century, *Adivasis* had called for the creation of a majority *Adivasi* state, a 'Greater Jharkhand', in the region (Corbridge 2002). The central state responded by creating not one but three states: Chhattisgarh and Jharkhand in 2000, and Telangana in 2014. *Adivasi* people were divided across these three resource-rich states, ensuring that they would constitute no more than a third of the voting population in any of the three. The gerrymander was clearly designed to guarantee resource access to the region, and arguably has been very effective. A Chhattisgarh advocate, Sudiep Srivastava, who has prosecuted many mining and environment cases, ruminates:

> Why was this state created? There was no demand for it . . . There must have been a reason for it. Some said it was to give *Adivasis* more rights but all that has happened is they have much less rights now than before. Who benefited? Only those who want mines. You work it out for yourself.
>
> *(Interview 2015)*

About a third of Chhattisgarh's population consists of Scheduled Tribes or *Adivasi* populations, about 10 per cent of the *Adivasis* in India (Ministry of Tribal Affairs 2013). Most are forest dwellers, including both tribal and non-tribal communities. Forests occupy over 40 per cent of the state and contain resources essential to *Adivasi* livelihood. In terms of mineral resources, the state is ranked second in the country for coal reserves and production, contributing over a fifth of national production. According to the government of Chhattisgarh's Mineral Resources Department, the state's thirteen coalfields contain 55,000 million tonnes of coal, with about 5,500 million tonnes in the Hasdeo-Arand field in Sarjuga and a further 12,000 million tonnes in nearby Korba (Government of Chhattisgarh 2017, 2019). Most of the available coal is considered to be of 'power grade' and has drawn the attention of coal power developers for several decades. Areas such as Korba have had power plants of the National Thermal Power Corporation (NTPC) and the Chhatisgarh State Electricity Board (CSEB) since the 1980s (see Table 2.1).

A factor that has both enabled and complicated coal mining in Chhattisgarh is that much of the coal lies under pristine forests (Greenpeace 2012). The Hasdeo-Arand forests (literally, 'forests of the river Hasdeo') spanning the Korba and Sarguja districts in the north of Chhattisgarh comprise some of India's most pristine and dense contiguous tracts of forests, with perennial water sources, rare

Table 2.1. *Hasdeo-Arand coal timeline*

2009	
December	Hasdeo Arand listed as No-Go for coal mining
2011	
June	Forest Advisory Committee (FAC) objects to loss of forest from PEKB mine
June	Environment Minister overrules FAC: PEKB mine on the 'fringe' forests
July	Forest Clearance (Stage I) granted by Environment Ministry
December	Environment Clearance for 10 mtpa PEKB coal mine granted
2012	
February	Forest Rights Committee alerts District administration of pending claims in the PEKB concession
March	Forest Clearance (Stage 2) for PEKB granted by Environment Ministry
March	Government of Chhattisgarh orders use of forest land for PEKB
2013	
March	PEKB coal washery granted permission
September	Grant of Community Forest Rights for Ghatbarra village in the PEKB coal concession
2014	
March	National Green Tribunal suspends forest clearance for PEKB coal mine and directs FAC to review its decision
April	Supreme Court allows interim coal extraction until further orders from the Environment Ministry
August	Supreme Court finds 218 coal concessions illegal including PEKB
September	Government of India seeks to open coal concessions, including PEKB
2015	
January	Village Assembly members reject coal mining under PESA and meet ministers and politicians in New Delhi
September	Ministry of Coal awards Parsa coal concession to RRVNL
November	RRVNL writes to District Authorities to cancel the Community Forest Rights (CFR) of Ghatbarra village

Table 2.1. (*cont.*)

2016	
January	State authorities reject Ghatbarra FRA application to make way for mining
June	Rejection of FRA claims in Ghatbarra challenged at Chhatisgarh High Court
September	Villagers send a legal notice to cancel public hearing for PEKB mine
September	Public hearing for PEKB is goes ahead without any response to villagers
2017	
January	Expert Appraisal Committee (EAC) defers decision on PEKB for non compliance of environmental safeguards
April	Site inspection by environment ministry's committee to review compliance
May	Police Compliant against the Hasdeso Arand Bachao Sangharsh Samiti
October	Public Hearing for Parsa coal concession
November	Notice to villagers for acquisition of land for Parsa coal mine
2018	
January	FAC states the Chhattisgarh State Government had not provided compensatory afforestation land for PEKB
April	Expansion of PEKB mine approved by EAC with additional safeguards
2019	
January	Environment Ministry approves RRVNL's Parsa mine
February	Environment Ministry recommends environment clearance for Parsa mine
July	Environment Ministry issues environment clearance for Parsa

plants and wildlife species, including elephants and leopards. The Chhattisgarh government, like other state governments, has played an increasingly significant role in coal mining and thermal power by setting up their own companies as well as joint ventures with the private sector (133 Memoranda of Understanding between 2001 and 2011) with a proposed investment of about RS 2000 billion (USD 26 billion) (State Investment Promotion Board 2015).

Chhattisgarh is at the nexus between coal privatisation and wider debates about climate change, fossil fuels energy security and development. For *Adivasis*, the most pressing issues are about land and livelihood. A member of a village Panchayat, Jayanandan Porte, told us:

> Our whole village is dependent on the forest for everything. As you can clearly see, farming is not the main source of livelihood for us . . . it's the forest that we rely upon . . . there is not a day when we don't go to the forest to get something or else. It's a part of our everyday life. *(Interview 2015)*

Legal and Regulatory Framework

In January 2015, representatives of twenty *Gram Sabhas* (village assemblies) of Sarguja, Korba and Raigarh districts in the central Indian state of Chhattisgarh met the ministers of environment and of tribal affairs in New Delhi. They demanded that the government stop the auction of coal mining licences in their districts to either the private or the public sector, as they would not consent to mining. As elected representatives of local village councils (*Gram Panchayat*), they were exercising their constitutional mandate as articulated through two prominent acts, the Panchayat Extension to Scheduled Areas (PESA) Act and the Scheduled Tribes and Other Traditional Forest Dwellers (Recognition of Forest Rights) Act, 2006 (FRA 2006). Village assemblies of Indigenous communities living in Scheduled Areas recognised by the Indian Constitution have the powers to reject mining proposals (Aggrawal 2015) (see Table 2.2).

These particular mining approvals were among the 214 mining licences that the Supreme Court of India revoked in 2012, as they had been allocated corruptly. After this 'Coalgate' debacle, the newly elected central government had yet to enact laws that allowed the re-auctioning of coal concessions to private bidders. This happened at a time when the central government was looking to promulgate new coal mining laws through which several of the mining concessions, earlier cancelled by the Supreme Court, could find new owners. An ordinance to this effect was soon passed, turning Chhattisgarh's tribal farmlands and forests into potential private mines. By September 2017, several of these coal concessions had been auctioned and were at different stages of approval, including applications for forest clearing and acquisition of village-owned land.

The consequences of this ordinance were immediate and punitive. In 2017, one *Gram Sabha* in Sarguja district was pressured to meet for the third time to decide on a mining project. They had refused to concede their land and forests to mining on earlier occasions. The president of the *Sarpanch Sangh* (Association of *Panchayat* Heads) in this area was angry:

> The officials sent us a notice that in these villages, they want the *Gram Sabhas* to give permission to acquire and mine in our land. This includes land given to the Indigenous people for farming, forests, rivers and lakes. Essentially it is a plan to displace us from our homes for coal.
>
> *(Interview2015)*

In January 2018, Adani Mining indicated that it wished to acquire 115 acres of land and forests to mine coal in fourteen villages in the Tamnar Concession of Chhattisgarh. Reports revealed that members of the *Gram Sabhas* in these villages were threatened with arrest if they refused to comply. By 2019, at three *Gram Sabha* meetings, people had voted overwhelmingly against the move to acquire their lands. Savita Rath, a popular movement leader in this region, said:

> There are eight coal mines and fifty-six power plants in this region. The resulting environmental pollution affects not only the villagers but even farming, the forests and

Table 2.2. *The mining approval process in India*

1. **Mine Allocation Licence:** corporations bid for licences by providing mining plans. Allocations are decided upon by either the Ministry of Mines or the Ministry of Coal (in case of coal mines) at the level of the central government.
2. **Mine Prospecting and Mining Lease:** Ministry of Mines or Ministry of Coal grants or rejects mine prospecting licenses and mining leases for undertaking mining activity. Applications need to be submitted through the Indian Bureau of Mines or by the State government. A mine lease is typically issued for thirty years.
3. **Land Acquisition:** state government acquires land by issuing a prior notice for acquisition. The District Collector facilitates the acquisition proceedings, including the determination of compensation amounts and rehabilitation. Consents of landowners may be required depending the law being used to acquire land.
4. **Forest Diversion and Tree Felling Approvals:** project proponents submit applications to the state forest department, which either rejects the application or forwards it to the Environment Ministry based on site verification. Environment ministry grants (with conditions) or rejects these applications. If approved, the state government can order for forest diversion.
5. **Consent of Forest Dwellers:** is required in all cases where land is being acquired in Schedule V tribal areas granted special protection by the Constitution of India. In other areas consents of *gram sabhas* (village assemblies) are required as prior to final approval for forest diversion.
6. **Environment Clearance:** applicant submits a Detailed Project Report and supporting documents to the environment ministry (if above 50 hectares) or state impact assessment authority (if below 50 hectares). An appraisal committee grants the terms of reference to prepare an EIA. The project proponent prepares the EIA and submits it for a public consultation. All documents are appraised together by the appraisal committee, which recommends (with conditions) or rejects an environment clearance.
7. **'No Objection' for Water Use:** is required for any surface or ground water use for mining and related ancillary activities. For surface water use, applications are made to the state water resources department. For ground water use, state or central ground water authorities issue 'no objection' certificates.
8. **Pollution Control Consents:** is to be secured from the State Pollution Control Board for setting up a mine. Consents to operate mines need to be renewed within the time period specified by the Board.

wildlife. If the government refuses to listen to us, the people's representatives here are ready to take the fight to the courts, alongside building a popular movement.

(Interview 2015)

In India, the main instrument for acquiring land has been the colonial Land Acquisition Act, 1894 (replaced by the Right to Fair Compensation and Transparency in the Land Acquisition, Rehabilitation and Resettlement Act, 2013). In addition, the Coal Bearing Areas (Acquisition and Development) Act 1957 applied specifically to coal extraction (Bedi 2013: 102), and most of the land acquired previous to 2015 in Chhattisgarh was under this Act. In December 2014, the central government moved to hasten coal mining and the acquisition of rural land from individuals and communities by corporations. After it failed to pass its controversial coal mining bill in the *Rajya Sabha* (Upper House) of Parliament, it re-issued two ordinances in 2015. The first was related to coal mine auctioning, and was enacted under the Coal Mining (Special Provisions) Bill which allowed auctions of over ninety coal concessions to permit the commercial mining of coal (Phukan 2015). The other federal ordinance sought to dilute the land acquisition provisions, especially in relation to consent and social impact assessment requirements under the Right to Fair Compensation and Transparency in the Land Acquisition, Rehabilitation and Resettlement Act, 2013 (Madhavan 2015). This was contested and eventually shelved (though state authorities subsequently sought means to achieve this separately) (Kohli and Gupta 2017).

As noted earlier, PESA (1996) and the FRA (2006) were two landmark pieces of federal legislation which transformed discourses around the ownership, governance and management of forests in India, making some attempts to ameliorate the continuing injustices suffered by *Adivasis* and other forest-inhabiting communities since the time that the forests were 'reserved' under colonial rule. PESA mandated consultation with *Gram Sabhas* (village assemblies) or *Panchayats* before land in Scheduled Areas (recognised under the 5th Schedule of the Constitution) could be acquired for development projects or any activity involving acquisition/alienation. Implementation has been partial at best. In its 2009 report, 'Development Challenges in Extremist Affected Areas', the Planning Commission noted that PESA was 'powerful legislation . . . but implementation of this law is weak and ineffective' (Planning Commission 2008: 44). Compulsory acquisition of lands for coal has been a particular problem, as coal is defined as a national interest matter, part of the state's 'eminent domain' (to be acquired and transferred to private players) (Lahiri-Dutt, Krishnan and Ahmad 2012). Yet, as state authorities have devised a multitude of means of sidestepping the protections, the legislation has become a rallying cry, unifying struggles locally and nationally in new and potentially transformative ways.

The FRA was co-written by *Adivasi* activists, and the Preamble to the Act spoke of remediation:

> Forest rights on lands and their habitat were not adequately recognised in the consolidation of state forests during the colonial period as well as in independent India, resulting in historical injustice to the forest-dwelling scheduled tribes and other traditional forest dwellers who are integral to the survival and sustainability of the forest ecosystem. (Ahmad 2014)

The FRA put in place a clear legal mechanism for recognition of rights at both individual and community levels for forest-dwelling communities, including forest workers, who had lived in a designated forest area for seventy-five years or three generations. Members of Scheduled Tribes could claim up to 4 hectares of Scheduled land for dwelling and cultivation via Individual Forest Rights, provided they occupied that land and were dependent on it as of December 13, 2005. Non-*Adivasis* would have to prove their families' residence in the vicinity of forest land for seventy-five years prior to December 2005, in addition to this requirement.

Equally important, the Forest Rights Act recognises and vests secure community tenure on 'community forest resources' in *Gram Sabhas*. These include rights for seasonal and continuous access to and settlement in common forest land for forest communities within the traditional or customary boundaries of the village. For pastoral or nomadic communities, it safeguards their seasonal use of traditionally accessed lands, including reserved forests, protected forests and protected areas such as sanctuaries and national parks. These communities also have rights to the ownership, management, use and disposal of forest produce (including water bodies); the protection and management of forest resources; and rights to biodiversity and intellectual property (Ministry of Tribal Affairs 2006, 2012).

Adivasis have vested enormous hopes in these two Acts; one of our interviewees said:

> This is a huge power that *Gram Sabha* from tribal areas have ... according to the Forest Right 2006, *Gram Sabha* will have ownership on all forest resources. So by exercising these rights we are saying that, we do not want mining here. So there should be no mining activity here.
>
> *(Interview 2015)*

This is an exaggeration of *Gram Sabha* powers. The FRA does not confer absolute ownership of all forests. What emerges from both Acts is a partial and complicated bricolage of use rights, ownership and management of forest land, depending on the nature and recognition of claims.

Like the Liverpool Plains and the Lausitz cases, approvals for new mines or extensions of existing ones can be appealed at both High Court (state) and Supreme Court (federal) levels. In India, there is another legal body, the National Green Tribunal, that has a powerful influence on the creation of mines, protection of the environment and the alienation of land. The Tribunal was established on October 18, 2010 by the central government to provide a specialised forum for effective and speedy disposal of cases pertaining to environment protection, conservation of forests and compensation for damage to people or property due to the violation of environmental laws or conditions specified while granting permission. It has the power to hear all civil cases relating to environmental issues, including environmental protection, conservation and control of pollution, and can order relief or compensation. The Tribunal's decisions have to comply with the principles of sustainable development, the precautionary principle and the polluter-pays principle, and its remit is to examine the merits of each case in the context of natural justice.

In an interesting inter-colonial circulation of archives, the former Minister for the Environment, Jairam Ramesh, told us that the Indian Forest Rights Act was influenced by the New South Wales Land Rights Act, and that the National Green Tribunal was based on the Land and Environment Courts of Australia and New Zealand.

> It is from the Australian model. Yes. Australia and New Zealand actually. We are the third country after Australia and New Zealand . . . Well, you know, we learned . . . we looked at different models and then finally, after talking to various people in the courts, we settled on this.
>
> *(Interview 2015)*

These acts and the opportunity to appeal to the courts or the National Green Tribunal means that contentious mining applications are contested both through legal means and local mobilisation. A minority of mining-related cases reach the National Green Tribunal, about a tenth of 2,051 judgments in 2010–2016 (Rangarajan et al. 2018), but many are contested in other jurisdictions.

These conflicts create their own narratives of rights and responsibilities, of life-worlds and livelihoods. Mine proponents argue that *Adivasis* have a responsibility to the nation, not just to themselves, and that their livelihoods will be enhanced by economic development. *Adivasi* counter-narratives are about marginalisation and oppression; by the colonial state, by religion, by the hyper-narratives of development and modernity. In their narratives, they articulate an alternate modernity that does not transmute the nature that they inhabit into natural resources, their peoples into populations and their lived knowledge into expertise. One of the elders of Salhi village said:

> We are growing rice and filling the godowns. Are they growing it? So they are giving that rice only back to us, are they doing us any favour? All the profits that they earn on food, clothing, and so on is due to the resources from our lands. They are befooling us and filling their coffers in the name of our development. The development is of outsiders and foreigners, we are getting destroyed.
>
> *(Interview 2015)*

Adivasi Communities in Salhi and Ghatbarra

In the Hasdeo-Arand forest area, where Salhi is located, the villagers are 80 percent *Adivasi* Gond. They have three forms of livelihood: subsistence agriculture, grazing animals and access to forest produce which they use themselves and sell in local markets. These livelihoods are intricately linked to the forests and water sources. The forests are interspersed with paddy fields – the primary source of food security – as well as grazing commons, critical for their livestock. Forest produce, such as *mahua* (a plant that is fermented to produce alcohol; most households have stills, though home brewing of alcohol is nominally illegal), *amjem* oil seeds, *tendu* leaf and *khunkdi* (mushrooms), is a source of year-round food and income for local residents. Other daily essentials from the forests include firewood and grass. Villagers fashion a range of products from more than thirty different species of grass, including brooms, ropes and mats. As a village elder commented,

> All the money that we get is from the forests. … All the seeds from our forest are our source of income. Forests are our source of income. If these forests are gone, then we shall die. There will be nothing left to survive.
>
> *(Interview 2015)*

These Hasdeo-Arand villages were likely to be affected by projected new coal mines. The PEKB coal mine, central to this ethnography, was unaffected by the Supreme Court's de-allocation order; two others adjoining it, Tara and Parsa, were affected. As of 2018, the process for acquiring land and determining forest rights was under way for both these mines, and for PEKB's expansion. The major company proposing these mines is the Adani Group, in a joint venture with the Rajasthan Rajya Vidyut Nigam Ltd (RRVNL), a state government undertaking. The PEKB mine is in the Hasdeo-Arand forest; as mentioned above, it is one of the largest intact forests in central India and also an important watershed of the Hasdeo Bango reservoir on the Hasdeo river, providing critical water supplies to local farmers (see Figure 2.1).

The narratives invoked by the villagers in their struggles against mines were simple but powerful. One central narrative consisted of their claimed rights to '*jal, jangal, jameen*' – 'water, forest, land'. This slogan was imbued with their fear of the loss of home, livelihood and habitat. *Adivasis* were keen to tell us what losing their forests meant to them, not just the destruction of paddy and grazing land, the pollution in the rivers and the air, but also the disappearance of their religious rituals in which the forest was essential, of the gods buried in the unquiet woods who emerged in terrible anger when their holy sites were damaged. A new generation of *Adivasi* poets, writers and artists have given these concerns a poignant eloquence:

> Leaving behind their homes,
> Their soil, and bales of straw
> Fleeing the roof over their heads, they often ask:
> O, city!
> Are you ever wrenched by the very roots
> In the name of so-called progress?
>
> *(Jacinta Kerketta 2016, 31)*

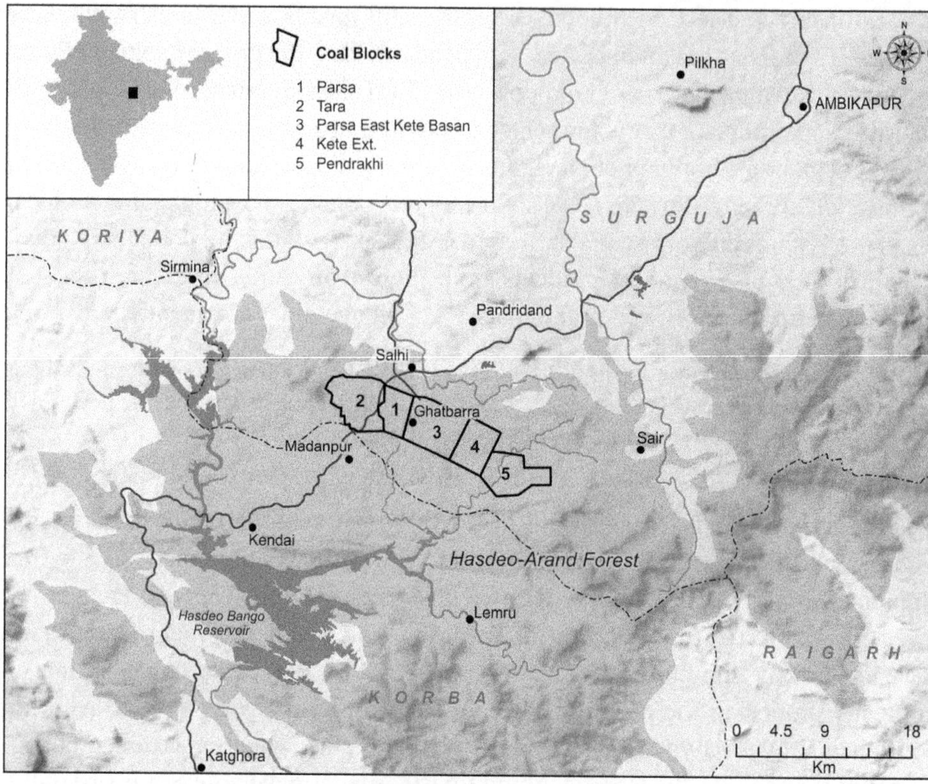

Figure 2.1 Hasdeo-Arand coal concessions.
Source: prepared by Olivier Rey-Lescure, Cartolab

The mining sector, with the state and central governments that support it, counter this particular script with the slogan of 'development' or '*vikas*'. The Adani Group, a key player in this area, links its operations with 'nation building', claiming, 'We live in the same communities where we operate and take our responsibility towards and the betterment of the society very seriously' (n.d.). The villagers have turned this slogan on its head. They say that what is happening is 'not development, but destruction': '*yeh vikas nahin, vinash hai*'.

Overall, the various levels of legal architecture combine to create a set of processes and an arena where *Adivasi* consent to mining is both necessary and coerced. Lack of *Gram Sabha* consent can create lengthy delays in mine approval; the National Green Tribunal can hold them up; the courts may hand down suppression orders. However, the relative weakness of civil society, the lack of compliance processes and a culture of impunity as far as extra-legal actions are concerned mean that *Adivasis* are often presented with *fait accomplis* and little redress. The priority in this context may be to maintain the continuity and dignity of struggle, as reflected in the unofficial motto of the legal NGO Janhit: 'No walkovers. We may not win, but we will fight.'

We are accompanied in our fieldwork by Alok Shukla of the NGO Jana Abhivyakti, who, for close to a decade, has worked with *Adivasis* in this area to safeguard their lands from mining. He has endured police harassment and surveillance. In the tiny office that sometimes doubles as a sleeping shelter for *Adivasi* activists, he points out that some *Adivasi* traditional activity is already compromised. In protected lands and national parks, hunting is completely banned (though many *Adivasis* ignore this prohibition, as we saw later):

> Hunting is almost stopped, it does not happen. Hunting is completely banned in this area. The non timber forest produce like *mahua*, *tendu*, they collect these and these are very important for their economy. Selling this out helps them financially. There are six such months in a year in which non-traditional forest produce helps them in their livelihood. For six months it's forest-based livelihood . . . For the rest of the months [it's] agriculture work. So the whole year, the livelihood is somehow forest-based and agriculture-based.
>
> *(Interview 2015)*

The forests also contain holy sites, or *deyurs,* usually marked by groves of trees, essential to religious and cultural practices. *Adivasis* are often categorized as Hindus in the Indian Census, but they practice animism. According to Jayanandan Porte,

> The *Adivasi* community worships nature. For instance, we worship trees and our deities and gods reside in forests. I'll give you an example . . . There is a deity called Boodha Dev in the forest of Salhi village. It appeared in my dream . . . there was also a pool where weapons were kept . . . So we decided to go to the particular spot I had seen in the dream and worship the deity. Since then, the deity keeps appearing in my dreams and warns us about the future through different signs.
>
> *(Interview 2015)*

In another village, Khotkhorra, we encounter some of the quotidian impossibilities that accompany development. This is a poor village; they seem not to have understood their rights under PESA and FRA and were the victims of covert coercion, being first displaced by a dam. No land was provided for rehabilitation, so they informally occupied an area uphill from their original habitation. Within a couple of years, the water table failed. They now have to bring water from a seepage well located 3–4 kilometres away from their homes. Access to the village is via one very steep dirt road. If the mines planned in the surrounding forests go ahead, that access will be removed and they will be uprooted again. The Khotkhorra villagers blame the disappearance of their water and the looming prospect of further dislocations on the relocation of their gods from their original site. One of them says that the gods are angry because they have been moved:

There is one [place] in our old village in the neighbouring forest where we worship Mahadev. We believe that like us, he is also dependent on the forest and is there to serve us. I can tell you that if the authorities try to force their way in the forest, they will not be spared by the deity. It's our belief that the deity will punish them if they commit any wrong.

(Interview 2015)

In another village, we meet an old man about to go into the forest for his daily forage. He has a catapult in one hand, an axe hanging from his waist. He insists that we take his photo. 'I have everything I need here', he says, 'a catapult to get my dinner, an axe for my firewood or any edible plant.' While we photograph him, we see a variety of domestic animals wandering off into the forests to graze. Ramlal, our guide, shakes his head. 'Here they are ignoring everyone's rights from an ant to so many other species.' He talks of all the animals that live in the forest: deer, bear, jackal. As we walk through the forest, we ask him what he would do if we met a bear. 'Run', he says casually, much to our consternation.

The application for the extension of the PEKB mine in 2014 stirred up the Salhi community. At least ten villages were affected. They were sure that their *Gram Sabha* would not consent to the extension, and the recent judgment in the Vedanta case in Orissa (against a bauxite mine) made them optimistic. Yet they were aware of the various ways in which they were being short-changed. The local administrator organised a *Gram Sabha* at Udaipur, 22 kilomentres away and out of the *Panchayat* area, which is illegal according to PESA. Furthermore, the letter announcing the meeting was written in English that most villagers did not understand. People – bureaucrats, politicians – came frequently to talk to them, ostensibly about their best interests. At the Salhi meeting, the women were both feisty and suspicious:

Why should we trust you? You will take all these interview notes and go. Then another person will come to do the same. Your views are different. They say brokers from outside are coming to the village.

(Interview 2015)

We asked whether the people of the village were unanimous in opposing the mines. Had any of them taken the compensation to buy other land or migrate to the city? The general consensus was that the mine operators were spreading money around many villages to create dissent. Jayanandan said passionately that those who sold their land to the mining corporations would not thrive:

I can tell you from my own experience that money alone does not bring prosperity to your life. The people of neighbouring village got *crores* (ten million) of rupees last year. A few managed to build houses and all but 75–80 per cent of the population is completely ruined. They have bought cars and there have been so many accidents since then … so many widows … So based on that, I feel that the coal mine would lead to our destruction rather than development ... That's what we are fighting for. We don't want destruction ... We want the government to develop our region without pushing us out of our home.

(Interview 2015)

At two morning meetings , we found three *Adivasis* who were completely intoxicated. In each case, the rest of the meeting asked us to ignore them. They had money burning a hole in their pockets, they said, after selling land to the corporation.

And look at them now. There is a saying here that if you sell your land, you will be reborn as a jackal, and we don't want that for us. These mining and other projects are an insult to our motherland, and we don't want to participate in that. This land supports so many creatures and life forms, and it is a mass murder and a crime.

(Interview 2015)

The villagers of Salhi and Ghatbarra appeared to be more or less united in their opposition to the mines. We didn't meet any villagers who openly supported mining and mine extensions (except for the three intoxicated men mentioned above). This may be because we made our contacts in the area through grassroots NGOs opposed to the mine. However, on one occasion, in Ghatbarra, we got a sense of dissenting opinions when the villagers requested, very politely, that we excuse ourselves from a meeting where disagreement and controversial opinions were likely to be expressed.

There did not appear to be much disagreement over the strategies for opposing the mines. Alok Shuka was vehement that they would utilise all of the rights available to *Adivasis* in the Constitution: working at the *Gram Sabha* level to withhold consent, applying for individual and community forest rights, contesting environmental and other violations before the National Green Tribunal, and taking cases of malfeasance and misappropriation to the courts. In addition, of course, there were civil actions, meetings, demonstrations, participation in *Panchayat* elections and alliance-building at the state and national levels to force *Adivasi* rights onto the political agenda (see Figure 2.2). As in the Lausitz case, the villagers and activists knew that their actions, at most, would delay rather than stop mining operations in a context where illegal appropriation of land and despoliation of forests were frequent and common. Umeshwar, who won a *Panchayat* election, recounted that successful anti-mine candidates from the Chhattisgarh Bachao Andolan had to go underground immediately after election results were announced. This was because the major parties (e.g. the Congress and the Bharatiya Janata Party) began to pressure them to defect.

They do pressure, but if we had no organisation, then they would have pressured more. They know we have an organisation, a huge strength ... during ... *Gram Sabha*, the secretaries were pressured more. Also some villagers who work in these companies are

Figure 2.2 Hasdeo-Arand village protest, 2016.
Source: Alok Shukla, photographer, with permission

bribed and told to take an agreement from the villagers. The forest department works under their [company] pressure only. They work under company pressure to ruin the forests. Earlier, also in 2008, a public hearing took place for opening of a coal mine. During that time these dense forests were recorded as shrub forests. The way of cutting the trees for re-growth is a way to ruin the forests. Forest department ignores it, around 33 per cent of trees are to be cut, but they don't pay attention and reduce the density.

(Interview 2015)

The tensions and disruption created by the threat of mining brought the villagers together. Most of them emphasised their long-standing relationships to the land and forest and have clear historical and familial memories of their ancestors' locations before the British Raj. The Forest Rights Act codifies this moral discourse of belonging for the public and national audience of India. *Adivasis* often express it as a form of historical kingship, 'our ancestors were kings', asserting a form of control and autonomy over land that is non-transactional and non-commodifiable. Like many Indigenous peoples, they chart their links to their lands and forest through the sacred, and the forests' plenitude in providing all necessities for living. In modern India, *Adivasis* have been compelled to learn and articulate a new idiom of rights to carve out a space in the national imaginary. The modern nation-state that they inhabit is both rights giver (through instruments such as the PESA, FRA and Schedule V of the Constitution) as well as rights taker through the often coerced and illegal appropriation of their lands in the cause of modernity and development.

Partha Chatterjee (2008) writes that the democratic public sphere in India, since the economic liberalisation of 1991, displays two discernible realms: civil society and political society. The former is constituted by the bourgeois middle class, which taps into and benefits from the neoliberal economy in terms of jobs and upward social mobility. It participates in elections and (mostly) adheres to the rule of law. Meanwhile, the large informal sector in the country, which remains outside the rule of law and depends on welfare, constitutes the political society (Chatterjee 2011). Although Chatterjee does not justify the nomenclature of this realm, he notes that it makes claims on the state alongside civil society, thanks to the electoral politics of the country. But *Adivasis*, he notes, are excluded from the political society because their small numbers do not have a substantial impact on electoral politics. *Adivasis*, NGOs and the numerous forums working for *Adivasi* rights might constitute an *Adivasi* society, following Chatterjee's framework (Chemmencheri 2015). This *Adivasi* society does not function in isolation, however, and is establishing crucial links with civil and political society organisations. *Adivasis* participate in umbrella campaigns such as the Narmada Bachao Andolan, Campaign for Survival and Dignity, and Ekta Parishad. Community sector organisations like the People's Union for Civil Liberties have maintained close contact with *Adivasi* society, running regular features in their bulletins on the implementation of the Forest Rights Act, for example. *Adivasis* have been able to build alliances for their struggles through these partnerships, but the stage on which these politics play out is still national. Their struggles have not caught the global imagination.

Jal, Jangal, Jameen

Devleena is talking to Jacinta Kerketta, an *Adivasi* woman from Jharkhand, whose passionate and angry poetry has become the artistic voice of *Adivasi* movements. Jacinta is eloquent and articulate; the capitalist system, she says, is based on profit-making industries and commerce which monetise basic needs like food, clothing and shelter. 'But even this artificial organisation of economy is based on the resources provided by Nature. Industries require water, forest and land.' The *Adivasi* struggle, she says, is not a struggle for the interests of just one community. It is for the entire country, for the entire world. Her poems are recited at protest meetings, their style resonating with the predominantly oral cultures of the Adivasi community:

> We're here at the bazaar!
> What would you like to buy, the shopkeeper asked.
> Brother, a little rain, a handful of wet earth,

A bottle of river, and that mountain preserved
There, hanging on that wall, a piece of nature as well.
And why is the rain so dear, pray tell?
The shopkeeper said – This wetness is not of here!
It comes from another sphere.
Times are slack, have ordered just a sack.
Fumbling for money in the corner of my sari,
I untied the knot only to see
In place of a few folded rupees
The crumpled folds of my entire being.

(Kerketta 2016, 33)

The slogan '*jal, jangal, jameen*', or 'water, forest, land', was first raised by Komaram Bheem, one of the most significant Gond *Adivasi* leaders of the country, during the British Raj in the early part of the twentieth century. He demanded that *Adivasis* should have total rights to their forests because, as Jacinta Kerketta says, in *Adivasi* areas there is a 'healing power'.

When people come here, they feel a flow of real power in mind and body. The human appears to turn a little more human. Here, there is not so much pollution of the mind. When people who come here are reacting like this, then it is because this is an area where many *Adivasis* live. The air of the *Adivasi* areas touches the inner self of a person.

(Interview 2015)

Our conversations with *Adivasis* made one thing clear. All of them feel that this connection to nature is absolutely essential for their communities. It is the major reason for their struggle against mines, to preserve their forests. Many people in Salhi tell us of the Gond artist Jangarh, whose paintings now sell for huge sums in Europe, and the price he paid for allowing himself to be torn away from his roots. Jangarh's problem, says one of them, was that he was removed from the local habitation and environment that produced his art:

Adivasi society is connected with Nature, and the entire organisation of their economy is in relation to Nature. They have survived for a very long time by supporting themselves through keeping animals, practising agriculture, collecting forest produce, etc. They take from Nature only as much as there is immediate need for them. They do not consider Nature as easy prey to their greed.

(Interview 2015)

The entirety of their village community is essential for *Adivasi* emotional, mental and physical well-being. The potent force of their locality does not reside in its opposition to the national or global, or in the fact that it is ahistorical or apolitical, but rather because it is politically, discursively and historically constructed (Gupta and Ferguson 1997). Their home is constituted of a continuous and dialectical process of the transmission of knowledge, information, beliefs and practices and the trajectory of customs and values proceeding from one generation to another. *Adivasi* concepts of home are vulnerably linked to an entire network of personal, community, social and cultural identifications. Their notions of home and identity are not static, mired in unchanging tradition; rather, they resemble the artistic device of pentimento, a thinking and re-thinking of historical and contemporary political and social experiences. Jayanandan illustrates this in his account of the name of his village:

> I can tell you how the village was named. It's a story that I have heard from old people in the village. Our village is located between Sarguja and Korwa district. People from Sarguja used to cross the Banyan (Bargad) tree that was located in our village whenever they had to go out to import and export ration and other things. On their way back, they would halt and sit under the tree to check their belongings. This practice of checking was called 'Ghaat Chenkna'. So the name Ghaatbarra came from the combination of Banyan (Bargad) tree and the practice of 'Ghaat Chenkna'. That's the story of Ghaatbarra's name. So Gonds and Manjhwaars started settling here. Then Yadav, Uraon, Penka, Rajwaar and many different communities settled here ... People in those days used to walk all the way to the other end to import and export lots of things. It used to take them no less than a week to walk all the way to the other end and return ... These were the people who named the village ... How can we let anyone destroy such an old village and not say anything about it? That we have been around for more than seven generations is what people remember of the history ... the actual duration of Gonds and Manjhwars inhabiting this place might be longer than that.
>
> *(Interview 2015)*

In contemporary India, *Adivasis* are located in an unstable present between a past history of deprivation, oppression and marginalisation and an unpredictable future where the rights supposedly available to them retreat like a mirage. Their present acquires its meaning within these disjointed and conflicting temporalities. Gramsci refers to the 'strangely composite' nature of identity 'which contains prejudices from all past phases of history' and deposits 'in you an infinity of traces without leaving an inventory' (Gramsci 1971: 628). *Adivasis* are constantly involved in different forms of negotiation, between their traditional life-worlds and developmentalist discourses, their families and communities and the Indian nation-state. Their imaginary of 'water, forest, land' mediates the past and present, the local and the national. Corporeality is at the heart of their meaning-making; the *Adivasi* body represents that liminal space between India's colonial past and its modern developmental future. The *Adivasi* has become a spectre haunting the national imaginary; as anomaly, as threat and as object of uneasy reflections about the nature of tradition, progress, technology and environment. As Jayanandan states,

> An *Adivasi* community cannot be split into separate individuals. Wherever one person may be, he or she is connected to the other people, to the blood relatives, to the jungles and hills, to the water courses, to the cattle and birds, to the ponds and fields, to the threshing grounds

and to the religious places, to the burial places, to the village meeting grounds, to the learning places for the youths: all this is connected. To deprive a community of all these things, and to dump them in some other place: how can that be a development for them? *(Interview 2015)*

Though coal mining has been part of the history of Central India, it is relatively recently that the mines have come to Hasdeo-Arand. Jacinta's words above remind us of a conversation we had in Podi village with a courageous young woman, Babli. She stood firm against the forced acquisition of her home in the face of the steadily advancing open-cut mines. When we visited her village in the Ghevra district, we were confronted with a looming moonscape. The mudbrick houses clung precariously to an unstable island surrounded by a dystopian architecture of tall, skeletal mining equipment, in a strange rural inversion of the Blade Runner universe. Eighteen months later, she was forcibly dragged by her hair out of her house and beaten with batons for refusing to vacate the village. Podi has now been erased from that landscape. The tiled mudbrick homes, the narrow alleys, the wells, the paddy fields and fruit trees, the vegetable patches and the forests for grazing, hunting and foraging have vanished from history. Like Horno in Lausitz, Podi is one of the symbols of both the resistance to the mines and the victory of coal. The image of these women dragged out of their homes by the police remains vivid in the *Adivasi* imaginary.

Alternative Modernities or Development without Jobs?

During the Raj, the Raniganj-Jharia coal-producing areas created an urban belt that serviced the primary colonial enclave of Calcutta but did not stimulate the social and economic development of the immediate hinterlands (Lahiri-Dutt, Williams and Imam 2014). The same trend continues in modern India where coal mining has produced extensive urbanised regions but has not necessarily benefitted rural coal communities. According to Kohli, '[T]he development model pursued in India since about 1980 is a pro-business model that rests on a fairly narrow ruling alliance of the political and economic elite' (Kohli 2007: 113). Since the neoliberal model was introduced in 1991, the level of government intervention has not fallen, but has rather been re-orientated, in favour of domestic private-sector interests. This elite development alliance is united by strong economic and political incentives in order to exploit mineral reserves in *Adivasi* land. *Adivasis*, however, do not receive the benefits that are supposed to flow from such development (Oskarsson 2013).

The former Minister of the Environment, Jairam Ramesh, admitted in our interview that environmental debates are political debates:

> I think now, environment is fairly and squarely in the political debate of the country . . . I think it's now firmly embedded in the development agenda . . . the nature of the environmental issues in India is such that they relate to fundamental issues of livelihood – land, water, forests and so on and so forth. So, you know the livelihood issues are very important. Also, I think, increasingly, environmental issues are becoming issues of public health, particularly air pollution and chemical contaminations. You can't afford to neglect that.
>
> *(Interview 2015)*

With the current emphasis on national rates of economic growth, several states in India have attempted to institute aggressive developmental policies which compromise human rights and justice (Sengupta 2010: 29). The Salhi villagers were eager to point out that they were not necessarily anti-development. In fact, some villagers had agreed to the first PEKB mine on the assumption that it would not affect the residential part of the village and provide infrastructure (such as schools and hospitals) and employment.

> When the news of the mine came, we felt . . . we would all benefit financially. When the coal started getting shipped out of here, then we realized the wealth of this place is going elsewhere and here only destruction is happening, so we started protesting . . . Initially, they told us that the mines will acquire only the farm land and the residential space will be left out. They kept us in the dark. Similarly in Kete, the people there were informed that only forest land would be used to mine coal and residential space will not be touched. So they gave their consent to the mine. It was not taken by force, and the people followed what was given in the proposal. It's only after starting of the mine that we realized the whole village will be displaced.
>
> *(Interview 2015)*

In 2014, these villagers brought the mining activities of Adani in PEKB mines to a complete halt. According to the *Indian Express*, local villagers began a *dharna*, or sit-in, on the premises in August 2014, demanding the promised compensation, rehabilitation and jobs and forced the company to suspend all operations (*Indian Express*, 2014).

A villager, Bholenath Singharmo, pointed out that the forest in the area was an elephant corridor, so that animals too would be affected. The impact on forest dwellers and Adivasis was significant:

> Before the mining production, the rights of the tribals and forest dwellers in the area must be settled. We rely on tankers to get drinking water, there is no facility of school or dispensary that were promised. Now mere word of assurances will not work. We want action on the ground.
>
> *(Interview 2015)*

Activists like Jayanandan challenge government and corporate stereotypes that *Adivasi* communities are custom bound, traditional and inimical to change. In our conversations, he articulated sophisticated alternative notions of development:

We worked towards improving the economic structure of the village. Our focus was on flattening the agricultural land and making it more productive for the benefit of local population. The traditional way of farming does not yield a lot of produce. So they trained people on how to increase the agricultural produce on the same land. I went to Hyderabad for training and learned new ways of cultivation. Paddy cultivation, for instance, is much better if you do it the 'line to line' way. It's a scientific method that involves less capital, lesser number of seeds, saves time and yields much more produce as compared to the traditional method. People tend to think that the hybrid method gives more production, but that isn't true. The local paddy yields the same, if not more, when cultivated through the scientific method.

(Interview 2015)

Jayanandan emphasizes that the 'type' of development is in question, not development per se.

When the Adani company came here for their coal mine, we could see that there are two types of development . . . One thinks about the long-term welfare of the public whereas the other one wants to pursue its own agenda by focussing on a handful of people and displacing the masses . . . so this is a difficult situation for us . . . All of us decided that we are only beginning to learn new ways of farming and we should not let the mine displace us . . . I wish for consistent development. I have a question for those who define development in terms of better jobs, better housing and other such things . . . I want to ask them: Why do they have to uproot us from our place in the name of development? We, the *Adivasis*, are dependent on forests and natural resources for our livelihood. If you are going to keep us away from these forests, then what development are you talking about?

(Interview 2015)

Another of our interlocutors is Sudha Bharadwaj, a lawyer, who founded the legal NGO Janhit to represent *Adivasis* whose land has been illegally alienated. She considers that employment opportunities in *Adivasi* areas worsened with coal privatisation. Previously, with government-controlled enterprises under Coal India Ltd, there were permanent jobs in public-sector coal mines. Now automation is proceeding rapidly and the available work, mostly unskilled, goes to poorly paid and unorganised migrant labour. In 2014, a union leader in Chirmirri, which has one of India's oldest underground coal mines, told us categorically that he wouldn't let his sons become miners:

This work is against nature. We know that Coal India is going to lay off three to four hundred thousand workers in the next three years. There is no future for us here.

(Interview 2015)

According to the villagers, the jobs offered by the mining companies were unskilled with low pay, for cutting trees, running errands (*peons*) or other 'menial' tasks. There was no training available for sophisticated equipment even for the few villagers who were educated:

They have not trained anyone on the machines, just hired us like shepherds or *peons*. Those who have come from outside have good jobs, as people in our village are not educated. Even if some are educated, then also we have not got dignified jobs. The people from outside earn twenty-five to thirty thousand Rupees while we get five or six thousand rupees. Now, is this development for us or for outsiders?

(Interview 2015)

The *Sarpanch* of Salhi claimed that the skilled jobs, including those in the 'officer' category, went to migrants from the neighbouring states of Jharkhand and Bihar:

The people with positions, influence or means are in a pursuit to acquire every place that belongs to people like us. All over they are planning either power plants or industries. Now we are understanding why people in cities look down upon villages. Why don't they displace people in cities? They can put power plants there as well as coal must be available there too, it's not that coal was deliberately put underground [where] the villages [are] only. We want to know: why is this so?

(Interview 2015)

It was difficult, if not impossible, to talk to Adani mining executives. It was also potentially politically and ethically compromising given our close involvement with the villagers. However, government and company rhetoric about development clearly took a different view. Adani's website, for instance, claims:

Through Adani Foundation, we ensure development and progress is sustainable and inclusive; not just for the people living in these areas, but the environment on the whole. At Adani, we believe in delivering benefits that transcend our immediate stakeholders.

(n.d.)

Adani's message echoes the vision of India's Ministry for Rural Development:

The vision and mission of the Ministry is sustainable and inclusive growth of rural India through a multipronged strategy for eradication of poverty by increasing livelihoods opportunities, providing social safety net and developing infrastructure for growth. This is expected to improve quality of life in rural India and to correct the developmental imbalances, aiming in the process to reach out to most disadvantaged sections of the society.

(Ministry of Rural Development n.d.)

In Chhattisgarh, Adani Mining used social media platforms to greenwash themselves, lauding their protection of livelihoods and the environment. Videos and stories disseminated daily recounted the ways in which mining in Sarguja helped local villagers form income-generating enterprises, run plant nurseries and plant trees in partnership with the company. This message, that the company is a responsible miner, is directed at both national and international investors and governments (and as a counter to campaigns against their proposed Carmichael mine in Australia) (ABC 2017).

In Chhattisgarh, the visions of development presented by the government of India and mining corporations have not been realised for displaced *Adivasis*. Poverty has not been eradicated, livelihood opportunities have worsened and neither social safety nets nor growth infrastructure have been created. Consequently, there is no intrinsic loyalty to mining as a profession for displaced villagers who are virtually never given real jobs in the mines. The upper echelons of mining bureaucrats are usually from other states and live in the cities. There seems to be less and less common ground between these two points of view.

> Agents of mining corporations
> Knock on every village door.
> And no sooner is uttered a desperate sigh of hunger,
> Then disease, unemployment and helplessness,
> Are shoved down their throats
> Grains, medicines, utensils, and clothes.
> And the family carried away
> As labourers, for a pittance pay.
>
> *(Kerketta 2016: 75)*

Protests in Sarguja: '*vikas nahin, vinash hai*' ('not development but destruction')

According to Bhardawaj, the *Adivasis* are now in a worse situation than in colonial times because of the privatisation of mining enterprises. She explains that the British Land Acquisition Act distinguished between acquisition for public purpose, under 'eminent domain', and acquisition for companies. In the latter case, there were stringent restrictions on acquiring agricultural land, including demonstrated efforts to source alternatives or offer outright purchase. Now the presumption is that any application for acquisition for land by a company is for public purpose and can be dealt with under the current Land Acquisition Act.

The villagers' grievances fall into three categories: (1) that due compensation is not received for land acquired for mining, nor is rehabilitation mandatory; (2) that land acquisition is often unsafe, illegal or coerced, contrary to the wishes of the *Gram Sabhas*, violating forest rights and (3) that socio-ecological change caused by the mines, such as pollution of the waterways and the impact on wildlife, is not ameliorated.

Compensation and Rehabilitation

It is clear from interviews and published literature that lands for large-scale resource or infrastructure projects are frequently acquired through dubious processes, and that compensation, rehabilitation and resettlement are implemented partially, if at all. Opposition to mining in the areas we investigated was often based on bitter experience, of promises made and broken by mining companies in neighbouring districts. Many villagers recounted the experiences of the inhabitants of neighbouring Kete and Parsa who had lost their farmlands and forest land to Adani Mining. As mentioned above, the compensation promised, monetary and in the form of employment and infrastructure, was slow in coming (if it came at all):

> Look, there is one coal mine there. Parsa East Kante Basan coal project. It is a huge mine, around 2,700 hectares. But because of this mining, people who are displaced from their villages will not get any land for agriculture. Side-by-side livelihood dependence on forest is also getting destroyed. A number of villages are destroyed due to mining, there is straight displacement. Because of this project, a total of five villages will be affected, out of which one village is already being displaced, and rest of them will be displaced in the future.
>
> *(Interview 2015)*

Ram Pravesh, an *Adivasi* who gave up 2 acres of his ancestral land to Adani, told NDTV (New Delhi Television, a commercial broadcaster) that he was paid only 100,000 rupees as compensation, though the land rate at that time was 600,000–700,000 rupees per acre. The local administrator 'promised us jobs, houses but it's been six years and . . . promises have not been fulfilled', said the villager who now works as a daily wage labourer in the city (Das 2015). In the area we investigated, up to sixty villages were to be displaced by mines. The villagers were unconvinced that the administration was capable of such large-scale rehabilitation and resettlement:

> The administration cannot resettle one village, how will they resettle innocent tribals from sixty villages? These people cannot survive outside of this region, as they do not know anything besides farming.
>
> *(Interview 2014)*

There was general agreement that compensation was not adequate to remediate the loss of land and livelihood. In fact, many villagers pointed out that several people who had sold their land had later lost all their money to outsiders. The previous government had, at the time of the interviews, mooted a substantial increase in compensation for land acquired. The villagers, however, were adamant that cash money was not acceptable:

> No, the people here won't take money, even if in *crores* (ten million) . . . See, if they give us money, we can't eat that. We eat grains, rice, which we grow here. For how long will we purchase and eat? We can diversify our crops by growing tomatoes, potatoes, cauliflower, etc. We can add anything to it with our hands.
>
> *(Interview 2015)*

Most villagers agreed with Narad, an articulate and engaging village elder with an eloquent turn of phrase. We first heard from him the phrase that we later heard repeated often in the villages, '*yeh vikas nahin, vinas hai*' ('this is not development but destruction'). The villagers understood development as a contradictory and contested term and were acutely aware of the differing priorities of the government, urban areas and their own needs.

> They are fooling us and filling their coffers in the name of our development. The development is of outsiders and foreigners, we are getting destroyed ... Do these office-bearers in big cities produce rice or pulses that they eat? We feed them by ploughing these fields. If they can eat the money they earn from their factories, then we will feed them money ... Don't they need to eat rice? He who is interested in digging coal will eat coal only. We don't want to eat coal.
>
> *(Interview 2015)*

Government and corporate sources often assumed that the wellspring of opposition came from older villagers who, due to their age and traditions, were unwilling to change. Jayanandan went to Delhi in January 2015 to meet the Minister of the Environment who hinted that Jayanandan's son would have agreed with the minister's point of view:

> When we met the Environment Minister, he told me that I am speaking like an activist and asked me to call my son. I told him that by the time he grows up and coal mining starts, we all will be dead and what will he discuss with you? Is development at the cost of destruction?
>
> *(Das 2015)*

According to Salhi villagers, their young people were also opposed to the mines. Certainly no one at the village meetings we attended spoke in favour of the operations. As mentioned above, some women were suspicious of us as city people who might be abusing their trust. They were used to officials, journalists and bureaucrats descending on their villages and hoping to convince them of the 'development' benefits of mining. They were unsure whether our conversations would later be used to support 'development' arguments.

At the beginning of this chapter, we mentioned the twenty villages in the Hasdeo-Arand area who passed a formal resolution against government plans for coal mining in their traditional forest lands and also demanded that the requirements of both PESA and FRA be implemented, mandating *Adivasi* involvement in decision-making about natural resources, including obtaining consent to proposals for destruction of forests for developmental purposes (Das 2015). A villager said:

> We have raised our voices for what has happened in the previous [mines] that are running now. We demanded that they be closed if not operated as promised. They must operate as per the consent given. The employees from here must get increased salary. We have

organised ourselves and demanding Rs 10,000–15,000 per month salary . . . none of the twenty villages in our organisation want to take favours from the mining companies. We are firm in our protest and won't accept even their tea. They had promised to give Rs 10,000–15,000 at least, so as agreed, they must take us in that grade. Instead they have given us peon jobs.

(Interview 2015)

Unsafe Land Acquisition – and Eviction

The villagers and other interviewees were particularly concerned that PESA and FRA, which were supposed to protect their rights, were being flouted. PESA mandates that *Gram Sabhas* should be consulted before land acquisition. In practice, *Gram Sabhas* are seldom informed, people are terrorized into silent acquiescence, or 'No Objection' certificates are forged. One villager commented that fake 'consent letters' were often produced:

Then you show us the consent letter from the *Gram Panchayat* taken before the diversion. You have done it without any consent, meaning in a fake manner. So we are planning to take this whole issue in the high court.

(Interview 2015)

Sometimes, the methods used for land acquisition are truly Machiavellian. The *Gram Sabha* of Premnagar, another village in Sarguja, passed resolutions refusing land for a power plant on fourteen occasions. There was vociferous opposition in the environmental public hearing and, when the village leaders were arrested, there was a massive *gherao* (blockade) of the police station, forcing their release. The administration then decided that the village was not a village (or *gram*) but a town (or *nagar*) and set up a *Nagar Panchayat* (town council), thus abolishing the village council and the rights of the *Adivasis* under the FRA. This case was reported in the newspaper *The Hindu* (Sethi 2011).

Another case in Sarguja involved the inhabitants of Choura village, who protested the compulsory acquisition of their lands by the South Eastern Coalfields Limited, a public-sector mining enterprise. The plaintiffs alleged that not only was the PESA Act violated in that the *Gram Sabha* was not consulted before such acquisition, but a forged *Gram Sabha* resolution was submitted to obtain clearances. About 5,000 *Adivasis* of nearby villages decided to march to the Mines Offices to protest on 26 December 2009 (*Gram Ganrajya Divas*, or Village Democracy Day, the day the PESA Act was first notified). South Eastern Coalfields Limited, which had begun its mining operations, filed a civil suit for the loss of production on that day against six villagers for the recovery of over 3.5 million Rupees with 9 per cent interest (Bharadwaj 2014).

It is difficult to gain recognition under the FRA, which functions through the recognition of pre-existing rights. 'Claims' are submitted at the neighbourhood level in a village council. This is the grassroots interface at which *Adivasis* participate in the process of becoming complete citizens or subordinated subjects of the state. However, the distribution of community claims has been abysmally low. It is possible that some individual claims may be rejected due to insufficient proof; the same explanation cannot be extended to community claims, as they are held in common by the entire *Adivasi* community for the purposes of fishing, grazing and collection of forest produce. Archival or written documents may not be available, but community memory and oral history, as demonstrated in the examples above, are strong.

The reluctance of the Forest Department to relinquish rights over community forestlands emerges as a plausible explanation. While the 'participatory process' of claim submission calls on the *Adivasi* citizens to access the law, the subsequent stages of surveying and mapping the land claimed are monopolised by forest officials (Chemmencheri 2013). Thus, *Adivasis* have no knowledge of what transpires between claim submission and its acceptance or rejection by the higher-level committees and the basis on which final decisions are made. There is no transparency, and the decision-making process is monopolised by elite forest officials. The state also controls local livelihoods, as it is the sole purchaser of minor forest produce, on which *Adivasis* depend. While the FRA proposes complete right of access to this produce for *Adivasis*, this has still not been uniformly applied (Shrivastava 2015).

Evidence from the implementation of the FRA shows that, even when *Adivasi* land claims are recognised, the area they are granted is smaller than the area claimed. While the Act prescribes recognition of up to 2 hectares, Sarker (2011) points out that, on average at the national level, half an acre per successful claim was distributed. These national-level figures give a warning signal that the FRA, which was supposed to correct the 'historic injustice' against *Adivasis*, could become a new source of dispossession and repression. The village head, or *sarpanch,* at Salhi commented:

> The senior district magistrate called the *sarpanchs* of the villages asking them to come and collect their titles. But when they went, they realized the titles are not the community titles. One acre, one or two hectares of land for cattle grazing, cremation ground, and so on is there. But law clearly says that whatever forest resources comes under the traditional boundary, whatever is your natural right, you will get that. So the *sarpanchs* protested and refused those titles. Now we are drafting a letter for the district magistrate that the titles he has made are not as per the Act. We will take them as per our claim, and a copy of this letter will be sent everywhere from Chief Secretary to Ministry of Tribal Affairs.
>
> *(Interview 2015)*

The FRA ostensibly sought to reinstate rights to *Adivasis* in forested lands which the British gazetted as 'State property', with forest dwellers defined as 'encroachers'. The critics of the Act rightly point out that it both limits and individualises ownership (Bharadwaj 2014), and that implementation is both partial and flawed. These problems reflect its character as a means of juridically distinguishing between legitimate and ostensibly illegitimate landholders. The rejection rate of claims is above 50 per cent; in Chhattisgarh alone, 461,590 of the 890, 240 claims filed were rejected (Ministry of Tribal Affairs 2018; see also CFR-LA 2016). There is also evidence of direct manipulation. Analysis undertaken in 2018 revealed a 74 per cent rejection rate for FRA applications in coal-rich Sarguja and Korba (Saldanha 2018).

Rejection under the FRA provides a pretext for legally formalising the de-recognition of existing rights. In an echo of British law (using pre-independence legal precedents), in February 2019, the Supreme Court ruled that people were trespassing if they continued to access land claims rejected under the FRA. The case was brought by conservative Indian conservationist NGOs using the FRA to protect 'pristine' forests, and the government, which has responsibility for implementing the FRA, failed to make a counter-submission (suggesting tacit approval). The court ruling and a later order enabled the legalised eviction of at least two million forest dwellers, close to half a million in Chhattisgarh. This would effectively clear the forests for mining (Dutta 2019). Following widespread protests, the order was stayed on request from the central government, to allow the states to respond to allegations that the FRA process had been misapplied, opening up a new national field for contestation on FRA implementation. Already in 2019 the move was generating a major *Adivasi* upsurge and international outrage.

A high court judge (Interview 2014) commented despairingly that, though the Indian legal systems often delivered landmark judgments, the implementation of these legal remedies was flawed, nor were there audits as to whether there was compliance with judgments, especially those in favour of the poor and underprivileged. We may add that well-intended legislation fails not only in the implementation but also in its conception, especially where it empowers the authorities to exercise greater control over the people it is ostensibly designed to benefit, in this case in the adjudication of FRA claims.

India's Coal Rush and Socio-Ecological Change

India's rush to exploit coal began in 2004 with Prime Minister Manmohan Singh (simultaneously Minister for Coal), who granted several hundred coal concessions, many in dense forests. When a map of India depicting coal concessions was superimposed on the map that displays forests, 38 per cent of the new concessions, nationally, were in the Hasdeo-Arand forest. Later, in 2010, the Coal and Environment Ministries in India jointly marked areas in forests as 'go' and 'no-go' zones for mining. Of 582 coal concessions, over 600,000 hectares (49 per cent) were declared as 'no-go' zones. Coal mining was to be prohibited in these areas, which would become 'critical energy reserves'. The Ministry of Coal raised the requirement of tree cover for designation as a 'high-density' forest, yet the twenty coal concessions in the Hasdeo-Arand area were still in the 'no-go' zone.

The Ministry of Coal and the Prime Minister's Office opposed the 'no-go' zones, and in 2012, the then – Minister of Environment, Jairam Ramesh, made an exception for three coal concessions: PEKB, Parsa East and Tara. He granted mining approval on the basis that these were on the 'fringe' and 'not in the biodiversity-rich Hasdeo-Arand forest region'. Forest clearance was approved on the condition that the state government 'shall not put forth any new proposals to open the main Hasdeo-Arand any further for mining purposes' (Gupta and Paul 2018).

The PEKB decision had a major impact on the village of Salhi. The villagers were certain that coal mining destroyed their natural environment. They objected to the impact of mining on local flora and fauna, and to the pollution of air and water. They suspected that the water table would drop severely when the mines near their villages began full operations. One outlined how water supplies had already been affected:

> This time of the year for three months we let our cattle free to roam and graze around and we tie them in the evening. Now the water is not fit to drink and is all black. Though they are mute animals, still they understand that the water is not fit to drink. We also go near the river to farm. Earlier we used to bathe there, and now we bathe at home. The water is so polluted, who will bathe in coal water? The birds and animals have no water to drink.
>
> *(Interview 2015)*

Another villager added:

> But when we see the impact of mining, it is not only about displacement; there are so many environmental impacts as well. Ground water is contaminated because of the depth of these mines. Pollution because of blasting and transportation is also huge. There are a lot of health impacts there because of this.
>
> *(Interview 2015)*

The Hasdeo-Arand forest is also a crucial link in a 600-kilometre wildlife corridor connecting various animal reserves and national parks. In 2010, the Elephant Task Force of the Ministry of Environment, Forests and Climate Change concluded that the central Indian habitat of the elephant is one of the most fragmented and degraded. A detailed report in *The Hindu* (Bagchi 2012), pointed out that six decades ago, elephants were 'inhabitants' in Achanakmar National Park, whereas now they were 'outsiders', finding their way into Achanakmar from the forests fragmented by coal mining in the Korba district.

The Ministry of Environment and Forests and Climate Change approved around 450 square kilometres of an intact, uninhabited forest block as the Lemru Elephant Reserve in 2007, acting on a resolution passed by the Chhattisgarh State Assembly in 2005 (Greenpeace India 2012), but this approval has never been enacted. In February 2008, the Chhattisgarh state unit of the Confederation of Indian Industry (CII) wrote to the forest department saying that 'the area in and around the (elephant) sanctuary has been established as coal bearing. The proposed sanctuary, if finalised, will block at least 40 million tonne per annum of coal production' (Sharma 2011). Caving in to industry pressure, the state government made the entire area available for coal and has since ignored reminders from the central government to notify the reserve. Instead, the Chhattisgarh government is proposing an industrial rail corridor through the heart of the Hasdeo-Arand forest. The rail lines would effectively divide what is currently a contiguous forest area into smaller parcels to facilitate the opening up of coal concessions. This will have serious repercussions given the forest's importance as a wild elephant refuge and a crucial watershed. Ritwik Dutta, an environmental lawyer who challenged this decision in the appeals court, told us that a judge asked the state authorities if elephants in Chhattisgarh were able to fly, as the proposed railway would cut the reserve in two with no corridor between them (Interview 2014).

On our 2016 visit to the Achanakmar area, we came across captured and chained wild elephants. They had rampaged through the villages, and the frightened inhabitants attacked them with Molotov cocktails. Some villagers had been contracted to look after the elephants (named Raju and Madhu) and were cooking giant vats of lentils and vegetables for them. Because of the loss of forest cover, elephants now routinely travel through villages destroying houses and grain stocks and often trampling villagers. Yet there is a pervasive feeling that rampaging elephants were preferable to mines. According to one villager,

> Yes, here elephants [come] . . . An elephant killed a man here, and then they say it is not an elephant corridor. Buffalos of 2–3 people were bitten by tigers here. People in Adani [the coal-mining company] say there are no wild animals here. But lions, bears, jackals, deer all are there. They want to destroy the whole forest.
>
> *(Interview 2015)*

Dealing with the elephants and other wildlife that were being displaced by industrial encroachment was a problem, but it was manageable when compared to dealing directly with the mining companies. Another villager commented:

> If there are any houses in their way, they [the elephants] destroy them and eat all grains and everything. They would kill any animal and human in their way. They come every year . . .

> Of course when elephants come while my son and my family are sleeping, we feel angry. [But] elephants are ok, we will coexist, and tiger is also ok . . . It is their forest as well as ours. Our ancestors managed with them and we will do the same. But we do not wish to give our land and forest to Adani. They will destroy it completely. In fact, with elephants, lions, jackals we wish to stay like friends.
>
> *(Interview 2015)*

Villagers reported tigers in the area, as Hasdeo-Arand forest has links with the Achanakmar Tiger Reserve. Since the tiger is an endangered species, a sighting would have an impact on environmental clearances in the area. In fact, on one of our field trips to Sarguja, villagers were excited because a tiger had mauled one of their buffaloes. We tracked the buffalo to its watering hole and took photographs of the wounds. The villagers later provided these to the local Forest Guard, who apparently showed no interest and did not record a tiger sighting.

Strategic Themes in the Hasdeo-Arand Struggles

Our investigation of coal contestation in India's Hasdeo-Arand forest highlights a range of strategic manoeuvres. These parallel the findings in Australia and Germany (Chapters 3 and 4), suggesting an emerging common logic for advancing anti-coal agendas. This centres on the emergence of what we summarise as delaying, alliance-building and articulation with climate politics; a fourth aspect, the mobilisation of incommensurable *Adivasi* identifications, is discussed in the conclusion.

Delay as Struggle

Alok Shukla from Jana Abhivyakti made a poignant statement in one of his interviews: 'For *Adivasis*, the law is that moment between birth and death which allows us to take a breath' (Interview 2015). Recourse to the legal system may delay acquisition of land for mining. Shukla was adamant that the protests organised against land and livelihood alienation should be legal. He himself has borne the brunt of the endemic police and Intelligence Bureau surveillance. Local police or authorities often dub protesters as Maoist or 'anti-development'. This can have serious repercussions, as suspected Maoists may be imprisoned for years on remand without bail.

Shukla's strategies have involved protest demonstrations, legal remedies and sponsoring candidates for *Panchayat* elections (Interview 2014). Both Shukla and Sudiep Srivastava have been involved in numerous legal challenges to government decisions. For example, Jairam Ramesh's approval of mines in the 'no-go' areas was challenged in the National Green Tribunal which quashed the decision in

March 2014 (National Green Tribunal 2014). The bench questioned the entire basis for regarding the forest area as 'fringe' and directed the ministry to review its decision.

Another legal challenge has been mounted against the refusal to grant community forest rights to Ghatbarra, one of the villages in which we worked. The reasoning for the refusal in January 2016 was that 'the exercise of these rights' (to access the forests and collect forest produce) was 'in the way of mining' (Kohli and Shukla 2016). This appeal, lodged in 2016, is currently pending in the High Court of Chhattisgarh (Kohli 2019). A villager said:

> Sudiep (Srivastava) had already filed a case challenging the forest clearance [here]. In November 2013, the National Green Tribunal passed a judgment cancelling the forest clearance here. This was on environmental grounds because the elephant corridor and various such issues were ignored. This was already cancelled, so we did not challenge it . . . doing it again did not make sense. The issue was pending, and suddenly, on 27 January (2015), Ghatbarra village *panchayat* received a notice stating that their title of community rights is being cancelled.
>
> *(Interview 2015)*

Those fighting the case maintain that this decision raises two related issues. Firstly, whether this was legally permissible under the Forest Rights Act which lays down procedures for the recognition and vesting of rights but no provisions for their revocation. Secondly, since the community objected to the mine, how could it have been approved, in the first place, under the Forest Conservation Act 1980? In fact, the mining company is in the way of the community's forest access, rather than the community barring access to the mining company.

In May 2016, the Chhattisgarh Bachao Andolan had a partial victory. The Union Ministry of Tribal Affairs, responding to a right to information (RTI) application filed by Alok Shukla, concluded that:

> The reason for cancellation of the community title as provided by the District Collector, Sarguja, by saying that the forest land was already diverted before the issue of community title to Ghatbarra is not a ground for cancellation of the title and cannot be accepted.
>
> *(Interview 2015)*

However, the ministry did not direct the state government to revoke this order. Meanwhile, in the Hasdeo-Arand forests, mining operations continued unabated, and the forest-dependent people of Ghatbarra were gathering themselves to fight for restoration of their legally recognised rights to use and conserve the forest area. The High Court decision regarding the cancellation of the Community Forest Rights was still pending at the time of writing.

There is a third local issue in the offing. In September 2017, environmental clearance for the expansion of the PEKB mine was challenged by the Hasdeo-Arand

Bachao Sangharsh Samiti on the grounds that Adani failed to comply with the legal safeguards required by the first approval. The ministry expert committee has deferred the decision and made it subject to an on-ground enquiry and specialised legal opinions (Koshy 2017).

Despite these legal manoeuvres, according to Bharadwaj, the abrogation of rights are common. Besides the rejection of 50 per cent of claims under the FRA, provisions in the Act that explicitly mandate the determination of rights prior to displacement are being violated with impunity. Bharadwaj points to the cases of *Adivasis* displaced from various Reserve Forests such as Achanakmar (district Bilaspur), Udanti (district Dhamtari) or Badalkhol (district Jashpur) (2014). The Forest Department is involved in this extinguishment of rights because, as one NGO put it, 'It means loss of control: no bribes . . . to the DFO [divisional forest officer]' (Seetharaman 2015).

Alliance-Building

Established NGOs at state and national levels assist local civil action groups at the village level to mobilise large campaigns to bring together villages across the region and enable national linkages. An organiser from Sarguja recalls:

> We organized a rally on 3 March 2014 in Raipur, the capital of Chhattisgarh. In addition, twenty people from Sarguja and Korba went to Delhi on 3 March to protest. In Raipur, they submitted a memorandum to the governor's personal assistant protesting against the Adani mines in Sarguja, but had received no reply. Later all those who had gone to Raipur and Delhi got together to share what happened in both places with other village residents. It is important to share to keep the motivation high of the organisation and to discuss what more needs to be done to make the movement stronger. My uncle had gone to Delhi, [and] informed [that] a national-level consultation was organised. He learnt from there and shared with us that it's not only us [but] many regions across the country are affected.
>
> *(Interview 2015)*

Several organisations worked actively on the ground with the villagers of Sarguja in defence of their rights. We were most in contact with Jana Abhivyakti, working out of Madanpur, though we also consulted Janhit, a legal NGO. Jana Abhivyakti supports and works with two organisations in research, documentation, training and awareness campaigns. One is the Chhattisgarh Bachao Andolan, a network formed in 2009 as a broad democratic alliance of twenty-two groups (including people's organisations, trade unions and other independent people's movements). It focusses on grassroots issues. The other is the Hasdeo-Arand Bachaao Sangharsh Samiti, which was formed under the banner of the Chattisgarhh Bachao Andolan to oppose the reallocation of coal concessions in the region. The villagers themselves work through the Chhattisgarh Bachao Andolan to raise their issues at the state level.

Several candidates aligned to these movements contested the 2015 *Panchayat* elections with some significant success. One activist told us that, while addressing people during awareness campaigns, he cited the example of the hardships faced by his in-laws, who had been displaced by mining, receiving no compensation. According to Shukla,

> People have made their group and this organisation – Hasdeo-Arand Bachaao Sangharsh Samiti . . . It is a mass organisation of the twenty affected villages. They regularly do different programs of actions against mining – be it any conference, protest or rally. They regularly organise these kinds of events and protests. Hasdeo-Arand Bachaao Sangharsh Samiti takes all the decisions very democratically and they carry forward their protest via *Gram Sabhas*.
>
> *(Interview 2015)*

Continued opposition from the *Gram Sabhas* remains central, and the authorities have made it increasingly difficult for the villagers to maintain their veto. The Hasdeo-Arand Bachao Sangharsh Samiti has had to organise its participation in back-to-back *Gram Sabha* meetings and public hearings. This has posed several challenges. They have to respond to and engage with these processes on very short notice, with little time to prepare responses, which generally require extensive research. Members of the Chhattisgarh Bachao Andolan and Jana Abhivyakti have aligned with national-level support groups to regularly track and work with the Samiti members to make required submissions. Local activists are under pressure from the authorities, and Adani mining has filed a case alleging loss of revenue against three villagers, including one of our chief interlocutors, Jayanandan Porte.

International NGOs such as Oxfam also work in the area with local partners. For example, Chaupal Grameen Vikas Prashikshan Evum Shodh Sansthan (Chaupal) is a combination of four people's organisations, founded in 2005 and led by an *Adivasi* grassroots activist. These are predominantly tribal organisations which also worked on the Right to Food campaign. Chaupal's previous campaigns on the right to food and work established good links with village *Panchayats*, which helped them to work together on forest rights. Oxfam supports Chaupal's work at the state level, including coalition-building, brokering links with local and national officials, and information dissemination. Campaigns included supporting the formation of the Community Forest Rights Manch (platform), consisting of like-minded organisations to discuss the challenges and difficulties at the state level and devise new and joint strategies; creating a direct link with the state tribal department for follow-up and coordination; helping with timely dissemination of information, such as government orders, presentations and circulars; and working at the national level.

The mobilisation of local-level alliances in defence of the Hasdeo-Arand forest, for *Adivasi* rights, and against the manipulation of the FRA has had a major impact.

Until 2018, the Bharatiya Janata Party had been in power in Chhattisgarh since its creation. In the November 2018 state elections, there was a 29 per cent swing against the BJP in favour of the Congress Party, which, for the first time, stated it would fully implement the FRA and PESA, including 'collective rights' for *Gram Sabhas.* The FRA became a 'core' commitment for the Congress, which launched a series of large meetings in Adivasi constituencies, termed a 'Jungle Satyagraha', asserting Congress as the party that had instituted the FRA.

The Congress Party was voted in by a large turnout in twenty-seven of the twenty-nine *Adivasi*-dominated constituencies (Saldanha 2018). The election signalled a major backlash: the betrayal of the FRA, and the persistent mobilisations in defence of its principles, created a unifying dynamic, spilling over from the affected villages, into state-level politicisation and creating opportunities for Congress and for the local campaigns (Koshy 2019). In 2019, the campaigners we interviewed for this project were seeking to make good their electoral promises (Aggarwal 2019).

Through 2018 and into 2019, there was further spillover, as the Chhattisgarh actions were correlated with actions in neighbouring Jharkhand. There, *Adivasi* communities took forest rights into their own hands and, from 2016, had begun establishing large stone slabs, traditional *Pathalgadi,* inscribed with quotes from the FRA, PESA and the Indian Constitution, to assert and mark out *Adivasi* lands and emphasise their status in the Indian constitution. The movement was repressed by the military from 2018 with a wave of arrests state-wide, creating a crisis of legitimacy for the Jharkhand state (Kiro 2018). The 2019 Supreme Court decision mentioned above, which required the eviction of *Adivasi* 'encroachers' not recognised under the FRA, could not have come at a better time for the growing movement, as it created a national spillover and enabled the politicisation of land-grabbing and the failing FRA on the eve of a national election, as discussed in the conclusions to this chapter.

Climate Articulation

There is certainly a growing movement against coal mining and for *Adivasi* rights in India, threatening the central governments's efforts at increasing coal extraction in the country. As outlined in Chapters 6 and 7, the government is very conscious of anti-coal campaigning and its potential to disrupt coal-focussed energy policies. By the same token, the renewable sector is advanced if coal is frustrated, and this probably offers the best hope for a reduction in the rate of emissions growth in the country. Arguably, the success of the wider climate movement, both in India and internationally, depends on the capacity of *Adivasi* peoples, and their allies, to prevent a new domestic coal boom in India. Local problems with coal resonate:

coal is widely accepted as a local curse, not a boon, to be visited on parts of the country (i.e. *Adivasi* forests) that can be more easily 'sacrificed'.

Clearly anti-coal struggles are central to climate strategy. It is not so clear whether, vice versa, climate concerns have a place (yet) in anti-coal campaigning. Climate change can be always a far-off concern and, especially in Central India, where more immediate impacts of extractivism are prioritized. Climate has no direct traction in the system of mining approvals, which centre on local issues of environment, livelihood, land and forest rights. In the Hasdeo-Arand case, the focus for campaigners has been on delinking coal from local development. Coal mining is delegitimised principally as a threat to local environments and livelihoods, land and forests. This delinking 'from below', as noted, could become articulated with delinking 'from above', as climate policy reframes fossil fuels. Yet local activists are rarely linked with international climate NGOs (and where they have emerged, the central government has legislated against them, as discussed in Chapter 6). Climate issues do not translate well into on-the-ground strategy and campaigning: climate concerns have only recently gained visibility at the national level and serious traction in opinion polling (see Chapter 7).

There are clearly different registers of climate change awareness and knowledge, in a broad spectrum from climate science to everyday experience of the weather. There is the scientific definition of climate change, as a process of anthropogenic global warming, of which people may or may not be aware. At the same time, there is the general popular understanding and lived experience of India's changing climate. The Hindi word '*mausam*' means both 'climate' and 'weather', hence 'climate change' means the same as 'weather change'. Not surprisingly, when asked whether there are changes in the climate/weather (represented by the one word '*mausam*'), most people talked about altered weather patterns. On the other hand, for those who are familiar with climate science, the process of global warming is not immediately associated with weather.

Climate change activists have not yet found a common language to express the terrible consequences of advancing climate change for India's rural poor, including in places like Chhattisgarh that are facing the brunt of coal expansion. The globally focussed movements for climate action and local movements against coal tend to move on parallel tracks. Certainly climate concerns have risen up the agenda: until mid-2000s, climate politics in India centred on a small group of government agencies and think tanks (Thaker and Leisowitz 2014). From 2005, there is some evidence of a 'crowding-in' effect: Ylä-Anttila and Swarnakar (2017) find 'frame extension' linking climate and development, and a growing engagement across a wide range of community-based organisations, from less than five in 2004 to more than eighty in 2009. At the same time, there was a rapid rise in the number of media articles on the topic, from about 100 in the four major newspapers in 2004 to about

4,000 in 2009. Concurrently, some grassroots climate campaigning emerged, with various broadly based public actions, such as climate caravans and peoples' climate tribunals, especially after the emergence of the 'Climate Justice Now!' network in 2007 (which had almost thirty member organisations in India). But much of the activity was centred on cities and amongst the relatively well-off, and did not necessarily link to anti-coal campaigning on the ground in rural areas. In this respect there may be important opportunities for both the anti-coal struggle and for climate advocacy, but this would require a scale shift and indeed a cultural shift, from the serried halls of global climate policy into the dirty politics of coal extraction. As noted, the experience of Greenpeace in India demonstrates some of the political taboos that the domestication of climate struggles can encounter.

In our discussions with interviewees, we explored linkages between coal concerns and climate politics. In the villages, our interviewees generally referred to the direct experience of climate change, as reflected in changing weather patterns. Jayanandan, for instance, commented:

> I have seen the same thing for last two–three years . . . Earlier the rain used to be on time . . . but now you just cannot predict as to when would it happen . . . the frequency varies and so does the timing . . . first it doesn't rain, and when it does, it doesn't stop and keeps trickling . . . all of this is happening because of the imbalance in the environment . . . the rain cycle is just one example of it . . . this, in turn, is affecting the farmers . . . it's also affecting our health as people are falling ill due to the uncertain seasonal changes. . . Look at the *Mahua* tree for example . . . If rainfall doesn't happen on time, the flowers will not grow on the tree. If the flower won't grow, then the fruit will not grow as well. Same is true for many other trees. Sal tree is another example. So the trees are also getting adversely affected.
>
> *(Interview 2015)*

These comments suggest the most effective pathway for engagement with climate change is through people's experience of its effects on ecosystems in the forms of changed weather patterns. Certainly, it has been the direct experience of global warming that is now motivating global climate policy (though the climate science has been known for decades). As mapped in Chapter 7, it has been the sudden realisation of the impacts of climate change that is forcing the central government to focus on global emissions reduction as a survival strategy for India (rather than as the responsibility of high-income countries). If for would-be expert policy-makers, why not for villagers in the Hasdeo-Arand?

The obverse is that, without climate impacts, we can expect complacency. At the coal market of Chandasi near Varanasi, coal is bought and sold on the formal and informal markets, a place with huge trucks unloaded by precarious workers, covered in coal dust, carrying shovels and bamboo baskets. Here, when asked about the changing climate/weather, they cited pollution, unpredictable weather, less rain, more drought and more heat. We explained that climate change driven by greenhouse gases was perhaps fifty to sixty years away. One of the workers smiled and replied:

> We'll drop dead long before that, when we reach fifty, and if we don't work, our children will die of starvation anyway. The coal dust does bother us, but we have no choice. It gets everywhere, nose, mouth, skin, however much you scrub when you return home.
>
> *(Interview 2015)*

The lived ubiquity of coal dust for these workers is paralleled by a metaphorical ubiquity of coal in the imagination of some expert policymakers. Among the city-based interviewees, global warming and its implications for India were generally understood and accepted. As Jairam Ramesh stated,

> Climate change is a reality. I don't think we can deny that climate change is here. India has multiple vulnerabilities to climate change – the monsoon, the glaciers, the coastal areas . . . you name it and we have the vulnerability.
>
> *(Interview 2015)*

Ramesh, and much of the policy establishment, however, continue to believe that increased coal consumption over the next decades is necessary to fuel the country's growing prosperity, claiming,

> [It] is the cold-blooded development reality that there is no alternative to coal. And you need the electricity, and as I said, even with the most aggressive of assumptions, you still require the coal. I don't see India reducing its absolute levels of emissions. I don't see that in the next 15 years.
>
> *(Interview 2015)*

For Ramesh, the climate imperative is weighed against India's ostensible need for more coal-fired power. Regrettably, Ramesh claimed, India could not supplant coal without abandoning the poor. Here we can see climate change inducing intense cognitive dissonance: the poor must be saved by coal-led development, and at the same time they must be swept away by the climate change it produces. For such policy experts, the rhetoric of modernity, with coal at its centre, retains remarkable power and resilience. For Nehru, dams were the temples of modern India (Verghese 2013). Is the Varanasi coal market the apogee of coal-led development today (Allard 2015; Hayden 2015)?

Others, such as the environmental lawyer Sudiep Srivastava, and representatives of energy research groups such as Prayas, insist that coal has had its day. In particular, they point to excess capacity in the coal-fired power sector and argue that India does not need new coal mines, nor does it need any new coal-fired power. Modelling is undertaken to demonstrate that India's energy demand can be met by existing mines and power plants if they were made more efficient (see Chapter 7).

Some of the local activists were aware of the issues, but climate change was not at the forefront of their struggle. When specifically asked about climate change, Alok Shukla said:

> Climate change is a big issue ... That is why we talk about the complete Hasdeo-Arand region and not about a particular mine. If mining comes there and the whole Hasdeo-Arand region is destroyed, then it will be a huge loss for the environment. That is why when we talk, we associate our fight with climate change. We do not only talk about shutting down coal mining, but we also talk about alternative energy. Because we believe that the more the production based on fossil fuels, the [higher] will be the impact on the environment. We talk about decentralized power and decentralized production.
>
> *(Interview 2015)*

Here he combines the narratives of energy transition with on-the-ground anti-coal struggles. The realisation of strategic leverage through region-wide mobilisation, for the Hasdeo-Arand forest, is linked to climate through the loss of carbon sinks, but also through the burning of coal, and thus to the possibilities for renewable, decentralised, 'alternative energy'. These kind of linkages are available and certainly being explored in what is a dynamic ideological struggle: the struggle for the FRA, for instance, could over time be seen as quintessentially a climate justice campaign, with wide resonance for all of Indian society. Certainly, it is from these kinds of campaigns that a new common language may emerge for global climate priorities and the urgent struggles on the ground.

Conclusions

In Chhattisgarh, many of the proposed mines that we discussed were still under legal challenge in 2019. As outlined in Table 2.3, there are public–private proposals for several new mines and mine expansions. Several remain heavily contested but have been approved, though delayed by other means. If they proceed, they will have a massive impact on the core Hasdeo-Arand forest.

In February 2019, the Federal Environment Ministry gave provisional approval for the Parsa mine in the Hasdeo-Arand, breaching the conditions in place for the PEKB mine that there would be no more mining approvals in the forest. The approval, in the context of the Chhattisgarh election and with the Supreme Court decision, has pushed local mobilisation to a new level. In February 2019, 150 *Gram Sabhas* in the Hasdeo-Arand met to declare their opposition to forest clearance and to mining. The group was planning a march on the state capital under the slogan of '*Vaada Nibhaao*', 'keep your promises', directed at the new Congress Party government. Collective outrage at the mining approvals, in the context of the Supreme Court decision, was combined with increased confidence in political capacity. As Jayanandan Porte said, 'Let the environment ministry do

Table 2.3. *Status of applications to mine the Hasdeo-Arand forest*

Name of Coal Concession	Total Forest Land	Total Non-Forest Land	Coal to Be Mined	Forest Clearance Approvals
Chotia	900 ha	300 ha	Expansion 0.7–1.0 mtpa 2018	Granted 2011
Kete Extension	1,745 ha	Nil	Nil	Permission for prospecting
Madanpur South	660 ha	53 ha	ToR 2017; EIA pending	Nil
Parsa	841 ha	400 ha	Approved in third application, for 5 mtpa, 2019	Pending Supreme Court decision
PEKB	1,898 ha	800 ha	Expansion, 10–15 mtpa, 2018	Granted 2011
Paturiya Gidmuri	1,466 ha	285 ha	Considered for ToR 2018	Submitted 2018

Source: Gupta and Bipasha (2018); with updates from Nandi (2019).

what it wants . . . If our *gram sabhas* collectively oppose mining, what the ministry does will be inconsequential.' The context had changed:

> Before the PEKB mine was cleared, villagers used to think, '*Yeh to sarkaar ka hai. Sarkaar toh ek din isko le hi lega.*' [The forest belongs to the government, and they will take it away one day.] But today, villagers believe that if we fight, we can protect the forests from mining. We are much more aware about the laws and our power as *gram sabhas*. People feel more empowered.
>
> *(Porte, in Choudhury 2019)*

Our interviewee from 2015, Alok Shukla, was quoted in the press calling the approval a clear violation of the FRA, predicting, 'The matter of mining in the whole Hasdeo-Arand region will be an important issue for voters during the upcoming *Lok Sabha* [federal] elections' (Aggarwal 2019).

Chhattisgarh was by no means the only state where the FRA and PESA were being undermined by mining interests. Parallel struggles had been erupting across India, including, as noted, in neighbouring Jharkhand. Analysis of the November 2018 assembly elections by the NGO Community Forest Resource–Learning and Advocacy (CFR-LA) found that the Congress had been more successful in Chhattisgarh, where it championed the FRA, than in other states. The group calculated the consequences for the national electoral landscape if the Chhattisgarh model was followed in national constituencies with *Adivasi* voters. They found that up to a quarter of the 543 national seats were vulnerable to an *Adivasi* revolt against mismanagement of the FRA, reflecting the potential impact of the FRA as a shared frame, for re-thinking national traction of forest rights violations.

Underlying these shifts, and as noted throughout this chapter, is the mobilisation of an incommensurable challenge from forest dwellers. *Adivasi* communities by definition cease to exist when dispersed by mining, and for them, anti-mining is an existential struggle. Mining cannot be made commensurable with *Adivasi* interests, and is vociferously and persistently opposed, especially when developmental promises fail to be delivered. This aspect of the struggle is fundamentally important for understanding the political challenge posed by *Adivasi* rights: it subverts the epistemic notion that everything 'has its price', that is, the idea of universal commodification at the heart of neoliberal developmentalism. In this, *Adivasi* peoples share something important with climate campaigners: both are fighting zero-sum conflicts; it is either win or lose. If climate wins, coal loses; if *Adivasis* win, coal loses; and vice versa for both. Or to put it another way, the survival of community and the survival of the ecosystem are both threatened by coal: resistance to coal is a fight for survival. As argued later in this book, the most strategic priority for anti-coal campaigns is delinking coal from development.

As Parajuli puts it, for the poor in India, the issue is no less than the 'right to life', while for the privileged few, the issue is the 'right to property' (Parajuli 1996). We returned to the village of Kete in the third year of our research. The dystopian paraphernalia of mining loomed over the village – almost as if it were about to pounce and consume it. There was coal dust on the fields, in the water, on the children who were running home from school. As *Adivasis* made clear to us, these forests are more than a collection of trees. They are complex ecosystems that sustain not only humans but also animals, insects, uncountable life forms that are intrinsically bound up with the ecology of the jungle. These are also sacred spaces, full of both inspiration and terror; loss of these spaces is a negation of *Adivasi* spirit, personhood and identity. Since nature is also an actor in the complex assemblage of eco-biological systems of this earth, the loss of *Adivasi* rights to the irresistible forces of resource extraction points to a bigger loss, those of the rights of the forests and of the life-systems, including humans, they nurture.

The last word, therefore, should go to an elder of Salhi village who put the case poignantly:

> This land is our mother and we cannot go to another land by selling her. We will not flourish; rather, we will face troubles and violence elsewhere. We have grown here just as our ancestors, and this land has given us everything from food [to] shelter, clean air, water, home, so considering all that, this land is equivalent to our parents and God, and we cannot sell them. We are willing to face arrows and weapons with our children instead of being ashamed of having to sell our land and live like beggars or wanderers.
>
> *(Interview 2015)*

3

Australia

Contesting Coal Capital on the Liverpool Plains

On 19 February 2015, an unusual event occurred on the main street of Gunnedah, in North West New South Wales. A gathering of about sixty people assembled outside the offices of Shenhua Watermark Coal Pty Ltd, Australian subsidiary of Chinese state-owned company Shenhua Energy. The company was planning a 10-megatonnes-per-annum open-cut coal mine in the midst of the Liverpool Plains: prime agricultural land and ancestral country of the Indigenous Gomeroi people. It was a Thursday, and the office was closed, as it was Chinese New Year. Members of Red Chief Local Aboriginal Land Council (LALC) had organised a protest rally against the Shenhua mine project. The protest was supported by Front Line Action Against Coal, an anti-coal climate activist group that was blockading the site of another new mine, also in Gomeroi country, on unique biodiverse forest north of Gunnedah.

Apart from the activists, a few members of the farmers' anti-mine action group, Caroona Coal Action Group, attended, as well as a local independent political candidate who was opposing the Shenhua mine. Our research team added to the small throng. Gomeroi elders performed an Aboriginal smoking and cleansing ritual among the Chinese New Year decorations bedecking the building entrance. A number of speeches followed, with Gomeroi speakers informing those present that the mine would destroy ancient tool- and weapon-sharpening megaliths, their 'war memorial site' from the period of colonial invasion, and that it must be opposed at all costs. Andrew Pursehouse, a local farmer, also drew on war imagery, reminding the audience that Gomeroi and farmers' fathers and grandfathers had fought together during two world wars, bonding their descendants to join forces against this new enemy.

The assembly then formed up and marched chanting down the length of the main street, Aboriginal flags and signs aloft, some with Chinese characters. 'Lock the gate to coal and gas companies.' 'Don't destroy sacred land.' 'Protect cultural heritage.' 'Human rights violated.' Shopkeepers emerged, and pedestrians stopped in their tracks to stare at this novel spectacle. It was an impressive action, culminating in an open invitation to morning tea at the Red Chief LALC premises, at the other end of the main street. There was an atmosphere of conviviality and righteous common cause as the participants enjoyed tea and biscuits together.

The protest, led by Gomeroi people joined by farmers and environmental activists in the main street of a conservative country town, has all the features of the unstable and unlikely alliances identified by many other researchers in regional Australia when normally antagonistic or disconnected groups join forces to fight unwelcome local development. The expansion of extractivist capitalism in rural Australia brings many such alliances together (McManus and Connor 2013; Sherval, Askland et al. 2017; Vincent and Neale 2017). The forces ranged against them can be formidable: states wedded to developmentalist ideology and unsustainable growth, transnational corporations, and powerful class interests in all major political parties.

Despite the entrenched power imbalances, the outcome of these conflicts is by no means predetermined. In NSW and Queensland, coal is the largest export commodity, and large swathes of rural land, also claimed as ancestral country by Aboriginal Australians, are taken over for coal and CSG mining. The Liverpool Plains has been a prominent site of resistance against local coal projects. Residents of the region, environmental activists, State and Federal politicians, countless technical consultants and public servants, lawyers, journalists and the broader public have been engaged in the debate over coal on the Liverpool Plains in some way for more than thirteen years.

This chapter is based on our field research from 2014 to 2016, which occurred at the same time as the ethnographic research undertaken for the Coal Rush project in Lausitz and Chhattisgarh. The research puts local opponents at the centre of the analysis. We begin with an introduction to different connections to land and place, as well as class, cultural and political differences, focussing on the lives and histories of Gomeroi Traditional Owners, farmers, rural workers and town dwellers. We then analyse the arrival of coal capital in the region in the form of two large greenfield coal-mining projects. As we recount, establishing ‘new coal’ on the Liverpool Plains has proven immensely difficult for proponents. We examine the focal points of contestation through modes of collective action and some examples of the counter-moves against the state’s efforts at enabling displacement and externalisation of coal mining’s destructive effects – a point of similarity with the research project’s other case studies. The chapter then considers points of intervention that opponents have created in their efforts to destabilise the coal commodity. We analyse opponents’ attempts to re-regulate by means of state and national planning regulations, environmental and Indigenous heritage protection laws, as well as direct appeals to Members of Parliament. We also analyse efforts at articulating anti-coal stances with wider environmental and climate concerns, finding various tensions between what we have termed the 'regional exceptionalism' of some opponents and the universal challenge to coal posed by climate change. The chapter concludes with some reflections on the extent of the challenge that the various modes of opposition have posed to the state's enabling of coal capital accumulation, the ongoing uncertainty of the 'stalemate', and the social and cultural transformations that ensue from this protracted and many-sited struggle.

Places, Histories and Lives on the Liverpool Plains

In NSW, rich Permian coal deposits in the Sydney and Gunnedah Basins are found underneath some of Australia's biggest coastal cities as well as in agricultural areas. Historically mined for domestic energy and industrial use, most of the black coal produced in over thirty coal mines now goes to the transnational coal trade from Newcastle, much publicised as 'the world's largest coal export port'. The reach of the supporting infrastructure of rail haulage has expanded to inland districts as far as Narrabri in the North West of NSW.

The main ethnographic research site for the study was the Liverpool Plains, located to the west of the Great Dividing Range at 31 degrees latitude. The Liverpool Plains is a floodplain of the Namoi River, a temperate woodland zone about 270 metres above sea level. The landscape is dominated by cropping agriculture and beef cattle on properties that are often thousands of hectares in size. The rich basaltic soils, underground water flows and benign microclimate have provided farming livelihoods since early colonial days. The original owners of the land, the Gomeroi Aboriginal people (also known as Kamilaroi), sustained their way life for at least 25,000 years before dispossession by European settlers.

Gomeroi Lives

Based on early colonial reports, O'Rourke (1997) estimates that approximately 10,000 people lived in Kamilaroi country[1] around 1820, with up to 60 matrilineal descent groups, each with 150–200 members, termed *taurai* (see Figure 3.1) *Taurai* also refers to descent groups' territory, organised around creek catchments (Macdonald 2017). The usual residential grouping as in other Aboriginal societies was the hearth group – parents and dependent children. In summer months, plentiful food supplies allowed multiple hearth groups to congregate in semi-permanent settlements near water sources. Colder months saw people breaking into smaller groups to hunt and forage in back country (O'Rourke 1997: 149). As documented for the rest of Australia, people were agents of environmental change in their territories, using fire stick farming, elaborate fish traps and other systematic

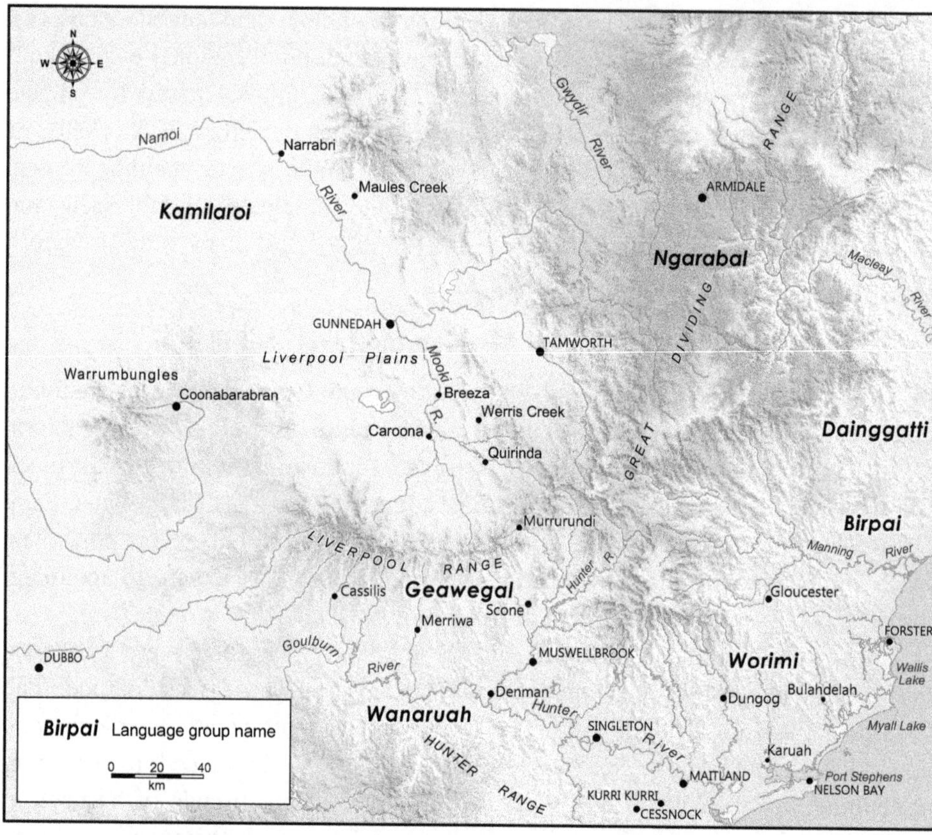

Figure 3.1 Indigenous language groups in North West NSW.
Source: prepared by Olivier Rey-Lescure, Cartolab

resource management techniques that maximised food supplies throughout the seasonal cycle (Gammage 2011; Pascoe 2014). Gomeroi people encountered Christian missionaries from the time of first contact, but they remain closely linked to the land through Dreaming connections, and have totemic bonds to living creatures, plants and many other features. Creative Ancestors include the powerful sky-dwelling Baiame, sometimes represented in the form of a giant human; Dharramulan, who is the creator of the *buura* ceremonies; and Kurrea, the water-dwelling Rainbow Serpent (O'Rourke 1997).

During the 1820s, the NSW colony began to expand as pastoralists crossed the Great Dividing Range seeking new pastures inland and relief from drought conditions. Violent land dispossession was associated with massacres of dispossessed Gomeroi people. To some extent this is documented in contemporaneous accounts, with, for instance, records of twenty killed in 1827 in Quirindi, six in 1835 near the Namoi River, both on the Liverpool Plains, a further eighty killed near Tamworth in 1836, and subsequent massacres in the wider North West region of NSW (Ryan

2019). Lost access to food and water devastated Aboriginal populations in the early colonial period, and just as significant were the epidemics of infectious diseases – smallpox, measles and influenza – to which the people had never been exposed and which brought very high mortality rates in some regions, causing the demographic collapse of many clans and tribes. Those who survived resolutely remained in their own country, often in farm labourer employment (Goodall 2008: 28; Macdonald 2010). As in other regions, resistance was tactical, intermittently effective and combined with strategies of negotiation and land demands (Goodall 1995: 66–67; Reynolds 2006: 156).

From the 1850s, Aboriginal people were brought into a system of NSW government reserves, some under the auspices of Christian missions (Blyton et al. 2004). The establishment of the Aborigines Protection Board in 1883 initiated a period of more paternalistic policies. Living conditions and civil rights declined further during the 1890s depression and the passing of the Aborigines Protection Act in 1909 (Norman 2015: 9–10). Aboriginal people on increasingly supervised reserves experienced control over all domains of life, including removal of children to institutions. Reserves with a predominantly Gomeroi population persisted in the Liverpool Plains into the late twentieth-century era of land rights and recovery.

As a result of Aboriginal people's long struggle for land rights in NSW, the Aboriginal Land Rights Act (ALRA) was passed in 1983. Aboriginal reserves, along with Crown lands that could be demonstrated to be unused or unneeded 'for an essential public purpose', passed into the control of LALCs or became subject to land claims under the terms of the Act (Norman 2015). There are now significant assets controlled by Aboriginal communities: 'a near-billion dollar investment fund and more than a billion dollars in land holdings' (Norman 2015: 247). Obtaining new land rights is never straightforward. Thousands of claims to tracts of land, large and small, have been lodged with the NSW government since 1983, but less than half of these have been successful and most have been protracted and/or subject to political interference (Norman 2015: 108–112).[2] Since 2016, Gomeroi people have lodged claims in the federal Native Title jurisdiction, and some claimant groups are negotiating Land Use Agreements with mining and CSG companies (Norman 2015: 245).

Gomeroi people retain their ancestral relationship based on descent group affiliation to particular land and sacred sites. They are Traditional Owners, a community-recognised identity. Scripts of Indigenous politics express a strong sense of enduring Aboriginal connection to country into the future, as expressed by one Gomeroi man we spoke to:

> We've been here for over 40,000 years. I might go tomorrow but I can guarantee you that our kids and their kids are going to keep taking the fight up to protect our culture and heritage. So they should.
>
> *(Interview, Shaun 2015)*

Farming Lives

The settler history in the western districts of NSW starts with the colonial explorers and surveyors. By the mid-1820s, explorers had found several passes through the Great Dividing Range to western NSW (Durrant 1994:10). The colony of NSW was well established and was entering a phase of pastoral expansion initially due to the growing demand for meat in the expanding colony (Denholm 2001) and in the 1830s associated with the wool boom that first established NSW as a commodity export economy (Merritt 2001). By the 1850s, the settler population of the Liverpool Plains was well established, with a mix of residents on pastoral properties and in small townships. The NSW and Victoria gold rushes in the 1850s ushered in the period from 1860 to 1890 that historians refer to as 'the long boom' (Merritt 2001). National economic growth came to a grinding halt in the early 1890s with a run by British depositors on colonial banks followed by a credit bubble and land values boom. The pastoral economy was deeply affected by the collapses of banks, land values and export commodity prices, which all contributed to the massive contraction of economic activity, sheep numbers, government spending and gross domestic product.

The Liverpool Plains was not immune from the effects. There was a dramatic decline in wool production that continued in the twentieth century. Large grazing properties were subdivided (Carter 1974: 115) as financially stressed landholders sold up. Producers diversified into mixed farming on smaller acreages as government policies of 'closer settlement' for small holders took hold (Merritt 2001). Anthea and Les, a landholder couple, now with farming grandchildren, had many vivid memories of rural life on the Plains from the 1950s – the strong social support networks of kin and neighbours, the rich social life, and the hard work. Anthea recalled the early days after the collapse of wool prices in the 1960s:

> When the wool industry collapsed, we had to get another option ... And of course irrigation had come for this part of the country, but because of the subdivision of the property, some of us were more setup for other enterprises, so we decided that we'd go into thoroughbred stallions. And we started because Les had a band of broodmares, so we bought in stallions, thoroughbreds and we bred thoroughbreds for many, many years and ran a stud here. So that was another option.
>
> *(Interview, Anthea and Les 2016)*

In the late 1960s and early 1970s, prospecting for underground water yielded an enormous reward: the discovery of vast reserves of high-quality water in a complex system of layered and interconnected aquifers. The development of bore drilling technology, innovations in tractor technology and new crop varieties facilitated the move to irrigated broadacre cropping. Dorothy Durrant, in her history of the district, wrote that, as a result of the aquifers discovery and technological change,

'A revolution in thinking occurred about what the district could grow, even without irrigation' (Durrant 1990: 9). Production remained subject to the vagaries of Australian weather, commodity demand and crop failures as well as politics. Droughts crippled production in 1965–1966, 1970, and 1980; severe floods occurred in 1971 and 1974.

Mining the socio-ecological 'gift' of the aquifers, combined with the expansion of export opportunities, was a boon for farmers in the irrigable areas of the Plains. Anthea reflected on the opportunities that opened up after the discovery of the big underground aquifers, and the good fortune of a couple of years of excellent summer rain in the early 1970s:

> We had this tremendous change. We could grow sunflowers and white sorghum, not just wheat and sheep and wool. Suddenly there was an option, the markets opened up. You know, people had gone to Japan because Japan suddenly became more interested and this big, anti-Japanese attitude[3] started to slip away.
>
> And then, we were doing markets with Africa. We were selling white sorghum to Africa. And Les's brothers got into corn, corn hadn't been grown here for god knows when, you'd only feed it to cattle or horses. You had Kellogg's and all those people, so you had all this growing of corn.
>
> *(Interview, Anthea 2016)*

Liverpool Plains agricultural production is organised on agribusiness lines, with properties typically held by family companies and trusts. Multinational agribusiness is a minority of holdings but the farming is highly capital-intensive. In contrast with earlier periods, there are fewer employment opportunities for labourers, as machines now do jobs like cotton weeding, picking and baling. With good agricultural services and access to a pool of casual workers in the towns, even large farms can now be run with a manager and two or three assistants.

Rural Workers' Lives

Prior to the era of intensive mechanisation in the 1970s, landholders were large employers of both year-round and seasonal labour. The countryside is dotted with villages, many of them once thriving small townships from the 1850s. In some places, only the name and a few derelict houses remain, while others have become small settlements, often bereft of commercial services. Some boast a pub, and there is often a park and a community hall, perhaps a church and a cemetery. Breeza, in the heart of the Liverpool Plains and the closest settlement to the proposed Shenhua mine, is one such village in our study area.

Breeza today has a stable population of about fifty. It is a sociable community, with longer-term residents and more recent arrivals living in cottages on large lots with plenty of space for trucks, sheds and animals. The main source of paid work is still casual farm labour and transport jobs for truck owners. Breeza residents commented that long-standing relationships with landholders are important for this:

Val: And you get the work from knowing the farmers, you develop a relationship, they know you and they give you a call.

Joan: They ring my husband up and say, 'Listen are you doing any work at the moment, can you, can you give us a week? So and so wants a week off, you know.' So he'll go and do a week, a week's work when somebody goes on holiday.

(Interview, Val and Joan 2016)

Class divisions between landowners and rural workers are marked, but exist within a quotidian framework of shared commitment to place, and values of cooperation and mutual support. Land rights and access to country are the deepest source of conflict, potential or actual, between landowners and Traditional Owners.

In Breeza, some Gomeroi residents who were born there are connected through ancestral ties to that place, which cannot be severed by property titles or mining projects. They speak of the strength of these ties, and links going back to early settlement, as in this exchange between two Gomeroi men and a neighbour:

Eric: I don't intend going. I was born and bred here and I'm not going.
Robert: And my ancestors come from here.
Val: He was born here, he's got no choice, he has to be here.
Eric: 1840s! 1840s we were here. . . . 1840s we go back.
Robert: We can go back a little further than that! (all laugh).

(Interview, Eric, Val and Robert 2016)

This question of who has the choice to leave and who has no choice but to stay is important when considering Gomeroi connection to country. Gomeroi country is not an asset that coal companies can compensate with the means to buy an equivalent asset elsewhere. Its value is incommensurable in these terms.

Town Lives

We made contacts and participated in events in several of the North West towns over the duration of the study. We selected Quirindi, the municipal centre of Liverpool Plains Shire, as the main site for the ethnographic study of town life. The shire population is 7,687 (ABS 2016) with about 3,500 people living in the town, some with ties to landholding families and established enterprises, others in short-term professional, service and commercial occupations. Quirindi has the character of a small country town that services the agricultural hinterland. The town's settlement goes back to the 1820s, and it flourished in the nineteenth-century 'long boom', particularly after the arrival of the railway in 1877.

There are many similarities between 'town and country' in the district.. There are shared party political affiliations, with most voting for the rural-based conservative National Party or for independent rural representatives. There are shared scripts of cultural identification with regional and rural Australia, co-dependence on rural industries, and shared participation in popular leisure pursuits and community service clubs.

At the same time, there are some significant divisions defined by large-scale landholdings of some farmers – in wealth, livelihood, sense of place, and economic opportunity. These often come to the surface in discussions of proposed coal mine developments. Gomeroi people have another experience of social difference. Their unique connection to their ancestral places, their experience of dispossession and generally low socio-economic status, set them apart from much of the social life of landholders and town. On the other hand, Quirindi and other North West towns have strong town-based organisations in the LALCs, Aboriginal Corporations and linked services. Like other Aboriginal groups in NSW, they have gained increased autonomy, corporate lands and local recognition in recent years, as part of the growing momentum for Indigenous rights in NSW and Australia (Norman 2015).

The following sections elucidate how these various participants in social life on the Liverpool Plains experienced coal capital's arrival. The actions of different groups and alliances to derive advantage or avoid harm were significantly transformed, and transforming, in the intensely political engagements of citizen protagonists, coal companies and state agencies that took place over the duration of our study, and which are ongoing.

The Arrival of Coal

As with any major economic activity, coal mining shapes patterns of social life. However, particular and often divisive issues arise when societies are confronted with new coal developments on an unprecedented scale. Conflicts over coal instigate new forms of social affiliation and social action, and may consolidate or disrupt historical political allegiances (McManus and Connor 2013; Pearse 2016). These social experiences and imagined futures are articulated in collective cultural expressions or 'scripts' that form the rationales for protagonists' claims in political contests around coal mines (McManus and Connor 2013: 166–167; Vanclay and Enticott 2011).

A number of coal projects currently operate in North West NSW, and mining has long been part of the regional economy (see Table 3.1). As coal prices rose in the mid-2000s, owners of existing coal projects in Narrabri Shire sought to take advantage of the rich coal deposits in the Gunnedah Basin. New development applications for larger-scale mines were lodged. The largest and most contentious of these has been the Maules Creek project, majority-owned by Whitehaven Coal,[4] an Australian company with a number of smaller coal mines around Narrabri. Whitehaven received approval in 2012 to produce 13 megatonnes per annum (mtpa) at Maules Creek, making it the largest producer in the North West. The

Table 3.1. *Coal mines operating and proposed in the Gunnedah Basin*

Name DGRs issued	Majority owner	Type	Coal productionMt/yr	Status
Werris Creek 2005	Whitehaven	Thermal, open cut for export	2 for 7 years	Operating 2005
Narrabri Nth 2006	Whitehaven	Thermal, underground for export	11 for 21 years	Operating 2012; expansion to 13 Mt/ yr pending
Rocglen 2006	Whitehaven	Thermal, open cut for export	1.2 for 10 years	Operating 2008
Tarrawonga 2005	Whitehaven	Thermal/ coking, open cut for export	3 for 18 years	Operating 2006
Sunnyside 2006	Whitehaven	Thermal, open cut for export	1 for 5 years	Operating 2008
Boggabri 2006	Idemitsu	Thermal/ coking, open cut for export	1.5 for 21 years	Operating 2006
Vickery 2010	Whitehaven	Thermal/ coking, open cut for export	4.5 for 30 years	Operating 2014; extension to 10 Mt/ yr pending
Maules Creek 2010	Whitehaven	Thermal/ coking, open cut for export	13 for 30 years	Operating 2012
Caroona 2014	BHP Billiton	Thermal, underground for export	10 for 30 years	Withdrawn 2016
Watermark 2012	Shenhua	Thermal/ coking, open cut for export	10 for 30 years	Conditional approval; pending application

mine site is near cattle farms, and part of it is located in the Leard State Forest, on the northern boundary of the Plains, and not far from the pre-existing smaller Boggabri and Tarrawonga mines.

While several other coal projects were in the NSW planning development process at the same time as Maules Creek, including the BHP Caroona and Shenhua Watermark Coal Projects discussed in the next section, Maules Creek attracted most public attention during several years leading up to its planned start of operations in 2015. Local landholders organised against the mine through the Maules Creek Community Council from 2010, joined in a broad coalition with Gomeroi Native Title Claimants and anti-coal groups including Lock the Gate Alliance and Front Line Action against Coal. They built a long-running blockade from 2012 against the proposed mine, opposing it as a threat to Gomeroi burial grounds and other sacred sites, to endangered species of the forest, and to land and climate. While ultimately unsuccessful, the campaign against Maules Creek dovetailed with growing awareness of the impacts of CSG extraction on underground water, and helped mobilise farmers against both coal and CSG in the wider region, led by regionally organised groups such as People of the Plains and the Northwest Alliance, as well as the national group Lock the Gate Alliance.

As discussed in the next section, organised opposition to the Caroona and Watermark mines in the fertile black soil cropping region of the Liverpool Plains, began earlier and had a different character to Maules Creek, lacking sustained alliances with climate or anti-coal organisations. Yet some of the political visibility gained by the Maules Creek campaign helped to fuel growing public disquiet at the ever-expanding coal industry in the region.

Contesting the Caroona and Watermark Mines

The arrival of coal capital in any particular location can be a quiet but significant moment in the movement towards full commodification of the underground deposits of coal. In NSW, the formal process begins with the Resources Minister identifying a zone for exploration. The department then allocates an Exploration Licence (EL) to a firm, increasingly by competitive tender (see Table 3.2). Though not required by law to directly notify landholders,[5] the NSW government contacted Liverpool Plains farmers to organise a briefing by NSW government bureaucrats in October 2005 to announce the start of coal exploration in the region. As Anthea, the farmer introduced in the previous section, recalls,

> They [government officials] rang up and booked the Caroona Hall and I said, what for? . . . they said, 'we want it for a public meeting. We're talking about opening [the Liverpool Plains] up for an exploration licence for coal.' And I said, 'You've got to be joking. I don't think that's a very good idea.' So we had a significant discussion on the telephone. And of course they went ahead, and the hall was packed [with people from] everywhere. . . . [So] this was the government coming to us to say we are going to open up this area for an exploration licence for interested parties. . . . And they told them almost to a man in the community in that October, 'This is not a good idea.'
>
> *(Interview, Anthea 2016)*

Even in this early encounter with a representative of the NSW extractive state, the key script articulating the regional exceptionalism of landowners in the mine-affected area was stressed: this is not a good place for a mine.

Despite landowners' protests, in April 2006, BHP Billiton was awarded EL6505 for the Caroona Coal Project (see Figure 3.2). Costing A$100 million, the licence permitted extraction of an estimated 10 million tonnes of black thermal coal per annum over thirty years. The mine would be long-wall (underground), as the rich

Table 3.2. *Mining approval process in NSW*

1. **Exploration Licence:** corporations bid for Exploration Licences issued by the NSW Department of Resources. Minister issues licence subject to security bond and conditions.
2. **Development Application:** applications for mines on 'biophysical strategic agricultural land' must obtain a Gateway Panel certificate before submitting a full application to the NSW Department of Planning. Applicant submits a Conceptual Project Development Plan, meets Director-General Requirements for environmental assessment (DGRs) and undertakes an Environmental Impact Statement (EIS), including consultation with authorities and landowners, and engagement with the community. As a mine proposal, the application is designated a Major Project in the State Significant Development (SSD) category. It is put on public exhibition and submissions are published.
3. **Development Assessment**: NSW Planning Department review and recommendation. 'Controversial' applications are referred to an appointed Planning Assessment Commission (PAC) for review, including public hearings. The PAC makes a Determination Report, Minister for Planning approves with Conditions of Consent.
4. **Water Trigger:** Federal Government Independent Expert Scientific Committee (IESC) reviews water-related impacts of the proposed project under the Environmental Protection and Biodiversity Conservation (EPBC) Act. IESC reports to the Federal Minister for the Environment, who approves and determines any conditions.
5. **Federal Approval:** Minister for the Environment determines on projects defined as 'matters of national significance', including under terms of EPBC Act and Aboriginal and Torres Strait Islander Heritage Protection (ATSIHP) Act.
6. **Mining Licence:** NSW Minister for Resources determines the company passes the 'fit and proper person' test, and issues Mining Licence subject to security bond and conditions.

Hoskisson seam of the lease went up to 600 metres deep (Thompson 2008). At the time, the NSW government vision was of an almost limitless horizon of expanding revenue from coal, as prices kept hitting new highs. The NSW Premier celebrated the time-honoured scripts of state developmentalism: economic growth, increased export revenue, more jobs and new infrastructure projects:

> The commodities boom is delivering significant economic growth to Western Australia and Queensland; I am pleased NSW is in a position to share in the economic benefits of high demand for Australian commodities. . . . Large tonnages of coal from Caroona could also deliver a major boost to our export revenue given the continuing demand for coal, particularly from Asian markets. But most importantly it could have major benefits for the region through new jobs and up to $2 billion in capital works and infrastructure projects.
>
> *(Iemma in AAP 2006)*

BHP's main script in the finance news media was of an expanding horizon of profits from thermal coal exports. The BHP vice president of energy coal project

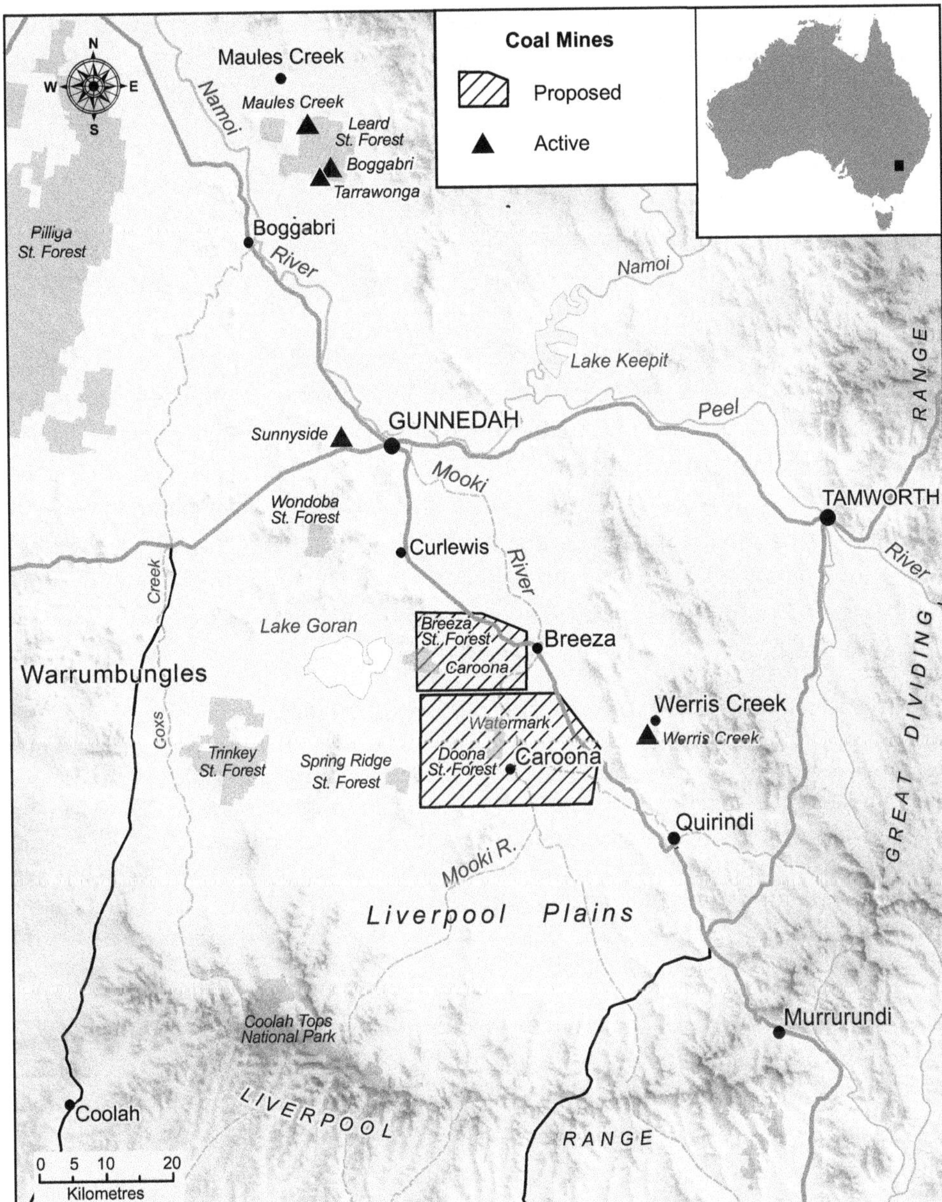

Figure 3.2 Liverpool Plains mine projects.
Source: prepared by Olivier Rey-Lescure, Cartolab

development, Phil Clark, told the press that his company had only begun analysing its first drilling results in the last few weeks, 'But it looks like it's a thermal coal to be used in power generation, and it looks like a very good quality thermal coal,' he said, noting most would probably be exported (Freed 2006).

Affected Liverpool Plains landholders and their supporters responded by forming the Caroona Coal Action Group (CCAG) in April 2006, when they realised they had a fight on their hands to stop BHP's mine (ABC Rural 2010). SOS Liverpool Plains, a women's awareness and fund-raising group to support CCAG, was formed in 2007 (ccag.org.au, accessed 31 January 2018). CCAG has been the voice of farmer opposition to mining on the Liverpool Plains for more than a decade, and during this time their main script, of Liverpool Plains exceptionalism, has been consistent, expressed in the slogan 'Wrong Mine, Wrong Place'.

Following the granting of the EL, BHP began to send geologists and a drilling team to set up test pits and drilling holes. In 2008, twenty-two landholders in the Caroona mine EL area received requests from BHP to access their property.[6] They went to the Mining Warden's Court to object and were unsuccessful (Interview, Catherine, May 2016). CCAG then blockaded BHP's drilling teams to prevent them accessing the Duddy family's property, Rossmar Park. This 615-day blockade was the first of a number of periods of heightened political mobilisation. Anthea vividly recalls the blockade, the neighbourly cooperation and the widespread support:

> We hemmed them in . . . They were supposed to give us 24 hours notice before they entered the property. And Les said, 'BHP's here.' And I said, 'But BHP can't be. They're not supposed to be here.' And he said, 'Well, they're down there digging a hole.' . . . And so we rang [our son] in Sydney, and he said, 'I'll ring Charlie [neighbour], Mum.' And he rang Charlie, and he said, 'Don't worry, mate. I'll take my machine down and I'll get Nick [son] to put his machine at your ramp.' . . . And BHP was just caught in there for months and months and months and couldn't get their stuff out.
>
> *(Interview, Anthea 2016)*

Two landholders challenged the NSW Mineral Resources Minister's decision to allocate the EL to BHP on the grounds that mortgagees had not been notified. Their case in the NSW Supreme Court was successful (ABC Rural 2010). The blockade played a significant role in delaying the progress of the BHP coal project through state and federal assessment processes, although the legislation was quickly amended to prevent further challenges (Kennedy 2017: 85–87).

The Caroona Coal Project slowly moved through several stages of the NSW government mine application process. A number of properties were acquired around Caroona. The local presence of the company, at a small office in Quirindi's main street, was never high. One woman living in town commented on the perfunctory nature of the public meetings:

> [BHP] held a number of community meetings at the RSL Club, with power point presentations reiterating already stated (in local media) edicts like 'we will only be

mining on the gravel ridges'. Answers to questions did not elaborate or extend beyond that already presented in the presentation.

(Notes Donna, 2015)

Affected landholders continued a vigorous campaign against the mine, with several rounds of appeals and legal challenges (Connor 2016; Kennedy 2017) as well as increasing pressure tactics on conservative government MPs.

The conflict heightened as another miner arrived. Parallel to the BHP coal proposal, Shenhua Energy entered the scene. In 2008, at the height of Australia's 'resource boom', when both thermal and metallurgical coal export prices hit their giddying peak of almost US$180 per tonne, the NSW government put out a tender for EL7223, in the Watermark area of the Liverpool Plains, 35 kilometres south east of Gunnedah (RBA 2009). In August, it was announced that Shenhua Watermark Coal Pty Ltd had outbid BHP Billiton, Xstrata and at least four other coal companies (Kirkwood 2008).

The Shenhua mine proposal was of a similar magnitude to the nearby BHP coal project. However, the scale of the coal resource was identified as much larger in a government report at the time, described as 'over one billion tonnes of in situ coal resources from near surface to greater than 500 metres depth of cover', being 'of domestic and export quality thermal coal' (DPI 2009: 29). Observers were left wondering what would happen to the remaining 700 million tonnes of coal, access for which would require deeper underground mining.[7]

Controversy surrounded the Shenhua EL allocation, which was overseen by then–Minister for Natural Resources, Ian Macdonald, whose 2017 conviction for misconduct in public office over the corrupt issuing of a mining licence in the nearby Bylong Valley was overturned in 2019 pending a retrial (Thompson 2019). If the mine goes ahead, Shenhua will have paid up to $675 million to explore for coal in the rich deposits of the Gunnedah Basin.[8] This is the highest amount a company has ever paid to the NSW government for the right to extract coal. Leigh and Alex, landholders located near the Watermark mine site, expressed the growing surprise and outrage that was widespread in the rural community as one coal mine project followed another:

Leigh: We first found out that they were looking to issue a coal licence there when, in 2006, [I came across] a 'Review of Environmental Factors' somewhere on the Internet. And I printed it out and I went, 'This is what these guys are doing?!' And I actually wrote submissions at that point in time to say, 'Get out of here.' You know, this is not a suitable land use for this type of prime ag[riculture]. . . . And this community was completely caught by surprise. They had no idea that this was even in the cards . . . Caroona was done in 2006. Watermark didn't go out to the market until 2007, I think it was. It then became murmurings . . . People started to understand, but there was still no information from the government at all.

Alex: We'd had a bit of a heads-up that, well, obviously they released Caroona and that was, like, a shock to this community here. And we all got very involved in protesting . . . You know, this just shouldn't be allowed! And then after that, Shenhua came, which was like we were really pole-axed between the ears with that one.

Leigh: So I think everyone just basically was in disbelief that. . .

Alex: That they'd do it.

(Interview, Leigh and Alex 2016)

While many town residents supported mining development for the jobs and business it would bring, the Watermark EL swelled the ranks of 'mine-affected landholders' in opposition. Through CCAG, they mounted a strong campaign on every possible front relevant to the agricultural economy, consistently articulating the importance of the 'black soil plains' to the food security of the nation and the threat to priceless water resources, as well as its 'wrong place' location. The landowners are well connected to rural industry organisations like the NSW Farmers Association (NSWFA) and Cotton Australia, and these groups were publicly supportive. Farmers never electorally rejected the National Party MPs in the regional seats, and persistently lobbied conservative politicians, despite the latter's pro-coal and anti–climate change policies. They foregrounded the impact of the two mines on local agricultural production, and sought to engage wider audiences with 'threats to food bowl' messages. The simultaneous reluctance to build formal alliances with national environmental groups so as not to alienate conservative political allies characterises the stance we have termed 'regional exceptionalism' – a pervasive element of the farmers' opposition since 2006 that builds on other successful locally based actions in earlier contests, especially in the fraught arena of NSW government water allocations (Pursehouse submission to PAC 2014). It provides a strong contrast with the 'globalising the local' strategies of the Lausitz villagers, who focussed on building strong coalitions with urban environmentalists, discussed in Chapter 4.

Protecting Land, Selling Land

By 2009, the expansion of coal and gas mining had become a focus of national politics and concerted local opposition. As coal prices stayed high, and EL applications proliferated, national political debate about the sale of prime agricultural land to foreign buyers brought Shenhua's 'buying spree' into the spotlight, and foreign investment approvals came under critical scrutiny. Debate centred on the Foreign Investment Review Board (FIRB), a non-statutory advisory body to the Australian government established in 1976 under the *Foreign Acquisitions and Takeovers Act 1975*. Land acquisitions made by Shenhua were examined by the wFIRB, and on 21 July 2009 the company was given approval for its purchases.

Some federal MPs, including Barnaby Joyce from the National Party, at the time a Queensland senator, were vocal in federal parliament arguing for greater restrictions on foreign investment into agriculture. In response to objections, company spokespersons argued that the strategy for acquisition in the EL zone would remove uncertainty for landholders (Clayton in Cubby and Wilkinson 2009).

However, from early on, the issue was understood as a question of whether the Australian government would limit foreign ownership of agricultural land across Australia. Two Senate Inquiries were held in 2009, the first about tightening rules of FIRB approvals and the second about food production in Australia. The latter included focussed discussion on the clash between agriculture and mining on the Liverpool Plains. Shenhua declined an invitation to attend the Senate Inquiry (ABC 2009).

No changes to foreign ownership rules, or to mining policy, came from these inquiries. But the pace of mining and CSG expansion in NSW and local tensions over Shenhua's land acquisitions encouraged the NSWFA and other organisations to favour revisions to NSW land use policy to deal with conflicts between mining and agriculture. In parallel, in some parts of NSW, there were intense campaigns against drilling for CSG on agricultural land, led by farmers mobilised through Lock the Gate (LtG) Alliance. These issues became a stake in NSW party political rivalry, and in the 2011 NSW state election campaign, the conservative Liberal-National Coalition (the 'Coalition') won on a platform that included a policy of protecting agricultural land from coal and CSG. This policy commitment translated into a series of measures that were negotiated with various stakeholders into 2012.

Ring-Fencing the Region

During the years of our research, 'ring-fencing' and 'no-go' zones were well-established political demands in the black soil plains. Most notably, landowners had engaged in a successful direct action against coal developments on their land during almost two years of the Caroona blockade against BHP in 2008–2010.[9]

In 2015, one of us visited a long-established landholder family at their property near the perimeter of the proposed Shenhua mine area. They discussed tensions and challenges of campaigning against the mine. Elizabeth explained CCAG's strategy in geographic terms – the aim was to 'ring-fence' the Liverpool Plains, making it a 'no-go' zone for coal. On this point, Elizabeth's reflection turned into a broader one about political legitimacy and coalition politics: it was important for some on the executive of the CCAG not be to seen to be part of Greens campaigns to stop coal in general. In practice, the landholders' reluctance to join wider anti-coal campaigns meant CCAG chose not to accept an invitation to join a coalition with environmentalists in the LtG Alliance.

Elizabeth shared that CCAG leaders perceived that joining with LtG would lead to rejection from Coalition politicians. Moreover, the larger goal to re-regulate coal uniformly on a state and national levels was less winnable than the ring-fencing strategy. Elizabeth and other landholders of our acquaintance didn't fully agree with CCAG's disconnection from environmentalists, or with the enduring electoral support most landholders maintained for the National Party, which had been ineffectual in changing state or federal government policies. We found that individual landholders were connected to LtG and other environmentalist campaigners for different issues and events, such as the Gomeroi protest that opened this chapter. However, when it came to efforts to protect their land assets, the focus of CCAG and the NSWFA was on state-wide policy reform capable of ring-fencing the Liverpool Plains as an exceptionally productive agricultural region.

The changes to state planning policy were brokered through an unusual alliance of the NSWFA and the Minerals Council of Australia (MCA), that in 2009 were invited by federal National Party politicians to develop a Strategic Regional Land Use Policy (SRLUP) for NSW. After two years of meetings and a change of government, the Stakeholder Reference Group broadened to include consultation with more NSW groups including representatives from the Aboriginal Land Councils, Nature Conservation Council and the Irrigators Council. Consultations broke down just prior to the 2011 state election, when the Coalition government allowed the NSW Minerals Council (NSWMC) to edit its policy draft before it was released to the NSWFA.

In 2011, the draft NSW SRLUP policy was released, introducing new scientific scrutiny of risks to alluvial soils and water resources from coal and gas mines. Not surprisingly, none of the uneasy bedfellows who had participated in its drafting was happy about the outcome. The NSWFA threatened to withdraw from the process. The NSWMC said the policy 'unnecessarily steriliz[e] the State's strategic mineral resources assets' (NSWMC 2012).

The criticisms continued when the final policy, with some amendments, was released (Denman 2012). Fiona Simson declared the policy was 'very, very disappointing' for farmers, lacking any robust legislative guarantees for protection of land and water (Fuller and Ingall 2012). The Minerals Council was dissatisfied because the policy was too robust. CEO Stephen Galilee, welcomed some rigour but commented: '[I]f you have too much regulation and new conditions and requirements as part of an assessment process you do run the risk of scaring away investment' (in Fuller and Ingall 2012).

The SRLUP created new layers to the coal and gas mine approval process, including new advising agencies and a 'Gateway' screening process[10] (see Table 3.2). However, it failed to ring-fence the Liverpool Plains. Landholders wanted the specific areas nominated in the Liverpool Plains and Upper Hunter legally protected, with an enforceable legal instrument under the State Environmental Planning Policy

(SEPP), and not just policy highlighting the significance of the region. Landholders often remarked to us, 'It's the Gateway process that doesn't have a gate.' CCAG President Tim Duddy stated:

> Well, if it's not protected it doesn't matter how much they draw on a map; the fact of the matter is it's not protected by this policy . . . There has been a State Environmental Planning Policy in NSW for seven years that is about the preservation of strategic agricultural land, and it doesn't get used.
>
> *(Duddy in Denman 2012)*

Although the SRLUP makes frequent reference to the importance of Aboriginal cultural heritage in relation to land use, there were no new or strengthened provisions. Gomeroi people, many of whom are registered Native Title Claimants, but not private landholders, have no new protections under the policy.

The SLRUP did, however, lead to additional review of the Shenhua and BHP applications, prompting Shenhua company representatives to publicly express frustrations with the ongoing delays and new layers of regulatory requirements. They declared that the delays on the Watermark mine had informed their decision to cancel $10 billion worth of major future mining-related investments in Australia (Aston 2012). This news came out via an anonymous government informant who told the *Sunday Herald:* 'companies are screaming about delays.' The government informant was reported being sympathetic with Shenhua's reasoning for capital re-direction:

> Why would an investor come to NSW, where it takes four years to get a project approved and into production, when you can do it in less than two in Africa? If [Shenhua] money is withdrawn, it sends an awfully powerful message to other investors when Australia and NSW [are] seen as a less-attractive option than Africa.
>
> *(quoted in Aston 2012)*

Land Acquisitions: Transactions and Emotions

While the diverse stakeholders were involved in the SRLUP negotiation process, Shenhua was steadily purchasing the properties it needed to start work on the mine unimpeded by landholder opponents. By June 2011, Shenhua had purchased forty-three properties covering most of the 19,500-hectare EL site, at a total cost of $213 million, with some properties purchased for more than ten times their previous sale price (Bita 2011).

In mine project localities, property acquisitions take their toll on the fabric of rural social life as a cascade of land sales creates new economic opportunities for some and potentially stranded assets for those who choose not to sell or whose property is excluded from the statutory designation of 'affected landholders'.[11]

Landholders excluded from this category who may wish to sell because of perceived impacts may be left without an offer, anticipating a bleak future of dust, twenty-four-hour noise and light, blasting, heavy truck traffic, and a stranded asset. Some of the farmers we spoke to felt themselves close enough to the mine to be affected but not close enough to be designated as having rights to request the company buy their property. This risk of one's home and business becoming a stranded asset was a strong motivation for those opposing the mine and the myriad uncertainties it would bring.

Transfers of private land to the coal company are a significant moment in the difficult drift toward coal commodification. Landholders threatened to extend the Caroona blockade to the Watermark mine before the lease was even allocated (Colvin 2008; Thompson 2008). However, the Shenhua mine project site attracted no blockading. This was largely due to Shenhua's successful early acquisition at very high prices of all the private land in the project area, after an initial phase of negotiating access agreements with the mediation of NSWFA (ABC 2009) during the exploratory drilling stage.

The decision to sell is a subterranean source of social tension. In the two and a half years we spent visiting the region, seldom did people discuss the topic of property sales to Shenhua. Most landholders are careful to respect their peers' rights to sell, particularly in light of the very large profits on offer from coal companies, seeing property sales as individual 'business decisions' (e.g. Duddy, cited in Winestock 2015). In the words of one farmer,

> [T]he only person that ever copped so-called flack for selling was the first guy that sold, and then when everyone realised how much money he received, everyone was very forgiving. That particular man tried to sell his land for about $750,000, and I believe he probably picked up about three or four million dollars for selling that same block of dirt to the Chinese.
>
> *(Interview, David 2015)*

Landowners are more likely to be directly criticised by Gomeroi residents. 'Always was, always will be, Aboriginal land' is a resounding chant from Gomeroi and supporters at anti-coal and CSG rallies. In conversation with us, several Traditional Owners expressed the stark inequities of the compensation regime:

Robert: If some of them [affected landowners] had said no, the mine could never have gone ahead.
Joan: I know two people who sold out.
Interviewer: You get disappointed in such things?
Eric: I know that other people say, oh look at the money they got, I don't care, I don't care.
Robert: One of the them, who got a significant amount of money, he said to me, 'Well if you don't like it, why don't you just leave?' I actually turned around and walked away from him because I was frightened of what I might say.

Eric: I would have said, 'Well there's no coal under my land.'
Robert: I should have said because I didn't get the proper pools of money that you got. You know, we're not getting anything.

(Interview, Robert, Joan and Eric 2016)

It is rare for farmers who have sold to speak to researchers (we only met one such landholder, in the Mid-West region of NSW), and it is not very often that they speak publicly. Upon sale the landholders may be asked to sign 'gag' agreements that prevent them from speaking publicly about the transaction (Thompson 2006). These kinds of secrecy agreements are common and in the Hunter Valley have produced sharp divisions between community members (Connor et al. 2009). Farmers and house occupiers who lease property back from the company in the period of exploration and review are also constrained by gag agreements.

In the Shenhua coal project zone, there has been some evidence of tensions in contexts where landholders who have sold remain in the community, often on their former property. However, this arrangement is not chosen by everyone. One landholder who sold spoke with the *Australian Financial Review*, describing relations with his community going 'cool' after he sold. This led him to buy a new property in the North West, but at a distance from the Liverpool Plains. 'It's too hard to live there. The emotions were too high' (Clift in Winestock 2015).

There have been other occasional public statements from families who have sold. For instance, in 2010, after selling to Shenhua, members of the Bailey family shared their reasons for selling with a reporter, highlighting the fear both of social isolation and of being left with a stranded asset. John Bailey stated:

> We felt we had no choice. Neighbours who have sold surround us. We didn't want to be left on a property next to an open-cut coalmine. It's the state government that caused this by selling the mining leases.
>
> *(Bailey in Myers 2010)*

Mrs Bailey added that their sale was a difficult decision, stating: 'The money means nothing. It is tainted money. It will never bring us joy' (ibid.). From this we infer that the decisions to sell are never taken lightly, and landholders in other regions have reported the stress associated with the process of engaging with coal companies.

As the Baileys' situation illustrates, the pressure to sell intensifies as more neighbours sell. The pool of opponents in a position to refuse the mine company shrinks. Those who are no longer defending their land and water assets 'move on', both psychologically and physically, and often, like the Baileys, with some anguish about their decision. As the Caroona Coal Project languished, some landowners lost enthusiasm for the struggle and focussed on their own enterprises. In an interview with us in 2016, prior to the cancellation of the Caroona EL, one farmer commented:

And some of the landowners that were really there in the beginning fighting the BHP licence are not so affected by the Shenhua licence. And the Shenhua licence has sort of gone ahead of the BHP licence in terms of when it's going to happen. And so those landholders have, sort of, felt that they've done their thing with the BHP, and they didn't need to keep doing it with Shenhua.

(Interview, Catherine 2016)

The cancellation of the BHP Caroona EL in 2017 removed a lot of landowners from the affected zone category. The connectivity of the underground water system, and the Shenhua mine's impact on agricultural productivity for irrigation farmers, remains a common worry but a less personally motivating concern than the prospect of remaining with a stranded property asset in a mining zone. At the same time, community concerns about the mine were never reducible to immediate local effects alone. In particular, there was widespread worry about the Shenhua and BHP projects providing a gateway for blanket mining expansion in the Liverpool Plains.

The quiet arrival of coal capital in the Liverpool Plains began with increases in international coal prices and political decisions that were invisible to landholders and residents. The subsequent tendering and issuance of licences to explore for coal, and voluntary negotiations of private property acquisitions between coal companies and landholders, began a reconfiguring of local economic and social relations. The stakes are high, and the possibility of loss and change keeps many people awake at night.

While landholders' decision to sell to the mine may be construed as an individual business decision to avert adverse consequences or to take advantage of highly inflated land values, the regional exceptionalism of the CCAG suggests something more was at stake. In their persistent efforts to re-regulate the coal commodity, NSW landholders sought to protect assets from engulfment by coal (and gas) capital by asserting an exceptional status for the region, as a highly productive 'food bowl'. The CCAG, with other regional and Gomeroi opponents, sought to assert an incommensurable local challenge to the mine, one that could not be negotiated away. In the next section we analyse the ways that opponents pursued this challenge through the state's maze of regulatory processes for approving coal mine developments.

Contesting Coal

The Watermark mine development process illuminates the politicisation of the state's role in regulating coal, and its failures in environmental and social protection. This section highlights how conflicts over coal involve community protagonists in necessary engagement with different parts of the capitalist state that are involved in regulating the coal commodity and how the horizons of these protagonists – their values, political actions, social relationships and expectations – take shape and shift in the development application process.

Coal-mining developments in NSW are regulated by the *Environmental Planning and Assessment Act* 1979 (NSW) (EP&A Act), the *Mining Act* 1992 (NSW), and the State Environmental Planning Policy (Mining, Petroleum Production and Extractive Industries) 2007 (NSW), colloquially known as the Mining SEPP. The EP&A Act defines coal mine proposals as 'State Significant Developments' (SSDs) in the broader category of 'Major Projects'. In a series of amendments, these developments have progressively been removed from the aegis of local government consent authorities, in a process that has facilitated privatisation and deregulation agendas by expanding Ministerial control of Major Projects (Connor 2016: 235).[12] Meanwhile, federal oversight is increasingly invoked in this and other environmental decisions in Australia, through the Minister for Environment.

Resisting the Mine, Not Opposing Coal

We found the claims being made by the CCAG were particularly influential in shaping the terms of regional debate over the Shenhua mine. Landholders are generally quick to identify the issues as hinging on risks to agricultural land, water and productivity. A dominant theme is the insistence they are 'not against mining', and 'not against coal' per se. Partly reflecting this, the CCAG does not campaign on the climate impacts of coal production, and does not have a position on the science of anthropogenic climate change, and the role of coal in it. This is not unlike other similar organisations, including LtG, for instance, which only makes glancing reference to the issue of climate change and coal production.[13] This reflected the still controversial politics of climate change in rural Australia, especially for National Party voters and the more conservative farmers.[14] The landholders' stance of regional exceptionalism did bring them into direct conflict with the state in terms of contesting the capture of state planning and regulation by mining interests, and in terms of asserting a re-balanced development model, that subordinated mining in the region to other social, environmental and economic interests, principally linked to agriculture.

In this respect, the farmers are similar to many of the 'reluctant activists' that become protagonists in contested local development issues but are reluctant to connect it to wider and often controversial societal debates (Peace et al. 2012). As noted, the landholders' key claims against the mine rested on the exceptionality of the Liverpool Plains as one of the most fertile food- and fibre-producing districts in Australia, a 'rich and rare' place, with 'the highest agricultural productivity in NSW' and some of the most fertile black earth soils, 'making up less than 1% of the nation's surface area' (CCAG 2013: Appendix). For the CCAG this simply was not a place to be mined; as one farmer put it, 'I believe that coal assets should be utilised only where there is a balance but in this case it is the wrong mine in the wrong place' (Juanita Hampersum, PAC submission, June 2014).

In general, this moderate stance conforms to the conservative political profile of many of the landholders opposing the mine, as drawn in one farmer's thumbnail sketch. Catherine commented: '[Most farmers are] staunch Nationals, staunch conservatives. Not particularly overly political, though. Not particularly overly anything, just all very level-headed, just getting on about our stuff (Interview, Catherine 2016).

As landholders discovered, mining capital and its state allies had no interest in maintaining the regional status quo. The objective for Shenhua, as reflected in its land acquisitions, was by definition to displace the landed incumbents. In these circumstances, ties to the conservative political elite were of little use. The Nationals remained resolutely pro-coal despite rhetorical flourishes to shore up their constituency. Ironically, as discussed below, the CCAG was better served by the independent local MP, Tony Windsor, who was willing to align with the Greens and Labor to put barriers in the way of coal capital's advance into the region.

Others advocated a more critical stance, born not of elitism but of marginality. For the Gomeroi Traditional Owners who opposed the mines (not all did), the destruction of their spiritual sites and ancestral lands, connected to cultural integrity and social well-being, is a recurring feature of their treatment in the Australian state since first contact. Gomeroi articulated a different form of opposition. Unlike the farmers, they did not argue that coal mining should happen elsewhere and instead asserted their overarching and a priori claim to Country, against the Commonwealth authority: 'We've had a gutful of the destruction of our culture; we'll rally together and march on Canberra' (Mitchell Neave in Daley, 2015).

The foundation of the Gomeroi claims resides in the uniqueness and non-convertible value of the places that constitute their cultural, spiritual and personal well-being. These places are unique in the same way that all Aboriginal places are unique. People are part of particular places, connected by birth, kinship, marriage and a host of other ties in relationships of mutual dependence of creation and sustenance in a sentient land. The long struggle of Gomeroi people predates coal's arrival by more than two centuries, in Indigenous striving for land rights and cultural survival since Australia's first settlement.

When the Caroona EL was awarded to BHP, community action was mobilised quickly. A public meeting, reportedly attended by 250 landholders and other residents, formed CCAG in April 2006. The organisation's messaging has changed over time, but the broad aims, as expressed in the words of official spokesperson Tim Duddy, are unchanged:

> We are not radicals, we are just a group of concerned farmers who don't want the land that we grew up on to be damaged. We want these plains preserved for future generations. . . . We are not anti-development, we are anti-damage.
>
> *(Duddy, 26 September 2006, CCAG website, accessed 12 July 2007)*

CCAG's 'Call to Arms' expressed the organisation's aims of mobilising a wide support group: 'local farmers and townsfolk, community leaders, industry groups, state and federal politicians and the Australian public' (CCAG website, 26 September 2006). In fact, from the vantage point of many town residents, the campaign against the mine was mainly a farmers' affair. One woman in town reflected on the long history of anti-mining campaigns since the arrival of BHP:

> Anti-mining sentiment and opposition has been piecemeal, elitist and too little too late. The 'them and us' attitude of townies vs farmers on the Liverpool Plains is older than the mining debate and was always going to prevent a unified response. Locals have lost coal-related employment over the past two years beginning with some Werris Creek–based train drivers and mine employees. There are no winners in small regional communities.
>
> *(Notes Donna 2015)*

The major parties, which supported coal mining and CSG expansion, were largely silent. Over time, as the visibility of the issue grew, National Party MPs, such as local member Barnaby Joyce, who was elected to the New England seat in 2013, were critical of the mine, while taking no effective action. Independent and populist minority party MPs who opposed the mine have gained some political capital by targeting the failure of the National Party to address landholders' concerns. Greens Party MPs have been allies for some landholder opponents of the mine, while strongly rejected by others. The Greens had been at loggerheads with the Nationals for many years: 'Greenie' is a still used derogatory term in the locality. Yet, with the Nationals staunchly opposing climate science and backing the coal industry, there is ambivalence. Independent MP Tony Windsor represented the constituency from 2001 to 2013, and supported the Labor–Green coalition government of 2010–2013. Doors had begun to open between local farmers and environmental organisations in the campaign against coal and CSG.

Overall, the scripts of most groups engaged in the struggle did not strongly thematise a blanket opposition to coal. Crucially, the 'local' scale of political claim-making is in part shaped by the narrow opportunities available within the state's regulatory framework which focuses on single coal mine projects in review processes, not cumulative impacts or regional effects on water, landscape or climate. The project application review process provides even less scope to engage in the larger questions that landholders and Gomeroi people wanted to be raised about national food security and Indigenous heritage, respectively, nor to address environmentalists' concerns about climate change.

The Planning Assessment Commission Review Process

Our first appreciation of social connections and divisions in the conflict over coal was at a public hearing held by the DPE Planning Assessment Commission (PAC) in Gunnedah in 2014. The PAC is a statutory body that reviews and makes determinations on State Significant Developments such as coal mine proposals.[15] PAC review panels for mine projects are committees of three people, usually retired senior public servants from the NSW government. They conduct public hearings, review documentation, undertake site visits and solicit information in meetings with the proponent, government bureaucrats and technical experts, to assist in making a determination under the terms of reference provided by the NSW Minister for Planning (see Table 3.2).

The PAC review of the Shenhua Watermark project brought Liverpool Plains opponents into a wider circle of interest groups in mining and CSG developments. Two PAC public hearings were held, with terms of reference for their review related to impacts on strategic agricultural land, water resources, health and amenity, and long-term land use. The first PAC hearing, held over two days in June 2014 at a community services club in Gunnedah, was a major event for mine opponents. It was preceded by a farmer-led rally and march down the main street of Gunnedah, with prominent yellow and black placards, 'Wrong Place, Wrong Mine' and 'No Mines on the Liverpool Plains', carried by a chanting crowd of about 150. A huge, fully loaded cotton-bale transporter truck was parked outside the Shenhua office, with slogans and messages in English and Chinese, such as 'Go home to China Shenhua. Don't destroy Australia's best farmland'.

At the hearing, there were over sixty presentations by individuals and group representatives, the majority opposing the development. Most of the presenters were landholders, as well as their local support groups and agriculture industry bodies, all with varying points of opposition to the mine. These speakers variously drew on independent scientific information, their personal histories of farming on the Liverpool Plains, and passionately worded statements about the bleak future for their communities if the anticipated risks were to materialise, especially risks to water sources. Catriona Simpson, a mixed grain and cattle farmer on the Plains, declared that co-existence of mining and agriculture was not possible:

> This is a fight about resources, about coal versus water, the environment, clean air and prime agricultural land. . . . We say ENOUGH is ENOUGH. We don't want to put at risk our future right to clean air, good health, water and rich agricultural land.
>
> *(Simpson, PAC submission June 2014)*

There were two Gomeroi people, an individual Traditional Owner and a representative of the Red Chief (Gunnedah) LALC, who both expressed concerns about destruction of Aboriginal Heritage and environment more generally. Four ENGOs – the Koala Foundation, The Wilderness Society, LtG Alliance and the NSW Nature

Conservation Society – expressed strong objections, and scientists from the nearby Observatory informed the PAC about the threat to their work from light pollution and dust. Technical experts, some commissioned by CCAG at considerable expense, presented counter-reports to Shenhua and the government on matters such as water modelling, koala numbers and conservation, and the company's profit projections.

The themes of opponents' presentations reflected scripts already well established during more than eight years of conflict over coal mine developments in the Liverpool Plains: the value that Gomeroi people place on their ancestral country as an indissoluble part of personal and collective identity; the exceptional status of prime agricultural land and underground water sources on the Liverpool Plains, not compatible with mining; the dubious nature of the company's scientific modelling of impacts on aquifers; the productivity of the food and fibre production of the pastoral and agricultural sectors, important to food security and well-being of Australians and overseas consumers; and the long-term profitability, sustainability and viable community fabric of agriculture compared to coal mining.

Mine supporters' scripts, including town businesses and their representative bodies, miners, service clubs and charitable groups, highlighted the economic development, badly needed jobs and enhanced regional infrastructure that the mine would bring, as well as the benefits to the local community from charitable donations and other 'corporate responsibility' initiatives. Most made passing acknowledgement of the need to protect water as the key resource underpinning regional survival and prosperity. Presentations from Gunnedah and Warrumbungles Councils aired mixed views, broadly favourable of the economic development and jobs but cautious about strain on local government infrastructure, as well as damage to water and black soil productivity, and the negative impact of land offsets under biodiversity regulation.

After the Gunnedah hearing, the PAC panel considered community presentations and submissions along with a raft of other proponent and government advisory documents. The PAC report in August 2014 approved the Shenhua development application, albeit with twenty-five conditional recommendations including proposed safeguards for water sources, the black soils, human health and koalas. Aboriginal heritage concerns were ignored. Landholder opponents and their support organisations, who had been confident of the strength of the case they had made, were angry and derisive, vowing to fight on. CCAG member Rosemary Nankivell told the regional newspaper:

> It's not over yet, this is a community that has a long history of fighting … In this day and age, an open-cut coalmine on the best agricultural land in Australia is pretty much nearly criminal.
>
> *(Nankivell in Tyson 2014)*

In the view of the opponents, the conditions placed on approval were inadequate and unlikely to be policed or implemented with the weak regulatory apparatus in place. The complex hydrology of the aquifers, on which some farmers were heavily dependent, was a major source of contention. This was a point when landholders' horizons and expectations, of the regulatory process, and their prospects within it, notably shifted to a strong sense of injustice in procedure and outcomes, as Amanda Kennedy (2017) has analysed.

Both the company and the Department of Planning were strongly critical of the strict conditions laid out in the report's recommendations, which effectively become the conditions of consent for the mine's operation after final approval. In its response in October 2014, Shenhua criticised almost every recommendation and implied it was being treated unfairly. The chastened PAC went 'back to the drawing board', commissioning more water modelling and biodiversity reports, and further consultations with the company and relevant government departments.

The second round of public hearings, held in December 2014 with a different group of panel members, attracted a similar number and composition of speakers, and was followed up by site visits with landholders and Gomeroi at their request. By this time Gomeroi Traditional Owners had assembled a strong case critical of the Aboriginal Cultural Heritage Values Assessment (ACHVA) and the Aboriginal Archaeological Impact Assessment (AAIA) reports that are a mandatory part of the proponent's Environmental Impact Assessment (EIS).[16] They highlighted deep concerns about the inadequate archaeological surveys, the need to protect significant places, including burial sites, that may not have been discovered, and the harmful and culturally inappropriate removal of huge grinding stones that were in the middle of the eastern and western mining pits. The grinding grooves, which currently sit within private farm property owned by Shenhua, are worn into a rock face from tool and weapon sharpening. Some of the large slabs of sandstone are several metres across, embedded in the ground that is moist from underground springs.

In January 2015, the PAC approved the Shenhua development application. The final report acknowledged that most speakers and submissions were opposed to the mine, with the preeminent concern 'uncertainty of any potential impacts from the mine on the aquifers, which are a critical water source for agricultural enterprises in the Liverpool Plains region' (NSW Government 2015a: 4). In carefully couched bureaucratic language, most of the earlier report's recommendations were watered down in favour of the Department of Planning and Shenhua's preferences. Landholders were 'gutted', a phrase often heard in the aftermath of the approval. Tim Duddy, spokesperson for CCAG, forecast the end of agriculture on the Liverpool Plains:

> The farmers of the Liverpool Plains have had their death warrants signed by the PAC and they have condemned the Liverpool Plains to be mined forever. It shows that these

processes, such as the Planning Assessment Commission, do not work and the water resources will be destroyed, the agricultural region will die, leaving a legacy where there is nothing, forever. People are so tied to this place and people are so angry about these processes that we have participated in for the last eight years in good faith that our assets would be protected.

(quoted in ABC NSW 2015)

Gomeroi opponents expressed outrage at the gross disrespect for Indigenous heritage on the part of the mining company and government complicity in its destruction. In reference to grinding stones relocation, one Traditional Owner stated, 'Now every site tells a story and each site is unique in its own right. So you take stuff away from that site, it takes your integrity away from it' (Interview, Shaun 2015).

Having failed in their efforts to get a favourable outcome from the state government review process, landholders turned to the federal government's regulation of water resource risks under the EPBC Act. The Gomeroi turned their attention to the federal Aboriginal and Torres Strait Islander Heritage Protection Act 1984 (*ATSIHP Act*) (see Table 3.2).

Incommensurability, Displacement and Intervention

The task of the state in dealing with the existential threat posed by coal mining is to push through regulation that appears to transform this incommensurable challenge into the semblance of a co-benefit arrangement, creating co-existence, trade-offs and compensations. In the process, the state institutionalises displacement but, in doing so, creates new sites for intervention. In managing the social legitimacy of coal mining, ostensibly in the public interest, the state 'socialises' its risks and impacts, and ironically becomes the key site of conflict (see O'Connor 1998). While state and federal government agencies have proven important and willing supporters of the coal commodity, they are also (reluctant) agents of its destabilisation. Conflicts over individual coal mines like those we witnessed on the Liverpool Plains can become so politicised and significant that state practices can shift, at least temporarily, and, in doing so, begin to de-stabilise the coal commodity. This is part of an ongoing process of 're-regulation' whereby opponents aim to change the terms of state regulation in their favour – in the Liverpool Plains case, with the aim of limiting the availability of the coal resource in a particular spatial location.

For example, earlier in the chapter, we described the attempt to ring-fence the Liverpool Plains from coal and gas developments by pushing the state government to develop a more effective strategic land use policy. The outcome of the fraught three-year SRLUP process fell far below expectations, but it kept landholder interests centrally involved in a crucial policy reform agenda and caused further delays to mining approvals through more regulatory hurdles.

The SRLUP initiative is an example of a particular response to the socio-ecological displacements set in motion by coal commodification. Appropriation of non-human nature is essential to the process of coal capital accumulation, producing multiple kinds of disruptions and displacements. The violence of the coal commodity on the Liverpool Plains involves digging up Gomeroi heritage sites, removing habitats of endangered species and destroying the homes and economic base of many Breeza residents and landholders. If mining proceeds, a series of waste products will be created by the mine, from tailing dams filled with toxic water to greenhouse gases in coal production, not to mention the emissions associated with the export to and combustion of coal in China.

Some of these matters are formally recognised and managed by different parts of the state. As part of a series of residual social and environmental protections, multiple forms of often violent displacements are allowed, but 'controlled', as part of mines' Conditions of Consent. Many of these are evident in the Shenhua development. Gomeroi heritage sites and objects in the mining zone are subject to 'relocation', such as cutting up a huge rock face and relocating it to a public space. The management of biodiversity involves the 'translocation' of an already threatened koala population to another 'like' habitat that the company will construct. Land bought by the company as 'offsets' externalises the destruction of land value – fertility, biodiversity and sustainable use – that occurs at the mine site and can destroy forms of value at the offset site. Shenhua has purchased more than 4,000 hectares of land in the neighbouring Warrumbungles Shire. At the first PAC, the Shire manager unsuccessfully protested the 'bias in favour of the developer', citing the hardships caused by the uncompensated externalities of offsetting, including depopulation and decline in community life as working farms are sold for conservation offsets, and loss of property tax income to the shire (Loane PAC submission, June 2014).

There are big gaps in the management of other externalities: consideration of greenhouse gas emissions is barely existent in state environmental law, only in federal law; risks to underground water are subject to state regulation, but not federal. Some externalities go unrecognised: derelict farms and unkempt properties owned by the company with managers on short-term contracts; reduced access to traditional country by Gomeroi who must now negotiate with a company bureaucracy for permissions; and the psychological distress of communities riven by sell-offs.

Below we discuss three sites of social and environmental protections that became important points of intervention for opponents: Gomeroi heritage; koala habitat; and underground water resources.

Removing, Relocating: Gomeroi Grinding Stones

Just as they have done since the nineteenth century, Gomeroi are resisting another round of enclosure and destruction of Indigenous heritage from the Shenhua mine. In an interview after the mine development approval, one Gomeroi man was critical of Shenhua as a foreign company that 'show no respect to us as the first people of this country':

> These grooves are highly significant to us, it took Europeans over 100 years to conquer us because we turned around and . . . fought a resistance against those settlers at the time. Now these areas are like retreat areas where the Aboriginal people retreated back to sharpen spears and stuff like that and then turned around to keep that fight going. Now every site tells a story and each site is unique in its own right. So you take stuff away from that site, it takes your integrity away from it.
>
> *(Interview, Shaun 2015)*

The treatment of the grinding stones became the public symbol of the chain of Aboriginal dispossession and destruction, especially at the second PAC, by which time the Red Chief Land Council had organised more effectively for the review process. The PAC panel, which had made no recommendations in its first report regarding Aboriginal heritage (which did not appear in its terms of reference), accepted an invitation from Gomeroi Elders to visit the grinding groove sites (NSW Government 2015a: 5). In its final report, the PAC expressed its sympathy for the feelings of 'the Aboriginal community', but determined it was 'in the public interest' to 'relocate' the grinding grooves:

> The Commission acknowledges the concerns and deep hurt that the Aboriginal community expressed during the visit to the grinding groove sites, and wishes to thank the community for sharing their knowledge of their history and their concerns for these sites. The Commission notes that the location of the two sites, being within the central parts of the eastern and western mining pits, makes preserving these in-situ impractical if the mine goes ahead. It is not evident how the mine could be altered or redesigned to avoid the two sites.
>
> The Commission accepts the significance and importance of these two sites and agrees they should not be destroyed. While not ideal, the Commission considers that the excavation and relocation of these two sites should be permitted as it will protect the rock grooves in perpetuity and therefore, on balance it would not be in the broader public interest to prohibit the mining.
>
> *(NSW Government 2015a: 13)*

A Heritage Management Plan, requiring a series of actions for 'protecting, monitoring and/or managing' any 'Aboriginal heritage items' found on the site, including relocation of the grinding stones, was included in the final Conditions of Consent for Shenhua's development application (NSW Government 2015b: 20–21).

The logic of these conditions is an affront to those who understand that these objects are intrinsic parts of unique places that are integral to Gomeroi cosmological experience and cultural identity. People are deeply pained by the removal of grinding slabs from another mine near Boggabri to the town park, where they have deteriorated with moisture loss and the clambering of children and dogs. They are adamant that the proposal to remove the grinding grooves from the Shenhua mine site for the life of the mine amounts to destruction: 'Once you take it out of the ground where they are and shift it somewhere else, it's already destroyed' (Interview, Robert 2015).

Gomeroi Traditional Owners took their case into Federal jurisdiction. In 2015, they submitted an application for 'last resort' protection and preservation of their cultural sites within the Watermark project area, under Section 10 of the Aboriginal and Torres Strait Islander Aboriginal Heritage Protection (ATSIHP) Act (Razaghi et al. 2017). This was followed by a second application in 2017. An independent review was requested by the Minister for Environment, and a community consultation took place in November 2016. There was no further response until July 2019. After a brief visit to meet with Gomeroi Traditional Owners and view the sites, the new minister, Sussan Ley, rejected the application to protect the sites despite acknowledging the sites' 'immeasurable cultural values' and significance for Aboriginal people. While stating the 'difficulties in measuring or otherwise quantifying the value of Indigenous cultural heritage and in comparing the value of such to potential economic or social benefits of the mine', the decision affirmed the pre-eminent economic value of mining, yet another iteration of the dispossession that Gomeroi have experienced since first contact. The NSW EDO announced it would be acting for Gomeroi Traditional Custodian Dolly Talbot to appeal the decision based on the minister's incorrect application of the ATSIHP Act (EDO NSW 2019).

In the official process of dealing with the Gomeroi grinding stones and other Aboriginal heritage, there is no form of life, object, amenity or place that (so far) is able to establish any moral, ontological or economic primacy over the imperative of coal capital accumulation. Effectively, the coal commodity is part of a non-linear cosmology in which time can be reversed. Within the ethos of corporate capital, all risks can be managed and everything can be 'put back together again' after the mining finishes. This is accomplished through the displacement and externalisation of risk that is the foundational logic of the state's planning and environmental legislation, and its corporate manipulation.

Translocation: Koalas

The plans to relocate the Liverpool Plains colony of koalas illustrate the perverse forms of legislation that accelerate the demise of non-human sentient beings in the name of conservation. The Liverpool Plains is home to a significant population of koalas, under immense pressure from anthropogenic change. Since colonisation, widespread land clearing, urbanisations, road kills, dogs and introduced feral animals have threatened koala populations. In the last fifteen years, major environmental changes have led to further drops in the population, such as the Millenium drought in the ten years up to the mid-2000s and the current severe drought in much of inland NSW.

Scientists and advocates for the koalas argued at the PAC public hearings that the Department of Planning and Environment failed to consider significant impacts of the mine on a viable population of koalas, as is required by the *Environmental Planning and Assessment Act 1979* and the Threatened Species Guidelines. Part of what was contested was the inadequate baseline evidence for the koala population in question. Shenhua's EIS estimated 12,753 animals for the entire Gunnedah Shire, a gross overestimate according to independent experts. Shenhua's numbers allowed the koalas to seem less vulnerable than they actually are. The Australian Koala Foundation (AKF) estimated that there are only 800–1,300 animals in the Shire (Australian Koala Foundation 2014).

The mine development requires 847 hectares of koala habitat (a small area of Breeza State Forest amidst farmland) to be cleared (see Figure 3.2). Shenhua's presentation to the PAC assumed the company would successfully control koala relocation to an offset tract away from their accustomed home. The Koala Plan of Management proposes to encourage the koalas to move 'naturally' to a 'new, young Koala habitat' with trees planted by the company over ten years. Failing that, a forced 'translocation' program will be undertaken, where animals are captured and moved to a new location. The AKF submission included evidence that there is a mortality rate of between 30 per cent and 90 per cent in relocation programs.

The final PAC report offers cursory recognition of the plight of Australia's iconic native animal as a 'significant issue' and makes no comment on the marked disparity between company and AKF statistics on koala numbers and relocation mortality. The final report found in favour of the company, with a string of Conditions of Consent relating to planting of feed trees and a lengthy discussion of the provision of a company shuttle bus to transport employees to and from the mine site so that they would be less likely to run over the koalas while commuting.

In mid-2015, in response to the deficient PAC determination, Upper Mooki Landcare, a local environmental group, in partnership with public-interest environmental lawyers, challenged the company and Planning Department in the NSW Land and Environment court (EDO 2016). This was a judicial review case, the only form of appeal now possible to opponents under the EP&A Act. The litigants argued that the PAC had not given due consideration to the scientific evidence for koala demographic vulnerability and translocation mortality. The case was dismissed with the judge finding the development approval was valid. A farmer involved in the Landcare group articulated the injustice on behalf of the koalas:

> It is not enough for the Baird government and mining giant Shenhua to cross their fingers and hope that koalas survive 'translocation', which experts judge carries a high risk of failure. … Unleashing this mine on the remaining koalas ratchets up a notch what is already a desperate situation for the estimated 262 koalas that now live where Shenhua wants to put its mine.
>
> *(Ranclaud in NCCNSW 2016)*

'Getting the Science Right': Scaling Up Water Regulation

Neither the koala case nor the Gomeroi legal appeal under federal Indigenous heritage legislation elicited public comment from the company. However, there was a strongly negative business response when independent federal MP Tony Windsor, a Liverpool Plains farmer himself, worked with the Greens and Labor to secure an amendment to federal environmental protection law in 2013. The 'Water Trigger' amendment to the *Environment Protection and Biodiversity Conservation Act* 1999 (EPBC Act) gave new powers to approve or deny mine developments, or impose specific conditions relating to water management for mines approved by the federal Environment Minister. In circumstances when the Water Trigger applies, an Independent Expert Scientific Committee (IESC) undertakes a review of the risks to water, and plans for its management.

The Water Trigger amendment was first introduced into federal parliament in March 2013 and was passed in June of that year. It was instantly controversial, with Coalition MPs and business groups opposing it. The Minerals Council of Australia (MCA), Australian Petroleum Production and Exploration Association (APPEA) and the Business Council of Australia (BCA) opposed the reforms as being too onerous, predicting they would discourage investment in gas exports (APPEA 2013; Lloyd 2013).

Strong public criticism came from the Shenhua leadership in April 2013 at a business forum attended by the former Prime Minister Julia Gillard. Liu Xiang, chair of Shenhua Australia, addressed the forum:

> From our own perspective the regulatory environment is different today than it was when Shenhua first invested in the Watermark project in 2008 … At a macro level, the investment environment in Australia remains attractive. However, a degree of caution still needs to be exercised by policymakers so that unexpected changes in legislation and regulation do not impact investor sentiment about this market.
>
> *(Liu in Wen 2013)*

This statement demonstrates the extent to which Shenhua believed its key bargaining chip was Australia's claim to be 'open for business'. Allegations of sovereign risk, and the related invocation of capital flight, no matter how glancing, directly translate into political risk, especially for Labor governments.

The Water Trigger was also criticised by its presumed beneficiaries – the agricultural industry. The NFF distanced itself from the reform, expressing concern that it could set a precedent, leading to future regulation where the agricultural industry might become subject to the same kinds of federal government review as the mining industry.

Tony Windsor, the Water Trigger's sponsor, was the most enthusiastic advocate of the amendment, and staked his political fortunes on it. His enthusiasm was shared by landholders when their lobbying resulted in referral of the Shenhua application to the federal minister for review under the EPBC act in February 2015. The minister referred the review to the IESC, thus 'stopping the clock' on the time limits for the assessment process. Tim Duddy's response, on behalf of CCAG, was diplomatic:

> The weight on the Commonwealth Government from the Directors of the Chinese project will be enormous at this time and the stopping of the clock enables them to do a proper review of the things that are outstanding in this project... That is something that needs to happen and I'm very grateful that it's occurring.
>
> *(Duddy in McOwan and Thomas 2015)*

When the Shenhua mine proposal was reviewed, the IESC's advice became hotly politicised. Notwithstanding criticisms of the process, which resulted in a weak supportive report, the Federal Environment Minister Greg Hunt announced conditional approval for the mine in July 2015, citing IESC advice that risks were 'manageable'. The minister was strongly criticised in the media by landowners and their supporters. When berated by influential conservative radio host Alan Jones on the nationwide 2GB *Alan Jones Breakfast Show*, the minister declared he would take the unprecedented step of referring the Shenhua water management plan to the IESC for further review (Hunt in Mitchell 2015).

The Water Trigger, and the Biodiversity Management Plan that was also part of the Minister's conditions of approval, created more hurdles for Shenhua, setting in train a number of unresolved legitimation issues concerning the impact of mining on the black soils and the underground aquifers. Four years later, Shenhua still had not submitted the water or biodiversity management plans to the federal department for IESC review.

The three points of intervention we have discussed in this section are significant attempts by local opponents at re-regulating the coal commodity on the Liverpool Plains. While the case against the translocation of koalas was unsuccessful, the other two challenges are still unresolved, evidence of the effectiveness of opponents' persistent efforts to achieve reregulation. There is much at stake. The defensive counter-moves against the appropriation of land, country and livelihoods has elicited a chain of ad hoc and indecisive responses from the state.

Alliance-Building and Climate Articulation

Alliances among local groups contesting coal and CSG in North West NSW have been in place for sometime. In the Liverpool Plains, there is ongoing collaboration between CCAG and the Red Chief LALC. In the broader North West region of which the Liverpool Plains forms the southern part, a range of alliances between local groups and environmentalists began to emerge from 2010, with the formation of LtG Alliance, organised opposition to the Maules Creek mine, and the ongoing actions against CSG around Narrabri in the north. Such alliances have become a long-standing presence in the North West, for instance, with the creation of regional organisations such as the Northwest Alliance and People for the Plains, both linking farmers and environmentalists.

The campaign led by the CCAG against the Shenhua mine has generally not been conducted in alliance with environmental organisations. Some landholders, at a low ebb due to the setbacks of 2015, briefly formalised a Liverpool Plains Alliance involving the CCAG, existing local allies and national environment organisations including the Wilderness Society, 350.org and LtG. It was launched in November 2015 with a 'Harvest Festival' weekend gathering of several hundred people at Breeza on the property of one of the long-standing CCAG members and vocal mine opponent, Andrew Pursehouse (Murphy 2015) (see Figure 3.3). Speakers included the NSW Greens MP Jeremy Buckingham, Gomeroi elder Dolly Talbot, populist Tasmanian senator Jacqui Lambie and Fiona Simson, head of the MSWFA.The initiative for the Alliance came from the Liverpool Plains Youth (LPY), a group formed in November 2014 with members mainly from farming families and local agricultural businesses (Liverpool Plains Youth 2016). A proposal was developed through meetings of LPY members with activists from the Newcastle branch of the national conservation NGO, The Wilderness Society. According to Maddy Coleman, one of the founders of Liverpool Plains Youth, linking with environmentalists was 'definitely tough on a lot of people', but, as she said, the Harvest Festival had shown the Alliance was 'really powerful' (Interview, Coleman 2015).

CCAG member and landholder, Andrew Pursehouse, who hosted the Festival, confirmed farmers were 'pretty uncomfortable' with aligning with environmental organisations, but stressed the need to 'do whatever it takes'. For him the Alliance was a product of frustration with existing political channels. As he said, 'For our National Party at the moment to be not fighting this, I just cannot believe it. ... I just can't believe that we have farmers now that are having to support the Greens' (Interview, Pursehouse 2015). Pursehouse stated that he and his fellow farmers felt

Figure 3.3 'Protect the Plains' protest at the harvest festival, Liverpoool Plains, 2015.
Source: Jeff Tan, photographer, with permission

'abandoned', adding, 'We know we should be voting for the National Party . . . but how can you vote for a National Party that won't support protecting the Liverpool Plains.'

The Alliance had its parameters, and not all landowners supported it. At the time Pursehouse stressed farmers were leading the Alliance, and that it maintained the 'wrong mine, wrong place' stance, stressing, 'It's all about coal mining on the Liverpool Plains. It's not about all mining' (Interview, Pursehouse 2015). The place-based strategy, for 'dining, not mining', was echoed in the Harvest Festival theme, and the campaign videos emphasised repeatedly the limited life span of a coal mine in comparison with agriculture. As one CCAG landholder said, 'This land will continue to produce food for the rest of the world forever; now that mine over there is going to operate for 30 years' (Interview, Hamparsum 2015).

Despite the high energy and optimism of the Harvest Festival and media productions, a focussed, coalition-style campaign against the mine never eventuated. Like the state's ambivalent, undecided response, the would-be LP Alliance did not come together in concerted action. The Alliance website has shut down, and only occasional social media activities register on the LPY group website. This is not to say that such collective action is not possible in the future. However, the transient nature of landholder/Gomeroi/environmentalist coalitions is a reminder of how difficult sustained collective action on coal can be due to the many differences in play.

Yet there were substantive shifts underway. In mid-2015, several months prior to the Harvest Festival event, speeches by NSWFA president Fiona Simson stated that the association had shifted its position on climate change to accept the science and call for a 'transition from fossil fuels such as coal and gas towards more renewable energy sources' (Hannam 2015). A NSW policy was not formalised, but the following year Simson successfully led a similar initiative in her new role as head of the National Farmers Federation (NFF). A rift opened up with the National Party, which continued to reject climate science and, as noted, was generally supportive of coal mining, including the Shenhua mine. In contrast, the new NFF policy clearly acknowledged the reality of climate change, stating it 'poses a significant challenge for Australian farmers'. The policy is equivocal, however, affirming agriculture's potential to contribute to emissions reduction while aiming to protect farmers from costly carbon emissions policies, (NFF 2016).

More widely, farmers were adopting renewable energy technology, both for on-farm and household uses, and were less likely to view fossil fuel–based energy as the only available option. For at least one member of CCAG we interviewed, there had been a shift in thinking, towards renewable energy over coal-fired power:

> Look, I suppose in view of the way we're moving now with alternative energy, it's getting better and better with the technology. I guess in the past I've worried the fact that we still like to turn the lights on and we still haven't had an alternative for baseload power and a lot of the other countries haven't either. But it's wonderful to see that the alternatives are really powering along.
>
> I can see a future where we won't need coal and I guess my comment on the fact that we're not against coal mining ... should be more refined to no more new coal mines. Obviously our existing coal mines are going to see us through for the next 20 years. But I guess it's no more new coal mines is probably a better way to put it.
>
> *(Interview, Pursehouse 2016)*

Another CCAG member we interviewed took the view that delaying mining development so that climate policy and renewable energy expansion would make coal less viable was an important part of the group's strategy:

> You could probably say we were trying to hold the process up a bit, to allow alternative energy to get a foothold. We could see it coming ... And climate change, you know we're farmers, we don't deny that it's happening and we're very concerned about it. So we just thought more people will become educated, more people will become concerned about where we're getting our energy from and alternative energy will come and become cheaper and therefore coal won't be so in demand.
>
> *(Interview, Hamparsum 2016)*

Such views, however, were never publicly expressed by CCAG spokespersons. Some members support climate change policy and environmental action, but climate change is a divisive issue, and climate change scepticism is common, reinforced by the National Party stance (cf. Connor 2016: 82–92, 111–117). Landowners also complained to us about the extensive delays as a period of 'limbo' during which they have not been able to make critical investments to grow their assets.

Affected Gomeroi Traditional Owners have always struggled within their much longer history of dispossession, and their alliance-building with environmental groups is directed towards protecting the integrity of their land and sacred sites. Climate change time scales were not foundational to their public stance, which emphasises a sense of continuity with the land in an enduring and qualitatively different timescape. The Gomeroi presentation to the second PAC in 2015 expressed this inter-generational connection with statements across five generations, from children, the young and middle-aged, as well as from Gomeroi Elder, Uncle Neville Sampson.

Sampson's statement strongly emphasised the 'devastating effects' of the mine on the 'social fabric', the 'glue that has made Breeza the place it is today – the people, our communities – the Aboriginal and non-Aboriginal people who give the area its identity' (Sampson, submission to PAC 2015). He linked past and present communities through the presence of the grinding grooves, in a powerful statement of their meaning and significance for today:

> Decisions are being made by people behind desks or by Ministers who have not come out on country with Elders like myself to see what it is what will be destroyed – in but one place there is an amazing legacy of our ancestors – there is a very large amazing grinding groove, it has over 100 spear-making grooves – deep and perfectly formed – this is the legacy of our great warrior community, a culturally important industrial community, a wonderful men's site, a site which has seen repeated use over many generations of Gomeroi people. The amount of time it takes to rub these marks into the stone is over many years and many users. Yet this can be destroyed and the mitigation proposed is to cut it all up and move it on.
>
> *(Sampson, submission to PAC 2015)*

Conclusion

We finished writing this book in 2020, fourteen years after the arrival of coal capital in the Liverpool Plains, and there has been no coal mining on the Liverpool Plains. Affected groups and observers alike understand the situation as a stalemate. Different state agencies and jurisdictions are implicated in various ways in the ongoing stalemate. From mid-2016, the NSW government announced it was 'in negotiations with Shenhua about the future of the Watermark mine project'. Shenhua's EL expired for the second time in February 2016 and, in an extraordinary delay, was not renewed until July 2018 (Furlong and Haydar 2018).

The struggle continued into 2019. In late December 2018, under the shadow of the upcoming holidays, the state government announced it would alter its development approval to allow 'pre-construction' work on the proposed mine site, pending management plans as required under the Water Trigger. The CCAG expressed outrage and followed with its own commissioned report in January 2019, which showed the Shenhua's Environmental Impact Assessment had grossly underestimated the impacts of drought on the aquifers (Anderson and Howe 2019). The report came in the context of an officially declared severe drought affecting all states. The state and federal governments had announced extensive drought relief, and the issue was high on the political agenda. The Chair of the CCAG, Susan Lyle, stated, 'Australia cannot afford to risk any water, anywhere' (in Kelly, 2019).

At one level it is remarkable that Shenhua has maintained its commitment to the project. In August 2016, BHP Billiton had taken a full compensation package to cancel the Caroona EL. However, it seems Shenhua was not seeking such an arrangement. Instead, in July 2017, the NSW government paid Shenhua $262 million for a buyback of 51.4 per cent of the EL area, on the basis that this would prevent any proposal for mining on the black soil plains, ostensibly leaving the higher-ground land for the mine (Ker 2017). CCAG spokesperson Tim Duddy claimed it as a partial victory, 'testament to the huge community effort to protect the area', while noting the Watermark mine was still on the table, despite it being 'incompatible' with agriculture (Murphy 2017). LtG spokesperson Georgina Woods was less restrained, declaring that the decision was 'half-baked and cowardly', and would not ensure an end to mining (Murphy 2017).

The partial EL buyback, which did not impinge on the mine disturbance area or restrict mining in any way, produced only further uncertainty. It was a most unusual development. The NSW state government essentially disposed itself of more than a quarter of billion dollars in public revenue with no significant effect on the mine development or impacts. Local people were not reassured, and Shenhua only reluctantly accepted the arrangement. Possibly the company viewed this as compensation to buy their silence. Certainly, there have been no further public pronouncements from Shenhua about problems in the approvals process, or about the claimed implications for investment security.

The record of thirteen years of mining projects in the Liverpool Plains without a single tonne of coal being mined shows that state agencies cannot easily do the bidding of coal companies. We chose the Liverpool Plains case because it presents an important illustration of the difficulties faced by coal capital when it seeks to displace an influential and materially powerful local elite, in this case associated with highly productive land and (subterranean) water. The case was always going to be a test of wills, between the two industries and their respective state advocates and industry lobby groups. At one level the opponents have democracy on their side. Many landowners are active political party members in electorates like New England where National Party MPs can be challenged. The Gomeroi Traditional Owners are supported by the NSW Aboriginal Land Council and national Indigenous rights groups. Climate change, coal and conservation activists are part of diverse networks of civil society organisations, of different types and at different scales, with strong influence in state and national arenas.

The state's efforts at managing anticipated harms from the mine have the political effect of shielding Shenhua from political responsibility, allowing it to maintain a legal identity as a socially and environmentally responsible corporate citizen, despite significant public outcry about the project outcomes. In effect, the state's environmental and social protections served a legitimation function for coal capital. Non-negotiable risks for the opponents – the social fabric, community cohesion and historical belonging, underground aquifers and threatened species, Aboriginal heritage and wider climate effects – are all interpreted as negotiable by the state, which still refuses to rule out the mine all together. However, as demonstrated in this chapter, the state has not delivered a seamless legitimacy for the project, and not all objections have been fully contained. Coal capital is by no means fully hegemonic, and can come under sustained challenge. Indeed, while the state has not said 'no' to coal capital on the Liverpool Plains, it has not (yet) said 'yes'.

Landholders, Gomeroi and other residents opposing the Shenhua mine have shared their deep feelings of anger and loss at various junctures, both publicly and in private conversations with us. Gomeroi know that heritage has already been destroyed forever by exploration activities, and as Elder Uncle Neville Sampson put it, 'Once you remove a sacred site, you can't restore it again' (Sampson in Razaghi et al. 2017). The mobilisation of these and other intrinsic values, from community and livelihood to heritage, country and environment, and the capacity to mount an incommensurable challenge to the developments, has been at the core of the continuing ability to mobilise and block mine projects. Given its intrinsic and non-negotiable logic, the struggle is at no small cost in terms of individual exhaustion, and as noted, in terms of the cultural and social distress that it brings. The stakes for those experiencing the existential crisis that the mine has brought can be very high. For years people have lain awake at night imagining scenarios of mass mobilisation and resistance – last-ditch citizens' stands against a destruction that is world-scale for those living through it.

The account in this chapter is revealing of the role of the state in enabling and legitimating the coal commodity but in the process providing avenues for mine opponents to create opportunities, albeit limited, for contesting the proposed new coal mines. This contradictory character of the coal–industrial complex, which we detail in the second section of this chapter, is paralleled in the other two case studies of new coal developments, discussed in Chapters 2 and 4. Insofar as the state remains ostensibly dedicated to the public interest, it will institutionalise the exercise of legitimacy, and thereby offer up, in a contradictory way, the means for contesting it.

The analysis also brings into sharp relief the spatial claims that result, including most notably the Gomeroi connection to ancestral country, and the landowners' 'wrong mine, wrong place' mobilising slogan. The use of existing political channels as well as the marshalling of Indigenous rights legislation, scientific and legal expertise, and the legitimacy of agri-industry have had a remarkable impact in terms of ousting the Caroona mine project and delaying approval for Shenhua. In one reading, this is a great victory; in another, any success achieved solely for these mines is spatially confined, and thus vulnerable. Coal and CSG projects continue to vie for strong footholds in nearby districts of the Liverpool Plains, and threaten to consign it, much like the neighbouring HunterValley, as a sacrifice zone for coal.

Despite this vulnerability, mobilisation of opposition, drawing together challengers across varied sites of resistance, over a long period of time, is itself a feat of political activation. In the specific context of the Liverpool Plains, there are sharp cultural and political differences to navigate in the debate over coal. These reflect the history of capitalist developmentalism in the region and the very different material circumstances, such as those of town residents and farmers, Indigenous people, rural society and the dominant metropolitan culture, National Party stalwarts and the few exceptions. There have been some exceptional feats of alliance-building and collective action across antagonisms, although these have been necessarily defensive. The opponents have constituted and made visible new constituencies, and have validated and privileged existing practices, especially around agriculture and Indigenous heritage. No transformative agenda for a post-coal society has emerged, although the values and themes that might underpin it are being invoked.

Questions of political agency, material social relations and lived experience have been the focus for our investigations across the three country cases in this book. At the centre of the *longue durée* of holding back coal in the Liverpool Plains is a group of resilient people who have been resourceful opponents over more than a decade of struggle. They have achieved much in terms of their capacity to frustrate and delay coal capital and in the process create the political space for alternative pathways. All this they have achieved whilst dealing with the now inter-generational uncertainty about the future loss, and the loss of future, that Shenhua's coal mine will set in train if it goes ahead.

Notes

1 Gomeroi/Kamilaroi country is coterminous with the North West and some adjacent regions of NSW as well as south-west Queensland.

2 These statistics bear comparison with the equally poor rate of successful land rights claims by *Adivasi* people in coal-affected areas of northern Chhattisgarh, discussed in Chapter 2.

3 Anthea is referring to the aftermath of Japan's entry against Allied forces during World War II in the Asia Pacific.

4 In 2012, Whitehaven Coal merged with another Australian company, Aston Coal, original owner of Maules Creek Coal Project (www.whitehavencoal.com.au/maules-creek-mine/)

5 For many residents and landholders, newspaper notices are usually the first message received that coal mining, and the dramatic change it can bring, is on the horizon. Neither mining companies nor government are legally obliged to directly announce a new EL to landholders situated within an EL area. A notice of the EL application must be advertised in local and state-wide newspapers within forty-five days of lodgement with the Department (Mining Act (NSW), 1992: s 13A; Mining Regulations (NSW), 2010: cll. 15(11), 21(11)).

6 Landowners, who do not own the rights to mineral resources on the land, which are vested in the state, do not have the right to refuse exploration access indefinitely (Kennedy 2017: 85).

7 This remains a seriously long-term worry for farmers given their concerns about aquifer damage.

8 MacDonald announced that the agreed EL price included $300 million for the exploration licence, $175 million payment towards a long-awaited new rail crossing to Port of Newcastle through the Liverpool Ranges, and another $200 million upon the granting of a mining lease (Ryan 2008).

9 The LtG Alliance, established in 2010, became a vocal advocate for this approach among NSW and Queeenland landholders, although it was not a significant presence in the Liverpool Plains (Lock the Gate Alliance 2019).

10 The SLURP instituted a new Land and Water Commissioner, a Mining and Petroleum Gateway Panel (the Gateway Panel) and a Gateway process to scientifically assess new coal and gas mine proposals for strategic agricultural lands; an Aquifer Interference Policy; and two Codes of Practice for gas well integrity. Strategic Regional Land Use Plans were drawn up for the Upper Hunter and New England North West regions of the state. Important for the landholders, biophysical strategic agricultural land (BSAL) on the Liverpool Plains (part of the New England area) was defined in the policy as having unique soil, water and land characteristics which have high agricultural value to the state (NSW DPI 2012: 16).

11 When the state Department of Planning & Environment gives approval for a mine, the Conditions of Consent may require the company to make offers to purchase properties within the 'zone of affectation' identified as being impacted by the mine in different ways, e.g. noise and dust. The company may also be required to make an offer if any landholder in this zone requests it.

12 The aims of the Mining SEPP are 'to promote the development of significant mineral resources' and, broadly, to ensure a 'balanced use' of land for competing purposes (NSW Government 2007).

13 The Lock the Gate Alliance has a series of policy objectives. None relate to climate change except Item 7, which calls for 'Independent and rigorous research into greenhouse gas emissions from coal and unconventional gas mining to make sure they are properly and fully paid for' (Lock the Gate 2019).

14 The majority of landholders vote for the National Party, which has had an unofficial but vocal climate change denial stance for many years (Coorey 2018).

15 The PAC was established in 2008 as part of a series of major amendments to the EP&A Act between 2005 and 2011 (Connor 2016).

16 The consultants' reports (AECOM 2012; Connect for Effect 2012) draw on various historical, geological and archaeological surveys as well as the information provided by Aboriginal people who are Traditional Owners, members of LALCs within or near the mining site, and others with a claim of personal association with the area. These persons are invited to act as Registered Aboriginal Parties (RAPs) for the consultation process. In the case of the ACHVA for the Watermark project, there were 145 RAPs – a diverse and unusually large group.

4

Germany

Globalising the Local to Reach the National, Protest against Coal in the Lausitz

On a warm Saturday in late September 2014, thousands of protesters from twenty countries converged on the normally sleepy village of Kerkwitz in the Lausitz (Lusatia) in Eastern Germany. Some of the protesters had already been camping in a field behind the local fire station and participating in the 'climate camp' – *Lausitzer Klima und Energiecamp* – during the previous week. Others were local people from Kerkwitz and nearby villages and towns. Their numbers were swelled by large crowds which began arriving at the small local train station from early on the Saturday morning. They proceeded to form a line along the road from Kerkwitz to the river Neisse, about 3.5 kilometres away, which marks the border with Poland. A festival atmosphere prevailed: an amateur string quartet played by the roadside as protesters strolled past, villagers with hand-made signs marched alongside the banners of Greenpeace, Friends of the Earth and other major environmental organisations, and the local fire brigade helped to direct traffic.

From around midday, the protesters began linking arms to form a human chain, reaching all the way from Kerkwitz to the river. At the same time, another group of protesters on the Polish side of the border was forming a similar chain from the village of Grabiće to the banks of the Neisse. At around 2 p.m., bells rang on both sides of the border. A small number of protesters entered the river from either side and, standing at a shallow spot, linked arms, completing the chain, which stretched a distance of 8 kilometres and consisted of around 7,500 people. They held up banners in Polish and German which read 'Together against Coal: Our Future Is Renewable'.

Why had so many people come to this relatively remote border region to join in the protest? The immediate focus of the action was to rally against the demolition of three local villages, Kerkwitz, Atterwasch and Grabko. Since 2007, the villagers had been fighting a proposed expansion of the nearby Jänschwalde lignite mine, owned at the time by the Swedish company Vattenfall. Vattenfall had lodged an application to extend the area of the mine by 2,000 hectares, which, if approved, would have enabled the mining of an additional 200 million tonnes of lignite over twenty years. On the Polish side of the border, the state-owned company PGE was seeking to commence mining operations which would have swallowed fifteen villages and 3,000 hectares of forest.

On a broader level, the human chain was a protest against coal itself and its contribution to climate change. The human chain was supported by international environmental organisations such as Greenpeace and Friends of the Earth, and by a large number of smaller climate NGOs from Eastern and Western Europe. They came together with local and regional citizens' initiatives, church groups and inhabitants of the threatened villages to co-ordinate the protest on the ground.

In an interview on the day, Thomas Burchardt, one of the organisers of the protest from the nearby village of Drehnow, and spokesman for the citizens' initiative Klinger Runde, said he was 'overwhelmed' that so many people from all over Europe had joined local people to demonstrate for 'a liveable future without more coal' (Interview Burchardt 2014). Kuba Gogoliewski, a Polish campaigner from the organisation CEE Bankwatch, who joined his German wife Julia Huscher in the middle of the river to mark the symbolic climax of the protest, described it as 'a sign that people on the ground can find a common language much sooner than their governments can' (Interview, Gogoliewski 2014).

This was the first time that a major protest against coal mining had taken place in Eastern Germany. As a 'cosmopolitan event' (Beck 2010), it was a successful media spectacle that was widely reported in local, national and international print and electronic media. From the perspective of the climate movement, it was a further step towards the creation of a pan-European – and transnational – movement which clearly identifies the halting of coal extraction at its source as a crucial element of climate action.

The human chain protest was also the beginning of our intensive fieldwork in the Lausitz, which continued for more than two years, concluding with the *Ende Gelände* protest in Welzow in 2016. These two – very different – protest actions frame a period of intense national debates and political controversy about the future of coal in Germany, and the clash between continuing coal reliance, the German *Energiewende*, or energy transition, and Germany's climate goals.

To understand the developments in German coal mining, this chapter takes the Lausitz as an exemplary case study. It starts by introducing the history of the Lausitz as a coal-mining area. We then outline the regulatory framework surrounding coal mining in Germany, the legal and bureaucratic context within which our local case study unfolds. Our analysis of the case study material centres on the strategies which people in the Lausitz adopt to voice their opposition to, or support for, a continuation of lignite mining. Through our sustained ethnographic fieldwork, and the process of gathering material for a series of radio documentaries, we have sought to develop an understanding of the motivations and reasoning of the different actors, and the scripts or narratives which guide them.

Our fieldwork, and this chapter, thus concentrates on mine opponents in Kerkwitz, Atterwasch and Grabko, but also draws on statements and perspectives from mine proponents and people in other parts of the Lausitz. The focus on three villages of altogether 900 inhabitants allows us to analyse how the threat of relocation to make way for coal mining impacts local social structures in German rural communities. Through a micro-perspective on aspects of the social life of the three villages, we outline the ways in which villagers organised to resist the mine extension, and the strategies and rituals of protest they have adopted, which are framed within a global debate about climate change and environmental protection. The proposed mine extension at Jänschwalde-Nord has not only created conflict and division within villages but also sparked collaborations across village borders that were previously rather unusual.

In terms of scripts and narratives guiding the stakeholders involved, we identify *Heimat* or home as a central one that is invoked by both opponents and supporters of mining. Local concerns on both sides revolve around the fear of losing *Heimat*, of losing the Lausitz and what it means to both sides respectively. Some of the villagers who oppose the mine extension explicitly frame their struggle as one which is not just about defending *Heimat* as their homes, farms and fields, but defending the *Energiewende*, which they experience as already embedded in the landscape and the fabric of everyday life. Local mine opponents argue that they are already 'living the energy transition', and that any expansion of coal mining would betray or undermine – literally – the goals of the federal government and its energy policy.

On the mine proponents' side, *Heimat* is also a relevant script. Decisions made by the federal and state governments are vital for their future as workers in the German coal industry. *Heimat* is conceptualised here on a more regional level and centres on familiarity, social structures and economic security.

Returning to the opponents' strategies, the chapter next turns to the ways in which they have sought a wider constituency and support for their cause, which they found in the globally connected German climate movement. In collaboration with local mine opponents, a range of actors in the German climate movement has been able to interpolate the global discourse of climate change into the local struggle against coal mining.

Overall, we argue that local activists and national-level environmental organisations have – largely – successfully pursued several strategies, which allow them to 'globalise the local' in order to resist an expansion of coal mining in the Lausitz and intervene in national debates about coal and its contribution to climate change. There is a clear articulation of coal and climate, through a self-conscious strategy of delay in anticipation of climate and energy policy that will supersede the need for coal. To achieve this in the long haul there is a process of mobilising incommensurable values and identifications, centred on the assertion of an irreplaceable sense of place, of home and community belonging. This is then interlinked with and expressed through wider alliances on issues of energy and climate justice.

The Lausitz as a Mining Area

The Lausitz is a region rich in lignite. As a geological region defined by its large coal seams, it extends from the easternmost parts of Germany through large areas of Poland. Life in the Lausitz has, for much of the last two centuries, been synonymous with living from and with coal mining. Coal mining began here in 1844 and expanded rapidly with the industrialisation of the region from 1870 onwards; between 1930 and the present, some 7 billion tonnes of lignite were extracted from mines in the Lausitz covering an area of more than 800 square kilometres (von Bismarck 2010).

Historically, the Lausitz has been the settlement area of the Sorbs, a West Slavic community that migrated to the region in the late first millennium. After the Congress of Vienna in 1815, the Niederlausitz became part of Prussia. Even though migration of Germans into the Lausitz had led to a dilution of Sorb preponderance as early as of the Middle Ages, Prussian rule led to an accelerated assimilation of the Sorbs by the end of the nineteenth century.

At the same time, industrialisation set in, and the rural character of the area started to vanish. While the first discoveries of lignite in the region date back to the eighteenth century (Krümmelbein et al. 2012: 53), the second half of the nineteenth century saw an expansion of mining here, which was supported by the construction of numerous railway lines between 1860 and 1880 (Förster 1968: 16) and the general economic boom. From the 1840s to 1860s, mining was still characterised by numerous small-scale businesses mining in small open-cut mines, providing raw coal for the nearby businesses of cloth production and glass kilns, which were shaped by early industrialisation processes. In the 1870s, mining became a professional business, attracting investors from nearby Berlin and other areas. They acquired land from local farmers on a larger scale and opened underground mines, which soon fell short of satisfying the ever-growing demand for energy in the Lausitz and beyond. Companies such as the two major players – Eintracht Braunkohlenwerke und Brikettfabrik AG, founded in 1887 as an incorporated company, and the Ilse Bergbau AG, founded one year later – erected briquette factories next to their mines, where coal was pressed into briquettes for local use or shipment to Berlin and other areas. The companies soon took to larger-scale open-cut mining that allowed a mechanisation of the mining process (Förster 1996: 11). Innovations in excavation and draining technology and electrification of the processes increased production. The open-cut mines grew further in size and efficiency during the first decades of the twentieth century. Since investors wanted to keep costs at a minimum, there were no relocations of settlements for mining purposes until 1924.

Nevertheless, early industrialised mining in the Lausitz had vast impacts on the social structure of the area. On the one hand, the expansion in mining caused the immigration of large numbers of workers into the Lausitz. On the other hand, the number of independent companies declined, as did the number of full-time farmers (Förster 1996: 12). Mining provided better-paid jobs, causing people to seek work in the mines as an additional income, or full time. Thus, coal mining also transformed agriculture, away from small-scale farming with independent farmers working on their soil to miners partly or wholly dependent on wage labour. The lowering of the water table in an area with low soil fertility and the purchase of land for mining further contributed to these transformations. The number of miners in the area multiplied more than sevenfold between 1871 and 1889 (Förster 1968: 21). The rural character of the area disappeared by the 1880s, and the beginning of the twentieth century brought the erection of large-scale power plants and high-voltage transmission lines. A contemporary writer described the Lausitz in 1923 as characterised by pits, dumps, local railway, cable railway, electric lines, brown streams, steaming chimneys and briquette factories, among them glass and brick factories (Maier 2002: 149).

In the late nineteenth and early twentieth centuries, the Lausitz became synonymous with a certain kind of industrial modernity, which arose elsewhere in Germany over the course of the nineteenth century (for example, in Saxony, northern Bavaria and what is now North-Rhine-Westphalia), but which contributed in particular to the rise of Berlin as the national capital and a symbol of German technological progress. As Rolf Kuhn, Director of the International Architectural Exhibition (Fürst-Pückler-Land 2000–2010), has put it, 'Without the Lausitz and its lignite industry, Berlin would have had no heating, no electricity and no light. Whenever one sees images of the glittering Berlin of the 1920s, those images would have been unthinkable without the Lausitz' (Interview, Kuhn 2015).

Coal mining in the Lausitz also spawned the development of the first large cohort of industrial proletariat in the area. While the large inflow of migrants made the employment of women and children mostly unnecessary, conditions for those working in the mines were characterised by extremely low safety standards, numerous accidents, insufficient medical and hygienic provisions and twelve-hour or longer working days (Förster 1990). Before the formation of the German Reich in 1871, only a change in workplace could mean a change in these conditions, but freedom of association and the continuing growth of the socialist workers' movement and the Social Democrat party brought a consciousness of the prospects of organised engagement and struggle. Even though the monopolies Ilse AG and Eintracht AG started to build so-called charitable institutions in the 1880s, namely company housing and barracks, such philanthropy could not prevent the first larger union-organised miners' strike in the Lausitz in 1904. While it ended with the prosecution and eventual conviction of two miners (defended by Karl Liebknecht in a public lawsuit exposing the existing dreadful conditions of mine work), two years later union workers and miners renewed their call for better wages and working conditions, leading to another major strike in May 1907, which resulted in partial improvements. Large strikes in 1920 and 1927 eventually caused the mounted police to be called in from Berlin, the recruitment of strike-breakers from Western parts of Germany, and subsequently a slight improvement in both working conditions and wages (Förster 1990).

After the Nazi regime took power in 1933, large numbers of unionists, communists, social democrats and other active mine workers were imprisoned. Coal mining became an industry important for warfare, and compulsory purchase of land for purposes of public utility became possible in 1937. At the time of the Second World War numerous foreign forced labourers were working in the Lusatian mining area (Förster 1990: 104ff.).

After the Second World War, and three years before the GDR was founded in 1949, all mining companies in the Lausitz were confiscated from their former owners. This set the course for the subsequent state monopoly in lignite mining in the GDR (Förster 1996: 15). The country's energy policy focussed on self-sufficiency and developed the Lausitz into its role as a prime coal and energy hub. This included the erection of multiple thermal power stations adjoining the mines or further away, such as the Jänschwalde and Boxberg power plants in the 1970s, the Berlin-Klingenberg power plant in the 1980s, as well as numerous smaller ones in the area (that are no longer in operation today). Lignite was the primary energy source of the GDR for much of its forty-year history. In the 1980s, the GDR was the world's largest producer of lignite, with an annual yield of 256 million tonnes, or 28 per cent of total world production in 1981 (Nawrocki 1981), reaching a peak in production in 1988 with 310 million tonnes.

In 1951, the government named so-called protected areas, and scheduled the villages therein for relocation and demolition within the next twenty years. Construction activity was henceforward no longer allowed in these areas, which were furthermore subject to numerous changes and extensions in the following decades. Between 1945 and 1989, seventy-one villages were demolished and a total of 13,453 people forcibly relocated to make way for mining, with an increase in numbers after the oil shock of 1973 (Förster 1996: 18). The government did not give much consideration to ecological concerns, or cultural and ethnic objections by the Sorbs. However, as long as it did not interfere with mining, the GDR promoted the Sorb language and culture in numerous ways. Several institutions, which in part exist until today, fostered Sorb culture and research. Equal rights of the Sorbs were written into the constitution in 1949, and between 1966 and 1989, seven festivals of Sorb culture were held (Stiftung für das sorbische Volk 2009). But mining and energy production brought simultaneously more and more German workers into the Lausitz. In line with the GDR's energy policy, mining and energy production was continuously increased and developed. Technical and scale improvement was promoted, as was engineering expertise in the processing of lignite. Mining, already established as part of Lusatian identity, was glorified in the person of the miner during GDR times, and became cemented as a basis for identity construction throughout the whole area and beyond.

The region still provides one-third of the lignite mined in Germany, which, with 178 million tonnes per annum, remains the largest producer worldwide (DEBRIV 2015). But coal has been both a blessing and a curse for the Lausitz. The region's reliance on coal as the foundation of its economy and industrial culture has come at a cost, both in its impact on human health and the destruction of villages, landscapes and social structures. It has, moreover, made the region's economy especially vulnerable to changes in the fortunes of coal. German reunification in 1990 brought with it a dramatic decline of lignite mining in the Lausitz. The region went through a radical restructuring process (von Bismarck 2010), which resulted in the loss of tens of thousands of jobs and weakened its economy. In 1989, at the end of the socialist period, 79,016 people used to work in the mines, power plants and directly related industries (DEBRIV 2015). By 2015, only 8,316 were still employed in lignite mining in the Lausitz. Of the seventeen Lusatian open-cut mines which existed in 1990, only four remained in operation in 2017. The amount of lignite mined decreased from 168 million tonnes in 1990 to 62.5 million tonnes in 2015.[1] The state-owned mines were privatised and subsequently consolidated under the name Lausitzer Braunkohle AG (LAUBAG).

In 1994, the LAUBAG was sold for 2.1 billion Deutschmark to a consortium of German energy companies; seven years later, the Swedish company Vattenfall became one of the owners, and in 2002 the sole owner, of the Lusatian mines and power plants, forming Vattenfall Europe Mining AG and Vattenfall Europe Generation AG. In 2015, Vattenfall decided to sell its mining assets, completing the sale to the Czech-based energy company EPH and the investment firm PPF Investments late in 2016. The remaining mines and power plants are running now under the name Lausitzer Energie Bergbau AG (LEAG). The company planned to continue mining lignite, but beyond the mid-2020s this would only be possible through the extension of existing mines or the opening of new ones. The proposed mine extensions are the Welzow-Süd II field and the Nochten II mine south of the

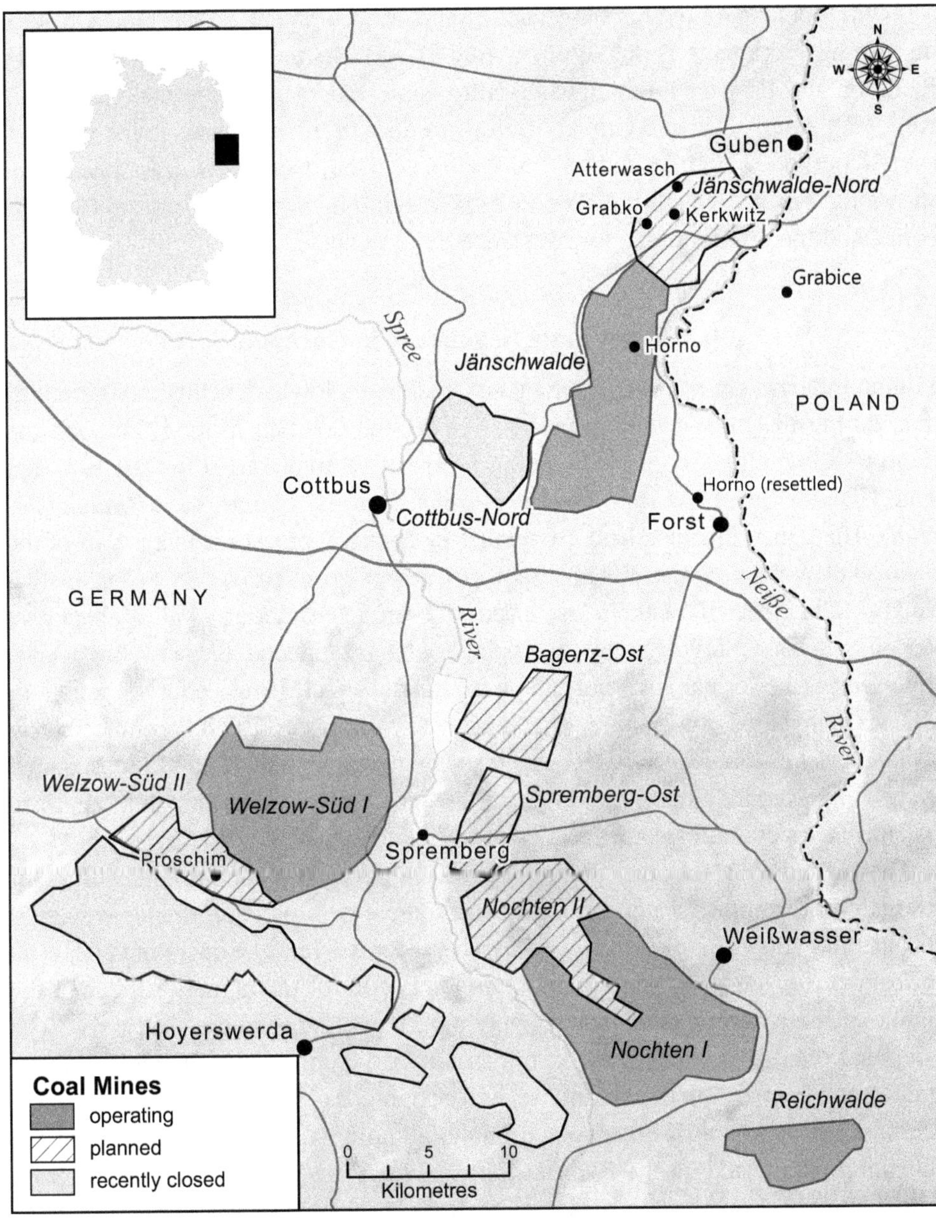

Figure 4.1 Proposed coal mines in the Cottbus area, Lusatia.
Source: prepared by Olivier Rey-Lescure, Cartolab

regional capital Cottbus, and up until 2017 also the Jänschwalde-Nord mine north of Cottbus (see Figure 4.1). Also, in the original application made by Vattenfall in 2007, Spremberg-Ost and Bagenz-Ost are proposed as new mine sites to be opened up in the 2030s.[2]

In the context of overarching coal-mining development in the area we now discuss developments at the Welzow-Süd II and Nochten II mines, but mainly focus on the proposed Jänschwalde-Nord mine extension, near the villages of Kerkwitz, Atterwasch and Grabko. Before we turn to the responses in the villages, a brief outline of the regulatory framework will be useful, not least because it shows the hurdles which the proponent of a mine or mine extension must overcome, and the opportunities for resistance by opponents.

Coal and State Regulation in Germany

Mining in Germany is a heavily regulated business. Nowhere is this more obvious than during the mine planning process. Under the German Mining Law and the Land Use Planning Act, mine planning needs to be approved at both federal and state (*Länder*) level. At state level it is centred on the lignite plan (*Braunkohleplan*). The lignite plan is a land use regulatory approval procedure that is part of the regional planning program. When proposing a new mine, or a mine extension, the first step has to be a search for alternative means of energy generation as well as alternative locations. This is followed by a scoping of environmental impact assessments, followed by the formal environmental impact assessment. If relocation of people or villages is involved, a social impact assessment is also necessary. Environmental and social impact assessments as well as their scoping need to include public consultation at specified intervals. A positive review of the lignite plan would result in its approval (Akademie für Raumforschung und Landesplanung 2000).

The second stage of mine planning involves detailed planning procedures, for example in relation to water rights and environmental protection rights, as well as the operating plan (*Betriebsplanverfahren*) at federal level. The operating plan is an instrument for the preventative and continuous control of mining. Similar to the lignite plan, environmental and social impact assessments are necessary. The operating plan needs to be made public in affected communities, including appropriate time frames for objections, several scoping dates and hearings. The plan requires the approval of all involved public authorities. A positive review of the operating plan results in the *Planfeststellungsbeschluss* (approval of the operating plan). This is equivalent to a licence to mine, which is granted generally for a maximum of fifty years (Kremer and Neuhaus 2001; www.gesetze-im-internet.de/bbergg/index.html).

The whole mine-planning procedure usually takes between six and ten years and offers multiple points of intervention. Before a mine can open, the plans for excavating the overburden, and then for mining itself, followed by rehabilitation and recultivation, have to be pre-approved. An authorisation to mine also includes the right to compulsorily acquire private land, usually involving the compensation of the owners on the basis of market prices. The advantage of agreeing to selling privately owned land to a company prior to the approval of the operating plan is often better monetary compensation and – at least in the relocations carried out by Vattenfall – a certain degree of voice in the actual relocation of (willing parts of) whole villages, their facilities and infrastructure. Neither today's legal options for intervening in mine planning nor the range of options for negotiating relocation have been there in previous systems.

German mining law is one important framework for current coal mining in the Lausitz. Another equally important framework is set by political and policy agendas at both national and state level The national *Energiewende*, as discussed in Chapters 6 and 7, is designed to shape energy policy but is open to political negotiation. At the Länder level, the Lausitz is located in both South Brandenburg and Saxony. Decisions at this level are less predictable, as there is serious political dispute over the future of coal for the region.[3] In Brandenburg the Christian Democratic Party (CDU) states that coal is indispensable and investment in power plants is necessary; the Social Democratic Party (SPD) has a history of arguing that coal is necessary for regional competitiveness and to provide baseload power; the Left Party (Die Linke) opposed coal mining in the region but moved away from this position when they went into a governing coalition with the SPD. In 2014, for instance, Die Linke agreed to extend the Welzow-Süd mine, defying their own federal leadership.[4] The agreement was a clear breach of the promise of 'no new mines', with an exit from coal mining by 2040, which Die Linke had promoted in their 2014 election programme. The Green Party (Bündnis 90/Die Grünen), which had 6 of the 88 seats, was the smallest faction in the Brandenburg state parliament, and the only party that was consistently anti-mining.

These various positions for or against coal mining at the local level do not necessarily run along party lines. In Atterwasch, for example, the CDU member Monika Schulz-Höpfner has, contrary to the party's official position, taken a clear and energetic stand against coal mining, while being a member of the Brandenburg parliament. Thus, in the particular instance of coal mining in the Lausitz at least, confusion about and mistrust in political decision-making should not be interpreted as the result of a general disenchantment with politics, which is often cited as a reason for current (particularly right wing) protest movements in Germany (Dostal 2015), but is rather the consequence of concrete instances of broken promises and policy reversals over a number of years. As we shall see, the now legendary pronouncement by the former state premier of Brandenburg that 'Horno ist das letzte Dorf' – 'Horno is the last village' [to make way for a coal mine] is a particularly salient example of this trend.

The lack of coherence in political decision-making is magnified at the national level and within the larger frameworks determining the future of coal mining. The most important of these is Germany's climate policy, and its centrepiece, the *Energiewende*, or 'energy transition'. These are discussed in more detail in Chapters 6 and 7, but a brief sketch of the *Energiewende* is necessary here, as it is a crucial element in the villagers' strategy of opposition to the Jänschwalde mine expansion. The *Energiewende* has been characterised as 'one of the most ambitious national energy transition initiatives worldwide' (Moss et al. 2014: 1), foreseeing 'full decarbonization of the economy' by mid-century (Fabra et al. 2015: 51). Laws introduced by the German federal government in 2011 and passed in 2012 mandate a target of 35 per cent of national electricity to be generated from renewable sources by 2020, and 80 per cent by 2050 (Hager and Steffe 2016). The Fukushima nuclear accident was the catalyst for these laws, and was a crucial turning point in the evolution of German energy policy: Germany committed to phasing-out all nuclear power plants by 2022 (Hager and Steffe 2016; Renn 2011: 13). The *Energiewende*, however, is not simply a technocratic initiative, but a social process, which Ottmar Edenhofer, co-chair of working group III of the IPCC, describes as 'one of the greatest social experiments there has ever been in Germany, comparable with the process of reunification' (Focus-Online 2011). However, as Felix Christian Matthes points out, the energy transition is the continuation of a policy approach which began in the early 1990s but did not become the 'official headline of the new German energy paradigm' until 2011 with the decision to exit from nuclear power (Fabra et al. 2015: 51).

Crucially, the energy transition has had bipartisan support from the major political parties in Germany, the CDU (Christian Democrats) and the Social Democrats (SPD), as well as the Greens and the Left Party (Die Linke). Public support for the *Energiewende* has generally been strong: research conducted by the Institute for Advanced Sustainability Studies in 2017, based on a survey of 7,500 households, indicates that 88 per cent of the German citizens support the *Energiewende* in both urban and rural areas, and across all levels of education, income and political preference (Setton et al. 2017). But there are signs that this support may be eroding: almost two-thirds of citizens now believe the cost burden of implementing the energy transition has not been equally shared, with citizens bearing more of the cost than business and industry. From 1998 to 2016, the price of electricity for domestic consumers rose by 34 per cent in real terms, driven largely by fees and levies associated with energy transition; as Fischer (2016: 1584) notes, this had a particularly negative impact on the lowest income groups. The authors of the IASS study argue that energy policy should focus more on social acceptance and support for low-income households if the *Energiewende* is to remain socially sustainable in the long term. Delays in constructing needed high-capacity power supply lines, failure to develop adequate storage facilities, a highly questionable electricity tariff and network policy and the federal government's decision to abandon its own policy of imposing an emissions levy on power stations (the *Klimaabgabe*, or climate contribution) reinforced the impression of a lack of political will to implement an energy policy which is environmentally friendly and furthers the government's own climate goals.[5]

The Lausitz as a Theatre of the 'Social Drama' of Climate Change

The complex and relatively onerous regulatory framework described above has meant that the approval process for the Jänschwalde-Nord mine extension – and for other mines in Lusatia – has moved very slowly since Vattenfall's initial application in 2007, despite strong support for the extension from both the mining trade unions and the state governments of Brandenburg and Saxony (whether led by the CDU or by the SPD in coalition with Die Linke). This has given the villagers and their supporters breathing space, time in which to organise, form alliances and build solidarity (see Table 4.1). On the other hand, it has also subjected both opponents and proponents of the mine extension to prolonged uncertainty about the future.

In the following, we describe the concrete ways in which the struggle against the mine extension has played out, at the village level and in the region more broadly. We show how the social structures and rituals of everyday life in the villages have been affected by the conflict and continuing uncertainty over the mine and examine the motivations of individuals on both sides.

Over the ten years of waiting, both opponents and proponents have developed narratives or scripts which inform and sustain their struggles. These scripts are not necessarily discrete. They may overlap and interweave, and some are mobilised by both opponents and proponents of coal mining. They bring into play narratives of home and identity, ecological modernisation, climate change, struggle and solidarity, local and global. The contest over the future of coal in Lusatia can be seen as a struggle over who controls these narratives. In a broader sense, it is a contest between competing modernities, or competing visions of modernity; one urban, regional and industrial, in which the coal industry continues to sustain mass employment and prosperity for the 'silent majority' and nourish a sense of pride and identity; the other rural, localised and post-industrial and high-tech, in which the energy transition has become integrated into the fabric of rural life. Many of those who invoke this latter vision of modernity explicitly place it in the context of what Smith and Howe call the 'social drama' of climate change. Climate change, they argue,

> exists in a complex field of stories defined by multiple, competing genres. Its discursive environment is deeply layered. It is not simply a discourse about nature, energy production,

Table 4.1. *Jänschwalde-Nord timeline*

Events	Planning in Theory
2007	
Press conference Vattenfall and state government of Brandenburg: intent to open Jänschwalde-Nord	*Braunkohlenplan* Search for energy locations
Direct Democracy I: *Volksinitiative* – collection of more than 20,000 signatures -> state parliament has to take the mining issue on to the agenda	
2008	
Protest March (*Sternmarsch*); subsequently every year	
Direct Democracy II: *Volksbegehren*: attempt to collect 80,000 signatures to have a referendum on mining, failed	Environmental impact assessment
Vattenfall submits first documents for the lignite plan	Social impact assessement
2011	Plan approval order
First scoping	*Rahmenbetriebsplan*
Lausitzcamp; subsequently every year	Social impact assessment
2012	Environmental impact assessment
Positive decision on scoping	Statement of all involved administrative bodies
Village Fête (*Dorffest*); subsequently every year	Plan approval order
2014	
Vattenfall decides to sell his mining assets in the Lausitz	
Human Chain as part of the Lausitzcamp	
Klimaabgabe: minister of economics announces a plan to make industries pay for emissions	
2015	Land acquisition / Relocation
Kapazitätsreserve: minister of economics announces compensation for shutting down parts of Jänschwalde and other power plants instead of *Klimaabgabe*	
2016	Pre-cut
Ende Gelände as part of #BreakFree2016 and Lausitzcamp	
EPH buys mines and power plants in the Lausitz; promise to keep workers until 2020; state politicians welcome the buyer and miss the chance to demand a funds for recultivation as fixed assets	

Table 4.1. (*cont.*)

Events	Planning in Theory
2017 EPH declares that it will not proceed with Jänschwalde-Nord	Coal production for up to 50 years with subsequent recultivation
2018 German government convenes the 'Coal Commission' to work out a plan for ending coal mining and combustion	
2019 The 'Coal Commission' recommends an exit from coal in 2038 and 40 billion Euro financial assistance for affected regions over the next 20 years	

policy, or scientific facts. It is also a reflexive narration in which the representation of climate change itself is analyzed, dissected, and subject to storytelling.

(Smith and Howe 2015: 24)

For at least some of the participants in our case study, the social drama of climate change is being acted out in microcosm, at the level of everyday village life, and in the struggle to defend it against the encroachment of coal mining. We begin our ethnographic analysis with a sketch of the village community as it comes together for an important social ritual.

The Village Community

It is loud in the Kerkwitz inn, the Dorfkrug. People chat and drink while the band plays hits from the last four decades. Their repertoire caters to the taste of the villagers, and soon people start dancing. In pairs, young and old, they move across the dance floor of the large wood-panelled room adjacent to the restaurant. Some people are still eating, enjoying traditional food – schnitzel, fries and mixed vegetables, oscillating somewhere between memories of a popular cuisine of the 1990s and German all-time favourites – and countless shots are ordered at the bar. Parents dance with their grown-up kids, sometimes women with women, and exchange gossip. It is *Kirmes* – a village fair held annually with the beginning of autumn – and like *Fastnacht* or *Zampern*, it is one of the yearly occasions for villagers to come together, drink, chat and dance. There is no talk of coal mining tonight, but people laugh and drink and enjoy themselves until late at night.

The *Kirmes* is one instance where the village's social life finds expression. It exemplifies how the villagers come together as a community that shares experiences and traditions. Kerkwitz, Atterwasch and Grabko are medium-sized villages, with populations of around 500, 240 and 145 inhabitants, respectively. Villages in Germany still bear traces of close social contacts and neighbourly help that originate – amongst other factors – in the village's spatial structure. Due to spatial contiguity, life in rural areas was, and to an extent continues to be, defined by common experiences of everyday life as well as special occasions, traditions and celebrations. The villagers share everyday occurrences and participate in the life of their neighbours. Neighbourly rights and duties used to be exactly determined: the duty of disclosure, for example at the time of harvest, or the duty of greeting were fixed rules (Henkel 2014: 143f.). While these rules no longer apply, neighbourly help and collective engagement remain important aspects of village life. People in German villages often participate at their neighbours' rites of passage and other celebrations. It leads to a strong identification with the community, and to the development of what is called the village community (*Dorfgemeinschaft*). While identity and closeness were previously determined mainly by circles of relatives and people of higher rank living in the villages, today they are strongly influenced by numerous associations and clubs. The oldest associations in German villages are the marksmen's clubs and the fire brigades, which already existed in part in the Middle Ages. Today most German villages feature a number of cultural clubs, sport clubs, village clubs, fire brigades or ladies' circles (Henkel 2014: 159f.). Working in a village association is often considered a social obligation. Consequently, social cohesion is generally considered to be stronger in villages than in cities, with a positive emotional tie to the village. The other side of this coin is a tighter social control, also relating to power relations, hierarchies and demands, as well as a more direct social sanction of violations of norms.

The villages of Kerkwitz, Atterwasch and Grabko in many aspects resemble the aspects of rural life as Henkel describes them. People share important events, and have several peer groups based on clubs, kinship and own preferences. The *Kirmes, Zampern* and the erection of the Pentecost tree are important traditions. Some people can trace the history of their family in the village back several centuries. Ulrich Schulz, who owns a farm of around 750 hectares in and around the village of Atterwasch, can trace his family's association with the village back to the time of the Thirty Years War (1618–1648), and is proud of the fact that the three generations of the Schulz family who run the farm today are the only remaining people in the village to make their living solely from agriculture.[6] The nearby village of Kerkwitz recently celebrated its 500th anniversary by publishing the village chronicle in a new edition. The villages, however, are not unchangeable entities. Villages have experienced in- and out-migration over time. There are certainly also social disruptions, animosities and potential for social conflict. Yet, the majority of the villagers identify as belonging to their respective villages; young as well as older folks call themselves rather proudly ‘Atterwascher’, ‘Kerkwitzer’ or ‘Grabkoer’. Traditions are cultivated, and the social cohesion of village life is regularly reproduced.

The announcement in 2007 that the three villages would be demolished to make way for the Jänschwalde-Nord mine extension affected the village community in several ways, which seem contradictory at first glance. On the one hand, it strengthened community spirit, heightened participation in village life and let the village stand united. At the same time, it produced a contrary effect, which in some cases weakened the village-bound connection to place and caused subtle tensions based on claims to power to rise to the surface. These several changes in social structure arise from the threat of being resettled, and need to be contextualized and explained in more detail.

The people in the three villages received the letters advising them of the prospect of relocation in September 2007. One of the first reactions – after several moments of shock and disbelief – was the founding of numerous action groups. Roswitha K., who has been engaged in the struggle against Jänschwalde-Nord, and whose family has been living in Kerkwitz for generations, recalls the time well:

> The public relations committee of the group Agenda 21, of which pastor Berndt is the leader now, that was actually founded immediately, in the first year. That must have been the case, because in January was the first *Sternmarsch* (protest march). That takes place every year. … The Klinger Runde … was founded already in May 2007, after the Clausthal survey [the basis of the future Brandenburg energy concept, naming the potential new mining areas]. They said we definitely have to do something against it. In the twenty-first century one cannot simply demolish villages anymore.
>
> *(Interview, Roswitha 2015)*

In addition to the public relations committee (*Öffentlichkeitsausschuss*) and the Klinger Runde, the villagers founded a number of further action committees for a range of specific purposes (some of which were later dissolved). What is more important than the number of committees is their general agenda regarding the proposed mine extension, and their ideas about how to reach common goals, which caused the village community and conventional social structures to be scrutinized.

There were some residents in one of the villages who sought to negotiate with Vattenfall to secure resettlement, and argued the village as a whole should do this. This directly undermined social cohesion in the village community, especially when in one of the committees those who had decided to leave tabled a foundation agreement for future resettlement for the whole village, a step that was opposed by the majority. What followed was described by one of the opponents of the mine as ‘running the gauntlet’. Internal decision-making structures and social unity within the village were fractured, not least because of suspicions about the intentions and motivations of the villagers who were willing to sell and to negotiate with Vattenfall. The mine opponents consequently needed to mobilise and tighten existing networks within the village community to reach a point where opposing the mine extension could safely be communicated to the outside as a common point of view, and a direction had been agreed upon. This process was marked by conflicts that also overflowed into verbal aggression during public meetings, and consequently lead to social sanctions within the village community as people were no longer included in private gatherings. Even the social obligation to exchange greetings when meeting on the street was abandoned for those residents who had opted to negotiate with Vattenfall. In the context of a close-knit rural community, violating the basic rules of politeness demonstrates a crucial rupture in social relationships.

Less harsh were the disagreements over how to achieve the common goal of stopping the mine extension, and thus preventing resettlement. Yet, also in this regard, tensions developed within the village community but were carefully held within the village and not communicated to the outside. The contentious issues here were the means and pace with which to oppose the mine extensions. The two main thrusts could be termed proactive contestation versus defensive temporizing.

It must be stressed that the unity the villages present to the outside world is rather more united than these internal politics might suggest. While in personal encounters the residents who actively oppose the mine openly state that there are a number of villagers who are not positioned at all, but remain indecisive, and a handful who are in favour of the mine extension (which many villagers who are active in the protest say they can accept and understand), the representation in the media is one of a united stand by the affected villages and surrounding areas in opposing the mines. The *Dorffest*, the village fête in Atterwasch, which has taken place every year in late October since 2012, as well as the yearly *Sternmarsch*. the yearly protest march starting simultaneously from the three affected villages that has taken place in January since 2008, are prime examples, as they are distinct statements against the resettlements. They draw the attention of the regional media; and disputes within the villages and dissenting views are not exposed here.

Besides the potential for latent conflicts to surface or new ones to evolve, the proposed mine extension has also had positive effects on social networks in the villages. The process of opposing resettlement had strengthened the sense of historical belonging and attachment. The length and continuity of ties to the place were mobilised as a way of legitimizing and authenticating the right to stay, while welcoming 'newcomers' who likewise identified with the place. For Roswitha, who not only knows the village history by heart but also traces her ancestors back for several generations, the sense of belonging was open-ended:

For someone who is not so attached to *Heimat* [home], it might not be so bad if he or she has to move somewhere else. Maybe . . . I do think that if you moved here only twenty years ago it is different from being born here.

Q: Even though twenty years can be a long time.

A: Yes, yes, there are always people who, so to speak, do not warm to the place, and others move here and integrate very fast into the village community.

(Interview, Roswitha 2015)

Christian H., one of the members of the public relations committee (*AK ÖV*) living in Atterwasch, echoes this perspective in this description of how social relations in the village had changed:

On Monday next week we are sitting in here [in the Dorfkrug] and well, we'll have our Christmas celebration for the committee (AK ÖV). We have to see it this way: If the coal [mine extension] hadn't come, I wouldn't have got to know all these people. Of course, we do live in a village, next to each other. But the people that I've got to know through this issue, in the normal run of things, I would not have got to know better, if it hadn't happened. [. . .] That is, it welds us together. The ones who *want to* get welded together. [. . .] And by now we also feel connected as humans, because we know each other and learn to appreciate each other. [. . .] And that's true of the ties between the villages, as well as within villages. [. . .] Before we would not come up with the idea of driving to Kerkwitz and helping the people there with something. But now it is normal.

(Interview, Christian 2014)

The threat of being relocated demanded of the villagers that they take a stand, and furthermore that they not take that stand alone, but in close collaboration with their neighbours and the residents of the other affected villages. They established new social ties or intensified loosely existing ones. As Christian put it, the resistance against coal mining welded individuals together, if they were open to that. The common experiences establishing a village community were enhanced through a shared fight for the same goal, a strategic and long-lasting interaction that was performed in the village inn, the Dorfkrug, during public and semi-public meetings, at protest marches and through an intense discourse on a shared concern. The threat of the mine extension allowed for social ties to be established in response to that threat, but those ties now reach beyond the immediate context of that threat, enabling new forms of social action and mobilisation as people got to know each other and interact on a more personal level.

Furthermore, their social connection to place, which was previously limited to the single village, has been widened. Shared memories are now associated with the three villages and allow for the generation of a site-specific identity that takes the area potentially affected by mining as its frame of reference. Alongside the distinction and even rivalry between neighbouring villages (Henkel 2014: 139) a notion of 'being (in this) together' emerges across the boundaries of one's own village.

Thus, despite the fact that, or precisely because, the Kirmes dance at the Dorfkrug is an event where people do not talk and think about coal mining, there are distinct social networks which determine who joins in this form of social interaction and who does not – networks which have been formed by the 'coal question'. Village limits still play a role, so that it is distinctively a Kerkwitzian event, yet these boundaries are permeable. Social ties on a personal level, as well as those established on the basis of the common fight against coal mining, open up this village ritual to people who would normally be 'outsiders'. At the same time, the struggle against mining has closed doors for some members of the village community; it has made insiders into outsiders. Belonging, as expressed in a place-centred concept of 'home' or *Heimat,* plays a central role in the way these social dynamics are played out, at both the village and regional levels.

The Village as *Heimat*

The church bells are ringing in Atterwasch, calling the people to church, which is about to be held in the red brick building dating back to the seventeenth century. The oldest part of the church dates back to 1294. On Reformation Day, 31 October, an important festival day for German Protestants, the church not only draws elderly people from Atterwasch and the neighbouring villages but opens its doors for a mixture of young and old, some of them travelling to Atterwasch from Berlin and beyond, but most coming from Atterwasch or the nearby villages of Kerkwitz, Grabko and others. All settle in the wooden benches dominating the whitewashed interior of the church. The pastor speaks to an attentive audience and makes references to God's creation and the injunction on men not to destroy it.

After the sermon people flock to the open space in front of the church, where the country women (Landfrauen) have already placed freshly brewed coffee and trays of cake on folding tables. People contentedly sip on a cup of coffee in the slightly chilly autumn air, hopeful that the weather forecast of sunny skies will prove true later on. A handful of environmental activists and a publisher have put up small stalls with information leaflets and publications on coal mining and its impact, pollution control and the history of the area. In the relaxed atmosphere people exchange the latest news and opinions on the coal mines and their potential extensions, on plans for the future or simply gossip. Most people seem to know each other, and local residents engage in conversations with activists from Greenpeace, who arrived in the morning. Later, the small stage becomes the centre of attention as local politicians, a representative of the farmers' association and other stakeholders give short speeches taking up the issue of coal mining. A few hundred people are assembled here, all drawn by the idea that they do not want the villages of Kerkwitz, Atterwasch and Grabko to become part of the list of 'lost villages' being resettled and demolished for coal mining. Thus, the village fête (Dorffest), organised by the 'Bündnis *Heimat* und Zukunft' (Alliance [for] Home and Future) every year since 2011, has become an established venue for the supporters of the threatened villages here in the Lausitz.

Julia A., a woman from Atterwasch in her early twenties, had spoken at the village fête a few years earlier; she used the term '*Heimat*' when she summarized her speech, as follows:

> Yes, essentially I said that we have to fight until the end. We must not give up. The main thing is that we are fighting for our village, because it is our *Heimat* and we will never get a new *Heimat*. So, it is essential that we keep up [the fight] and focus on our aim. And our aim is to preserve our *Heimat*. Yes, that is what I said.
>
> *(Interview, Julia 2015)*

Julia states here that the reason for action, for fighting against coal mining, is *Heimat* – home. *Heimat* needs to be protected and preserved, and it is inimitable and unique. There is a strong emotional aspect attached to it, which finds further expression in relation to the possibility of losing a personal sense of home that lends cultural meaning to life:

> [If the mine goes ahead,] my *Heimat* would be gone. The place where I grew up, where lots of things happened in my life, and which I'm always happy to go back to. It would make me very unhappy. I remember watching, more or less, when the people in Horno [an already relocated village approximately 10 kilometres from Atterwasch] were relocated. I thought it was terrible, how the people from the surrounding villages would go and take the tiles from the roofs of the houses that were left. It was like they were just taking stuff from a junkyard. People had built something up over years, and all of a sudden it was gone. It was awful.
>
> *(Interview, Julia 2015)*

Julia expresses *Heimat* as the idea of an irreplaceable space that she grew up in. It is a place consciously and unconsciously experienced and now deliberately remembered. Significantly, this idea of home is mobilised as having intrinsic and thus infinite value: its origin is constitutive, and its potential loss is posed as existential. In a distinct way, with strong parallels with the *Adivasi* villagers displaced by mining in Chhattisgarh, and the Indigenous landholders (and to some extent the farmers as well) on the Liverpool Plains, the Lausitz campaign draws its strength from posing an incommensurable challenge to the proposed mine. The capacity to do so owes much to the specifically local, face-to-face concept of belonging, of the village-based *Heimat,* that is mobilised.

In everyday contexts, the idea of *Heimat* is the place that someone relates to and calls home. Yet, to translate *Heimat* literally with the English concept of 'home' does not capture adequately all the resonances *Heimat* carries. In its colloquial use, *Heimat* implies meaning, expectations and aspirations; it is the familiar space that people experienced and created through inhabiting it. It bears notions of belonging, intimacy, certitude, and spatial and social closeness. Often the location of one's childhood days, it is more than a childish memory. It is an important source of identity-building and reassurance, as home, house, protection and sedentariness resonate in it. In spite of its vagueness and different connotations, it remains a term that relates to the precise space in time. It is a place of intimacy, and the emotional feeling for that place is constructed through experience.

Yet the German word *Heimat* has a dark history and has been deployed for ideological purposes in the past. In the literature of the mid-nineteenth century, *Heimat* related to the countryside and village life. *Heimat* was the 'idyll of local communities, close family harmony, and a domesticated, friendly nature' (Applegate 1990: 9). By the end of the century, *Heimat* had also taken on political connotations; it became instrumentalised, as a useful term for national integration after the formal unification of Germany under Prussian leadership in 1871 (ibid: 11). The concept of *Heimat* expanded its reference frame, speaking no longer of hometown, but rather of territorial state and consequently of nation (ibid: 13). During the Nazi period, the nationalist connotations of *Heimat* intensified. The term was no longer associated solely with an autonomous local life, but was absorbed into Nazi ideology. It became a term closely linked to the central themes of race, blood and German destiny (ibid: 18). Once ideologically loaded in this way, the word *Heimat* remained contested after 1945. The philosopher Christoph Türcke discerns a 'consensus in dissent' between today's right-wing parties and the autonomous left in seeing national pride as an essential element of *Heimat*. For the latter, any such nationalistic associations of *Heimat* would be understood per se as hotbeds of fascistic mentality (Türcke 2006: 71). Türcke, like other German intellectuals before him (Mitscherlich 1971), argue for a rehabilitation of *Heimat*, and a separation from nationalism. However, the term remains contested and subject to scrutiny and instrumentalisation.

Less contested is the notion that *Heimat* gains relevance in moments of its loss. Türcke goes even further by stating that *Heimat* is constituted only *a posteriori*: children conceive their place of belonging with its social contexts and defining character usually only after they have left home. Only in retrospect do we apprehend the joy of those childhood places (Türcke 2006: 25), do we understand what we had. The loss of *Heimat* or the threat of losing it brings *Heimat* to mind, makes people aware of the emotional and spatially defined notions of belonging.

Thus, in the Lausitz, where the place literally faces the threat that it could be erased and vanish from the face of the earth, *Heimat* becomes a strong impulse in the struggle against mining. If the mines were to go ahead, some 3,400 people will lose their homes when they are forcibly relocated and their villages demolished.[7] The whole landscape would be dug up to make way for mining, and all the tangible markers of *Heimat* will be lost. Houses, streets, trees, cemeteries and churches, farms, the whole stretch of land with the meanings inscribed, will disappear. Mathias Berndt, the Protestant pastor of Atterwasch, put this prospect very forcefully in an interview in 2014, just before he retired. Sitting in the garden of his church rectory, Berndt describe the scene around him.

> Well we do indeed live in very a beautiful countryside here, all around us there are green meadows, and woods, with lots of old trees in them, and little valleys with streams running through them.
>
> The plan is to open up an open-cut brown coal mine, right here, fifty metres from where we're sitting. The mine would swallow up this village and go all the way to the river Neisse, that's about 7 kilometres from here. [. . .] The church here, which is eight hundred years old, would be blown up and destroyed. [. . .] The lake would vanish, the woods would vanish, everything would be turned into grey ash-heaps, and nothing more would grow here for a hundred years or more. The good life that we live here in nature and with nature would be destroyed.
>
> *(Interview, Berndt 2014)*

Berndt went on to say that the villagers had been 'living in fear' for seven years, since the initial application for the mine extension was made in 2007. Should Atterwasch and the two neighbouring villages be destroyed, the villagers would be 'torn out by the roots . . . and we know that when you cut off peoples' roots, you also cut off their future' (Interview, Berndt 2014).

Heimat as people experienced it sensually, emotionally and mnemonically would not change gradually, but be intentionally and knowingly destroyed in a relatively short span of time. These threats of relocation occur against the background of a long-standing history of the place, but also of a more recent history of relocation and the trauma that came along with it. Residents and activists refer to the demolition of villages to make way for coal mines, which was common practice during the socialist period in the former GDR and prior to it, so that by 1990 a total of 136 villages had been destroyed or devastated in the Lausitz for coal mining (Archiv verschwundener Orte 2009). The memories of the places for local residents are still alive, yet now ultimately tied to a feeling of loss and damage. Thomas Burchardt, for instance, witnessed the building of the Jänschwalde power plant in the 1970s at the age of twelve, and saw the destruction of Sorb villages to supply the power plant with coal:

> I remember sitting on the steps of the old church which belonged to the village of Groß Lieskow. The church was already half in ruins. A man came out, walked about ten paces, pointed out into the flattened landscape and said 'that used to be my house right there'.
>
> *(Interview, Burchardt 2014)*

It is important to stress here that the real and imagined landscape invoked by the villagers is one in which coal, and the region's history of coal mining, is physically and symbolically present, quite literally embedded in the fabric of everyday life.

The existing Jänschwalde mine lies only a few kilometres away from the three threatened villages, and on a clear day white columns of steam rising from the cooling towers of the Jänschwalde power plant are clearly visible over the low hills of the surrounding countryside. Hence, should mining also be regarded as part of the *Heimat*? Martin D., an activist now based in a larger city some 200 kilometres away, remembers growing up in Jänschwalde in the 1980s:

> The power plant was visually always very present. That is, whenever you moved around somewhere in the surroundings the power plant was a big industrial construction, with the tower of clouds always a land mark, I would almost say. And the power plant was so – it somehow belonged to it, you can't put it differently. Because I was born there, also grew up there. As a youngster, adolescent, one explored the area with the bike a lot. One went to the lake, through the woods. One had a look around, at what happened in the neighbouring villages. [. . .] I can go back even further. I once went with my parents when I was still a kid of 8 or 9 or 10, definitely still a school kid, to a devastated village. That was still GDR-times or shortly after the reunification. That [village] was already emptied. And there were cracks in the road, from the earth settling. And we went through the village and went to the edge of the mine with my parents. It was quite an adventure, a Sunday afternoon outing. I can remember it very distinctly, this ghost village, empty houses, somehow. And in the road already cracks where a foot could go in. [. . .] That was when I first recall consciously noticing the mine landscape.
>
> *(Interview, Martin 2014)*

Mining is experienced visually and sensually; people also remember the dust and almost black air when briquette plants unleased exhaust fumes, regularly causing layers of black coal dust to cover everything. Coal mining and its sensory impacts, especially in terms of local pollution, were a familiar part of the Lausitz, one that the residents lived with and necessarily included into their view of the place. For those opposing the mine these experiences are remembered as part of their past, under the GDR especially, and as a constant threat in the present. In contrast with the regional adherents of coal mining (discussed below), they do not celebrate that past, but wish to leave it behind.

'Horno ist das letzte Dorf' – A Cautionary Tale

The local story of the destruction wreaked by mining is closely linked with the recent local history of reunification and democratisation. Eastern Germany has experienced many limitations of reintegration and tales of disappointment play a cautionary role, acting as an allegory for the present. One such tale, often told by opponents of the mine, is the story of Horno. Horno was demolished to make way for the Jänschwalde mine in 2004, following a fifteen-year campaign, dating pre-1989, against its destruction by many of its inhabitants, who were resettled in 2003–2004.[8] Horno has become iconic for numerous reasons. For one, it was the first (and supposedly last) village that was destroyed to make way for the Jänschwalde mine after the reunification of the GDR with the FRG.[9] Manfred Stolpe, the then Premier of the state of Brandenburg, is said to have proclaimed in 1998 that Horno would certainly be the last village that has to give way to lignite.[10] That promise was not kept, and '*Horno ist das letzte Dorf*' ('Horno is the last village') has since become an allegory for the opportunistic and nearly unpredictable decision-making of regional and national politicians.

Narratives of emotional attachment to places lost forever are common in the Lausitz, where, as mentioned, 136 villages have been demolished since coal mining began (see also Wolf and Kuhn 2011). But Horno, because of its closeness to the threatened villages of Kerkwitz, Atterwasch and Grabko, and the fact that many local people witnessed its devastation, represents a very immediate case of struggling for and eventually losing *Heimat*. Roswitha expressed the powerful sense of loss, and foreboding, in this way:

> In 1990 one drew hope, because our [then] State Premier Stolpe said, 'Horno is the last village to make way for coal.' And I imagined back then, 'How should that be?' One had heard before of villages that were dug up, but these villages were always far away. But Horno, there I could put faces to the people who lived there, because I went to school with them. That was something totally different, wasn't it?
>
> *(Interview, Roswitha 2015)*

The story of Horno also resonates with local people because it unfolds in the immediate aftermath of German reunification, and the hopes which many citizens of the GDR cherished for greater democracy and participation after 1989.

From the early 1990s on, people living in villages which had been scheduled as potential mining areas or 'sacrifice zones' in the former GDR were once more permitted to build on the land they lived on, and to renovate or expand their homes. The restrictions on building in mining areas, which were inscribed in GDR law, could now be erased from the land charge register, an option many people seized. Moreover, the change from state socialism to Germany's 'social market' capitalism in a broader sense seemed to promise more ways for civil society to articulate its concerns. Thus, people in Horno could actually voice their protests against coal mine extensions, use different means of staging protest, public presence, and appearances in court – instruments that were not available in the GDR, or only to a limited extent.

The eventual destruction of Horno thus embodies the dashed hopes of people in the Lausitz. It revealed that in the new system people could still be displaced by the mines despite protesting against them: they could not prevent forced resettlement and demolition. Horno became a sobering lesson in the limits of participation and democracy in reunified Germany, and the accompanying disillusionment with politics in the new system. But interestingly enough, it did not become a reason for local people to conclude that protest was futile. Sabine N., another resident of Atterwasch, sees the struggle to preserve *Heimat* as a matter of historical responsibility – even if that struggle ultimately proved fruitless:

> You shall not surrender. You are always responsible to the next generation. Even if someone says to us today, "Well in Horno it also didn't work, so you don't need to bother." But the people from Horno can look their grandchildren in the eye and say, 'We tried with all means available to us.' And the same goes for us.
>
> *(Interview, Sabine 2015)*

Reflecting this, Horno itself becomes, in its absence, a symbolic strategic site. It is not only an icon of loss and defeat, but a reference point, an important script animating resistance to new mining. The sentiment resonates very strongly with the sense of historic responsibility and dignity expressed equally powerfully in the other two cases, as discussed in Chapters 2 and 3, most especially the insistence of 'no walkovers' in Chhattisgarh, and of continuity across Indigenous struggles in the Liverpool Plains. It demonstrates a strategic practice of refusal to concede, as a demonstration of democratic legitimacy, and of intergenerational responsibility.

As a reference point it inspires action in the present. According to activist Antje K., who grew up in the Lausitz, and now lives in the regional centre Cottbus, the people of Horno have inspired solidarity amongst protesters throughout the region:

> Because they showed that one can fight. That it is worth fighting. Of course it is also a bit ambivalent because you see that the people of Horno fought but lost. [But] the mayor of Horno accompanies the [current] resistance in spirit, and he spoke a few years ago at the Sternmarsch [. . .] He said, 'Sure, it might be your turn now, as well. But the first thing you have to do is to stay together, because we wouldn't have made it if we had not stuck together. And for you and for your fight time is on your side.'
>
> *(Interview, Antje 2015)*

The residents of Horno carried on their fight at numerous levels of government and legal jurisdictions, and even appealed to the European Court of Human Rights to prevent eviction. People in the Lausitz threatened with resettlement today also try to tap the full potential of judicial measures, a complex process allowing for formal objections and complaint at several stages in the process of opening new mines. These judicial measures allow, if not for a protection of the place against its destruction, at least for a delay in the mining process. There is strong sense that 2003 was different from 2018: Antje's reference to the Mayor's comment about time being 'on your side' is centrally important for the articulation of wider energy and climate dynamics with the future of coal in the region.

The Region as *Heimat* for Miners

The idea of the Lausitz without the coal industry is contested by those who assert the region's proud history of mining and power production. As noted, local people have grown up on the doorstep of the industry, and many have relied on it for employment. For mining advocates the industry has forged the region and defined its community and history: rejecting mining is tantamount to rejecting the community. The delay in mining approvals increases the sense of uncertainty for miners and their supporters, who already sense their understanding of the region is under threat from the national move away from coal under the *Energiewende*. In this context they deploy a different script of losing *Heimat*, that may be no less intensely felt. As Marco B., an electronics technician in his twenties who works in the Jänschwalde power-plant, explains,

> [Coal] means a lot to me. A real lot. In principle, it means being able to stay here in my home. Without brown coal we'd lose most of the jobs in this region. If there were no more jobs here, I'd have to move away. For that reason, coal is important, because it means I can continue to live here, where I feel at home. It means I can build a house with the money that I've earned. That's very important to me.
>
> *(Interview, Marko 2015)*

For proponents of coal mining, the Lausitz is the home of miners and mining. It is *Heimat* experienced and understood as a region, with its characteristic industrial landscapes, not as an individual village. Lena K., a nurse in her early thirties and active for Pro Lausitzer Braunkohle, an organisation set up to lobby for the continuation of mining, describes *Heimat* in terms of her regard for natural places: this includes rehabilitated mine sites, many of which had been reforested and converted as popular lakeside communities, and had been made 'more attractive':

> *Heimat*, well, *Heimat* is a swath of land where you feel at home. [. . .] It is a liveable area here. [. . .] I am a person close to nature. I have a horse, there are woods here where you can enjoy riding. All of it is actually very nice. And then you additionally have to say that we have the Spree forest on our doorstep, which is very nice. And then some things developed here in the context of post-mining landscapes, like the Seenland [lake area], which I have to say also makes this area way more attractive.
>
> *(Interview, Lena 2014)*

Like Lena, many proponents of mining – whether they were born in the Lausitz or had moved there – see themselves as fighting for their regional home. This regional *Heimat* is the combination of the villages, the cities of Cottbus and Spremberg, and particularly the natural environment surrounding them. It does not so much refer to the open pits and the dug-up landscape as to the lakes created in the course of re-cultivating the mining areas by flooding the disused pits.

There are also social networks centred on the mining industry, which bind people to the region. These networks revolve more around kinship, socialisation and chosen friendships established in context of a life of working in the mining and power industry, rather than from proximity to a particular village or place. For Stefanie W., in her early twenties and working in the coal mine, the loss of mining for the region would mean leaving behind not just a familiar place but also a set of relationships that centre on financial security:

> The problem is that you have friends here, you have family. You know what's what and where things are. You know your way around. [. . .] Or you think, if I invest anything here now, I want some sort of future. If I buy a car, I definitely want my job to be secure until it's paid for. If I build a house somewhere now, I want to know that I don't have to leave it after ten, twenty years because I have to go to Bavaria or Dusseldorf, somewhere else, to work.
> *(Interview, Stefanie 2015)*

For supporters of mining, the economic and demographic upheavals in the Lausitz since reunification overshadow any physical destruction of the landscape and individual villages. These upheavals have brought with them a dramatic decline in the size of the coal industry and the number of people it employs. Since reunification, the number of mines has decreased, as has the number of jobs in mining, energy and related industries. A quarter of the population left the region looking for jobs in the larger cities and in Western Germany, and this process of economic atrophy continues. A common theme amongst proponents of mining is the loss of young people and, with them, the future of the region. As Wolfgang Rupieper, head of Pro Lausitzer Braunkohle, says,

> We don't want skilled workers leaving the region, and we don't want to lose all our young people. Every year Vattenfall takes on 250 to 300 apprentices in the coal industry. They learn a range of trades, and they earn good money when they're finished. Sure, they could leave and find jobs elsewhere in Germany – but then Lusatia would be depopulated.
> *(Interview, Rupieper 2015)*

The lignite industry has shrunk but is still an influential economic player in the region. Given the hardships, which the region has experienced over the last two and a half decades, it is hardly surprising that workers in the coal industry, their families, unions and local businesses fight to save the remaining jobs, even if they are only a fraction of the number coal had employed before reunification.

Arguments about coal's centrality to the economy of the region are omnipresent for mining proponents. Not surprisingly, a survey by the German research institute Forsa in 2013, that was commissioned by the mining union, the IGBCE,[11] found out that 92 per cent of Lausitz residents who completed the survey thought that the lignite industry had a strong or very strong meaning for the region, and that 63 per cent considered the lignite industry to be an important economic aspect of the Lausitz and East Germany (Forsa 2013).[12] For the Pro Lausitzer Braunkohle group and other supporters of mining, any further job losses in mining are considered to be not only a *Strukturwandel* (a process of structural transformation, unfolding over time) but a *Strukturbruch* – literally, a structural break, with connotations of a violent rupture. The region has already experienced one such traumatic structural break after reunification. They argue that a further shift away from coal would bring the region to its knees. The representative of Pro Lausitzer Braunkohle, Rupieper, recognised that mining required relocation:

> Of course *Heimat* is important for all human beings, it touches us emotionally, and therefore anyone who loses their home is going to be emotionally affected. That's true of anyone who might be affected by the mine extensions, who might lose his or her home, and be relocated. But these [to-be-relocated] people, these citizens, will be compensated. They'll get a house and land somewhere nearby, in good condition. They won't be financially disadvantaged, and they can stay in the Lausitz, just in another place.
>
> *(Interview, Rupieper 2015)*

Relocation for villagers was a minor and relatively commensurable inconvenience: people would be compensated and could stay in the region, 'just in another place', in a new house with land. In contrast, the loss of mining for the region spelt disaster for those working in the industry. They would have to quit the region entirely to find new work, and in this respect, the loss of mining poses an incommensurable challenge to their livelihood and hence their ability to remain in the region. As Rupieper puts is,

> On the other side are x-thousand workers and their dependents and colleagues who depend on coal for their livelihood, and who won't have jobs anymore if the industry declines. These people and their families will have to go somewhere else in Germany or Europe to find a job, and they won't be compensated. They have to bear the risk.
>
> *(Interview, Rupieper 2015)*

In this script the material consequences of resettlement are minimised, as compensation is paid, and the people to be resettled are involved in the process of resettlement and compensation. Villagers would not lose their regional attachment, as the sites offered for resettlement are in close proximity to the old villages, and the resettled people can influence the process and planning for the new village. Proponents of mining argue that people who have been resettled do not protest anymore or voice their discomfort, or will cease to do so after a generation at home in their new houses. Opponents of resettlement, by contrast, argue that these people never found a 'real' home, and that all the new comforts and material compensation cannot mask the fact that the emotional and historic bonds with the precise house or village are lost.

Importantly, the supporters of mining seek to relativize the potential losses of the villagers who oppose mining, rendering the destruction of villages commensurable with the mine expansions. In contrast, the potential loss of mining for the region is framed as posing a profound existential threat for mine workers and associated communities: they are not likely to receive compensation and have to find work elsewhere.

In sum, both opponents and proponents of coal and coal mining mobilise legitimising concepts of home or *Heimat* in the struggle to defend their interests and pursue their goals. Both antagonists assert their version of home as intrinsic and as facing an existential threat, either with the loss of villages or with the loss of mining. In an attempt to shift the logjam, defenders of the villages have in recent years sought to embed their struggle in the wider *Energiewende* and global energy transition. Here, ideas of home have become articulated very clearly with issues of climate change and energy.

The Lausitz as Home to the *Energiewende*

In the last decade the *Energiewende* has entered the Lausitz in both physical form, as visible renewable energy, and in the form of a set of ideas about energy transition and climate change. For the villagers, the project is a concrete, everyday reality: in our interviews with them they describe the numerous ways in which they are already living the energy transition. In this way the social and cultural traditions of rural life have intersected with the project of ecological modernisation that underpins the *Energiewende*. The concept of home as pursued in the villages becomes articulated with the wider historical project of addressing climate change. Monika Schulz-Höpfner, the former mayor of Kerkwitz and Atterwasch, and a Christian Democrat member of the state parliament of Brandenburg from 1994 to 2014, views the energy transition as a common goal that can bring together both opponents and proponents of mining:

> The common denominator must surely be to encourage progress and development in our region. The common denominator is climate policy. The very same climate policy which our federal government has promulgated: onwards with renewable energy! That's already a fact here! You can see it right here on my farm.
>
> Q: You're pointing to the solar panels there on your roof . . . that's what you mean when you say the facts already exist. . .
>
> Schulz-Höpfner: I mean the solar panels, I mean our windmill, I mean our electric car. What my family and I talk about, we live as well.
>
> *(Interview, Schulz-Höpfner 2015)*

Villagers appeal simultaneously to historical tradition, and to the practical steps which local residents have taken in implementing the *Energiewende*. Roswitha is keen to stress that her fellow villages are investing in renewable energy:

> If you look at the roofs of the houses around here – solar power is practically everywhere. A lot of the houses – definitely 30 per cent of them, maybe more – have solar on top. Local

people have done a lot for renewable energy. The fact that more and more brown coal is being burnt just doesn't make sense.

(Interview, Roswitha 2015)

Echoing the sentiment, local farmer Ulrich S. stresses the practical contribution that he and other farmers are making to the *Energiewende* – and their pragmatic reasons for doing so:

We earn our living from farming. Farming is a hard life, but it also offers many of us opportunities to get involved in renewable energy. [. . .] The biogas plant is over there, right next to the chicken coops, so that we can use the warmth generated by the plant to heat the coops. [. . .] We generate about 160 kW from the biogas plant and heat the farm buildings, the farmhouse, and the coops.

Q: So you're making your own contribution to the energy transition?

Yes, certainly.

(Interview, Ulrich 2014)

It is worth pointing out that our interviewees' everyday understanding of the *Energiewende* is generally more narrowly framed than that which informs policy debates at the Federal level or the energy transition laws passed in 2011 (Hager and Steffe 2016). Broadly speaking, the energy transition is understood at the local level of the village or region as a transition to electricity generation from 'clean' renewable energy sources (such as solar or wind), and often in explicit contrast to 'dirty' coal-fired power. This contrasts with what might be termed the 'expert' framing of the energy transition as a larger set of abstract targets and policy instruments encompassing areas such as energy efficiency and transportation, whose ultimate aim is a transformation of the entire German, and indeed European, energy system in the context of climate change. As we shall see, however, these contrasting understandings do not mean that climate change is absent from the understandings and motivations of local actors.

Global Protests and Socio-Ecological Relations: New Alliances in the Lausitz

As noted at the start of this chapter, the people taking part in the human chain protest of September 2014 – local, national as well as international mine opponents – were not protesting against the Jänschwalde-Nord mine extension alone. In fact, they followed the call from a range of environmental organisations that had mobilised people on the basis of environmental injustice, climate damage and climate change.[13] Simply put, the motivation of many environmental and political activists who came to the Lausitz that day was that coal mining, and the burning of coal in power plants, has a major impact on the climate, and its effects are felt globally. As Falk H., one of the activists who grew up in the nearby city of Cottbus but now lives in Berlin, explains,

> We didn't want to make it only a local issue, we wanted to make it like a global issue because mining is the worst thing that we can do to this area here and the worst thing we can do in terms of climate change.
>
> *(Interview, Falk 2014)*

Mobilising on a large scale could not be done individually, or by the civil action groups which had formed in the Lausitz right after the announcement of the proposed mine extension in 2007. Rather, it required help from established NGOs and other 'outside supporters'. The human chain involved Greenpeace, Friends of the Earth, campact!, Klimaallianz Deutschland, the Lausitzer Energie und Klimacamp, Berliner Energietisch, Naturfreunde Deutschlands, Anti Atom Berlin and the Polish Stowarzyszenie Nie Koplani Odkrywkowej. On the more local level, the previously mentioned Klinger Runde also joined as an official organiser.

The local opposition to coal mining in the Lausitz had found new allies through large-scale protests like the human chain, but also through a continuous process of engagement and collaboration in smaller but regular events such as the annual Lausitzer Klima- und Energiecamp which was initiated in 2011. As a climate camp, it has been a place for political action and for people to imagine ecological alternatives to current energy production, and has been offering workshops, theatre performances, seminars, demonstrations, protest actions, public debates and other low-threshold activities centred on energy politics, environmental and climate related issues (Feigenbaum et al. 2013) (see Figure 4.2). It aims at informing locals as well as visitors in conceptual and practical hands-on formats. Last but not least, it creates the logistical framework for larger-scale protests.

The Lausitzcamp and the human chain form part of a growing German climate movement, which involves lobbying groups such as the Klima-Allianz, as well as Left-orientated social movement organisations, such as ATTAC, that combine environmental protection with a critique of the political system and the pursuit of climate justice (Kössler 2013). Protest groups trace a lineage from the anti-nuclear and pro-renewable 'New Left', but they also draw on a new generation of young, ecologically motivated people. The new cohort builds on the expertise and infrastructure from its predecessors but works more on a networked basis, centred on issue mobilisation rather than organisationally based. The various alliances and coalitions for environmental protection and climate justice tend to be contingent, not clearly hierarchically ordered, and based on mailing lists and offline and online networks rather than organisational membership. The *Ende Gelände* alliance, for instance, which became active in 2015 in the Rhenish mining area, became a driving force, if not of the German climate movement, then at least of the anti-coal movement. *Ende Gelände* is in its own words,

> a broad alliance of people from the anti-nuclear and anti-coal movements, the Rhineland and Lausitz climate camps and the Hambacher Forest anti-coal campaign. We are from

Figure 4.2 Lausitz protest against coal.
Source: Photo by Markus Pichlmaier, with permission

> grassroots climate action groups, large environmental organisations, left political groups and many other campaigns, groups and networks. We all share the belief that to stop climate change we need to take action ourselves, using civil disobedience as a powerful signal for real action to put our climate before profit.
>
> (Ende Gelände 2016)

In May 2016, *Ende Gelände* staged a large-scale protest action in the Lausitz, bringing not only national and international protesters and their agendas to the Lausitz but also civil disobedience as a new form of protest in the anti-mining struggle. With the slogan 'Stop Coal, Protect the Climate!', the alliance organised a protest weekend against mining in the Lausitz, openly and publicly announcing a mass blockade of the Welzow-Süd coal mine and the adjacent power plant Schwarze Pumpe, south of Cottbus. Around 4,000 people came to join the protest on the weekend, and while it included an officially approved demonstration march and political speeches, drawing a broader civil society of around 1,500 people on a Saturday afternoon, the main action which attracted most media attention was the occupation of diggers, conveyor belts, railway tracks and the power plant entrance, which lasted from a Friday afternoon to a Sunday afternoon.

Around 3,500 people, mostly dressed in white 'Hazmat' suits to highlight coal as a health hazard, took part in the occupation, which was well organised, using tactical and infrastructural knowledge that had proved successful in the anti-nuclear movement. Based on an agreed-upon consensus, all action was deliberately not directed against the power plant workers or the police, but was aimed at symbolic action without inflicting property damage. This consensus, combined with excellent planning and organisation, led to the successful blockade of the mine and the power plant for nearly forty-eight hours. As a precaution, Vattenfall halted mining in Welzow-Süd and reduced energy production at the Schwarze Pumpe coal-fired power station. The occupation was symbolically successful and largely non-violent. The police, too, mostly avoided escalation. Police only intervened with force when a few hundred of the several thousand protesters demolished the power plant's fence and rushed onto the premises.[14]

While the civil disobedience tactics were not wholly supported by local opponents of the mine, they all noticed that the protest, as well as several smaller initiatives and media campaigns initiated and realised with the help of national NGOs, helped to advance the visibility of their local campaigns. The NGOs meanwhile were able to use lignite mining as a tangible symbol of CO_2 emissions. The local campaign against the mines allowed the NGOs to converge in the Lausitz and give concrete expression to their focus on 'keeping fossil fuels in the ground', which, according to Princen et al. (2015: 7), has until recently been unthinkable in mainstream policy and academic debate.

For the villagers, the protests created unprecedented public support. The *Ende Gelände* 2016 protests were coordinated as part of the global 'Break Free from Fossil Fuels' campaign, thereby making the Lausitz part of a globally coordinated resistance against fossil fuels (Ende Gelände 2016). These large internationally networked protests, in 2016 with Ende Gelände and in 2015 with the human chain, gave the villagers of Kerkwitz, Atterwasch and Grabko an important morale boost. Reflecting on the impact of the human chain a year later, Roland Lehman, the mayor of Kerkwitz, commented on its impact:

> An experience like that, when you realise that so many people have come from so far away, more than 7,000 people, that they've come here to our little Lausitz, to support us and add their strength to ours, that makes a deep impression on you. [. . .] And surely it helps to raise consciousness about what's happening here, not just in our backyard but at a national level and beyond. Because it's an issue that is starting to get attention worldwide, and in my view should get attention worldwide.
>
> Q: Why is it so important that this gets attention at a local, national and international levels?
>
> Well, one crucial point in all this is climate change. And of course burning coal or other fossil fuels to generate electricity is a huge factor in climate change. For that reason alone it's an urgent necessity to stop doing that.
>
> *(Interview, Lehmann 2015)*

Connecting the Global and the Local: Climate Change as Script

The *Lausitzcamp*, the human chain and *Ende Gelände* 2016 aimed not only to shed light on the regional problem but to frame it in a global perspective. The local can serve as a means to understand and address the larger issues of climate change, and vice versa. The camp organisers and protesters continuously stressed the global impact of lignite mining in terms of emissions, global warming and climate change. They connected the locally felt impacts of mining with questions of global climate justice, asserting claims well beyond a more localist 'not in my backyard' response. Considerations of global impacts of mining have indeed found their way into the awareness and arguments of some local mining opponents. When Christian H. is asked whether ecology is a relevant topic at all, he replies:

> For some [villagers] it is. And, well … even the most ignorant person must now be noticing that we really play fast and loose with our planet. [. . .] I would wish for more people to think about it ecologically. Because for me it is a very important topic, because the impact can be felt here directly. [. . .] I am 44 years old. Previously I never experienced a winter without snow. But last year we had such a winter. We had one day of clearing snow, a sunny day, and that was it for this winter. And as I said, someone wants to tell me that this isn't connected?! This cannot be explained with climate variability in Germany any more, that here in our part of Germany with the continental climate there is no snow any more. [. . .] If you think about it, for just five minutes, you notice that it is a global issue.
>
> *(Interview, Christian 2014)*

Such reflections on the changing climate are common in the other two cases, in India and Australia, as a way of comprehending the material effects of a changing carbon cycle. The linkages between local and global environmental concerns certainly have become more prominent in the wider discourses on coal mining. While local threats, such as the leaching of iron hydroxide into the waters of the River Spree, resulting in what is known locally as the 'brown Spree', and the decline of the water table are immediate effects of mining in the Lausitz, the indirect consequences through global warming are also related to the emissions produced in coal-based energy production. Roland Lehmann amplifies on this:

> Certainly in the first instance it's about saving our villages. But everybody knows today that it's not just about that, if you look beyond your own backyard it's about a lot, lot more. It's not just about a village here or a village there that might vanish from the earth. In the end, we'll all be affected, not just those of us whose villages get dug up. The bill for what happens here will have to be paid eventually. Not by us, not directly, but by our children, and their children. And we can't let that happen.
>
> *(Interview, Lehmann 2015)*

This statement expresses very clearly the fundamental and irreconcilable collision between coal and climate, and the sense that there is no possibility of one accommodating the other. The clash is zero-sum and incommensurable: the 'bill … will have to be paid'. Similar concerns are expressed by Mathias Berndt, the pastor from Atterwasch, who describes his motivation as follows:

> A famous professor here in Germany said that the energy transition is the Reformation of the twenty-first century, and the energy transition can't be achieved with words, but only

through deeds, just as Martin Luther was a man of deeds in 1517. So I've tried to act in such a way that I don't just talk about the energy transition and the preservation of God's creation, which are really the same thing, but actually to realize them through my deeds. [...] And in my view it's an important part of this change, this transformation, that the democratic grass-roots are involved more strongly.

(Interview, Berndt 2014)

It is not surprising that the *Energiewende* and climate change are expressed in local arguments against coal mining. Some commentators argue that, for the majority of the German population, the primary meaning of the *Energiewende* is societal, with the exit from nuclear energy and the expansion of renewables being the main theme underpinning their endorsement of the energy transition; climate change plays only a secondary role (see Morton and Müller 2016).

Contestation over climate and coal is converging though. Protests against lignite mining in the Lausitz, such as the human chain in 2014, brought together national and international NGOs with a focus on climate change, protesters from the villages and local climate activists like Falk H. His statement that 'mining is the worst thing that we can do to this area, and the worst thing we can do in terms of climate change' articulates one of the central insights behind climate activists' focus on extraction, rather than the 'global management formulation' of the problem of climate change (Princen et al. 2015: 6). The diverse activist groups and environmental organisations who converged on the Lausitz for the 2014 human chain protest were putting this insight into practice, seeking to project it onto the 'public screen' (DeLuca and Peeples 2002). From 2014, that agenda was further asserted with, for instance, the 'coal kills' human sign organised by Greenpeace in front of the Jänschwalde power plant in August 2015, and, as mentioned, the *Ende Gelände* protests in May 2016, which were part of the global 'Break Free from Fossil Fuels' campaign, across twenty escalated actions on six continents, orchestrated, among others, by the 350.org and its local action group Fossil Free Berlin. The protest escalated in successive years, and has firmly positioned coal extraction as the main driver of climate change.

The climate–coal nexus, and its growing salience, does not mean that climate change or the energy transition has become the key line of argument among villagers in Lusatia threatened by the mine extension, or that they are all necessarily sympathetic to the environmental protesters. Some remain sceptical about environmental arguments: panegyrics about the global impact of coal mining are still not easily accepted in an area where mining has shaped identities for such a long time, even for those opposed to mining. Coal has been part of the history of the region and, as noted, there is a strong consensus over its importance. Overcoming coal has to proceed with the involvement of affected communities, not defined as requiring their destruction.

In October 2015, however, the global dimension of damage through coal mining found its way to one of the more strictly local rituals of village life, the autumn village fête in Atterwasch. Melvin Purzuelo, an environmental activist from the Philippines, and Hindou Oumarou Ibrahim, a climate expert from Chad, shared the stage with two Lusatian speakers. Invited by Greenpeace and the Bündnis Heimat und Zukunft, Purzuelo and Ibrahim were introduced as people affected by climate change, and they told of their experiences and the way climate change was understood in their home countries. They expressed their belief in a common struggle against environmental destruction, which needed to take the local as well as the global into consideration in order to prevail. Thus the 'appeal for solidarity with the suffering of the distant stranger' (Arnold 2012) was brought together with the local experience of the concrete impacts of coal mining.

The long years of resistance to the mine extensions in the Lausitz by local people and their supporters from beyond the region, culminating in *Ende Gelände* in 2016, have been informed by the growing intensity of climate change, and have become part of wider global narrative, in Germany and beyond. The intensity of this engagement reflects Smith and Howe's argument discussed in Chapter 1 about climate change as social drama, where place is central in creating and mobilising a constituency for climate action. This intersection is often understood as the subsumption of the local by the global, as climate change impacts, whether anticipated or experienced, come to reconfigure local social relations. In important ways there is evidence of a reverse flow in the context of the Lausitz as local people opposing the coal mines link their struggles with the global effort to reduce greenhouse gas emissions and in the process find a wealth of new alliances and gain strategic leverage over a national state ostensibly committed to overcoming fossil fuel dependence as part of its climate policy commitments. In the process, the local opposition is helping to construct a moral geography of climate action, what Smith and Howe describe as one of the central tasks for climate activism.

Conclusion

On 30 March 2017, nearly ten years after the initial application by Vattenfall, the mine extension plans were cancelled. EPH, the new owner of the mines and power plants (now called LEAG), announced that it would not proceed with Jänschwalde-Nord. Announcing the decision, the CEO of LEAG, Helmar Rendez, said the decision not to proceed with this mine extension (neither with Reichwalde nor with parts of Welzow-Süd II) would enable the company to plan its mining strategy for the next twenty-five to thirty years in a predictable way, and would provide a foundation for it to expand into other areas of the sector. LEAG would still proceed with the extension of Nochten II Sonderfeld Mühlrose, meaning the relocation of

Table 4.2. *Recent coal mines in the Lausitz*

Name	Start	End	Output	Status in 2019	People (to be) resettled
Jänschwalde	1975	2023–2025	8–10 million tonnes/year	Operating	1,170
Jänschwalde-Nord	2025		250 million tonnes	Stopped (in 2017)	900
Welzow-Süd I	1962	2027	18–23 million tonnes/year	Operating	3,550
Welzow-Süd II	2027	2042	204 million tonnes	Planning on hold, to be decided in 2020	810
Nochten I	1973	2026	16–19 million tonnes/year	Operating	740
Nochten II / Teilfeld Mühlrose*	2020s	2045	310 / 145 million tonnes	In planning	1,700 / 200
Reichwalde	1985-1999, 2010	2045	12–13.5 million tonnes/year	Operating	260
Bagenz-Ost	2030s		220 million tonnes	Stopped (in 2017)	-
Spremberg-Ost	2030s		220 million tonnes	Stopped (in 2017)	-
Cottbus-Nord	1975	2015	4–16 million tonnes/year	Closed	900

Source: LEAG Tagabau, 2019; Bund, Friends of the Earth Germany 2019. (*plan modified and size reduced in 2017)

200 villagers in the village of Mühlrose, and would reserve any decision on the Welzow-South II extension until 2020.[15] As outlined in Table 4.1, some mines are proceeding, some are on hold, and others are halted in what is a very uneven process across the region (Table 4.2).

Villagers in Atterwasch, Kerkwitz and Grabko breathed a huge sigh of relief. They had won an important victory. Their battle had been successful after a decade of living with the threat of forcible relocation. When the planned extensions had been announced, they had immediately begun to protest. They feared the loss not just of their physical home but of the sense of belonging, of memories, certitude and spatial and social closeness, what several described as their sense of home, or *Heimat.* The fear of losing *Heimat* is also inherent in any possible exit from coal mining in the Lausitz, since miners worry that this would mean the loss of their jobs and incomes, bringing with it the necessity to move to an area economically better off. Regional contestation over the mines is hence also a form of contestation over the meaning of locality, in terms of its development trajectory, whether with or beyond coal. The need to develop the third option of a new development trajectory which would enable employees in the mining sector to prosper, and stay in the region, is critical.

More generally, locally based protest against the relocations was not enough to prevent the mine extensions. Recent experiences, such as the fate of Horno, as well as the history of coal mining and expansion across the Lausitz, demonstrate very clearly the limitations of protest confined by locality. Ten years of struggle by the villagers of Kerkwitz, Atterwasch and Grabko, as well as recent protests in other villages, have led to an acknowledgement that the fight against coal mining needs cooperation with new allies. As Roland Lehmann put it,

> Today in this digitized world it is possible – and I see this here as an advantage – to connect with each other. [. . .] And yes, we took action ourselves to draw attention to our misery. And I think many things were successful. There is the Sternmarsch every year. Then there was the week of the climate camp, and the human chain which followed it. [. . .] Interest in that issue is tremendous. [. . .] And then the whole issue takes different dimensions. It's not only regional any more. That's of no interest to anyone. [. . .] Instead we achieved that [when] it reached a larger public somehow. [. . .] And then the whole effort was already not in vain.
> *(Interview, Lehmann 2014)*

Solidarity and support strengthens the fighting spirit of local protesters, and it raises awareness of the issue beyond the villages. Alliance-building and collaboration can be a means to gather the attention of the media, and consequently of decision-makers, to an issue that would otherwise be an easily dismissed local matter, 'of no interest to anyone', as Lehmann puts it.

A focus on local environmental impacts could be self-limiting, as the impacts can often be ameliorated, at least ideologically. Vattenfall had, for instance, insisted that all of the negative local effects could be managed, whether it be noise, subsidence, coal dust, impacts on the water table or the pollution of local river systems (Vattenfall Europe Mining AG 2005). But as noted, climate change offers a zero-sum irreconcilable challenge to coal mining: more burning means more warming. The confrontation between climate and coal is in this respect of a different order – it cannot be managed.

In part this explains the power of the alliance-building under way in recent years in the Lausitz: the company can reduce its local impacts, but there is literally nothing it can do to remove its emissions from the equation. The alliances have enabled an elaboration, connecting the incommensurable challenge from those asserting the legitimacy of their home villages with the incommensurable challenge posed by climate change. In the process there has been much cross-fertilisation: the

German climate movement is made up of both ecologically sensitive activists and left protesters with an anti-capitalist agenda, and their positions can serve as starting points for a debate with local coal protest movements, both to address the concerns of local mine workers – for instance, in terms of regional diversification and 'just transitions' – as well as to develop broader arguments that go beyond the immediate effects of coal mining in the area.

Today, villagers identify climate change as a factor in their opposition to coal mining. As noted, they not only talk about climate policy commitments and the national *Energiewende* but also point to the local solar panels, windmills and biogas plants that are part of the rural landscape. They are seen as evidence of the lived reality of the *Energiewende* – a reality that they argue is inconsistent with continuing to burn coal for electricity generation. But it still is the climate movement, coming to a large extent from urban areas, that voices a more wide-ranging and fundamental critique of coal's contribution to climate change as the foremost concern. Concepts of climate justice and a related critique of capitalist order are brought into the fight against coal mining from that side, too.

Several villagers reflected on the impacts of having the climate movement as a partner and ally, as a reframing process that crystallises their own thoughts, hopes and fears. Climate change is a powerful line of argument that delivers a new resonance for their struggle. Crucially, that engagement with climate concerns enables the fight against mining to fundamentally breach the logic of local ideological confinement, and elevate the struggle to a different level. Protest in the Lausitz shows how it may be possible to reach national-level decision-makers by relating a local conflict to a global narrative of struggle against climate change and for climate action. It could be a way to combine a bottom-up approach with the hopes of embedding top-down movements.

Notes

1 Coal Industry Statistics, Statistik der Kohlenwirtschaft e.V., Essen. Source: www.kohlenstatistik.de

2 See www.kein-tagebau.de/index.php/de/drohende-tagebaue/weitere-kohlefelder/spremberg-ost. In 2017, LEAG announced it would not proceed with either Spremberg-Ost or Bagenz-Ost, nor with Jänschwalde-Nord.

3 See, for example: www.politische-bildung-brandenburg.de/node/9615; www.deutschlandfunkkultur.de/die-lausitz-letzte-bastion-der-braunkohle.1001.de.html?dram:article_id=390956; www.zeit.de/2015/06/vattenfall-braunkohle-lausitz-landschaft-energiewende/seite-2

4 See www.tagesspiegel.de/braunkohle-streit-in-brandenburg-bundes-linke-macht-front-gegen-ihre-landespartei/9981416.html.

5 See, for example, yearly summaries of Agora Energiewende at www.agora-energiewende.de

6 'We can prove that our family has been here on this farmstead for 500 years. My ancestors had contact with the Swedes at the time of the Thirty Years War. Our family has very deep roots here. Doubly deep, you could say, because we're the only ones left here who make our living solely from farming' (Interview, Schulz 2014).

7 Nine hundred of these are located in the named villages of Kerkwitz, Atterwasch and Grabko, due to the extension of the Jänschwalde Nord mine extension. Another 810 people in the Lausitz will be resettled due to the extension Welzow-Süd II, and 1,700 for the mine Nochten II. Numbers according to Grüne Liga, www.lausitzer-braunkohle.de.

8 See www.archiv-verschwundene-orte.de/de/ausstellung/themen/kampf_um_horno/67801 Also www.lausitz-bild.de/sonderthemen/horno01.html

9 Another ten villages were devastated for coal mines in the Lausitz after 1990 (Archiv verschwundener Orte 2009), yet these are not as prominent in the narratives in the affected villages of Kerkwitz, Atterwasch and Grabko, since they are further away and were not used as a symbol in political discourse.

10 It is documented that Peter Wagner, the then state party leader of the CDU, said these words: www.berliner-zeitung.de/archiv/ministerpraesident-stolpe-sagt-der-gemeinde-unterstuetzung-bei-umsiedlung-zu—pds-erwaegt-antrag-auf-verfassungsaenderung-laubag-und-spd-erleichtert-ueber-horno-urteil,10810590,9445032.html. However, they are in public and private debates attributed to Manfred Stolpe.

11 The trade union for mining, chemistry and energy. In the Lausitz, the majority of its members is employed in mining, establishing the union as an important agent in the fight to sustain mining.

12 In relation to these numbers, the total of 46% of the local residents considering lignite to be indispensable for the future energy supply seems rather small (see Forsa 2013).

13 Greenpeace, for example, on its German website does not mention the Jänschwalde mine at all, but focusses on burning of coal and names Welzow II as an urgent example of how mining as an environmentally disastrous and energy-politically unnecessary project proceeds; https://greenpeace.berlin/2014/08/anti-kohle-menschenkette-in-der-lausitz/. The NGO had been active in the Lusatian anti-mining protest for several years.

14 See 'Ende Gelände 2016 Mobilisation', Video (English Version): https://vimeo.com/162285020

15 www.niederlausitz-aktuell.de/niederlausitz/66170/leag-gibt-plaene-fuer-lausitzer-tagebaue-weitgehend-auf.html.

5

Laying the Foundations of the Coal Rush

The Post-war 'Coal–Industrial Complex'

The three preceding chapters analysed current contestations over proposed new coal mines. All three, in their different ways, highlight the centrality of national development models in conditioning outcomes. This chapter maps the national tendencies across the three countries as part of the global surge in coal extraction into the second half of the twentieth century. Across the three countries, coal-centred fossil fuel developmentalism became deeply entrenched in the aftermath of the Second World War. In each instance, the national state was a key agent in this process. The state's licence to approve and, not uncommonly, assume responsibility for the extraction of coal, placed coal as a dynamic force driving the national economy and, in different ways, in the remaking of the nation. Getting some sense of the enduring reliance on coal as a source of energy, and the centrality of the coal–industrial complex across the three countries, puts the anti-coal struggles on the Liverpool Plains and in Lusatia and Chhattisgarh into historical perspective, and is crucial to understanding their contemporary significance.

For Germany, coal was the bedrock of its advanced industrial development, with the coal miner cast as the embodiment of industrial ambition and the rewards for this enterprise evident in the large numbers (of men) who found employment in mines. For Australia, coal provided cheap energy for manufacturing and became a source of export earnings, consolidating the country's role as an exporter of primary commodities into world markets, and in the process cementing Australia's place in the international economy. For India, under British colonial rule, coal had been critical in feeding the fireboxes of the trains that traversed the rail network, providing the material links that gave meaning to the sense of a nation. Following independence, the state's assumption of control of the railways and of coal production became two of the foundational elements of the post-colonial national development project, and established the state as the single most important employer of labour.

The post-war coal–industrial complex in each of the three countries was underpinned by an economic and social order in which the state actively contributed to securing its hegemony. Despite this, the dominance of coal began to be questioned in the 1970s, mainly due to social and economic impacts, but it remained relatively uncontested until the 1990s. It was not until climate scientists' concerns about the potential of climate change garnered broader attention that the wisdom of the reliance on coal began to be questioned. Scientists led the way in the modelling that identified links between the combustion of coal as a major source of greenhouse gases, increased concentration of greenhouse gas in the global atmosphere, and climate change. It was only really then, after governments began to respond to the mounting evidence, endorsing climate research and setting up the IPCC in 1988, and establishing a means to act on it with the UNFCCC at the Rio Earth Summit in 1992 that non-government environmental organisations turned their focus to the issue of climate change. It would be another decade before climate movements emerged and joined calls for bringing an end to the coal–industrial complex.

In this chapter, we track the story of coal from 1945 to the 1990s, focussing on the processes of extraction and combustion, which have until very recently proceeded at an ever-accelerating rate. Some 2 billion tonnes of coal was mined across the world in the 1950s, climbing to 3 billion at the end of the 1960s, on the eve of the so-called Oil Crisis. Production continued to expand throughout the 1980s, levelling off during the global economic downturn of the 1990s to some 4.5 billion tonnes at the turn of the century. As noted in Chapter 1, by 2015, global coal production had almost doubled, to more than 8 billion tonnes: this extraordinary expansion built on the institutional developments outlined in this chapter, and occurred at exactly the same time as the emergence of global climate policy under the Kyoto Protocol. This more recent sharpening of the global coal conundrum is discussed in Chapter 6.

Coal and the State: Rights over Mineral Deposits

Following the Second World War, oil emerged as a catalytic force shaping the pace of development throughout much of the world, reordering strategic and military preoccupations in the global polity. Yet, even at the height of the oil boom, coal remained the main underlying source of world energy – the essential energy source for industrial capitalism and a significant element framing the trajectory of post-war development. This was especially the case for each of our focus countries, which possessed rich deposits of coal, both black and brown. While oil was increasingly regarded as the energy source of the future, each of the three states displayed an ever-deepening commitment to the mining and combustion of coal, whether to generate electricity, fuel the rail systems that were designed to bind together the nation, or fire the furnaces of iron and steel industries. Indeed, coal was decisive in shaping industrial dynamism in the three remarkably different economies of Australia, Germany and India. It became pivotal in framing the social order and shaping the unfolding political machinations and economic fortunes of these three countries. For much of the post-war period leading up to the negotiation of the Kyoto Protocol, and indeed beyond, the coal–industrial complex was hegemonic.

The primacy of coal as a potential resource rested largely on states exercising their rights over deposits. Ownership and the authority to mine was generally vested in the state, consistent with the long-standing and widespread (although not universal) convention that precious metal deposits, and gold and silver in particular, were the property of the crown, or territorial governments.

The rights of Germany's states (the *Länder*) date back to medieval times, and the authority of the Prussian states over deposits was specified in a series of laws adopted over the second half of the nineteenth century. In 1949, these were enshrined in the constitution, in the *Grundgesetz für die Bundesrepublik Deutschland*, or the Basic Law, for the Federal Republic of Germany (FRG) and the several *Länder* that were members of the FRG. This established the right of the *Länder* and the federal state to determine whether deposits could be accessed and extracted, or capitalised, and who could be granted rights to mine the deposit. It also reconfirmed the doctrine of eminent domain, that state authorities could override the interests of landowners to expropriate property when this was for the 'public good'. The state could procure properties, with just compensation, to enable coal mining to proceed in defiance of property holders' wishes.

The nature of state rights over mineral deposits was less well defined in Australia. The individual colonial governments acted on behalf of the Crown, and this was reaffirmed in the Commonwealth of Australia Constitution following Federation in 1901. Underlying the framing of law and policy was the principle of *terra nullius* – the colonisers' conviction that Indigenous peoples had not established settlements, and therefore could not have rights over land recognized. Aboriginal people were not recognised as citizens in the Constitution. This position began to be challenged in the 1960s when Indigenous struggles for political and land rights gained momentum. Aboriginal stockmen and their families walked off the Wave Hill cattle station in the Northern Territory, protesting at being underpaid for working on their own country. A federal Labor government later bought the station and gave the Gurindji people title to their country. In 1967, a federal referendum voted overwhelmingly to grant citizenship to all Aboriginal people. Indigenous Australians' campaigns for land rights continued, gaining some traction with the passing of the Aboriginal Land Rights (Northern Territory) Act in 1976, and an inquiry established by the NSW Labor state government that ultimately led to the

Aboriginal Land Rights Act 1983. Yet, the exercise of rights was to be circumscribed because the mining industry in NSW lobbied successfully for land rights to exclude rights over subsurface resources – including gold, silver and coal. Land rights claims under the Act were restricted to 'vacant Crown land', in line with the eminent domain doctrine, proscribing Indigenous communities from claiming land rights over areas deemed 'essential for public purposes' (Norman 2015: 62).[1]

The NSW Aboriginal Land Rights Act underscored state government authority over land use and its support for mining without question. But the absence of inviolable land rights was not restricted to Aboriginal Traditional Owners. Private landholders with freehold title were not immune from the restriction on rights over subsurface resources. NSW state mining laws, for example, enabled companies to apply for exploration licences that would permit entry onto private property, even in defiance of landholders' objections. This situation became increasingly politically contentious with the rapid expansion of coal and coal seam gas extraction in the early 2000s, leading eventually to the passage of the *Mining and Petroleum Legislation Amendment (Land Access Arbitration) Act 2015* (see Chapter 3).[2]

The legal foundations that underwrote coal extraction were also in evidence in India, which won independence in 1947. The protections afforded Indigenous communities and the environment are not significantly different from Australia, and this can largely be attributed to the developmentalist role of the state in promoting the coal industry. The eminent domain doctrine inherited from British colonial rule frames much of this developmentalist agenda. The main legal instrument has been the Land Acquisition Act 1894, which provided the state with the right to acquire private lands for public infrastructure. This and several other colonial legislative initiatives provided the legal pathways for facilitating access to, and the exploitation of, coal deposits. For example, the Indian Forest Act 1878 mandated state control over forests and empowered the state to remove forest dwellers, *Adivasis*, whose livelihood was dependent on foraging, to enable timber harvesting or coal mining to proceed (Gadgil and Guha 1992; Das Gupta 2009). This was despite the ostensible recognition of the need to afford some protection to 'scheduled tribes' and 'scheduled castes' in the *Government of India Act 1935*, carried over into the independent Indian Constitution.

Coal had been a critical resource under colonial rule, principally for operating the rail system which fed the British export and import trade. But coal had not been the engine firing manufacturing development in India that it had been in Britain. Newly independent India inherited an attenuated and underdeveloped energy system, and the new government saw the need to build and invest in a coal–industrial complex as one of the foundations of the post-colonial nation. India's First Five Year Plan period (1951–1956) stressed the need for increasing coal production through systematic and scientific development of the coal industry.

The first major step in this direction was the setting up of the National Coal Development Corporation in 1956, a government of India undertaking with the collieries owned by the railways at its nucleus that aimed to increase public and private investment in exploration, assert greater control over the supply of coal for the railways and increase domestic supplies to support industrial development. This became embodied in the declaration of coal and lignite as 'major minerals' under the *Mines and Minerals (Development and Regulation) Act 1957*, which reserved coal for the state and big companies. The government also privileged coal extraction through the *Coal Bearing Areas (Acquisition and Development) Act 1957*, 'which takes precedence over other legislative measures in matters of coal mining and subordinates all other land use to coal mining', including the right to unilaterally expropriate land for mining purposes (Lahiri-Dutt 2014: 10). The state's central role in the coal–industrial complex was further cemented in 1972, when the government began nationalising privately owned coal assets, firstly with the nationalisation of coking coal mines in 1972, followed by other coal mines in 1973 and establishing the state-controlled Coal India Limited (CIL).

The State and the Capitalisation of Coal

Historically, the exploitation of coal was contingent upon the imprimatur of the state. While national governments in India and Germany – and, to a lesser extent, in Australia – spearheaded increases in coal production, other levels of government also helped in creating and shoring up the coal–industrial complex. All three countries are federal states, and in each of the three countries, state governments generally have constitutional responsibility for land use and thus play an active role in securing opportunities for coal extraction. In India, the setting up of CIL was based on partnership with a number of coal-mining enterprises owned and controlled by state governments. Many municipal governments have also played their part, chiefly in investing in the infrastructure for coal-fired power plants and for delivering electricity to industry and households.

Historically, however, the national state has played a central role in the exploitation of coal-fired power for electricity generation, a role partly explained by the magnitude of funds required, the risks involved in investing in the infrastructure to produce and distribute electricity, and the long and uncertain time frame for the amortisation of such investments. The public good nature of investment in infrastructure to produce and deliver electricity to communities and industry is no doubt also a key factor in understanding why states have played such a critical role in establishing the impetus for exploiting coal. This is particularly evident in Germany, but also in Australia and India.

In India, for instance, the government of Andhra Pradesh assumed control of the Singareni Collieries Company Ltd. (SCCL) in 1956. The setting up of CIL was based on partnership with a number of coal-mining enterprises owned and controlled by state governments. In Germany, federal, *Länder* and municipal governments often invested in and managed the infrastructure to generate and distribute electricity. Municipal governments invested directly in coal mining or set up companies to take charge of mining. The legacy of this approach can be observed in the ownership structure of some energy corporations today, as well as several grassroots campaigns for municipal governments to engage in a new generation of renewable energy sources.

States have also intervened in industrial relations to ensure continuity in the exploitation of coal. In Germany, a model of co-determination which brought together the management of mining companies with worker representatives on works councils was established in the Ruhr coal fields early in the twentieth century, and provided an architecture for mitigating conflict at the coal face.

Abolished by the Third Reich, works councils were formally reinstituted in 1951 with the Montan-Mitbestimmungsgesetz, the Coal, Steel and Mining Codetermination Law, which was adopted in the face of a threatened mass strike. The law mandated codetermination works councils in businesses with more than 1,000 employees and provided for workers' representatives to make up one-half of the supervisory boards. The consultative process also extended beyond these parties by involving the *Länder* and industry associations alongside mining companies and unions. The *Mitbestimmungsgesetz* became one of the keystones of liberal democracy in the post-war FRG, and helped to underwrite the hegemony of the coal-industrial complex.

Critically, this post-war revitalisation of coal mining in the FRG also involved other European powers. Re-establishing Europe's industrial might necessarily meant boosting and organising the production and distribution of coal. Several states – France, Italy, the Netherlands, Belgium and Luxembourg – joined forces to establish the European Coal and Steel Community (ECSC) (Hanrieder 1989; Duchêne 1990). Launched in May 1950, and based on what was to become the organisational template for the EU, the ECSC enabled the pooling of coal and steel production largely to ensure its founding members could have access to German resources and thus some measure of energy security.

The ECSC underwrote the consolidation and expansion of coal production in Germany. However, locking in the commitment to coal was also a very expensive solution to the European challenge of securing a degree of energy self-sufficiency. German black coal was, by world standards, expensive. The increasing depth of deposits mined meant that German coal could be undercut by cheaper imports. If the industry was to have a future, and be the mainstay of Europe's energy security, state support was essential (IEA 1982). The ECSC resolved to guarantee production by providing subsidies to the industry (Hanrieder 1989; Duchêne 1990). These arrangements remained in place into the twenty-first tentury. Throughout the life of the ECSC, and after its dissolution in 2002, Germany remained the largest recipient of European state aid. The German government committed to continue subsidising domestic coal production while also providing funds to support mine closures and mine worker redundancies (IEA 2002).

Meanwhile, the increasing cost of coal mining in West Germany was forcing the state to rationalise and restructure the coal industry. Rationalisation resulted in coal mining in the FRG being dominated by three enterprises: RAG and *Saarbergwerke AGI*, which was jointly owned by the FRG and Saarland; the coal and steel conglomerate *Preussag AG*, also owned by the FRG; and the electricity generator *Vereinigte Elektrizitätswerk Westfalen AG.*[3] Additional support for the coal–industrial complex came from government-guaranteed long-term supply contracts with German steel companies, the imposition of import quotas and a system to compensate coal buyers for the much higher cost of domestic coal compared with imported coal (IEA 2002). Supply arrangements were also secured for electricity-generating utilities within Germany, the overwhelming number of which were owned by the federal and municipal governments as well as state governments. Power utilities passed on the cost of more expensive German coal to consumers through higher prices.

Through the 1950s and into the 1960s, a process of rationalisation also occurred within the power generation sector, which became more and more dominated by large energy companies.

Industrial mergers and increased concentration in the energy sector proved a comparatively uncontroversial process. The inclusive character of governance through the works councils, alongside industry assistance and support for retiring or redundant workers, contributed to the continuing popular support for the industry, and enabled depoliticised management of its restructuring. The orderly restructuring of the industry went hand-in-hand with ensuring the place of domestic coal production as the key to national energy security in Europe.

The history of coal in the former GDR was quite different. In the immediate post-war period, the Soviet-Occupied Zone in East Germany experienced a significant fall in production, albeit relatively short-lived. The extraction of lignite, the main coal type in the east, had been one of the mainstays of employment before 1945. Lusatia was a leading mining region, with seventy mines operating in the early 1930s and producing as much as 300 million tonnes of coal annually, primarily for thermal power stations, although the lignite was also used in the production of gas and in the chemical industry. Post-war, the scale of mining in the East was dramatically cut as manufacturing activity was set back by war damage and the severing of cross-border economic relations with western Germany, then under occupation by the Allies. The Soviet Union avenged its wartime losses by dismantling as much as a third of industrial plants, removing mining equipment, as well as a number of briquette factories, and relocating these to the Soviet Union in lieu of reparations. Military industries and state-owned enterprises were confiscated. Some 4,000 megawatts of capacity disappeared, and the economic and social malaise was exacerbated by the exodus of German citizens to the west, resulting in the closure of several mines (Burrant 1987; Irfan 2014). A substantial number of the more than 100,000 miners lost their jobs, and the worst features in the already inefficient and highly polluting energy industry were exaggerated.

However, starting in 1949, the newly formed GDR undertook measures to escape this malaise, and turned its attention to rebuilding the economy. Expanding coal production was pivotal to this, and images of the industrial mining hero were called into service. Drawing on the celebration of the Soviet coal-mining hero Alexei Stakhanov, the GDR proselytised the industrious efforts of Adolf Hennecke, a fifty-one-year-old miner from Zwickau, who mined almost four times his normal daily quota in a much-prepared experiment. The 'Hennecke movement' was projected as evidence of a renewed spirit of solidarity and industry in the efforts to build a socialist East Germany (Kopstein 1997). Some semblance of recovery was in evidence by the mid-1950s, when coal production returned to prewar levels of 60 million tonnes.

This recovery was consolidated with the adoption of the Second Five Year Plan 1956–1960, which set in train the ambition to 'modernise, mechanise and automate', and the New Economic System of 1963, which fostered cross-border trading relations under the COMECON, ending the GDR's economic isolation (Burrant 1987). But, unlike the development of the coal-fired electricity sector in West Germany, the GDR's electricity supply industry attracted relatively little investment and remained 'unmodernised, inefficient and polluting' (International Directory of Company Histories 1992). As the scale of coal mining recovered, the GDR explored other energy options with the Second Five Plan announcing the intention to construct a series of nuclear power plants. The GDR began mining uranium in 1947 (and became the world's third-largest supplier, for Soviet weaponry, and also fuel), and activated its first nuclear plant in 1966, in Rheinsberg, followed by a further four reactors at Greifswald from 1973; a large plant was constructed at Stendal but never opened.

In Australia, municipal governments in the major urban centres had led the way in investing in electricity generation and its distribution. Over the course of the twentieth century, state governments consolidated the municipal utilities into large state-owned and -managed utilities. Every Australian state government assumed responsibility for investing in the technology to generate and distribute electricity.

Hand-in-hand with this, governments also became directly involved in coal mining. It was generally accepted that this was part and parcel of the state's role in building the nation, in progressing the developmentalist project by capitalising on the black coal deposits in New South Wales and Queensland and lignite in Victoria and South Australia. State control of coal secured the fuel that fired the state-owned electricity-generating plants to provide relatively low-cost power for industry and major urban population centres, thereby constructing the coal–industrial complex and securing the hegemony of the social and political order upon which it rested. Moreover, in some respects this was not all that dissimilar to the German model, with the state establishing an industrial relations model designed to mitigate conflict in the industry. The federal Chifley Labor Government passed the Commonwealth Coal Industry Act in 1946, and in conjunction with the New South Wales Labor government established the Joint Coal Board to regulate the industry and ensure the maintenance of coal supplies in New South Wales (Fisher 1983; Lee and Draper 1988; Productivity Commission 1998).[4] The government set up the Coal Industry Authority and local coal authorities to mediate industrial conflicts. The Joint Coal Board also became directly involved in coal mining, purchasing a number of open-cut mines to become the largest coal producer in Australia at the time (Fisher 1983).

However, the process of capitalising on deposits of coal underwent a dramatic transformation towards the end of the 1960s. State governments in Queensland and New South Wales played a crucial role in supporting the extraction of coal by encouraging private corporate investment in new mines to develop coal as an export commodity. The Commonwealth also sought to underwrite this new industry with the express purpose of exporting coal to Japan and other East Asian economies. This export orientation dated back to 1961 when the Menzies government funded increased port capacity in Newcastle, New South Wales, and developed the Gladstone port facility in Queensland (Menzies 1961; Gabriel 1985). The expanding international coal trade recast Australia's place in the global political economy, and the fortunes of the Australian economy became increasingly bound up with developments across Asia.

State intervention in coal mining in India, and its determination to increase extraction, was an inescapable corollary of the government's decision to take control of electricity generation, with the objective of increasing the pace of economic development. The nationalisation of electricity-generating capacity, through the formation of the National Thermal Power Corporation Ltd in 1956, linked with state initiatives to increase coal production, which in turn were tied to transformations in the technology of mining, as the emphasis shifted from underground to open-cut mining. This necessitated the occupation of larger land areas to manage the overburden as well as the increased size of coal pits, hastening the displacement of forest communities from customary lands. This was especially the case in Chhattisgarh, which has the largest proportion of *Adivasi* peoples of any state in India (Amnesty International India 2016). However, with laws expressly restricting the formal channels through which decisions regarding land acquisition and displacement could be challenged, perfunctory consultative processes that masqueraded as being consistent with legal requirements, and a judiciary that interpreted the *Coal Bearing Areas (Acquisition and Development) Act* as overriding the rights of communities and environmental impact assessment processes, there were few options available for communities to challenge the hegemony of the coal–industrial complex. Besides, the fact that CIL, with almost 600,000 workers in 1974, had emerged as a major employer – second only to the Indian Railways – created a formally employed industrial workforce that politically overshadowed the disparate and little-organised *Adivasi* and other communities dependent on forests for informal work and livelihood who opposed land expropriation and displacement.

The Oil Crisis and Coal's Renaissance: State Power and the Capital Dialectic

The political economy of energy was radically transformed by the formation of the Organisation of Petroleum Exporting Countries (OPEC), a coalition of the major oil producing countries that curtailed global oil supplies and forced up the price of oil in 1973 and 1974, and again with the Iranian revolution in 1979. The inflationary effects of the oil price hike presented an immediate concern and questioned the future of energy security. The high-income bloc of countries, the Organisation for Economic Co-operation and Development (OECD), responded without hesitation, establishing the IEA in 1974 with the primary purpose of coordinating responses to the escalation in oil prices. Member states resolved to reduce 'dependence on imported oil for meeting energy requirements and to encourage the development of alternative sources of energy such as coal' (IEA Governing Board 1979). With this, increasing the production and use of coal came to be seen as crucial for future economic security (IEA 1982: 161–163). The need for a coordinated response was all the more urgent because of the dramatic and deleterious effects the oil price hikes had on the balance of payments situation of the oil-importing economies of Germany, India and Australia. Paradoxically, in the rush to promote coal as a solution to the energy crisis, the IEA noted there were some environmental concerns with coal. However, in surmising that 'in general, achieving current environmental standards is not incompatible with increased use of coal', the IEA Coal Advisory Board (1982: 13) played down the risks and regarded them as manageable.[5] It would be another three decades before the IEA conceded that this position was untenable.

The response across Germany, India and Australia was predictable. Coal's importance as an energy source in the GDR had declined temporarily in the late 1960s, due to the availability of cheap oil imports from the Soviet Union. In the wake of the oil crisis, Moscow increased its exports to Western Europe and increased oil prices for COMECON countries such as the GDR. The SED (Socialist Unity Party) government of Erich Honecker launched a program to increase coal production in the East: new mines were developed in the Lusatian district of Brandenburg and the Central German district of Saxony and Saxony-Anhalt. By 1981, the West German newspaper *Die Zeit* was reporting that the GDR had become the world's largest producer of lignite, with an annual yield of 256 million tonnes (Nawrocki 1981). Employment in mining expanded to over 10,000, although this came at some considerable cost because the expansion in mining entailed the substantial displacement of hundreds of villages to make way for open-pit mining (Appunn 2016). This, alongside mounting pollution generated by outdated power plants, contributed to social disquiet and mounting anti-government sentiment, and contributed to activities that would result in the fall of the Berlin wall (Major 2010). The GDR's rise to world dominance in lignite production prefigured a trend that would continue after 1989, as hard coal mining declined in Western Germany, and lignite became the principal source of power generation.

India's experience was similar to Germany's. With no domestic sources of oil, India was totally reliant on imports. The presumption that, as a leading member of the Group of Non-Aligned Nations, India would receive preferential treatment from OPEC was not realised, so the oil crisis proved extremely costly. The cost of annual oil imports was equivalent to some 40 per cent of India's export earnings at the time, and the inflation of oil prices was reckoned to result in a threefold increase in the total cost of oil imports to the nation (Manoharan 1974). National development plans thus intensified efforts to increase domestic production of coal. Under the overarching management of CIL, eight of its coal-mining subsidiaries doubled production over the next decade, principally for use in generating electricity. Total coal production increased by 25 per cent over the course of the oil crisis, and ratcheted up in the remaining decades of the twentieth century.

The inflation of oil prices had profound consequences for coal as a global energy source. World demand for coal increased markedly as did production, by 50 per cent in a decade. Australia's resources sector was perhaps the most significant beneficiary of the increase in world demand, with coal production and exports increasing twofold in the space of two decades (IEA 2015). Australian mining companies tapped into the growing Japanese demand for coking coal, supplying the rapidly growing Japanese steel industry as it responded to OPEC's oil-supply constraints (Gabriel 1985).

This period also brought with it a crucial shift in the emphasis of Australian economic policy, closely linked to the rise of the extractivist state and the coal–industrial complex. With an eye on growing demand in Japan, South Korea and Taiwan, at the federal government level, free trade became the *cri de coeur*. Protectionist industry policy for manufacturing was wound back in favour of state support for the promised minerals export boom. New mining technologies, increases in the scale of mining, including more open-cut mines, and a growing number of large international companies spearheaded the expansion of coal production, establishing coal as the nation's single most significant export earner.

This development was accompanied by a significant shift in the relationship between state governments and corporate mining enterprises, and nowhere was this more evident than in Queensland. Two companies figured prominently in the early expansion of coal mining in the state: Theiss and Utah. Theiss had discovered substantial coking coal deposits in the Bowen Basin in the early 1960s, and secured mining rights from the Queensland government with plans to export to Japan. Utah soon followed, again with the Japanese market in mind, and a more careful prospecting foray by Utah yielded richer lodes. Utah was granted leases over several sites.

These developments brought with them a change in the state's engagement with capital and the regulatory framework for mining. Rather than requiring companies to apply for separate exploration licences and development approvals under the terms of Queensland's Coal Mining Act, the conservative government sought to create a region-wide approval process, in the form of a franchise agreement that would grant access for the mining company.

This instrument had been proposed by the companies that pioneered exploration and mining in the Bowen Basin. They argued that the scale and duration of mining at particular sites would be much greater than previously, and would require investment in rail and port infrastructure, necessitating more substantial and longer-term financial commitments for mining projects (Gabriel 1985). Legislated franchise agreements would provide the certainty that their operations would not be encumbered by any other government regulations. Much of the authority for the negotiation of such agreements was placed in the hands of the premier and relevant minister for resources. This was of critical significance for the structure of state–capital relations: although mining franchise agreements were brought before state parliament, the development of Queensland's coal-mining industry was increasingly within the discretion of the executive and the premier.

Not only did this process create fertile ground for clientelism; it also effectively garnered the authority and power of the state to ensure that any obstacles standing in the way of the development of coal mining were erased, and there was no public record of negotiations (Fitzgerald 2001; Galligan 1989). The State stood to benefit through the payment of royalties, set at 5 cents per ton, but this was considerably lower than rates in New South Wales. The lower royalty rate, according to the Queensland Treasurer, was in some measure a strategic decision by the government to make investment in coal more attractive in Queensland than in New South Wales (Galligan 1985: 75). However, this was subsequently offset by companies being charged to transport coal on the State rail system.

The transformation in the scale of coal mining in Queensland and New South Wales was extraordinary. Queensland exports increased exponentially at 10 per cent a year, from 1.2 million tonnes in 1965 to 5.7 million tonnes, when Utah began producing, to 21.3 million tonnes in 1980 and 53.5 million tonnes in 1987, delivering 40 per cent of exports (Gabriel 1985; Galligan 1989).

The steady increase in Queensland's coal exports ignited the New South Wales government's interest in capturing a share of the growing Japanese market. New South Wales promoted private investment in the industry, and invested heavily in transport and port infrastructure to augment the state's capacity to ship more coal. New coal fields were established, and the scale of mining was increased. New South Wales was, in effect, competing with Queensland to develop the export industry.

Across the three countries, the value of the coal resource lay in its capacity to fire the steam turbines which generated electricity. The extraction and burning of coal for power generation were subsidised in West Germany. It was mined as a low-cost energy alternative to oil in East Germany, India and Australia, and then as a low-cost export commodity in Australia. In each of these instances, the state was pivotal in the capitalisation of coal, and in entrenching the coal–industrial complex and its hegemony post-1945 – a process which accelerated in the aftermath of the OPEC oil crisis.

Coal Capital Contested?

Beginning in the 1970s, coal came under challenge. Its dominance became increasingly visible and contestable, initially due to socio-economic concerns, and later due to climate and environmental impacts.

In Australia, the dramatic development of coal mining and coal exports shifted the centre of gravity of the economy. The increased economic significance of the mining sector, and its advocacy of trade liberalisation, ran counter to protectionist industry policy for the manufacturing sector. The exchange rate effects of a burgeoning export industry served to aggravate the competitive pressures facing manufacturing. In the early 1970s, this incited the first serious challenge to the mining sector's unfettered development and to the hegemony of the coal–industrial complex more generally. Anti-mining sentiments were further reinforced by the dominant position of foreign capital, and particularly American corporations, in the expansion of mining. In part, this dominance reflected the narrowness of Australian capital markets; in other respects, it flowed from the capacity of established mining corporations to draw on their financial strength and technical capabilities to take advantage of the opportunities. Critics, including unions representing manufacturing industry workers, challenged the ascendancy of foreign capital in mining, accusing the federal government of selling off the national estate, of uprooting the national economy and of becoming a client of American capital (AMWSU 1979; Wheelwright and Crough 1982).

Insofar as this growing opposition to mining focussed on the power of international corporations, it anticipated a later argument that railed against the negative consequences of globalisation and economic liberalisation. Claims that the national estate was being sold at fire-sale prices to foreign capital had already gained some traction during the 1970s. The federal Whitlam Labor government moved to impose restrictions on coal exports and the issue of mine licences, legislating to require 50 per cent Australian ownership in all new resource developments and imposing an export tax levy to capture some of the windfall profits arising from the surge in coal prices. These initiatives were endorsed by the conservative federal Fraser government following its election in 1975 (Gabriel 1985). Some foreign companies – Utah and CRA – opened their share registers to permit Australian shareholders to acquire an interest in them, thereby 'Australianising' the companies.

The flood of investment in coal, not only in Australia but in several countries around the world, had the not-unexpected consequence of increasing global production capacity, resulting in a world oversupply and plummeting prices. Thermal coal export prices declined from a little over $US60 a tonne at the beginning of the 1980s by some $US20 a tonne in the middle of the decade, recovering half the lost ground by 1990. Coking coal prices followed a similar trend, although the magnitude of the decline was not as pronounced. However, following a lobbying campaign led by the Australian Coal Association and coal-mining giants BHP-Utah and MIM, the system of export controls that had been introduced in 1978 to contain the impact of price volatility was set aside by the Hawke Labor government in 1986. 'King coal' still held some sway, although its economic strength was weakened as the large Queensland open-cut and low-cost operations, which accounted for over half of coal exports, cut prices for coking coal. As New South Wales open-cut mines followed suit, the more costly underground mines closed and several planned developments were suspended (Lee and Draper 1988).

In Europe, mounting concern with the cost of subsidising the extraction of hard coal was manifest in the increased production of lignite in Germany. This increasing reliance on coal as a source of energy, however, coincided with increasing disquiet about the environmental costs that its combustion was generating, and this was particularly pronounced in Germany, most obviously in the West with the formation of the Green Party in 1979 and the election of Greens to the Bundestag, but also in the East where an underground environmental movement was rallying against the coal-based industrial complex that had transformed the GDR into the most polluted place in Europe.

In the FRG, the environmental movement initially concentrated on campaigning against nuclear power and taking that struggle into the German parliament; coal was a relatively incidental concern (Hockenos 2015).[6] Following the 1980 publication of the book, *Energie-Wende*: *Growth and Prosperity Without Oil and Uranium* (*Energie-Wende – Wachstum und Wohlstand ohne Erdöl und Uran*), the environmental campaign shifted to a clearer focus on advocacy for renewable energy. Written by three anti-nuclear activists who had worked with the renewable energy pioneer Amory Lovins in the United States, the book presented renewable energy as an alternative both to petroleum and nuclear energy as sources of power. It became the subject of study groups across Germany and was adopted by the Greens and other progressive groups as positing a platform for the future. Abandoning nuclear was the driving force of this political agenda, reinforced by the Chernobyl nuclear plant meltdown in April 1986, which broadened political engagement with this cause. Oil was a secondary consideration given Germany's precarious reliance on imports; climate change and the future of coal as an energy source were, at this stage, subsidiary concerns. While *Der Spiegel*'s August 1986 headline story, *Die Klimakatastrophe*, fomented worries about climate change, hastening the end of reliance on nuclear power remained the paramount political objective. But phasing out nuclear power also served the renewable sector. Wide public disquiet about both coal and nuclear power informed Chancellor Helmut Kohl's Christian Democrat Party government's 1991 Electricity Feed-In Law (*Stromeinspeisegesetz*), which aimed to encourage investment in renewable sources through the introduction of a feed-in tariff for renewable energy (Hockenos 2015).

In the late 1980s and early 1990s, however, precisely at the same time as the international community was beginning to engage more seriously with concerns around global warming, and to establish the foundations of a global governance architecture to address climate change, coal's place as the overwhelmingly dominant source of energy was being well and truly cemented. This was clear in Germany, where the magnitude of coal production continued to increase through to 1990, and the commitment to coal was even more pronounced in Australia and India, where coal output more than doubled over the decade and a half following the OPEC oil crisis. In India, the state's preoccupation with the developmentalist agenda prevailed, and remained relatively uncontested, fuelling endeavours to increase energy-generating capacity. Regulations allowing established Indian manufacturing enterprises to generate electricity – for their own production purposes only – had given them direct access to coal deposits, so-called captive coal. In 1991, these restrictions were relaxed, thereby extending the reach of captive coal–mining, alongside CIL's mandate to increase coal production in order to increase national energy-generating capacity. While policymakers focussed on consolidating industrial development, the ever-expanding expropriation of forest lands for coal mining increased pressures on *Adivasi* peoples and others dependent on those lands. This fomented novel forms of resistance, drawing very much on the example set by the Chipko movement, and documented in Chapter 2 (Shiva 1988).

Conclusion

Although the post–Second World War era is often characterised as the 'age of oil', coal was a critical element in the resuscitation of the FRG as an industrial power and in the GDR's recovery from the devastation of the war (and its aftermath). Coal drove Australia's aspiration to become a global trader in primary commodities, and also, markedly, India's post-colonial developmentalist project. In each instance, the state assumed a pivotal role in defining the pace and momentum of economic revitalisation endeavours, and was a driving force underpinning the coal–industrial complex. By asserting its authority and exercising its rights to exploit coal deposits, the state set the pace at which coal could be capitalised and thus utilised, whether as energy, industrial input or commodity for export.

We have argued that coal's central role as a resource framing economic momentum in these countries pivoted on a post-1945 coal–industrial complex, closely linked to the rise of an extractivist state. This does not presume, however, that this hegemonic complex was uniform in each country; rather, these nations' different social, political and economic circumstances, as well as the materiality of their coal deposits, contributed to the distinctive form and development of the coal–industrial complexes in each case.

Despite the hegemony of the coal–industrial complex over the post-1945 period, we observe instances in which its dominance has come under challenge. The challenges become more pronounced, and more universal and global in their airing, as environmental concerns are taken up internationally. In the early twenty-first century, worldwide dependence on coal for 'stationary energy', principally electricity, has become elevated to a first-order global concern.

In the following chapter, however, we examine a further element of the coal conundrum: the extraordinary growth in coal production that occurred over nearly two decades following the negotiation of the Kyoto Protocol, which saw annual global coal production almost double to over 8 billion tonnes by 2015.

Notes

1 This qualification of rights, which, for instance, restricts the rights of traditional owners to block commercial or industrial activity on recognised Indigenous land, is mirrored in the definition of Indigenous land rights following amendments to the Commonwealth *Native Land Title Act*.

2 The Act enables exploration to proceed subject to the approval of the landholder; if agreement cannot be reached, the applicant seeking an exploration licence can apply for a right of access to be arbitrated. The consequence is that there is very little a landowner or lessee can do to prevent mining from proceeding.

3 Interestingly, this process of centralisation and concentration of capital followed the abandonment of the Allied powers' post-war decartelisation (or *Entflechtung*) program with the institution of the Marshall Plan and the determination to support Germany's industrial recovery.

4 The federal government had assumed control of coal and mining following the commencement of the Second World War, to support the marshalling of resources as part of the war effort.

5 'Environmentally acceptable coal combustion does involve, however, the control of some significant pollutants which have potentially serious implications, some of which are not yet fully understood' (IEA 1982: 11).

6 The Australian Greens Party has to be credited as the first Greens Party to have a member elected to a parliament, in Tasmania. Like the German Greens, which were established essentially as a force opposed to nuclear power, the Australian Greens were at first not particularly focussed on climate change as an environmental issue. Their primary cause was campaigning against the harvesting of old-growth forests and the damming of wild rivers.

6

Kyoto and the Coal Boom

Coal's Climate Contradictions

The 1997 Kyoto Protocol seemed to signal the endgame for fossil fuels, particularly for coal. Yet, as soon as Kyoto was signed, world coal output began to rise. From the mid-1980s, global coal production had stabilised at about 4.7 billion tonnes annually, but from 2000 to 2012, there was a huge upsurge, with global production rising from 4.7 to 8.2 billion tonnes. Most of this growth was in non-OECD production, which more than doubled from 2.7 to 6.2 billlion tonnes. The primary driver was China, which increased production from 1.4 to 3.9 billion tonnes. India's increase from 0.3 to 0.6 billion tonnes was comparatively modest. Kyoto sought to constrain emissions in the OECD world, yet even in these countries coal production was maintained, at about 2 billion tonnes (BP Statistical Review of World Energy 2019).

We are, then, confronted by a fundamental paradox. The Protocol did next to nothing to arrest the expansion of coal-fired electricity – which is by far the most significant source of greenhouse gas emissions. On the other hand, as the single most significant driver of climate change, coal is front and centre in the fight against climate change. As the UN's IPCC acknowledges, if the world is to avoid runaway global warming, the extraction of coal has to cease by 2050 (IPCC 2018).

Coal continues to be the primary source of energy, and while its future as a source of electricity is certainly being challenged, the post-Kyoto coal boom makes clear that exiting coal is no easy task. This chapter explores the reasons why.

Navigating Coal and Emissions in the Shadow of the Kyoto Protocol

Concerns about the environmentally damaging effects of coal-fired power stations gained traction over the course of the 1980s. Disquiet among scientists, environmentalists and a number of governments around the globe was initially aroused by the problem of atmospheric pollution associated with the generation of sulphur dioxide and nitrous oxide, and especially particulate matter. Attention increasingly turned to transborder pollution issues relating to acid rain and the depletion of the ozone layer, and then to evidence of the increasing concentration of greenhouse gases in the global atmosphere, and thus to global warming. These concerns were taken up relatively quickly by the UN and found expression in the UN Conference on Environment and Development held in Rio de Janeiro in 1992, and in the international agreement to establish a 'Conference of Parties' (COP) for developing concrete policy action, under the United Nations Framework Convention on Climate Change (UNFCCC).

At this time some governments began exploring the possibilities for emissions reduction. Successive German and Australian governments figured prominently in these developments, while the corporate sector, and especially the emissions-intensive sectors, made a considerable effort to influence the direction of policy development. Governments could not, however, ignore environmental non-governmental organisations (ENGOs) and other social movements that were taking a growing interest in the threat of global warming. Indeed, the ENGOs' engagement with the climate change question injected a new vibrancy and political force into environmental movements as well as spawning a new wave of climate advocacy organisations, whose primary objective was to pressure national governments and international institutions to take action.

This made for an intensely contested situation, albeit heavily tilted in favour of coal capital, reflecting its pivotal and established role in national economic life. In Australia, coal was a guarantee of low-cost energy for industry and had already become a major source of export income. Germany's industrial power and the corporatist state structure relied on coal to maintain Germany as Europe's economic powerhouse, notwithstanding the massive subsidies this required. For India, coal was viewed as an essential input for a nascent manufacturing industry, and later for increased energy access. In each case, coal companies were able to garner significant public legitimacy, not least through their role as major employers of unionised workers, who strongly advocated for coal's future.

In Germany, the federal government sought to take the lead on emissions reduction in Europe, setting up the Federal Environment Agency and 'Advisory Council on Climate Change' in 1992 which liaised with a dedicated Inter-Ministerial Advisory Group, to develop a range of emissions reduction initiatives. There was an emphasis on applying new technologies, and on a corporatist model, with sectoral study groups in energy supply, transportation, construction, agriculture and forestry. The government joined with peak electricity, power and energy and chemical associations and relevant trade unions, to develop a cross-sector consensus in 1995, a 'Declaration by German Industry and Trade on Global Warming Prevention' (European Environment Agency 2016). The Agreement endorsed a strategy to reduce CO_2 emissions 25 per cent below 1987 levels by

2005. The Declaration focussed on voluntary emissions reduction targets, ostensibly to avoid the lengthy legislation required for compulsory reductions. It also included support for workers who would be displaced by the resulting cutback in coal mining. For business, there was merit in backing the Declaration, as the alternative was mandating emissions cuts by means of the imposition of a price on carbon. Significantly, the *Länder*, municipalities and ENGOs were not invited to participate in the negotiation of the Declaration, though some of their suggested modifications were adopted (Abraham 2017).

Corporatist climate policymaking secured business interests, including in relation to the emissions reduction target, which was reduced following the reunification of Germany (Mez 2012; Schreurs 2003). Yet, in the event, reunification brought a windfall in reduced emissions due to the dramatic collapse of the East German economy. Ironically, one consequence of the collapse was that the East German economy came to the aid of West German industry, relieving it of the requirement to cut emissions to meet Germany's commitment for the Kyoto period, 1990–2012. Black coal mining in Germany was threatened more by the removal of subsidies, as required under EU competition rules, than by climate policy per se. Production of black coal went into decline, while the production of cheaper lignite was maintained at approximately half the pre-reunification production level.

At a political level, support for German climate policy and the goals of the German energy transition has been broadly bipartisan, and at least until recently, both have also enjoyed high levels of public support. This has not been the case in Australia, where climate and energy policy became politicised along party lines in the 1990s. This process intensified in the second decade of the twenty-first century, with the emergence of a bitter and divisive public debate over the future of coal, and attempts by leading Australian politicians, including one prime minister, to undermine the credibility of climate science and the need for climate action.

In 1990, the federal Labor government had established an Interdepartmental Taskforce to formulate ecologically sustainable development goals for several industry sectors, including energy production, energy use, mining, agriculture, forestry, transport, tourism and manufacturing, with a mandate to include recommendations on the management of greenhouse gases (Rosewarne 1992). The tripartite committees, involving bureaucrats, industry associations, trade unions and NGOs, including environmental groups, aimed to achieve policy consensus, although invariably ENGOs found themselves marginalised. An overarching report charted a national greenhouse gas management strategy, which endorsed the government's proposal to cut emissions to 20 per cent below 1988 levels by 2005. In 1992, after signing the UNFCCC, the Labor government released the *National Greenhouse Response Strategy*, a mechanism to audit and facilitate measures to reduce emissions. One particular qualification that marked the

Strategy – that any action should not have a negative impact on the Australian economy or on Australia's international trade competitiveness – was to become an enduring precondition imposed on climate policy by successive Australian governments. In line with its tentative commitment to emissions mitigation, and mirroring the German strategy, the Labor government released the *Greenhouse 21C* plan in 1995. Not unlike the German version, this included provision for major companies and industry sectors to voluntarily sign onto the *Greenhouse Challenge* to commit to emissions reduction targets.

In late 1996, the government reviewed its *Response Strategy*, and concluded: 'the NGRS had little if any effect in achieving the necessary policy coordination and integration within and between jurisdictions; with few exceptions, greenhouse issues have not been considered' (National Greenhouse Advisory Panel 1996). The failure to introduce any concrete measures to mitigate industry emissions very much reflected the successful stymying efforts of emissions-intensive industries and enterprises. The Minerals Council of Australia, representing major global mining companies including BHP Billiton, Rio Tinto, Xstrata (now Glencore) and Peabody Energy, had marshalled their considerable resources, dedicating 'a budget of over $32 million and over 30 staff' to effectively block any policy initiatives that could have an impact on their costs or future expansion (Pearse et al. 2013: 135).

The Australian Coal Association was also well resourced, and the political force of these pro-coal advocates was underscored by NSW Minerals Council and Queensland Minerals Council lobbying. Coal-based power plants were represented by the Energy Supply Association, and a broad cross-sector coalition of energy-intensive industry associations was brought together under the Australian Industry Greenhouse Network, including most notably the Australian Aluminium Council, the Australian Petroleum Production and Exploration Association and the Cement Federation. Successful lobbying was aided by the ease with which these organisations appeared to penetrate the corridors of power within government, frequently engaging the services of retired ministers and recruiting staff from the core of parliamentary advisors, or courting senior staff in departments that were influential in charting government policy, and also in donating to the major political parties.

The combination of these various industry groups, in conjunction with the endorsement of unions representing coal miners and waterfront workers and the parliamentary representatives of regional communities where mines were located, and of course the mining companies, established the coal–industrial complex as a real force in defining the Australian political economy landscape. ENGOs felt the full effect of this as they were increasingly marginalised from policymaking forums through the 1990s, first under Labor in the context of the 1994 recession, and then from 1996, under the conservative Liberal-National Party coalition government led by John Howard. Howard removed funding and access for ENGOs, and in 2001 withdrew from the Kyoto Protocol, following the lead of US President George W. Bush. The paramount policy objective was to maintain Australia's international competitive advantage as a resource-exporting country, though there were some piecemeal policy developments designed to placate an electorate increasingly concerned about global warming: a target of 20 per cent renewable energy by 2010 was set for the power sector, and following pressure from financial institutions, there was a proposal for an emissions-trading scheme (ETS).

Labor returned to government in 2007. In the lead-up to the election, the then Leader of the Opposition Kevin Rudd gave a keynote speech to the National Climate Change Summit at Parliament House, Canberra, in which he declared climate change 'the great moral challenge of our generation'. Rudd went on to win the federal election in November that year in a landslide and moved swiftly to ratify the Kyoto Protocol. Labor commissioned the economist Ross Garnaut to conduct a review of climate policy, modelled on the Stern Review (Garnaut 2008; Stern 2007). The review recommended an ETS, which the government sought to implement with its proposed *Carbon Pollution Reduction Scheme* (CPRS). The policy proposed reducing emissions by 25 per cent by 2020 from 2000 levels and establish a *Clean Energy Initiative* to support the adoption of low-carbon technologies (Pearse 2018; Rosewarne 2010). It did not envisage an end to coal and instead recommended that emissions-intensive trade-exposed industries be permitted to continue emitting, and that compensation be provided for emissions-intensive industries more widely, including coal-fired power plants. Following continued industry lobbying, \$3.9 billion in adjustment assistance was to be provided to the coal-mining sector, yet business continued to lobby against the proposed policy.[1] The CPRS failed in the parliament when Greens senators, who held the balance of power, voted against it, arguing that it did not go far enough.

Rudd believed he could rely on support for the CPRS from the Coalition parties which were in opposition; the then Leader of the Opposition Malcolm Turnbull was a strong advocate of action on climate change. However, shortly before the second reading of the Carbon Pollution Reduction Scheme Bill 2009, Turnbull was replaced as Leader of the Opposition by Tony Abbott, a climate sceptic, in an internal Liberal Party leadership spill. Abbott immediately withdrew his party's support for the bill, and it was rejected. The rejection of the bill gave the Labor government a trigger for a double dissolution of Parliament and fresh elections, but Prime Minister Rudd decided not to use the trigger, and the legislation lapsed (Talberg et al. 2015).

In April 2010, after the failure of the Copenhagen climate summit, the Labor Cabinet shelved any further attempt to reintroduce the CPRS for three years. Rudd's popularity plummeted, and he was replaced as leader of the Labor Party in June that year by Julia Gillard. Further negotiations between the Gillard government and the Greens saw the passage of the *Clean Energy Act 2011*, which set in place a carbon pricing scheme that would evolve into an ETS. The government also established the Clean Energy Finance Corporation (CEFC) to assist renewables, along with the Climate Change Authority to provide independent advice, and the Renewable Energy Agency to assist the adoption of renewable energy technologies.

An extraordinarily vicious campaign against Labor's climate policy waged by the coalition led by Tony Abbott, in alliance with the mining lobby and the conservative media, resulted in the defeat of Labor at the 2013 election. The Abbott government abolished the carbon tax, but it was unsuccessful in dismantling the CEFC, the Climate Change Authority and the Renewable Energy Agency. It replaced Labor's policy with its 'Direct Action Plan', which rewarded enterprises for emissions reductions, including farmers for sequestering carbon. Labor's emissions reduction target of 26 per cent by 2030 from 2005 levels was reduced by the Coalition to a 'real 20 per cent', and an emissions baseline for high emitters to safeguard targets for emissions reductions was abandoned.

The conservative prime minister gave coal the government's unquestioned seal of approval for the development of a series of mines, including Shenhua's Watermark mine on the Liverpool Plains. In declaring coal as 'the foundation of our prosperity', Abbott insisted that Australia had a 'moral imperative to provide it to the world' (Milman and Jericho 2016). In what became an intriguing Machiavellian drama, Abbott lost the leadership of the coalition and the prime ministership to Malcolm Turnbull, who had sensed a public desire for stronger action to arrest climate change. Deposed, an aggrieved Abbott gave voice to pro-coal advocates and backed the Monash Forum,[2] formed by a faction within the coalition to pressure the government to underwrite the construction of new coal-fired power stations and support the continued expansion of coal mining. Coal became a touchstone issue, not only for this faction of the Liberal Party, but for conservative commentators, the Murdoch-owned media, and minority right-wing parties such as One Nation. Australian climate and energy policy entered a period of political paralysis which continues until the present day.

India, as a developing economy with one of the lowest per capita emissions in the world, was exempted from any immediate obligation to reduce emissions under the UNFCCC and Kyoto. It led the G77 in vigorously resisting pressure for developing countries to be required to commit to emissions reduction and opposed a legally binding emissions framework. However, unlike the conservative Australian government, it was keen to participate in the Kyoto Protocol. As a strong proponent of the principle of 'equity and common but differentiated responsibilities and capabilities', India looked to the potential benefits of being able to earn carbon permits, under the Protocol's Clean Development Mechanism (CDM), as a reward for adopting measures that would reduce emissions or otherwise avoid the magnitude of emissions that would be generated by 'business-as-usual' investment projects.

Ironically, the CDMs became an instrument for supporting investment in new coal-fired power plants in India. The national government backed investors to apply for CDM credits, and, not surprisingly, several of India's nascent energy conglomerates were among the major beneficiaries (TERI 2005). Adani Power was the first company to benefit from the CDM scheme, receiving carbon credits for constructing a more efficient 4,620 MW 'supercritical' power plant at Mundra, Gujarat, the 3,300 MW power plant at Tiroda, Maharashtra, and the 1,320 MW plant at Kawai in Rajasthan (Carbon Market Watch 2010). Adani was followed by several other large energy corporations, such as Jindal, Tata Power and Reliance Power, which all gained CDM credits for new 'clean' coal-fired power plants.[3] There were serious doubts whether CDMs were funding genuine emissions reductions, and in 2013, after several years of lobbying by climate NGOs, the EU restricted their use for some industrial gases and for only the least-developed countries (this did not include India) and coal-fired power (European Commission 2011).

The Indian government remained determined to work towards increasing national income and reducing poverty (as noted), but this priority did not mean that concerns about climate change were ignored. India announced its National Action Plan on Climate Change in 2008. This was reconfirmed at the COP15 in Copenhagen in 2009, with a goal of reducing carbon emissions per unit of GDP by 20–25 per cent below 2005 levels by 2020 (IEA 2012). The National Action Plan also resulted in the first serious focus on solar power with the establishment of the Jawaharlal Nehru National Solar Mission (JNNSM).

However, the need for expanded access to India's coal reserves to address anticipated energy shortages became a key element in the national development policy agenda, and an ambitious plan to increase coal mining was launched in the mid-2000s. To this end, Coal India Ltd was set ambitious output targets. For the first time, private enterprises were invited to bid for the right to exploit coal allotments. A production goal was set in 2006 with the *Integrated Energy Policy*, which mapped a program to increase energy capacity and which prioritised the expansion of coal-fired thermal plant generating capacity, requiring an increase in coal consumption from 500 million tonnes in 2007 to 1.475 billion tonnes in 2032. Domestic coal production doubled over the next decade, supplemented by increasing imports, increasing from 50 million tonnes in 2007 to about 190 million tonnes in 2017 (IEA 2018). Some Indian corporations began investing in offshore coal mining, including in Indonesia and Australia.

The Neo-Liberalisation of Energy Economies and the Globalisation of Coal Capital?

Liberalisation of Energy Economies: Capitulating to Coal Capital?

In 1997, as agreement on the Kyoto Protocol was being finalised, the world economy was gripped by a financial crisis centred on East Asia that threatened to morph into global financial contagion. Public investment to boost the regional economy was centred on coal as a critical combustible energy source, and ignited the way forward. The development pathway remained resolutely coal-centred: Figure 6.1, charting world coal production, highlights the failure of the post-Kyoto environment to hold back the ever-increasing tide of coal production and consumption and the consequent escalation in greenhouse gas emissions, but the story is an uneven one. Coal mining in Germany was proving incredibly costly: as Figure 6.1 demonstrates, the magnitude of black coal mined peaked in the mid-1980s as the European Commission and Germany developed plans to reduce coal-mining subsidies and exit mining for black coal. As noted, the collapse of the GDR resulted in a dramatic reduction in lignite mining; the scale of lignite mined recovered somewhat after reunification but never to pre-1992 levels. To an extent, imported coal substituted for declining domestic production. The growing trade in coal is captured in Figure 6.2, which illustrates the marked increase in the shipment of steaming coal from the mid-1990s, which accelerated post-Kyoto. The Australian coal industry was a major beneficiary, with the volume of export coal doubling in the fifteen years following Kyoto.The expanding coal trade reflected heightened corporatisation and privatisation in the coal sector, as well as rising demand for

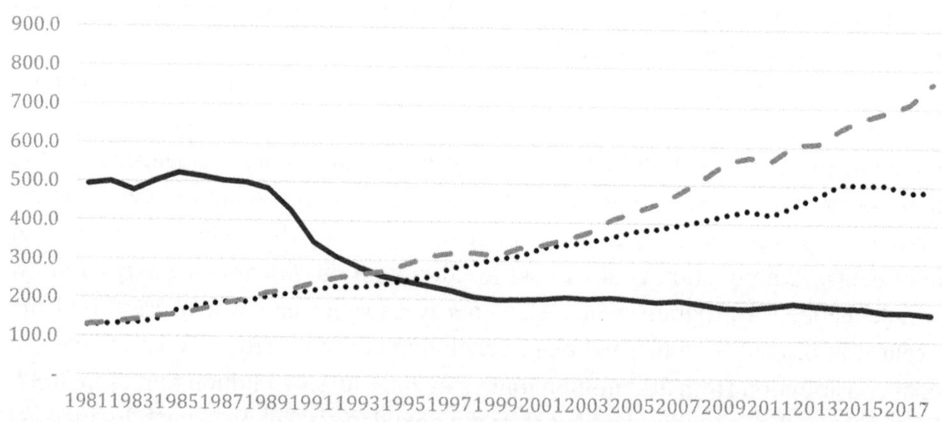

Figure 6.1 Coal production: Australia, Germany and India, 1981–2017, millions of tonnes.
Source: International Energy Agency *Coal Information*

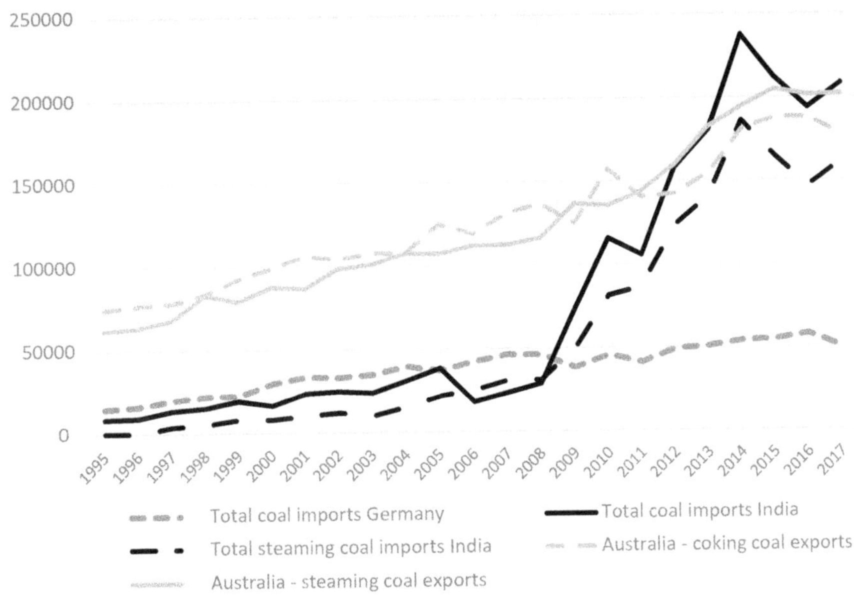

Figure 6.2 International trade in thermal coal, 1995–2017: Imports for Germany and India, exports for Australia, thousands of tonnes.
Source: International Energy Agency *Coal Information*

coal. At the same time there were efforts at weakening environmental regulations and other obstacles that could impede the rush to coal. The coal–industrial complex, well established across the three countries, was only strengthened as Australian, German and Indian governments each embraced energy market liberalisation.

In Europe, the momentum of the energy market liberalisation program picked up with the passage of the EU Directives on electricity markets in 1996 and 1998. Germany's National Energy Act 1998 called for a complete and immediate liberalisation of the energy sector to establish a single Europe-wide power market. The National Energy Act opened up the electricity market to competition, but the full force of liberalisation was somewhat circumscribed because of the influence of 'the network energy supply companies and their lobby organisations' (Catholic University of Leuven 2006; Thomas 2003). Unbundling the dominance exercised by the energy corporations and the division of the energy sector across the *Länder* were crucial aspects of the liberalisation project in Germany.

Ironically, national market consolidation was seen as spurring competition: the Federal Cartel Office accepted that its task of strengthening competition would be made more manageable by permitting the 'consolidation of the sector into four main companies' (Thomas 2003). This set in train an extraordinary restructuring of the energy sector. Over the course of 1999 and 2000, nine companies were transformed into four: E.ON, RWE, EnBW and Vattenfall. Further takeovers and mergers concentrated market power, amplified with the privatisation of East

German utilities and lignite mines following reunification. By the early 2000s, the four energy conglomerates controlled 95 per cent of Germany's generating capacity, with operations across the energy value chain, from production to transmission and retail. Each of the big four energy companies consolidated its market position, mostly through acquisitions, to secure coal's place in the energy system. Expanding generating capacity was crucial to this and included commitments to commence constructing new fossil fuel power plants that would generate an additional 24 GW, with a further additional 16 GW of capacity envisioned by 2020 (Catholic University of Leuven 2006; Hoffmann 2007).[4] For the Swedish state–owned Vattenfall, this represented a remarkable shift. In taking control of the greater part of Germany's lignite mines and lignite-fired electricity generators to pursue its expansion ambitions, with the support of the German state, Vattenfall abandoned its reputation as an environmentally aware energy corporation, becoming the third-biggest greenhouse gas emitter in Europe, accounting for 5 per cent of Europe's total emissions over the period 2005–2012, with RWE and E.ON generating 7 and 5 per cent, respectively, over this period (Bryant 2016: 59).

Corporate concentration helped to lock in coal as the critical element in electricity generation, but this consolidation of coal ignited a contradictory impulse: with plans announced for thirty-eight new coal-fired plants, the mostly local anti-coal campaigns gained a national focus. As discussed further in Chapter 7, the anti-nuclear movement was reorientated to spawn a nationally concerned anti-coal and climate change movement, and in 2007, the broad-based Climate Alliance was formed (Groll 2017).

In Australia, the federal and state governments were among the first in the world to privatise state-owned electricity generation and distribution utilities, as well as a range of other enterprises including banks and telecommunication entities. The liberalisation project had also seen the privatisation of the coal mines supplying fuel to power stations, a project that was launched in Victoria in 1993 and is still being worked through in other states (Cahill and Beder 2005). A corollary of the project was the establishment of a national electricity market, launched in 1998 purportedly to increase competition and efficiency in the production and distribution of electricity across the eastern seaboard states. In order to secure the necessary investment commitments to establish the physical means for a national market, the federal and state governments guaranteed that enterprises investing in the power distribution infrastructure – the poles and wires – necessary for delivering electricity across the participating states would be assured a minimum return on investments. The result was a dramatic and sustained escalation in the wholesale price of electricity. Significantly, this led to concerted efforts to maintain the existing base-load electricity-generating system and lock in the reliance on coal-fired power. In the post–Paris Agreement period, this has been being played out dramatically within the coalition government, with National Party members, whose support base is in regional electorates where coal is being mined, pressing for the government to provide funds to both maintain the existing fleet of privately owned power stations and to finance the construction of new coal-fired plants in northern Australia (Lowrey 2017; Murphy 2017).[5] The Minerals Council of Australia has spearheaded the idea, winning the backing of several coalition parliamentarians to advocate the proposal within the government (Massola 2017).

As outlined in the previous chapter, the national commitment to coal has been built on the foundation of a nexus between state and fossil capital, which (ironically) has intensified under 'liberalisation'. Both federal and state authorities have invested considerable quantities of public money to reduce the cost of freight and port charges, some key links in the coal commodity chain, most notably in the corporatisation and subsequent privatisation of rail and port facilities that have been sold off (Lucarelli 2011). Mining companies have been able to buy into these state-owned enterprises when they were subsequently partially or fully privatised – either solely, as was the case with Adani's purchase of the Abbot Point port facility in Queensland, or as a syndicate of several companies, as was the case with the Newcastle coal terminal port facility.

This state support for, and investment in, infrastructure reflects the centrality of the export trade, which has grown dramatically, and been the most significant catalyst for coal production. The expanded capitalisation of coal has been driven by the ever-increasing opportunity to sell coal into the international market. Global coal capital has determined the pace of this increase, with the amount of coal extracted in Australia more than doubling in the twenty years following the negotiation of the Kyoto Protocol. The then Coalition Treasurer Peter Costello captured this trend neatly when he declared at the G20 Summit in Melbourne in 2006 that Australia had become a 'global energy superpower,' a power that had contributed to 'global resource security . . . [by constructing] an energy and minerals freeway linking suppliers and consumers across the globe' (Costello 2006). Australia has developed into the world's largest exporter of both metallurgical and thermal coal, and the mantra that this helps other countries to develop, as well as Australia, has become engrained in the national rhetoric.

The great bulk – just under 90 per cent – of Australia's black coal is extracted for export. Exports remain the real driving force in the making of Australia's coal–industrial complex. The global market in coal has experienced a somewhat turbulent recent history, with world prices for thermal coal in particular falling substantially in the early 2010s, primarily because of the expansion of coal mining in China, and subsequently recovering as a consequence of some rationalisation of China's coal industry. The depressed prices had a detrimental effect on the profitability of several mining companies in Australia; some with a long history in the industry, most notably Rio Tinto, Anglo American and Glencore, considered exiting the industry. Rio concluded the sale of its remaining coal mine asset at the end of 2017 (Chalmers 2018), while BHP planned to exit thermal coal in 2019; several analysts described this ownership restructuring as marking a 'generational transformation' (Ker 2016b).

But while there was a write-down in the value of coal assets, there was no wholesale shift in ownership patterns.[6] The established mining giants acquired the mines up for sale, and several were retained when coal prices recovered (Carter and Friemann 2016b; Ker 2016a).[7] The partnership model, a long-standing practice linking mining companies with regional buyers, principally in Japan and Korea, remained in place. Japanese companies Mitsubishi and Mitsui, each partnering with BHP in several Bowen Basin mines, will maintain their respective interests partnering with BHP's successors. A number of Asian energy and steel corporations also directly own assets. Indian steel-manufacturing companies own coking coal mines in New South Wales and Western Australia.[8] Japan's large energy corporation, Idemitsu, owns and operates the Bligh mine, Queensland's third-largest thermal producer. KEPCO, the wholly owned subsidiary of Korea Electric Power Corporation, which generates 85 per cent of South Korea's electricity, is planning to develop the Bylong Coal project in New South Wales. And, as outlined in Chapter 4, the China energy giant Shenhua is still seeking to open a large thermal mine on the Liverpool Plains.

Offshore partnerships and direct ownership insulate players from volatile world coal prices and deliver energy security for large industrial conglomerates (Chambers 2016a; Rosewarne 2016). The investments point to an enduring and ever-expanding integration of Australian coal into global commodity chains. The boom in coal exports to China from the early 2000s demonstrates the speed with which such links can be forged, and how they directly affect socio-ecological relations on the ground in Australia. The first instance of Chinese capital joining the coal rush was when Yangzhou Coal Mining Company acquired Austar coal mine in 2004 and established Yancoal Ltd.[9] As the coal boom peaked, Yancoal acquired four mines from Felix Resources in 2009, before acquiring Cameby Downs in the Surat Basin and the Premier mine in Collie, Western Australia, in 2011, and then merging with Gloucester Coal in 2012 to become 'one of Australia's largest listed pure-play coal producers ... [and] the ninth largest pure-play coal company globally'.[10] Yancoal now owns and operates or manages nine mines in Queensland, New South Wales and Western Australia, producing metallurgical and thermal coal for export (KPMG 2012).

The continuing investment rivalry has to be understood in terms of the Chinese government's established internationalisation agenda, especially since it joined the WTO in 2001, with its *Go Global* policy. This was invigorated with the adoption of the '*One Belt, One Road*' (the *Silk Road*) initiative, which has prioritised investment in offshore energy projects. Coal has assumed a critical focus in this international investment drive, led by state-owned enterprises (Alon et al. 2014). Additionally, while mounting concern with particulate pollution from coal in China has seen a decline in domestic coal production, it has also contributed to efforts at improving the quality of coal burnt, in part by seeking offshore supplies (Fickling 2016; Walker 2016).

Shenhua, subsidiary of the state-owned China Shenhua Energy Company Ltd, the largest state-owned coal-mining enterprise in China, is driven by similar priorities in its efforts to open its coal mine on the Liverpool Plains (Hannam 2015c). Some critics argue that the production and consumption of coal in China have reached a peak and are now in decline, as concerted efforts to develop renewable energy sources bear fruit. Certainly, the Chinese government has restricted coal production and the construction of new thermal coal plants in order to address pollution problems; to stabilise the energy sector, it has also moved to combat illegal mining and close the more costly operations of small and inefficient mines and low-grade producers. The intense emphasis on the production of renewable energy sources adds weight to this argument, with China reaching peak coal while creating a national ETS, the first stage of which will be adopted in the power generation sector. These policy developments have contributed to a decline in China's coal imports, and critics contend that this points to an end to the growth in Australia's coal export trade to China, with Shenhua's failure to proceed with developing the Watermark mine as one manifestation of a now-established trend.

However, while Shenhua has implemented Chinese government policy, reducing coal production in its global operations in 2014 and 2015, stopping the construction of twelve new coal mines in China, and investing in renewable energy generation to increase the proportion of renewables in its energy mix to 15 per cent in 2020 and 20 per cent in 2030, Shenhua remains committed to 'clean' coal production as part of its '2045 clean energy development strategy'. It has joined with other major Chinese coal producers to consolidate planning and organisation as part of this strategy. Shenhua is also strengthening its value chain, with a stronger focus on upgrading company-owned mines and thermal power stations to increase the quality of coal produced and to reduce emissions (Reuters 2016a). It anticipates taking 'firm steps to globalize its resource allocation', including with the Watermark Coal Project in Australia, the Tsankhi project in Mongolia, the Sino-Mongolian railway project and the Zashulanskoye project in Russia (China Shenhua Energy Company Ltd 2014). In 2016, it 'raised its budget for building coal-fired power plants' (Fickling 2016; Ng 2016).[11] Clearly Shenhua was not anticipating an exit from coal, though it was diversifying its holdings into renewables, consistent with the National Energy Administration's five-year electricity plan as announced in November 2016 (Reuters 2016b; Spegele 2016). This does not preclude the possibility of Shenhua proceeding with the Watermark coal mine, which, indeed, came closer when the New South Wales government approved the renewal of Shenhua's exploration licence in mid-2018, and subsequently varied the approval conditions to allow mining to proceed (Furlong and Haydar 2018).[12]

Thus the continuing power and influence of the coal–industrial complex in Australia is closely linked to its enmeshment with global commodity chains and export markets.

A desire to diversify its coal supplies through imports has also been an important factor in the development of India's coal–industrial complex. India was subjected to a range of pressures to loosen state domination of the economy in the early 1990s, and the World Bank and IMF forced the issue in 1991 when a Bank and IMF assistance package was made contingent on the implementation of an economic liberalisation program. The World Bank played a direct and critical role in spearheading the liberalisation reform agenda in the energy sector, especially through India's states (Dubash and Rajan 2001). The Bank contended that problems in the Indian power sector were bound up with a conflict of interest, 'between [the] government's role as owner and its role as operator of utilities', and instead promoted power sector reform by offering financial support to states to restructure the electricity sector (Pargal and Banerjee 2014). Orissa was the first state to take up the Bank offer in 1993, separating generation and transmission infrastructure into distinct legal entities, but the state government was politically unable to authorise higher retail prices, thus rendering the exercise unprofitable and highlighting the extent to which electricity in India is understood as a civic common, and especially so for the rural poor (Dubash and Rajan 2001; Tongia 2003).

As was the case in Germany and Australia, opening up the power sector to private power companies was a key objective of India's liberalisation project, but the results haven fallen far short of ambitions. While there has been some limited privatisation, bureaucratic inefficiency and malaise as well as cronyism have defined the nexus between state and capital (IEA 2012). Most of the IPP (Independent Power Producer) projects either stalled during the approval process or did not reach financial closure.

Among the most criticised of these was the first major engagement involving private investors in electricity generation, the Dabhol power plant project in Maharashtra. The Dabhol Power Company, formed in 1992, was a project managed by Enron with GE, which would provide the turbines, and Bechtel, which would oversee construction of the power plant. Negotiations for the project were marred by a lack of transparency, and the Indian government questioned the terms of the contract, which had included agreement on an electricity delivery price that was quite exorbitant by industry standards. The contract was renegotiated by the

Maharashtra government, exposing extensive bribery and corruption (Bhushan 2001; Roy 2002a, 2002b; *The Economist* 2001). The project also brought significant human costs: community protest against displacement was met with violence and became the subject of much international censure (Human Rights Watch 1999). The scale of the Dabhol power plant was eventually reduced and the price at which electricity would be delivered was cut.

In 2003, with the passing of the Electricity Act, the government moved to open up the electricity market for private investment in an ambitious plan to expand generating capacity. In line with World Bank advice, the plan aimed to expand nuclear power plants and draw more power from renewables, such as wind and solar; but the emphasis remained concentrated on increasing thermal coal-fired power capacity (Joseph 2010). There was a rush of approvals for new power stations from 2007, doubling capacity (Ahn and Graczyk 2012; IEA 2014; Penney and Cronshaw 2015). A key element in this program was the approval of 'ultra-mega power projects', and ostensibly more efficient 'super-critical' coal-fired power stations able to deliver 4,000 MW or more.

Coal India, meanwhile, was restructured and corporatized, partly to expand domestic operations, but also to expand offshore. In 2006, it established Coal Videsh as a subsidiary to buy overseas coal mines, and in 2009, it joined an international venture with five leading steel and mining companies to acquire offshore coal (though this was short-lived) (Doherty 2012; Validakis 2013). In 2010, it was listed on the stock exchange with a public share issue equivalent to 10 per cent of its equity, to raise funds for expansion (PTI 2010). Also in 2010, CIL earmarked an investment fund of US$4 billion to finance prospective offshore ventures (PTI 2012).

The investment in electricity generation capacity also provided an impetus for the private energy companies to invest in coal mining, and in 2004, a large tranche of coal concessions was allocated to private companies. But the publication of details of the sale of the coal concessions for considerably less than their market value exposed systemic corruption involving politicians, bureaucrats and business leaders, and revealed practices that had a history predating, as well as postdating, the allocation (Comptroller and Auditor General 2012; Ghatak 2017; Ms 2018). What became known as the 'Coalgate' imbroglio thwarted progress in the industry's coal privatisation campaign. The 'Coalgate' contracts were rescinded, and several individuals were charged and convicted. Very few anticipated coal mines were opened, suggesting they had been speculatively acquired. Yet 'Coalgate' did not discourage the Modi government from pressing ahead with its developmentalist agenda and extending access for the private sector to expand coal production. In 2014, it sought to address some of the bureaucratic and organisational obstacles by integrating the ministries of coal, power and renewable energy to establish a new super-ministry (Ahn and Graczyk 2012; Inamdar 2014). The Prime Minister's Office also assumed a more interventionist role through the Coal Monitoring Group to expedite development approvals for new mines and related infrastructure projects (Infoline News Service 2015). Investment in railway infrastructure was tripled to fund the promise of a revolution in rail technology (ET Bureau 2018).

At the same time, environmental protections were further weakened, as communities' historic rights to land were sidestepped and a more aggressive approach to blocking resistance to displacement adopted. Breaking with the historical pillar of the coal–industrial complex, state monopoly control over the mining and sale of coal was dismantled (Jai 2016; Ms 2018; PTI 2018c).

Contesting the Power of the Coal–Industrial Complex

The rapid expansion in global coal production from 1990 to 2012, precisely during the Kyoto 'commitment period', spawned a range of tensions and contradictions which, notwithstanding the developments outlined above, have seriously weakened the coal–industrial complex. With the annual COP meetings under the UNFCCC, combined with the release of successive reports from the IPCC, the science and policy of climate change became increasingly prominent, and urgent. Debate over the future of fossil fuels moved to centre stage in global policymaking and underpinned the ever-increasing momentum of campaigns by internationally organised non-government climate movement organisations.

Climate policy, paradoxically, was made consistent with vastly expanded reliance on fossil fuels, and in particular coal. The rush to coal in low-emitting non–Annex 1 countries, with Kyoto effectively granting them a 'development window', or what Prime Minister Modi described at the 2015 Paris Climate Summit as 'carbon space to grow' – brought the globe much closer to dangerous climate collapse; the failure of high-emitting Annex 1 countries to substantially reduce their coal reliance and only to marginally reduce overall emissions only compounded the problem.

One element in this shift has been the more definitive findings of climate change research. The research undertaken for the UNFCCC and others provides an increasingly well-defined understanding of the impact of the increasing concentration of greenhouse gases in the atmosphere. As changing climate patterns are documented and confirm the predictions of climate science, a more critically informed popular appreciation has emerged as to how these changing patterns are affecting the human experience.

In this context ENGOs have kept alive the debate on the need to abandon coal. Groups such as Greenpeace, 350.org, Friends of the Earth and World Wildlife Fund have proved capable of developing new strategies for sustained leverage, through campaigning, supporting local struggles, mobilising people, coordinating movements across the globe and pressuring industry and government to decarbonise (Marx 2015). They have kept alive the momentum of climate change politics, exploring a host of different tactics to confront the resistance to tackling climate change. ENGO messaging appears to be gaining ground. Recent surveys suggest renewed popular acceptance of an urgency to act to reduce emissions if we are to avoid runaway climate change (Goering 2017). This has been particularly noticeable with campaigns directed at emissions-intensive industries that have, in turn, had to develop measures to mitigate emissions in order to maintain some degree of legitimacy as energy providers. The political force of the ENGOs has been underscored by a more explicit commonality of purpose. While they pursue a range of different tactics that are sometimes at odds, there have been concerted efforts to present a united voice: the 2017 Lofoten Declaration calling for an end to fossil fuel extraction is an illustration of this.

The broadly framed ENGO campaigns have occurred alongside campaigns that directly confront and challenge the mining or emissions-intensive operations of energy corporations. Protests that aim to block production at mine sites have featured in each of the areas in which the case studies were undertaken. Commonality of purpose has also been evident here, especially in the German case study. The human chain protest in the Lausitz in 2014 brought together national and international NGOs with a focus on climate change, protesters from the villages and local climate activists. Falk Hermenau, who had grown up in the Lausitz and taken part in climate protests as far afield as Australia, described his reasons for joining the human chain in stark and simple terms: 'mining is the worst thing that we can do to this area, and the worst thing we can do in terms of climate change' (Interview Hermenau 2014). Hermenau's statement articulates one of the central insights behind climate activists' focus on *extraction*, rather than the 'global management formulation' of the problem of climate change (Princen et al. 2015: 6). As Princen, Manno and Martin argue, 'the central problem is not about what is done *after* extraction and combustion; it is about extraction itself' (ibid.). The diverse activist groups and environmental organisations who converged on the Lausitz for the 2014 human chain protest were putting this insight into practice, giving concrete expression to an objective which, according to Princen and colleagues, has until recently been unthinkable in mainstream policy and academic debate: '*keeping fossil fuels in the ground*' (ibid.: 7).

The most recent large-scale protest in the Lausitz, named *Ende Gelände* ('closed ground'), in May 2016, was furthermore involved in the global 'Break Free from Fossil Fuels' campaign. This campaign aimed at a coordinated global resistance against fossil fuels, which simultaneously took place worldwide in twenty escalated actions on six continents (Ende Gelände 2016). This worldwide protest against fossil fuels and their grave environmental impact was orchestrated, among others, by 350.org, whose local action group 'Fossil Free Berlin' took part in the *Ende Gelände* protests in the Lausitz in May 2016 as well. More than fifty organisations signed *Ende Gelände*'s call for civil disobedience, and another sixteen declared their solidarity with the peaceful protest against coal mining. The common denominator for the wide range of locally, nationally and globally operating groups joining the protests against mining in the Lausitz is their awareness of climate change and environmental destruction that comes with coal mining. Lignite mining becomes a tangible symbol of CO_2 emissions as a main source for climate change.

In Australia and Germany, protests have been carried out not just at the actual sites of extraction but also in major business centres, with demonstrations organised to coincide with annual general meetings of energy corporations aimed at bringing the consequences of their emissions-intensive operations to the attention of shareholders and the general population. Climate activists have been able to take the challenge directly into the decision-making and reporting forums of companies through shareholder activism, corporate litigation and consumer or promotional boycotts. A myriad divestment campaigns have also been launched in many OECD countries to pressure investment, superannuation and pension funds – as well as other institutions such as universities and faith-based organisations that have invested capital – to withdraw their shareholdings in fossil fuel enterprises and coal-fired power corporations.

Campaigns calling for fossil fuel divestment were launched in the mid-2000s and have become a key strategy in challenging the hegemony of the coal–industrial complex, led by ENGOs such as End Coal, the Sierra Club, Coal Action Network, Greenpeace and Quit Coal. So successful were these campaigns that the mainstream business media began to display some alarm (Bell 2013; Scott 2014; *The Economist* 2015). The divestment campaigns were revived in the mid-2010s, including with German municipalities that held shares in some of the energy conglomerates (Marx 2015; Parkin 2016; Scott et al. 2018). The scale of the mobilisation of institutions and individuals has been extraordinary, with one 2016 report calculating that US$3 trillion had been withdrawn from fossil fuel investments (Carrington and Howard 2015). In 2018, the IEA reported that strong disincentives had emerged, discouraging investment in coal projects in the face of mounting opposition to coal: the upshot has been 'banks, insurance companies, hedge funds, utilities and other operators in advanced economies . . . exiting the coal business' (IEA 2018).

Another novel form of direct action to challenge coal has been to expose the business relations that underpin the coal–industrial complex. Challenging the role of financial institutions that provide the capital to support the business activities of emissions-intensive enterprises has achieved some traction. Actions organised against financial institutions have proved particularly successful in pressuring them to undertake climate risk analyses and withdraw funds that finance the development of coal mining and power stations. Climate activism groups, such as the Friends of the Earth–backed Market Forces or the Netherlands-based Bank Track, have pressured banks to desist from financing development of new coal mines and coal-fired power stations, and this lobbying has proved particularly successful, for instance with a swathe of international banks declaring they would no longer help finance the development of mines in a proposed new coal-mining region in Australia's Galilee Basin (Bank Track 2018; Robertson 2017).

Globally, the success is evident in the decline in total funding of developments supporting coal mining and coal-fired power stations, although there was some reversal of the withdrawal of coal financing in 2017 compared with the decline over 2015–2016 (Bank Track 2018). Major insurance companies have also indicated that they will limit the scope and scale of underwriting coal mines and thermal coal power stations (Insurance Journal 2018; Topping 2019). More specifically, over the last two or three years, premier banking corporations in each of Germany, India and Australia have announced their intention to no longer finance or underwrite coal mining and coal-fired power stations because they accept that climate change presents a real 'material financial risk' (Bank Track 2018; Market Forces 2019; Roddan 2019).[13]

There have also been less adversarial initiatives to engage corporations in emissions mitigation measures or to persuade them to exit the fossil fuel sector. For instance, since its formation in 2002, the Carbon Disclosure Project (CDP) has been an important institutional advocate, enlisting financial institutions, pension funds and insurance companies to voluntarily assess emissions intensity in appraising their business operations and those of corporate clients. The CDP has driven some quite positive reassessments of financial exposure. The Deutsche Bank, for instance, was listed as being among the world's 'greenest banks' as it concentrated its loan portfolio to back clean tech companies and 'continued its internal eco-efficiency efforts, achieving carbon neutrality' (Carbon Disclosure Report 2006; Deutsche Bank 2013). In 2017, the bank committed to reducing 'its exposure to thermal coal and to no longer grant project financing for greenfield thermal coal mines and new coal-fired power stations' (Bank Track 2018). The State Bank of India became a signatory to the CDP in 2011 (WWF 2011): having adopted a 'Green Banking Policy' in 2007, the Bank is investing in wind farms to reduce its carbon footprint.

The Bank joined a number of other Indian banks that are CDP signatories, including HDFC Bank Ltd., IDBI, IDFC, Reliance Capital, Tata Capital, IndusInd Bank and Yes Bank, and while they do not necessarily demonstrate the highest level of commitment to CDP reporting requirements, they are at least vulnerable to some leverage. Three of the largest banks in Australia are signatories to the CDP, and each committed to climate action at the Australian Climate Leadership Summit organised by the CDP in the lead-up to the Paris Climate Change Conference Summit (Cornell 2018; Ong 2015). In 2018, the CDP stepped up its efforts to enlist 500 companies to the 'Science-Based Targets' initiative to align their emissions trajectories with the Paris target, and has complimented Indian companies for signing onto the initiative (Carbon Disclosure Project 2019). The CDP works with more than 6,000 corporations as well as more than 550 cities and 100 states and regions, assisting them in incorporating effective carbon emissions mitigation in their operations.[14] Additionally, Climate Action 100+ was established through the CDP in 2017 to bring a somewhat sharper edge to lobbying the world's 100 largest emitters.

Complementing these are the more proactive initiatives of institutional investors organised under the umbrella of the Institutional Investor Group on Climate Change (IGCC). Formed in 2014 around a network of more than 150 European institutional investors overseeing more than €21 trillion in assets globally, it broadened its reach with the formation in 2014 of the Global Investor Coalition on Climate Change (GIC) in collaboration with four regional groups, the IIGC (Europe), INCR (North America), IGCC (Australia and New Zealand) and AIGCC (Asia). The coalition provides a 'platform for dialogue between and amongst investors and governments on international policy and investment practice related to climate change' (Global Investor Group on Climate Change 2018). Applauding governments that have set dates for phasing out coal, the IGCC has called on governments to step up action to address climate change, declaring, 'There is no place for coal in the clean energy future that is essential to addressing climate change' (UNEP Finance Initiative 2018).

A common reference point in these interventions has been the increasing awareness of the risks associated with coal-fuelled climate change. This narrative has become a concern for state regulatory authorities that have responsibility for oversight of corporate enterprise. There was a strong emergent emphasis on sound prudential and climate risk management, with agencies such as the Australian Securities and Investment Commission and the Prudential Regulatory Authority pressing companies to incorporate climate risk assessments, including potential exposure to legal action for contributing to greenhouse gas emissions. The Australian Securities Exchange and the Australian Accounting Standards Board have added their voices to the mounting pressure on companies to disclose such risks and to follow new international guidelines from the Taskforce on Climate-related Financial Disclosures (Potter 2019). In 2019, the deputy governor of Australia's Reserve Bank, Guy Debelle, stated that monetary policy may have to anticipate abrupt and disorderly transitions, which could cause economic shocks and threaten

Australia's financial stability, recommending businesses take immediate stock of the risks (Bagshaw and Bonyhady 2019).

In Germany, the sustained local struggles and concerted national-level campaigns against the use of coal in energy generation have heralded a watershed in the energy sector. Partly because of the unsustainable economic cost of relying on coal-fired power, partly moved by the political force of an anti-uranium movement campaigning against coal, and partly because investment in renewable energy technology provided new opportunities for the finance sector to revitalise the economy and strengthen Germany's status as a leading industrial powerhouse, this watershed became encapsulated in the *Energiewende*. As noted, the *Energiewende* imagined an end to coal as a major source of energy.

In Australia and India, the anticipated decline of coal has not been managed with anywhere near the same acumen. In both instances, the state has been, and to a large extent continues to be, a prisoner of the coal–industrial complex. Compounding mounting pressure on the corporate world to call it a day for coal, the capacity of governments, and various departments within the state more generally, to act in the public interest has been called into question. Local communities' opposition to mining has had to confront this reality. In many contexts mine approvals continue to proceed with remarkable ease. In New South Wales, the mining and resources sector and major mining companies continue to enjoy a virtual open-door in their access to ministers, their staff and bureaucrats (Evershed and Knaus 2019). And this is a reminder that the coal–industrial complex can provide a ripe atmosphere for malfeasance and corruption, as we have witnessed in India and Australia (Hutton 2013).

In Australia, the lack of confidence in the government's commitment to addressing the challenge of climate change has contributed in part to the growing popular support for renewable energy. It has also exposed the crude tactics employed by conservative factions that have desperately sought to block any move that would draw links between coal and climate change. These same political forces have actively campaigned for coal mining and coal-fired power as the basis for prosperity. In India, concerns about the rapidity with which some private corporations have grown and become dominant enterprises in the energy sector, apparently benefitting from close relations with leading political figures, suggest that personal connections come into play at an even more fundamental level to influence, or at least frame, investment practices and outcomes (Bahree 2014; Mehrotra and Witzig 2015). Again, of course, such relations are closely buttressed by developmentalist assumptions, that coal delivers livelihood and defeats poverty.

Clearly, positing the state as captive to coal does not have to be reduced to an argument about cronyism. The confidence in coal reflects broad and deep-seated structural links, the most general being the historical importance of coal as the principal energy source firing the momentum of the economy, the more direct and specific being the dividend returns to the financial institutions that have invested in coal and the significance of the royalties and taxes that are paid to state treasuries. It has been the promise of these immediate material benefits that provides some logic to the support for the coal–industrial complex – and the consequent sidelining of the anticipated cost of growing emissions because they belong to an ill-defined future that can be disregarded under the rubric of climate denial. That pragmatic viewpoint, of deferring the necessity for energy transition into the future, has suddenly unravelled: with rapidly accelerating climate change, the veracity of climate science is no longer seriously questioned, and the climate 'future' is already upon us.

Notes

1 The total level of support promised included some US$2 billion that had been allocated to underwrite research into carbon capture and storage technology.

2 The Forum is named after the engineer, and later First World War military commander, Sir John Monash, who was instrumental in establishing La Trobe Valley as a hub for brown coal–fired power generation in Victoria.

3 The financial benefits of being awarded carbon credits were considerable. For example, the value of certified emission reduction units awarded to Reliance Power had a market value of US$165 million (Fogarty 2011). Reliance Power had two registered power projects that would deliver 8,000 MW, and Adani two projects that would deliver 2,640 MW, resulting in the granting of more than 57 million CERs over a ten-year period, with a market value of some half a trillion euros (€556 billion) (Vidal 2010).

4 On 1 December 2014, E.ON announced that as of 2016, it would be spinning off its fossil and nuclear operations and focussing on renewables and distribution (www.cleanenergywire.org/factsheets/german-utilities-and-energiewende).

5 The former leader of the National Party, and Deputy Prime Minister, Barnaby Joyce, declared, 'it would be "morally prudent" for Australia to build new coal-fired power plants, potentially with taxpayer support' (Murphy 2017).

6 Indeed, many of the 'new' entrants are investors with an established association in the industry (Ker 2016b).

7 Glencore abandoned its earlier rumoured plans to exit coal mining as the price of coal has recovered. BHP Billiton, however, does not believe that the inflated price of $US300 a tonne for coking coal can be sustained (Chambers 10 Nov 2016).

8 Gujarat NRE owns and operates two mines in the Illawarra Southern coalfields; Jindal Steel and Power Limited has invested in coal exploration blocks in the Bowen and Surat Basins in Queensland, and Lanco Infratech and Griffin Coal bought into a coal mine in Western Australia.

9 Yanzhou Coal, which is the 78% majority owner of Yancoal, is a provisional state-owned enterprise and the fourth-largest coal miner in China (KPMG 2012).

10 Yancoal Annual Report, August 2018, 'Australia's Largest Pure-Play Coal producer', www.yancoal.com.au/.

11 Some local governments in China have assured Shenhua that its power plant projects 'will receive guaranteed power dispatch if they are completed by a certain deadline' (Ng 2016).

12 One possible qualification to this is the outcome of trade negotiations currently under way between the United States and China, which is placing pressure on China to revitalise the American coal trade. In 2018, Shenhua announced a US$117 billion investment in West Virginia (Needham 2019).

13 Once unleashed, the acknowledgement of climate risk becomes self-reinforcing, as can be noted by the Australian Prudential Regulatory Authority's efforts to raise awareness about climate risk appraisal, banks and insurance companies indicating that they now incorporate climate risk assessment in their management frameworks, and climate risk management, in effect, becoming mandated in prudential management (Roddan 2019).
14 Deutsche Bank, E.ON and RWE are signatories to the Carbon Disclosure Project.

7

Coal in a Climate-Constrained World

The Last Gasp?

In its 2018 *Coal Report,* the IEA reiterated its assessment that peak coal was in evidence, but that this had to be qualified because 'the story of coal was a story of two worlds'. World coal production had declined over the 2016–2017 period, the result of the multiple challenges to coal that have been noted in previous chapters and a massive upsurge of investment in renewable energy technologies. Despite this upsurge, the magnitude of coal produced increased in 2018. It was predicted to have peaked, reflecting the Paris Agreement commitments and the ensuing redoubling of efforts to reduce coal consumption in the old industrial heartlands – and a slowdown in the pace of expansion of consumption in China following its signing of the Paris Agreement and in response to the domestic pressures of atmospheric pollution and its related health effects (BP Energy Outlook 2018). Coal production and consumption in India are expected to increase at an accelerating pace through to 2040, notwithstanding an investment surge in renewable energy technologies. By contrast, the magnitude of world investment in coal is predicted to fall – with some exceptions, including in Australia, which is anticipated to maintain current export levels, expand existing mines and developing new sources, and likewise in India, which is allocating coal blocks with the objective of increasing production (IEA 2018).[1] Yet this tells only part of the story, because investment in renewable energy in both Australia and India currently exceeds investment in coal.

The story of coal is certainly being overshadowed by the increasing investment in renewables, but rather than conceive of this as the story of two worlds, our analysis of Germany, India and Australia suggests a more complex dynamic at work, and this is largely because coal remains such a contested commodity. The contest can be characterised as being arranged around four poles that reflect the political and material purchase of the different forces that have been seeking to chart the future course of energy production and consumption. One is framed by the ambitions to maintain a future for coal and to secure the power and institutional arrangements that have defined the coal–industrial complex and the system of energy-intensive capital accumulation. A second is defined by a reluctance to abandon coal as the driver of economic momentum. A third response is premised on exponents of coal-fuelled energy accepting or even embracing renewables but promoting a transition that defers the coal exit deadline, as can be observed with Germany's proposed 2038 exit date. The fourth advocates a much shorter time frame for exiting coal.

The role of the state has been critical to how each of these scenarios has unfolded. In Germany, a program for transitioning away from coal had been set as a result of public pressure to abandon nuclear power and transition to a low-carbon economy. This became embodied in the *Energiewende*, which was captured in the 2010 legislative commitment to reduce emissions by 80–95 per cent by 2050 relative to 1990 levels.

In contrast, governments in Australia and India defending the coal–industrial complex have tended to pursue more heavy-handed approaches, restricting the exercise of democratic rights by communities and ENGOs opposing the expansion of mining and displacement. In Australia, for instance, some state governments have introduced, or are proposing to introduce, laws that restrict the rights of citizens and climate NGOs to protest against the expansion of coal mining or the use of coal to fuel power stations (Donaldson 2014; Napier-Raman 2019; Slezak 2016a, 2017b). The federal government has been exploring measures to restrict the eligibility of environmental and other NGOs to make donations tax-deductible. Donations would be classified as supporting either advocacy work or activities deemed 'political', with the latter not entitled to tax write-offs. In India, the Modi government moved to block climate activists from travelling to speak at international forums, and to ban local ENGOs from receiving financial support from international organisations (Bidwai 2015; Bhalla 2016; Doshi 2016). Commitments to honour environmental standards and protect threatened ecologies by strengthening environmental approval processes are being frequently overridden in all three countries (Aggarwal 2017, 2019; Brändlin 2016; Hannam 2018; Watts 2017).

At the international level, pressure against coal from climate policy has been growing. The 2015 Paris Climate Agreement requiring net zero emissions by mid-century clearly signalled the death-knell for coal. Post-Paris, a range of contrasting scenarios for coal's future were laid bare. One grouping of fifteen national governments among those at the November 2017 COP meeting in Bonn formed the 'Powering Past Coal Alliance' and commited to phasing out coal-fired power generation before 2030. India and Australia did not sign, nor did Germany, which stated it would join once its Coal Commission had reported (discussed in Chapter 8) (Darby 2019). By 2019, there were more than fifty signatories, including a number of sub-national regional, state and local governments – including the cities of

Melbourne and Sydney – several US states, as well as ENGOs and other international organisations.

Against the growing post-coal bloc, the rhetoric of 'clean coal' and the dream of CCS remains the sector's lifeline. BHP, the world's leading mining company, for instance, has charted a pathway for itself as a 'responsible' miner: it has announced its exit from thermal coal, embraced CCS for metallurgical coal, resigned from the World Coal Association and questioned the adversarial pro-coal advocacy of the Minerals Council of Australia (Janda 2017). Technology is to solve coal's emissions problem, maintaining it as the world's 'energy foundation' (even as the world's climate collapses) (Evans 2018). This approach is reflected in the claim that coal is crucial for renewable energy, to produce steel turbines or to fuel electricity for hydrogen production (Constable 2019). Here, coal becomes a complement to renewables and, remarkably enough, comes to depend on the renewable transition (Bloomberg News 2017; Chowdhari 2018; Gray 2019; Iannucci 2019; Jamasmie 2019; Latimer 2016; Macdonald-Smith 2016; Yeates 2019; Wild 2017a, 2017b).

Australia's Coal Capital against Renewables and Climate Policy

At the UN COP meeting in Paris in 2015 and since, the Australian government remained an unapologetic champion of the old coal order. As then Minister for the Environment and Energy and now Treasurer Josh Frydenberg told the 2017 COP, 'Tens of thousands of Australians . . . rely on our coal industry and it does help lift people out of energy poverty in other parts of the world and provides billions of dollars of export income to Australia' (Bloch 2017). A year later, at the 2018 COP24 meeting held in Katowice, the Australian government attended a US-organised event promoting fossil fuels, intended as a precursor to a new 'Clean Coal Alliance' (Doherty 2018; Mathieson 2018; Merzian 2018). Only the US, Australia and COP host Poland attended.[2] While the US under President Trump did not attend any UNFCCC events, having frozen itself out with its decision to withdraw from the Paris Agreement, Australia valiantly sought to span the contradiction between coal and climate, maintaining an inside–outside stance.

Similar contradictions have paralysed domestic energy policy in Australia. After returning to the leadership of the Liberal Party in 2015 and winning the 2016 federal election, Malcolm Turnbull sought to re-establish consensus on energy policy, commissioning a report from Chief Scientist Alan Finkel, who recommended a 'clean energy target' consistent with emissions reduction. This was forced off the agenda by the conservative coal lobby, and Turnbull moved to 'Plan B' with a National Energy Guarantee (NEG) that would legislate for emissions reduction in the electricity sector as well as 'guarantee' affordability and reliability. The NEG was exhaustively developed by the government through 2017, but when it was introduced into Parliament in September 2018, it offered the trigger for a new revolt by climate sceptics in the Liberal Party, which then ousted Turnbull and installed a new neo-conservative, Turnbull's Treasurer, Scott Morrison.

These twists and turns have been remarked upon as signalling a new political instability in Australia (Eckersley 2015). The coal–industrial complex is proving signally resilient, to the extent of making it impossible to legislate on climate change, in the process threatening the legitimacy of democratic institutions. The coal upsurge, along with the wider mining boom, has brought a long-running resource curse that is eroding democratic values (Goodman 2008). Yet, at the same time, the fossil fuel sector has become increasingly isolated from wider business and commerce, especially the burgeoning services sector, which has become more orientated towards the renewable energy sector and associated industries. The imminent (and now actual) closure of Australia's privatised 'fleet' of ageing coal-fired power plants, as they literally become a danger to workers and too costly to repair or retrofit, has been a major precipitating force in this debate (Burke et al. 2019). Here, ironically, it is Australia's privately owned generating companies, along with some state governments, that have become the chief agents in forcing the debate on energy transition.

Renewable energy is swiftly becoming a key focus. By 2018, renewable energy in Australia was cheaper than even existing coal-fired power: the coal lobby needed a rationale for government intervention to overcome this price differential, and found it in the notion of reliability.[3] The NEG sought to achieve this by simply requiring generators to buy a proportion of 'baseload' or 'dispatchable' power, mainly from coal-fired stations, to supplement what was assumed to be intermittent renewable power. With the demise of the NEG, the government simply offered to directly subsidise the construction of new coal-fired power stations, again on the pretext of reliability (Karp 2018). However, this proposal remains to be tested against the power of popular sentiment, which in Australia has been staunchly in favour of renewables (Murphy 2018a; Parkinson 2018a).

Meanwhile (and partly reflecting this sentiment), there has been a surge in investment in renewables. The downward spiral in the cost of renewable energy has allowed households and businesses to use renewables to insulate themselves from unpredictable price variability on the grid. This alternative renewable energy dynamic has been in place for some time: Australia has the world's highest proportion of household rooftop solar, at 15 per cent, which has both reduced uptake and increased supply on the grid (Energy Australia n.d.). As energy demand has failed to grow as fast as predicted, plans for new fossil fuel power stations were being quietly shelved from the late 2000s.

Those national renewable energy agencies established under Gillard that survived Abbott's policy cull have played a key role in this transformation. Established in 2012, the Australian Renewable Energy Agency provides financial and other support for innovation and application of renewable energy technologies; and since 2013, the CEFC has provided debt financing for twenty major solar farm projects, which will add 1 GW of power-generating capacity (Clean Energy Finance Corporation 2017). The CEFC has supported a host of other clean energy projects, including wind power and hydro. State governments are also playing an active role in cementing the transition, by setting much more ambitious renewable energy targets than the federal government does. The previous South Australian Labor government, for instance, made substantial investments in wind and solar energy and electricity storage batteries, with the objective of generating 75 per cent of the state's power requirements from renewable sources (Parkinson 2018b).

AGL's decision in 2018 to proceed with the planned 2022 closure of its Liddell power station in defiance of the enormous pressure exerted by the coalition government is emblematic of a transition under way. Considered in the context of the acceleration of investment in solar and wind farms being undertaken by domestic and international financiers, households and small businesses – what one review described as a 'solar "tsunami"' – there has been a significant cultural shift in Australia with respect to energy generation that seems unstoppable (Hannam and Latimer 2018; Reuters 2019). The same cannot be said about the mining of coal for export. As outlined in the previous chapter, domestic energy policy and the steps being taken to transition from reliance on fossil fuel are a small part of the story of Australia's coal conundrum. In general, Australian coal production is closely articulated with export markets, and thus with the success or failure of global climate policy. Barring the unlikely possibility of a domestic coal moratorium, the future for Australia's export coal hinges on the success or failure of climate policy in the countries it exports to. Failure would doom the planet, though it would be a boon for coal–industrial interests. To the contrary, should there be a significant transition from coal-fired power to renewables, and especially in countries such as Japan, China and India, then the Australian export coal trade would finally be forced to close down. The prospects for this will be determined far beyond the communities now fighting the march of coal across Australia's (still) booming coalfields; but as we have argued, their struggles have become articulated with the broader struggle for global climate action.

India's Rush for Energy, with and beyond Coal

India's growth trajectory from the early 1990s was almost entirely powered by coal, the resulting boom in coal-fired energy (from 68% of the energy mix in

2000 to 75% in 2015) leading to a large increase in domestic coal production and coal imports. Yet growth under neoliberalism had been vastly uneven. Over two decades it had produced a 'Billionaire Raj', with more super-rich per capita than in China: remarkably, the income share of the top 1 per cent in India had risen from about 10 per cent in 1990 to about 22 per cent in 2014 (Chancel and Picketty 2017; Crabtree 2018). This was achieved on a per capita national income of about a third of the global level, and average energy use at about a quarter of global rates (Chikkatur et al. 2009; IEA Clean Coal Centre 2008). From 1990 to 2017, each 1 per cent increase in GDP had produced a 0.4 per cent decrease in poverty, contrasting with a ratio of 1:1.5 in China for the same period; in India, stunting in children due to malnutrition remained remarkably high in 2015, at 38 per cent of the population (FAO 2019: 82).

For the government, ironically enough, poverty reduction offered a ready mandate for intensifying the existing model and expanding coal: according to the established developmental script, prosperity depended on energy access, and this required coal-fired electricity (Sant and Gambhir 2015). Yet, by the late 2000s, with India's growing engagement with climate concerns, ever-expanding coal-fired power was increasingly being put into question. Debates about responsibility were increasingly superseded by a sense of necessity in the face of direct anticipated climate impacts. And most important, with growing access to low-cost renewable energy, the coal–prosperity nexus was starting to unravel. National policy shifts meshed with challenges on the ground; with coal being challenged both 'from above' and 'from below', there was some indication of a structural shift.

By the late 2000s, UN preparations for a new post-Kyoto climate agreement had sparked a growing debate about India's role. In 2007, the prime minister established a high-level Council on Climate Change involving representatives from the government, industry and civil society to coordinate plans for assessment, adaptation and mitigation of climate change. It reported in 2008, immediately prior to the 2009 UN COP in Copenhagen, and was tasked to develop proposals for the post-Kyoto scenario. The resulting 'Climate Action Plan' emphasised the need to maintain annual growth rates, for 'inclusive and sustainable development' while 'also serving specific climate change objectives' through a range of national initiatives for industrial efficiency and renewable energy (Government of India 2008: 13). The plan recognised the need to constrain emissions but stated it would only limit India's per capita emissions to OECD levels (though this made no sense for climate stability). Citing the 2006 Integrated Energy Policy, the plan proposed a threefold increase in coal consumption by 2032. Most significant, the 2008 plan still stressed uncertainties about the 'magnitude of climate change impacts' and throughout stated it 'could' or 'may' (not 'would' or 'will') have serious impacts, asserting that there was 'no firm link' between documented impacts and anthropogenic climate change (Government of India 2008: 15).

India's drive for coal was intensified with the 2012–2017 National Plan, which proposed expanding domestic production from about 660 million tonnes in 2010 to 980 million tonnes by 2020 and explicitly sought to achieve this by targeting '[e]nvironmental and forest clearances of coal projects' with a 'special mechanism for inter-Ministerial coordination ... to accelerate processing of these projects' (Government of India 2012: 33). But, as with Germany and Australia, the collision between expanded coal and climate change was starting to shift the policy agenda. A key aspect of this was the recognition that climate change was already having an impact on India, and as a result, the framing definition of 'climate justice' in terms of post-colonial carbon debts and development rights was substantially revised 'from within'. The resulting shift in climate policy redefined conceptions of energy justice based on fossil fuels (Bickerstaff et al. 2013).

The new position emerged in 2014 with the report of the 'Expert Group on Low Carbon Strategies for Inclusive Growth', which argued that to prevent further climate disruption, it was 'of utmost importance' that India ensure the emergence of an effective global agreement (Expert Group 2014: 5). The Expert Group tabled a proposal specifically for slowing India's emissions growth, principally by reducing dependence on coal and expanding renewables. This, they argued, could ensure that emissions would only double rather than triple by 2030 (i.e. grow from 1.7 billion tonnes to 3.2 billion tonnes, rather than to 5.2 billion tonnes, between 2007 and 2030; Expert Group 2014: 27). This was reflected in a doubling of the reduction in emissions intensity (from the business-as-usual −22%, to −42% between 2007 and 2032; Expert Group 2014: 27).

Elements of the Expert Group model were reflected in India's 'Nationally Determined Contribution' (INDC) under the 2015 Paris Agreement, which aimed to reduce in energy intensity by 35 per cent by 2030 and to increase 'non-fossil fuel based' energy to 40 per cent of electricity generation by 2030, allowing coal to fall to 53 per cent (Government of India 2015). The country's 2017 Draft National Energy Policy then projected a further reduction to 44–50 per cent in coal generation by 2040 with a slower increase in energy demand (NITI 2017). In this context the government embarked on a twin-track energy strategy, of continued expansion in coal-fired generation and coal mining on the one hand whilst at the same time seeking to greatly expand the fledgling wind and solar energy sectors on the other. With the difficulties in gaining access to domestic coal – acknowledged by the government in the 2012 National Plan – renewables started to substitute for coal expansion (Goodman 2016).

Certainly, climate concerns were being forced onto the national political agenda. Post-2008, in the context of growing international and domestic debates, climate issues gained some traction. Thaker et al. (2016: 3, 12) found a diversifying agenda, with 'climate change providing a space to engage with the government on broader governance issues': this was reflected in the language of 'co-benefits', and a focus on domestic vulnerabilities, especially for the rural poor, which 'has led some to reassess India's development strategy'. Dubash and colleagues demonstrate the unfolding agendas and highlight the resulting downward pressure on the coal industry (Dubash et al. 2019). The structural context for coal was shifting, and this was having impacts on the ground. Global Coal Tracker, for instance, finds that between 2010 and 2018, 491 GW in planned coal power was cancelled in India, more than twice the current operating capacity of 220 GW; only 57 GW was still planned to go ahead (Shearer et al. 2019).

Government efforts to boost coal were being re-contextualised. In 2019, the government was still seeking to boost coal production, encouraging private mining companies, allowing them to sell on the coal market and boosting private generation. There was a focus on further corporatising and commercialising CIL to expand production (Carl 2015; IEA 2012; Jain 2018). In 2018, the government was still fast-tracking mining approvals, aiming to produce 1 billion tonnes annually by 2020, in part to replace imports but also to feed rising demand (PTI 2018a). But the industry faced continuing logistical problems, in terms of transport especially; many coal-fired power generators under the NTPC were ageing and near retirement, and the coal itself was poor quality.[4] Over-hasty approval of large power plants had resulted in legal blockages over environmental or other development approvals; several of the plants are planned to rely on coal imports, and as a result were put into question by policymakers (Dave and Jai 2017). The anticipated upsurge in the demand for power was not manifesting, and instead, many coal-fired power plants were operating below capacity and new plants, as noted, were being shelved. Not surprisingly, in this context, there was flagging interest from the private sector, whether for mining or generation (Darby 2016; Jain 2018).

Most important, the development of new mines had not proceeded at all as planned. There were continuing disputes over allocations cancelled following the 'Coalgate' exposé and related disagreements over land rights (Energy World 2016). Community resistance to displacement remained a critical impediment (McDuie-Ra and Kikon 2016). Further, legal rights covered by environmental safeguards were being vigorously pursued. In response, the federal government with the sub-national states in coal-mining regions sought to dismantle or sidestep many of the provisions that protected local peoples and environments, including under the Forest Rights Act (as outlined in Chapter 2; Aggarwal 2019; Kohli 2012). Some projects were advanced: Jindal Steel and Power, for instance, was able to expand operations in Chhattisgarh by overcoming 'road blocks' (Mohan 2015).[5] For others, such blockages could simply be sidestepped or ignored.

Remarkably, in 2014, CIL itself was found to be operating two-thirds of their mines without environment clearances (BankTrack 2014).

In sum, the attempt at again recasting the coal–industrial complex was not delivering. Despite efforts at reinvigorating the coal–industrial complex, there has been little in the way of increased coal production or increased power capacity (PTI 2018c).

Towards a Renewable Energy–Industrial Complex?

While the interest in expanding coal production for thermal power stations appears to be wavering, the same cannot be said for renewable energy. Following Prime Minister Modi's declaration of a 'saffron revolution' in 2014 to spearhead the pace of economic development, there has been a sudden rush of enthusiasm from the domestic private sector and from international investors to invest in renewable energy projects. The seeds for this transition were sown with the establishment of the Jawaharlal Nehru National Solar Mission (NSM) in 2010 by the government led by Prime Minister Manmohan Singh.

The turn to renewable energy has involved state-owned utilities, private enterprises and international institutions. The Modi government pressed state-owned enterprises into service to invest in solar generating capacity (King 2014). A scheme was announced to establish at least twenty-five solar parks and Ultra Mega Solar Power Projects to add over 20 GW of installed solar power capacity, and this led to the construction of India's first 'ultra-mega' solar farm, the Charanka solar park in Gujarat (Carrington 2014a, 2014b). Around the same time CIL signalled its intention to invest in solar farms, dedicating up to US$1.6 billion for renewable energy projects (Saurabh 2016, 2018). In 2016, it announced the second phase of its solar energy expansion to construct 600 MW projects in the states of Madhya Pradesh, Chhattisgarh, West Bengal and Maharashtra, having commenced two 100 MW projects in the state of Madhya Pradesh (Chadha 2016; PTI 2016). The plants are to be allocated through reverse auctions with tenders issued by the Solar Energy Corporation of India. NTPC, India's largest generator, planned to have 32 GW of renewable capacity by 2032, comparing with its existing thermal capacity of 46 GW (and later aimed to expand this by another 19 GW) (Jain 2018). Big public-sector companies like NHPC, BHEL, Hindustan Salts and NTPC have all announced plans to invest millions of dollars in large-scale renewable energy projects. These projects include ultra-mega solar power projects with capacities up to 4,000 MW (Chadha 2014).

Private enterprises are investing in developing renewable capacity at a comparable scale, some in partnership with state governments (Nagarajan 2015; Pinjarkar 2016; Prasad 2015; PTI 2018b). All of the major Indian industrial-energy conglomerates are investing in large-scale renewable energy projects and discovering that this quite often involves competing with state instrumentalities (Chandrasekaran 2019). Reflecting the broad spectrum of enthusiasm for renewable energy, Tata Power Solar launched a project for the installation of solar panels on households (PTI 2019). Adani had constructed a solar farm in Gujarat, and in 2015 formed a partnership with the Rajasthan state to develop a 10 GW solar energy centre (Pathak 2015; Prasad 2015).[6] Tata formed a subsidiary to launch its investments in solar power, securing World Bank backing in the process (Tata Power 2018). It signalled the company's intention of having 30–40 per cent of its overall generating capacity sourced from renewables by 2025 (PTI 2016). Reliance expanded its power-generating capacity to include solar energy, gaining backing from the Asian Development Bank (Nagarajan 2015). Private energy corporations also expanded into renewable energy projects that were funded through partnership arrangements with foreign investors (Jayakumar 2018).

Backed up by a Supreme Court ruling on industry's recourse to renewables (Krishnan 2015), the enthusiasm is underwritten by a range of international financial institutions, multilateral aid agencies and development assistamce organisations (Centre for Financial Accountability 2018; International Finance Corporation 2019). There are more funds being provided for renewable energy than coal, and given the much shorter timelines between conception and execution for solar and wind farms (as compared with coal mines and coal-fired power), renewables accounted for 40 per cent of new capacity in 2018 (Quartz Media 2018).

In large measure, the greater-than-expected growth in renewable energy capacity can be attributed to the significant financial support provided by state agencies as well as by the private sector. There has been an extraordinary follow-up of expressions of interest in investing in renewables in India, with one estimate reckoning on an amount of between US$310 and $350 billion flowing into the sector in India over the next few years (India Brand Equity Foundation). The remarkable growth in renewables appears to be in competition with the still anticipated coal rush, and by 2019 India's leading Energy and Resources Institute had begun to grapple with the tensions of this twin track strategy, creating an Energy Transitions Commission specifically tasked with overcoming the growing bifurcations in India's energy and climate policy.

India's Transitioning as a Global Project

India's energy transition vision go well beyond the benefits that would flow from developing a less emissions-intensive economy. India was seeking to recast itself as an energy exporter in the wider South Asian region, whether of renewable or coal-fired energy. As the energy minister noted at an Indian Power Stations Conference in 2018, electricity in the region was relatively expensive, and countries such as

Myanmar, Nepal and Bangladesh were 'viable markets for export of power' (IANS bc/vd 2018). Mirroring the *Energiewende,* successive Indian governments envisaged developing a world-leading industry in research, development and production of solar technologies. This ambition has resulted in several international research partnerships, such as the agreement between the governments of India and the United Kingdom to work together in the fields of solar energy and nano-material research (India Brand Equity Foundation 2016), and the National Clean Energy Fund, which was explicitly created to provide a reliable source of revenue to develop the sector (Upadhyay 2016). The underlying objective was to establish a manufacturing sector that would produce solar technology and bring an end to relying on China in particular for imports of solar panels and other related technology.[7]

Modi has also promoted the global diffusion of solar technology as a basis for development in low-income countries, establishing the International Solar Alliance at the Paris UNFCCC to advance this goal and function as an equivalent to OPEC for the renewables sector (Ahmed 2016; McDonald 2016). With 121 countries supporting the Alliance, the Modi government assumed leadership for India as a 'renewables superpower' (Carrington 2014b). The Alliance was to have Indian headquarters at the National Institute of Solar Energy (NISE) in Gwalpahari, Gurugramed, and was to provide a forum for promoting greater cooperation in research to reduce the cost of finance and the cost of technology. Significantly, the Alliance aimed to mobilise more than US$1 trillion in investment to support the dissemination and application of solar technology across the developing world. India's Energy Transmissions Commission was expected to develop more concrete proposals to develop this (Ahmed 2016; International Finance Corporation 2019; The Energy Resources Institute 2018; United News of India 2018; Upadhyay 2016). India's engagement with solar energy was positioned as part of its commitment to emissions reduction, but it was also linked to industrial policy and to trade policy. Transitioning from fossil fuels to renewable energy is pointing to the substitution of the coal–industrial complex by a more environmentally benign development project. However, coal is not to be abandoned. Rather, at least for the Indian government, coal is to remain important for the time being (Roy 2015). Yet, paradoxically, as it diversifies into renewables, the coal sector itself becomes a catalyst for this transition (and not least CIL itself) (Pai and Handoo 2017; Roy 2015). The scenario of a coal-led transition from coal collapses the static concept of a coal conundrum into a much more dynamic process where the coal sector itself diversifies into renewables.

Germany's *Energiewende:* A Low-Emissions Accumulation with Coal?

India's turn to renewable energy has emerged as an industrial strategy to ignite the momentum of economic development and capital accumulation. The old coal–industrial complex has to a large extent been set aside, although coal will continue to be important in India's energy future. The transition is being engineered by the state and, in many respects, mirrors the German model for *Energiewende*. It too was designed to reinvigorate industrial capitalism and to globalise that dynamic by becoming a world leader in the manufacture and export of renewable energy technology.

For almost two decades, through the *Energiewende*, or 'energy transition', the state in Germany has sought to demonstrate leadership in setting the most ambitious emissions reduction targets in Europe. There were a number of important milestones on what Felix Christian Matthes calls the 'long political road' to the *Energiewende*, including the passing of the Renewable Energy Law (Erneuerbare-Energien-Gesetz [EEG]) in 2000 and the 2010 Energy and Climate Policy Package, which set out Germany's ambitious emissions reduction targets (Fabra et al. 2015: 51). Responding to strong and determined popular opposition to nuclear reactors, in 2000 the Schröder-led SPD–Green coalition government introduced a feed-in tariff system to encourage investment in renewable energy and negotiated with nuclear power utilities their eventual exit. Crucially, the *Energiewende* policy was not simply about setting an agenda for transitioning away from reliance on nuclear power and decarbonising the economy. It was also an industrial strategy, characterised by several observers as 'an innovation-oriented ecological modernisation project' designed to provide a new industrial focus for reinvigorating German manufacturing industry (Hillebrand 2013; Jänicke and Jacob 2004).

The promise was delivered with assurances of the long-term commitment to the feed-in tariff and an increase in the value of the tariff in 2010, and there was a fivefold increase in renewable energy-generating capacity over the following decade. Renewable energy created an industry that employed almost 400,000 workers and consolidated a 'highly developed national innovation system' (Jänicke and von Prittwitz 2010, in Buchan 2012; Hillebrand 2013; Hospers 2004). This established German manufacturing industry as a lead producer of renewable energy technology and, as a first mover, a significant exporter of renewable technology. As Hillebrand argues, the new eco-industry developed into one of the most dynamic sectors in Germany's manufacturing industry. Enjoying 'first-mover advantage' established a substantial competitive advantage in the supply of renewable energy technologies in international markets; it was also 'accompanied by the emergence of business associations that lobby for strict environmental regulation' (Hillebrand 2013: 668). With strong state backing and continuing support from the anti-nuclear movement and the Green Party, the new eco-industry presented an answer to concerns about energy security given the volatility of coal prices and reliance on Russian gas supplies, and thus represented a real challenge to the hegemony of the coal–industrial complex.

The development of the *Energiewende* also translated into a global industrial export strategy, underpinned by Germany's foreign aid program. The government-owned development bank, the KfW banking group, provided financial support to assist the development of the renewable energy sector in India in its early stages (KfW n.d.), and it has played a lead role in providing further funding for the development of the renewable energy sector in India following the Paris Agreement (ET Bureau 2017). Paradoxically, the 'first-mover advantage' is being lost to newcomers to the field, especially in the manufacture of photovoltaic panels, which has seen China assume an ascendant position. The upside to this is that Germany is benefitting from the import of cheaper Chinese-produced photovoltaic panels (Wehrmann 2017)

At one level, the *Energiewende* has been a resounding success: Germany has already achieved the target set in the energy transition laws, and renewables now account for 34.9 per cent of gross German power production, only just behind lignite and hard coal combined at 35.4 per cent (CEW 2019). In the first half of 2019, that figure rose to 44 per cent, well ahead of coal-fired power (BDEW 2019). But the adoption of the *Energiewende* did not mean the government was deserting coal. On the contrary, it became apparent following Chancellor Merkel's decision to expedite the closure of nuclear reactors after Fukushima that reliance on coal could not be abandoned so easily. It is generally agreed that the staged phase-out of nuclear power resulted – at least temporarily – in increased reliance on coal-fired power, as lignite became the only power source cheaper than renewables. Despite the introduction of the capacity reserve, Germany is still responsible for 35 per cent of total EU coal-fired power generation. One consequence is that Germany will likely miss the 2020 emissions reduction target of reducing emissions by 40 per cent from 1990 levels.

The reluctance to hasten the reduced reliance on coal also reflects the political pressure brought to bear by the union representing mineworkers, which has made a point of demonstrating the depth of opposition to closing mines and the loss of jobs that would result (Abraham 2017). Nor did the hesitancy simply reflect the desire to maintain the industrial accord that defined the corporatist system. The government was also responding to political pressure exerted by the lignite industry and coal-based communities. *DEBRIV Bundesverband Braunkohle*, the industry association representing German lignite producers, including RWE and Vattenfall, lobbied the government not to phase out coal production prematurely, and to maintain lignite mining and power generation to fill an anticipated power capacity gap when Germany's nuclear reactors closed in 2022 (Euracoal 2015). At the time, in 2014, the production of lignite in Germany had reached a record level, and even the government was sending signals that it did not want a too-hasty retreat from coal. Responding to rumours circulating that Vattenfall was assessing the future of its investment in lignite mines in Brandenburg and Saxony, the German Vice-Chancellor and Economy and Energy Minister, Sigmar Gabriel, wrote to Sweden's newly installed prime minister, appealing for his support to persuade Vattenfall not to withdraw from mining lignite to generate electricity (Clark et al. 2014). Gabriel observed that Germany remained committed to phasing out nuclear power, but that 'we also strongly believe that we cannot simultaneously quit nuclear energy and coal-based power generation', and accordingly the phase-out of fossil power generation would have to proceed 'at a gentler speed' (Clark 2014).

With a view to reconciling the government's failure to meet its 2020 emissions reduction target with its long-standing commitment to renewable energy, in 2015 the Merkel government sought to reassert its green credentials, launching the 'Climate Action Programme 2020'. This included specific measures for the electricity sector to decrease the use of black (or hard) coal and lignite. In 2016, the 'Climate Protection Plan 2050' was unveiled, setting out strategies to reduce greenhouse gas emissions by 61–62 per cent compared to the 1990 levels by 2030. The Protection Plan was intended to reinvigorate emissions reduction efforts but was confronted with some opposition. A proposed levy that would be imposed on, and result in the closure of, coal-fired power stations commissioned before 2000 was strongly opposed by the industry and unions (Abraham 2017). The peaceful transitioning that had distinguished some fifty years of coal industry restructuring appeared to be in jeopardy when the IG BCE announced plans for 10,000 mine workers to protest in front of the chancellory. The Economy and Energy Minister Sigmar Gabriel responded by assuring the industry that the plans 'would be phased in in a socially acceptable way' (Franke 2015). The levy was abandoned and in its place the government established a reserve system that would involve subsidising eight lignite-fired power stations to stay on standby – in 'cold capacity reserve' – able to refire should renewables energy capacity not meet demand. The Jänschwalde-Nord power plant in Lusatia, just a few kilometres from the threatened villages which were the subject of our case study, immediately had two of its five blocks placed on standby, and is expected to be closed altogether by 2033, if not sooner.

Notwithstanding this opposition, there have been some positive signs that the energy industry is engaging with the *Energiewende* more constructively. Each of the 'big four' energy giants has begun to invest in renewable energy projects. Vattenfall's decision to sell its interests in Lusatian lignite mines is held up as an exemplar for the future under the *Energiewende*. In a comparatively short time, there were also quite noteworthy shifts in the operational plans of the four major energy corporations.[8] EnBW[9] had announced in 2013 that it planned to produce 40 per cent its energy from renewable sources by 2020 (Appunn et al. 2015). At the end of 2014, E.ON reported that it was spinning off its nuclear and lignite-generating assets with a view to focussing on renewals and energy distribution. Vattenfall, pressured by the Swedish state, was withdrawing from fossil fuel–based power. Finally, in mid-2016, RWE, Germany's second-largest electricity generator and biggest CO_2 emitter, announced its intention to follow the lead of E.ON and separate its renewable energy business from its fossil fuel generation in order to raise the capital to fund its transition (Amelang and Wettengel 2016).

However, corporate engagement with the *Energiewende* should not be overstated. Vattenfall's divestment of its East German assets was almost a necessity if the company was to retain a presence in the German energy market as a leading power producer and distributor. The reluctance of the major energy companies to embrace *Energiewende* was demonstrated in E.ON, RWE and Vattenfall taking legal action against the German government for bringing forward the end-date for closure of nuclear reactors (Chazan 2016). While much has been made of the sale of Vattenfall's Lusatia mines to the Czech energy company EPH (Energetický a Pr myslový Holdings) at a peppercorn price, and Vattenfall transferring funds set aside for mine rehabilitation to EPH,[10] one feature of the sale contract that received almost no attention was that all forward coal sale contracts would be honoured with the revenue flowing to Vattenfall (Chazan and Foy 2016). This, in effect, meant that Vattenfall would continue to have skin in the game of lignite mining in Germany well after it had exited the industry and rebuilt its green image. E.ON meanwhile applauded the decision by the incoming Coalition government to postpone the 2020 emissions-reduction target (Clean Energy Wire 2018). RWE's decision to separate the renewable energy business from its fossil fuel operations had not, however, stopped the company from proceeding to clear parts of the Hambach Forest in order to extend mining at Germany's largest open-pit lignite mine and expand lignite production in Western Germany, and in 2018 dismantle what remained of the village of Immerath to expand its mine north west of Cologne (Brändlin 2016; Kuruvilla 2018).[11]

The upshot is that, for the immediate future, coal lives on in Germany, and this is engendering an intriguing scenario. With the increased generating capacity resulting from investment in renewable energy, and especially wind, Germany is now experiencing periods when energy supply considerably exceeds demand, and it is exporting energy to Austria and Switzerland (Agora Energiewende 2015). More investment in grid networks is enabling an even greater scope for exporting surplus energy (Agnihotri 2015; Richardson 2015). The substantial consolidation of the Czech energy company EPH in the German energy sector following its purchase of Vattenfall's Lusatia interests will enhance its profile as a transnational energy corporation. It is unclear what the company's future plans are with the Lusatia investments, but it is not beyond question that it could use the lignite mine and power plants as a springboard for strengthening its European presence by expanding electricity supply into the broader European energy market. This could well manifest in Germany becoming a transnational electricity exporter based on the coupling of lignite-fired power and the more variable generating capacity of the renewable energy sector, which would clearly have an impact on Germany's and Europe's commitment to accelerate emissions reduction.

The *Energiewende*, the transitioning to renewable energy, is occurring alongside the continuing commitment to coal as an energy source: energy security in this context has become a central basis for keeping the coal industry alive. The difference between Germany and Australia is that whereas the time frame for exiting coal in Germany is set in terms of years, the tendency in Australia has been to posit the time frame in terms of decades. This time frame becomes even more ill-defined when forecasting turns to Australia's future as a coal exporter, and when the justification for the continued production of coal and its export is reframed in terms of Australia's contribution to the economic progress of the developing countries of Asia, in terms of helping to relieve energy poverty and providing a cleaner fuel for energy than that that can be sourced locally (Hogan 2015; Milman 2015). The rationale for coal mining shifts with the rationale for renewables in what has now become established as an ongoing struggle over energy and climate policy. That struggle is now spreading across the globe as the climate crisis intensifies, and this is refiguring coal in new ways as a contested commodity.

Conclusion

We have argued here that the hegemony of the coal–industrial complex is being seriously challenged. With mounting evidence that the atmosphere's increasing concentrations of greenhouse gases are disrupting the global climate, the political mood has shifted in the direction of meaningful action. The current economic calculus of the costs of our reliance on coal as the premier energy source is clear. The risks of maintaining that reliance are increasingly acknowledged and are seriously affecting patterns of investment, be these in the corporate world or among households. Yet, as much as coal is being overshadowed by the enthusiasm for investing in renewable energy technologies, coal holds on, albeit subject to increasingly determined contestation.

Conservative political forces in Australia retain a confidence in coal as a key driver in the momentum of the economy, although the reach of this confidence is being challenged. Households and businesses are revolting against the inflation of electricity bills and are leading the world in the scale and magnitude of investment in the installation of rooftop solar panels and battery storage systems. State and territory governments are supporting this transition because of its political appeal.

This foregrounds a process of *energy democratisation*, liberating energy users from the monopoly of the transnational energy conglomerates that themselves are having to concede some ground with respect to the place of energy consumers in the industry.

Still, this transition has not brought an end to coal as a primary source of energy. The defence of baseload power is as much about diversifying the spread of investment in power plants as it is about reliability of power supply, but the energy conglomerates acknowledge that there will not be any further investments in large-scale coal-fired power plants, including the much talked-about ultra-mega-plants. The cost of building new power plants and the time it takes to build them does not pass the economic calculus test as compared with renewable energy technologies. The issue that is now on the agenda is the timeline for writing off coal power plant assets.

The question of mining coal for export is a different concern, but even that is being re-assessed and contested by prudential regulatory advisors and environment and planning authorities, and development approvals have been extensively delayed and, in some cases, withheld. Indeed, in the wake of the Paris Agreement, there appears to be a fracturing of purpose within the state with respect to its historical role in cohering the coal–industrial complex. In Western Australia, for instance, the Environmental Protection Authority issued new guidelines on emissions management in 2018 that, according to the EPA chairman, were 'necessary for Australia to meet its international obligations under the Paris Agreement': these guidelines would require big greenhouse gas emitters that produce more than 100,000 tonnes of carbon dioxide a year to offset their emissions on new and expanded projects.

This was viewed as a potential barrier to the rapid growth of the oil and gas industry, and energy corporations demanded that the guidelines be rescinded (Garvey and Williams 2019b; Latimer and Hastie 2019; Macdonald-Smith 2019a, 2019b; Macdonald-Smith and Thompson 2019). Within a day, the Western Australian Labor Premier advised that the state government would not be endorsing the guideline – because such restrictions would place new projects at a competitive disadvantage compared to existing projects and to coal and gas extraction on the east coast – and the EPA was pressured to withdraw the guidelines (Garvey 2019a, 2019b; Garvey and Williams 2019b; Hastie and Latimer 2019; Hewett 2019; Macdonald-Smith and Thompson 2019). Yet the guidelines have not been abandoned: it may well be the case that the Australian government's Paris undertakings has robbed the Australian Petroleum Production and Exploration Association of much of its ability to exercise leverage to minimise emissions offset obligations (Thompson and Macdonald-Smith 2019b).

The scenario in India is not much different, with investment in renewable energy overshadowing investment in new coal-fired power plants. Investment in coal is beginning to falter, with some of ultra-mega-plant proposals being mothballed. The assumed link between coal, development and poverty reduction is starting to break down. With renewable technologies able to be designed to meet a range of different scale needs, the engagement of renewables offers the prospect of meeting needs that hitherto have been overlooked or disregarded. While the Indian state has adopted an authoritarian demeanour in fostering the interests of coal, the ascendancy of renewables is being driven by an economic calculus more accommodating of a variety of interests. The success or otherwise of local coal contestation has become structurally articulated with these shifts in national energy planning. In India, as noted, climate change discourses were impinging on national-level policy, and with the growth in renewables there is a growing delinking of coal from development. Climate organisations that sought alliances with anti-coal movements were seen as a threat by the central government, but it was becoming increasingly difficult to take action against them.

The long campaign against coal in Germany has focussed on similar objectives, challenging the coal–industrial complex in the interests of combatting climate change and of scaling back energy production to democratise energy production and consumption. The debate on exiting coal also brings forward the issue of timing, with energy corporations petitioning for delaying the exit, as do many residents in East Germany such as in Lusatia where alternative employment options are less available and the plants are not as old as those in the Rhineland. This raises the critical issue of maintaining the dynamism of Germany's renewables industrial complex, both as an engine for economic development in Germany and for German leadership in global emission reduction efforts (DIW Berlin 2018).

Notes

1 Even China's powerful state-owned State Development & Investment Corp announced that 'it would no longer invest in thermal power plants and had quit coal altogether to focus on new energy sources such as wind power' (Smith 2019).

2 The paucity in attendance was attributed to the failure to engage developing countries in an alliance that poor countries were not sharing in the technology that could deliver clean coal (IEA Clean Coal Centre 2018).

3 The coal lobby spent more than any other stakeholder supporting the re-election of the Liberal-National Party in 2016 (Karp and Evershed 2018).

4 The Central Electricity Authority in its National Electricity Plan 2018 expects 48 GW of coal-based generation capacity to be retired by March 2027.

5 Jindal was granted a permit over land in 1996, making it the first private company in India to generate power.

6 Adani is also investing in several solar farm projects in Australia (Griffiths 2017; Ludlow 2017; Smyth and Mundy 2017; Vorrath 2017).

7 Modi established the seed-funding Prayas initiative, short for 'Pradhan Mantri Yojana for Augmenting Solar Manufacturing', as a project to support the manufacture of solar panels in India and replace the need to import panels from China.

8 This 'cultural' shift is no doubt a response to the decreasing profitability of electricity generated by lignite, which has seen the share price of energy companies drop dramatically (Brändlin 2016).

9 EnBW is 99% owned by the state of Baden-Württemberg. Fifteen per cent of RWE shares are owned by towns and cities in NorthRhine-Westphalia via a financial holding company, RWEB GmbH, while some cities hold additional shares directly.

10 In fact, Vattenfall 'gifted' the assets to EPH, which included a €800 million payment to EPH in return for EPH assuming responsibility for clean-up obligations (Wynn 2016). Vattenfall realised that the profitability of these assets would be affected by falling wholesale electricity prices consequent upon the increasing availability of renewable energy, so the divestment made good business sense (Chazan and Foy 2016). But the 'gifting' of the assets to EPH should not be interpreted as a 'fire sale' in the haste to exit a threatened sector. Vattenfall's sale agreement with EPH includes provisions for electricity supply contracts already negotiated to be honoured and for Vattenfall to enjoy revenue flows for some time after it has vacated the industry.

11 The Hambach lignite mine provides 5% of Germany's electricity, and RWE has a licence to mine through to 2040 (Brändlin 2016). However, a temporary stay has been issued to stop further clearing (Smith-Spark 2018).

8

Conclusion

Dynamics for a Post-coal Future

> The thing that gets me is when I watch the coal trains go past, and you've got 84 carriages, 200 tonnes per carriage going past, and I look at it and I think, how many hectares of rainforest is that going past me right now? As a farmer I look at it and I think, what are we doing? This is quite scary. If I was going to go out and say, 'Oh we're going to go and burn a million hectares of the Amazon forest', there would be an uproar.
>
> *(Interview Hamparsum 2016)*

The growing 'climatisation' of society is changing the meaning of coal. As demonstrated in this reflection from a farmer from the Liverpool Plains in Australia, interviewed for this project, the meaning of coal is being radically transformed. The quote exemplifies how the burning of coal has become the material embodiment of anthropogenic climate change. Viewing the coal in this way, as it passes by on the train, breaches local confinement and gains global reach, from the Liverpool Plains to the Amazon. It simultaneously invokes a temporal lineage, as part of geological time, from when the rainforest was first deposited. And finally, the presence of coal in the landscape, on the train between the mine and the furnace, is a sharp reminder of how climate is being changed. 'What are we doing?', he asks. In this rhetorical question coal is articulated with climate crisis, and with the necessity for a post-coal society.

John Hamparsum raised this question in an interview with us at a moment when he and others opposing coal mining on the Liverpool Plains felt they had won an important victory. The NSW state government had just announced that it would buy back the Caroona exploration licence from BHP Billiton for $220 million, meaning that one of the two mines proposed for this part of Liverpool Plains would not go ahead. The NSW Premier Mike Baird had said at the time that his government had determined that 'coal mining under these highly fertile black soil plains ... poses too great a risk for the future of this food bowl and the underground water sources that support it' (Hannam, August 11, 2016). The premier did not comment on whether the second mine, proposed by Shenhua, posed a similar risk, but Hamparsum told us that the cancellation of the Caroona project was 'an amazing breakthrough for us' (Interview, Hamparsum 2016).

In this book we have investigated campaigns seeking to halt coal mines across three countries, and analysed the national and transnational contexts in which they are played out. In large part the themes that emerge from these studies mirror Hamparsum's re-reading of the coal train. In this he spans some of the key dimensions of anti-coal struggles that we have explored in this book: the non-negotiable challenge posed by climate change and the impossibility of compensating for the permanent impacts of coal mining; the process of scale-shifting and temporal transformation; and the dynamics of institutional contestation. Taking the three cases of struggles against new coal mining, and setting them in the context of a disrupted nexus between coal and development, this book has sought to establish the possibilities for a post-coal future. This closing chapter draws together some of the themes from the cases outlined in Chapters 2–4, with the discussion of the coal–industrial complex in Chapters 5–7, asking what we can now discern in terms of the emerging dynamics for a post-coal future.

Three Struggles, Common Strategies?

In the context of advancing climate crisis, there would be little point in studying anti–coal mining protests unless we could identify what factors have contributed to their success or failure in slowing or preventing new mines, or mine extensions, from going ahead – and to what extent they might provide useful precedents or models for movements elsewhere, and for emerging global action on climate change. The three case studies investigated here suggest that the ability to challenge the meaning of coal for development is an effective means of delaying and even halting new coal mines. Drawing on the case studies, we suggest there are five modes of action and scripts for coal mining protagonists (Table 8.1).

First, the ability of the affected community to assert autonomy is critical. Mobilisation against proposed coal mines relies on the strength of existing representative structures and on the capacity to create new channels for political leverage. From the start, it is vitally important for resistance to coal mining to be able to assert the legitimacy of an alternative development pathway (often framed as an objection to the impacts of coal mining on local livelihood), and to highlight the costs, in terms of what is lost, of following the coal-based development trajectory. The embedded structures of Adivasi livelihood, culture and institutional recognition in Chhattisgarh are crucial in enabling the campaign against coal in the Hasdeo-Arand forest in India. Established landowners, along with Indigenous and environmentalist allies, have been crucial for challenging the advance of coal on

Table 8.1. *Actions and scripts for contesting new coal mines*

Dimensions	Proponents	Opponents
Capacity for contestation	Regional sacrifice, for the greater good, with compensation	Alternative development trajectory grounded in present-day capacity
Commensurability of the challenge	Co-benefit, amelioration, coexistence, replacement	Mobilising the loss/gain of intrinsic value
Structures of legitimation	The capture of state policy and support	Contesting legislation and regulation, and creating new blockages
Ability to force a scale shift	Confining concerns to a bounded locality	Breaching the local, to gain allies and resonance
Capacity to assert a temporal shift	Limiting mining to an immediate cost-benefit nexus of development	Projecting the destructive impacts of coal into the future (and from the past)

the Liverpool Plains in Australia. A pre-existing developmental commitment to post-communist *Energiewende,* the German energy transition, in the Lausitz has been important in helping to politicise and delegitimise proposals for new lignite coal mines in Germany: the affected villagers already see themselves as 'living the energy transition'.

Second, and partly reflecting the terms of developmentalism, it is essential that opponents are able to mobilise values and forms of identification that cannot be 'offset' or otherwise monetised in the form of compensation. Coal mining poses an existential threat on a number of levels, to land, culture, ecologies, communities and climate, as irreplaceable (and infinitely valued) aspects of socio-ecological life. The three campaigns effectively mobilise these irreconcilable values against the coal mines. Adivasi and other forest dwellers in Chhattisgarh have been campaigning to maintain the integrity of their communities and livelihood; Indigenous communities fight to protect their heritage and country from the ravages of coal and CSG extraction; and in Lusatia villagers defend both the past and the future, both halting the destruction of communities and advancing the post-coal transition. These goals are mobilised, presented and pursued as alternative ways or life, or development pathways, and allow the campaigns to sharpen the contradictions of coal-centrism. Creating and maintaining unity on intrinsic values, and resisting pressure to compromise them, can be very hard to sustain for activists and communities. This is an everyday struggle, of constant hard-fought battles, over decades in some instances.

In mine project localities, companies use their economic power to acquire land under conditions that can be socially divisive. This is documented in Chapter 3 for Shenhua's acquisition of all the land it needed to proceed with the Watermark mine. Despite these pressures, there are examples across the three cases where mining companies have been unable to find a means of buying off or displacing opponents. Villagers contesting coal in the Lausitz faced this difficulty very early in their struggle when some were willing to accept compensation and relocation; the capacity of the local village organisations to overcome this, in the name of the village community and locality, was centrally important. We saw similar dynamics in both Hasdeo-Arand and in the threat of violence from the authorities in Chhattisgarh. Gomeroi people in the Liverpool Plains, long dispossessed, continue to assert their inalienable right to their country. Myths of coexistence, between coal and Adivasi or Indigenous rights, or between coal and agri-industry, needed to be contested. There could be no 'middle road' or co-benefit with coal, if the mines were to be halted.

A third insight is that campaigns need to contest existing institutional structures that support coal, as much to expose their failure as to advance the cause. Coal has direct socio-ecological effects when extracted, in terms of direct displacement of people, impacts on land and water, and in transportation and combustion. As demonstrated across the three cases discussed in the book, state regulatory instruments become sites for intense political engagement and mobilisation, offering potential for stronger engagement and alliance-building. Opponents' campaigns contest the framework for mining approvals and challenge the capture of regulatory regimes by mining advocates. When challenged, the state can respond by creating new regulatory arrangements, ostensibly to accommodate public concerns. In the process, the impacts of mining are institutionalised by the state and 'socialised' as a matter of public interest and state responsibility (see O'Connor 1998). These themselves then become the target for public challenges to the mines. The 'water trigger' in Australia is a good example of this, as is India's National Green Tribunal; in Germany, the creation of various means to manage emissions reduction for the coal sector have also played this role.

A fourth aspect is the capacity to escape the limitations of localism. Those engaged locally seek strategic influence beyond the locality, so as to gain wider support and turn the tables on transnationally networked proponents. Mining opponents can find strategic leverage in the state's environmental, Indigenous and human rights legislation, and create organisational alliances to deploy this. These may emerge through engagement on shared agendas with non-local allies, for instance on forest rights, Indigenous rights or climate change. Localism can become strategic if it engages and levers open the dominant political opportunities. Agendas and possibilities emerge from mutual action around protest events and more sustained coalition-building in the face of counter-moves from coal advocates. There is extensive alliance building in the Chhattisgarh case, for instance, among villages, within region-level organisations and with national environmental and forest rights campaigns. In the Liverpool Plains case, the 'wrong mine, wrong place' model centres on an appeal to the distinctiveness of regional agri-industry, which we have termed 'regional exceptionalism', and on pre-existing linkages with national political elites. Efforts to create new alliances beyond regionalism, such as through the Liverpool Plains Youth, signalled some of limitations of the 'insider' approach. Alliance-building in Lusatia followed a similar pattern, as from the outset local opponents of the mine extensions invoked global dimensions of climate change as a way of gaining support from transnational climate activists and organisations, as exemplified by the 'human chain' protests of 2014 and the *Ende Gelände* protests in 2016.

Fifth, there is a parallel process of 'time-shifting', where protagonists engage in a contest over the temporal context for energy decision-making. Delay tactics seek to force a different timescale into the picture. Here, anticipated shifts in energy policy due to climate concerns are critical. Across the three cases the process of assessing the merits of mining proposals is linked, directly or indirectly, with timescale of transition to renewable energy under climate change. Articulation may be explicit, as evidenced in the scripts of corporates seeking to deny any link between coal production and climate change, when confronted by campaigns against the extraction of 'unburnable fuels'. Or, and in some respects more powerfully, the linkage may be embedded in the structural context in which coal mines are proposed. The re-contextualisation of coal under climate change creates new political space for anti-coal movements. Indeed, the articulation between local actions and wider civil society organisations in de-legitimising the coal commodity can become centrally important in achieving the shared goal of shutting down coal.

Protagonists enter a form of 'climate time', where efforts at either advancing or stalling a proposal rest on the shared assumption that coal projects can only become more difficult to justify over time, as climate concerns intensify (and renewables are adopted). This structural articulation of coal mining with the timetables of climate change is evident across all three cases.

In some respects, the coal advocates themselves, whether corporates or governmental agencies, are driven to pursue coal extraction in the knowledge that the window is closing on fossil fuels. The idea of 'emissions development space' for fossil fuels, as expressed in the Kyoto Protocol and also in the wide variation between present-day INDC's, reflects this notion that the window for coal may be closing. In Australia, for instance, the rush to open up a new coal mining region in the Gallilee basin in Queensland is at least in part driven by this awareness of a closing horizon for the industry.

By the same token the political leverage of anti-coal campaigns is conditioned by the emergence of climate policy and associated commitments to reduce emissions from fossil fuels. Whether they explicitly invoke the timescale of climate change and energy transition, as in Germany, or implicitly benefit from the growth of alternative renewable energy sources and the wider delinking of coal from development, the success of anti-coal mine campaigns in all three cases hinges on a recasting of timetables. This is most clearly reflected in the focus on delay, creating obstacles for mining approvals in the knowledge that the future can only bring more difficulties for coal advocates. In this context delaying coal becomes central in the unfolding process of climate change and global energy transition.

As outlined in Table 8.1, these five aspects can be conceptualised as dimensions in the struggle between advocates for coal mining, and their opponents. As in any political conflict, strategies and counter-strategies are in collision and can mirror each other. As we have argued in Chapter 1, the scripts outlined in the table above play into larger 'narratives of coal' which operate at both a national and a global level. The relationship is dynamic: global narratives of coal may shape the understandings and motivations of local actors, and local contests may also shift and reframe debates about the future of coal in national or transnational forums . Conflicts over coal mining have a particularly zero-sum logic, with no possibility of compromise over the loss of intrinsic and hence incalculable values. With the stakes so high, losing out to a coal mine produces existential threat.

Charting the Coal–Industrial Complex, and After

In opening the book we outlined some of the key issues in understanding the historical and contemporary role of coal. These are key to our purpose in this book, in terms of seeking to fully comprehend the barriers to a post-coal future, and thus the critical social transformations required. In Chapter 1 we outlined the socio-ecological dimensions of coal as a commodity or asset, in terms of its capacity to deliver thermal steam and then electric power, and in terms of its other impacts, ending with coal-induced climate change. Coal has acquired, and in part retains, a symbolic cultural role at the centre of dominant conceptions of social and economic development. In this process, state-led coal development has been central: it is the state that makes coal a resource, so it can be extracted and burnt for energy. This is reflected in the powerful institutional nexus, where coal and the state became imbricated in remarkable ways, as a *coal–industrial complex*.

Just as state capitalisation socialises coal interests, so the policy contradictions of the coal–industrial complex and growing climate crisis have socialised the problem of coal. The state has become part of the paradoxical process of both advancing industrial capitalism, and at the same time destroying the ecological foundations of that society. This expresses what O'Connor called the 'second contradiction' of capitalism (O'Connor, J. 1998; O'Connor, M. 1994b; Rosewarne 1997). As the state comes to exemplify this paradox, the question of coal is radically politicised, well beyond the local circumstances of extraction. This process is expressed in the changing meaning of coal, and is reflected in the political resonance that the struggles we document have been able to acquire. As outlined in Chapters 5 to 7 this is reflected in the disruption, and now apparent unravelling, of the coal–industrial complex. In each of our three country cases, coal enters a broad legitimacy crisis, which starts to infect the government agencies, corporate associations and investment groups that promote coal interests, as well as the coal corporates themselves.

Clearly then, any discussion of a post-coal future necessarily entails more than a socio-technical fix: it requires a process of unravelling assumptions about development, reorientating and reconstituting coal-centred political constituencies through just transitions policies, reordering state policy to overcome the power of coal industries, and defining alternative models for prosperity beyond the developmentalist state and the coal nexus. Efforts at diversifying coal-based localities and securing new modes of development are reflected in the German Coal Commission (discussed below) and the proposal for an Australian Just Transitions Authority; in India there are efforts at using the Forest Rights Act and other mechanisms to advance recognition and autonomy for Adivasi livelihood. All of these take the process of establishing a post-coal nexus well beyond the immediate context of coal and energy. Contestation on the ground meshes and clashes with the dynamics in national-level policy-making, corporate practice, and climate mobilisation. Efforts to challenge coal as an asset, range from sites of extraction, to global climate policy, to boardroom and investor risk assessment, and to community and even classroom outrage at the continued logic of coal dependence and coal-based destruction. Articulation of the struggle against coal across these multiple social fields is critical.

There is a large task, already underway, of revisiting energy production under climate change, to produce a wider societal transition to new modes of decarbonising development. In the study we have found powerful parallels between coal struggles under Germany's 'ecological modernity', India's post-colonial industrialism and Australia's extractivism. The contrasting outcomes reflect the degree of political space for meaningful deliberation about the implications of climate change. In post-industrial Germany, that space is relatively open, with major political forces recognising both the possibilities offered by climate action, as well as its necessities. In India, by contrast, the public sphere is dominated by industrialists and their advocates, with environmental and Adivasi NGOs reliant on legal means to gain traction, although there are signs that in recent years this is changing as transition is taken-up as an industrial strategy. In Australia, the ground is heavily skewed to the fossil fuel sector, with a mining industry that has in recent years claimed the capacity to change governments, though again, there are signs the sector may be being forced into abeyance by growing climate concerns and the turn to renewables. In all three cases, quite clearly the struggle is only in its early days, though the pace of change is quickening.

In all three cases, local manifestations of the 'coal–industrial complex' have come under severe pressure, demonstrating the extent to which the question of climate action now affects the policy field. Advocates for coal mining rely on scripts of national development, and specifically the claim that coal is the key to unlocking poverty, maintaining energy stability, or advancing development. Delinking coal from anti-poverty and development narratives is probably the most strategic priority for anti-coal campaigns, and this has been true in Germany and Australia as much as in India. The argument that coal is a necessary evil is, perhaps, the most powerful and insidious of all the arguments still made in favour of the industry. Yet the preconditions for overcoming the coal–development nexus are now, arguably, coming into place, and not least with the emergence of industrial strategies linked to renewable technology, principally wind and solar energy. Aross all three countries, renewable energy is offering an increasingly viable and lower-cost alternative option for energy access, for regional, community and household power. The development of such technologies has now gained its own dynamic independent of climate policy: countries are embracing renewables not to reduce greenhouse gas emissions so much as to access allied 'co-benefits', including for industrial development, as the Indian government describes them (NITI 2017).

Underlying the structural shift to renewables is a growing awareness that climate change is not any longer a far-off prospect, but a present force, transforming everyday lives and livelihoods. With advancing climate turmoil, and the continued inadequacy of climate policy, the contradiction calls forth new and deepened legitimacy problems. In each of the three countries discussed in this book, conflicting climate and energy policies spill over into national political contention. In the new dispensation, we can see the emergence of a decarbonised social imaginary and associated climate policy apparatus, positioned in direct contradiction with continued fossil fuel dependence. Even in Australia, where the two mainstream parties support coal exports, and conservative politicians keep broaching proposals for new coal fired power stations, surveys consistently report overwhelming public support for renewable energy (Climate Institute 2017). The policy contradiction is surfacing across multiple social fields, re-articulating social forces, contending social priorities and struggles, while creating new political spaces for delegitimising fossil capital.

Local Struggles and Global Agendas

Central to this book has been the question of correlation, across contrasting issues and concerns, at differing levels of engagement, from local to global. Correlated with local and national contention, debate about the future of coal is part of wider conflict with the international fossil fuel sector, involving large international advocacy NGOs, mainly in the science and environment sector. That conflict has been waged since at least the late 1980s, passing through a series of phases and levels of intensity, and has helped shape national-level contention across many countries. As discussed in Chapters 6 and 7 of the book, the wider national and international terrain is by definition in flux, caught in a process of transition and reaction, involving the apprehension of the impact of climate change and its carboniferous causes, as much as it involves socio-technical questions of decarbonisation. As we argue, it appears there is a transition underway, but the crucial question for strategists seeking to overcome coal dependence is how to articulate that transformation within localised contexts, so as to create the required paradigm shift.

UN climate negotiations, intensified in anticipation of the end of the Kyoto Protocol, and the assessment cycle of the Inter-governmental Panel on Climate Change (IPCC) charting growing alarm at the emerging climate crisis, have played a key role in forcing coal into question. The ongoing search for effective climate policy, played out in COP negotiations, has opened a political space for growing, diverse and vibrant climate change activism, which has been able to gain some leverage. The legitimacy of coal advocacy in international fora has constantly been contested, and this has unfolded across the political spectrum and policy fields – globally, within national jurisdictions, and in local communities. One consequence has been deepened political antagonism over climate, with the transformation of climate policy into a partisan ideological struggle. The efforts of energy corporations to sow misinformation about climate science were increasingly exposed and had the counter-effect of enlivening climate activism, as well as strengthening a reactive denialism. While *An Inconvenient Truth*, for instance, helped to turn the tables on the coal–industrial complex, more recent pressures for a 'Green New Deal' have put forward positive and sometimes radical agendas for a new development model.

In the process climate politics has migrated into national politics and fired up a recurring series of anti-coal campaigns that have marginalised the highly concentrated, oligopolised coal sector. Multiple sites of climate action have emerged, from consumer action to divestment campaigns. Climate litigation, for livelihood and conservation, against coal, has become a key political force. In the Netherlands for instance, climate campaigners have successfully sued their own government for ineffective action on climate and this has inspired similar actions in countries as diverse as France, Pakistan, Ireland and the United States (Coghlan 2018; Howard 2015; Nelsen 2014; Parker 2019; Timsit 2018). As noted, the direct health effects of coal extraction and burning are also being politicised, drawing new constituencies into the process of contestation. There are further fields opening up amongst labour movement organisations, by workers directly affected by climate change and climate policy. National-level initiatives on different aspects of climate change and climate policy have broadened the field of contention across multiple sites. This in turn has generated waves of international climate activism, most recent, in 2019, being the 'school strike for climate' and 'Extinction Rebellion' (Chang and Smith 2018; Taylor et al 2019).

Concerns about the role of coal in driving climate change have figured prominently, although not all struggles to block the expansion of mining and development of new coal mines have been driven by the assertion of the coal–climate nexus. As we have observed in Chapters 2–4, communities that are forced, quite literally, into living at the coal-face have mobilised to fight proposals for expanded mines or new coal developments, primarily through reference to local concerns, without necessarily referring to climate. In many instances, the momentum of the opposition to coal, and indeed the ability to sustain the opposition, has rested on the capacity of different social and political groups to join forces and draw on shared organising strengths. The assistance and support of ENGOs, has been critically important in helping to maintain these local challenges to the coal–industrial complex. And these local campaigns against the particular manifestations of coal's assault on the integrity of communities have provided grist to the mill for wider climate activism. The sites of contestation effectively dramatise and make concrete the wider struggle for a safe climate, and the end of coal. What could easily be dismissed as the more nebulous or distant threats of 'climate change' are materialised in these on-the-ground contests. Coal mining and coal-fired power become symbolically central as targets, played out in confrontations with quite tangible adversaries against the backdrop of increasingly refined and affirmed scientific modelling and evidence. By the same token, the ability to sustain these local struggles to defend the integrity of communities from coal's onslaught is bound up with the vitality of the more abstracted 'climate change' narrative. As parallel narratives, the two are structurally bound into one another and, as noted, can be co-articulated in unexpected ways.

The ethnographic case studies here have focused on the local struggles, but despite the specificity of these local contests, they are articulated with wider national and global developments. Moreover, just as the endeavours to resist coal's onslaught have been uneven in their outcomes, so the weight of the balance of forces has varied over time, and this is evident in the momentum of the increase in global coal production for instance. Reflecting developmentalist commitments across the globe, the pace of the rush to get coal out of the ground has been persistent and enduring. Certainly, for those who own and control coal assets, or gain revenue from their mining, there is profit-driven imperative to mine and burn as much coal as possible before the transition is put into law. Although unevenly experienced, the mining and combustion of coal now seems to be subject to a vulnerability without historical parallel in its history. We can now observe both the unfolding of large-scale organised opposition to coal as a major driver of climate change, and a serious challenge to the hegemony of the coal–industrial complex.

Post-coal Agendas: Early Tremors and Seismic Shifts

The cases we discuss in this book are embedded in a global process of apprehending climate change and acting on it. Action to enable climate stability, or 'purposeful' climate agency as Hulme calls it, challenges coal-based developmentalism often in the most unexpected ways. During our investigations into coal and development in India, Australia and Germany, we encountered and followed long-running cases of sustained mobilisation against new coal mining, and their role in the wider national-level transformations in the politics of energy and climate. Towards the end of our investigations, in the context of intensifying climate instability and ongoing failure internationally to meet the Paris Agreement targets, there were substantial developments under way in each of the national contexts, forcing the post-coal scenarios onto the national political agenda. Each of our case studies signals shifts that expose the climate–coal contradiction to wider publics, with the potential for a more inclusive climate action politics.

India – Post-coal Transition Commission

In India, transitioning from fossil fuel dependence to renewable energy has tended to pivot around a technocratic agenda. The promotion of renewables is embedded in a set of wider market-based incentives, consistent with neoliberalism and the idealised 'free market'. Among the more noteworthy initiatives has been the creation of the Energy Transitions Commission (ETC) (India), led by the Energy and Resources Insitute (TERI). ETC (India) brings together a high-level coalition of business repesentatives, policy makers, scientists, non-profit organisations and researchers to explore the obstacles to decarbonised power, and is financed by a range of EU-based foundations and companies, such as OPower, Royal Dutch Shell, Schneider Electric and Statnett (Energy Transitions Commission 2019). It describes itself as 'a unique, high-level, multi-stakeholder platform on energy and electricity sector transitions in India' focused on 'decarbonising the power sector' (ETI 2018).

ETC (India) is particularly significant in the Indian context because its explicit starting point and rationale it to enable the decarbonisation of power, and therefore the exit from coal. As such it builds on the recent work on India's coal transitions, for instance by the Indian Institute of Management in Ahmedabad, with the Paris-based Institute for Sustainable Development and International Relations (IDDRI) (Vishwanathan et al. 2018), and at The Energy Research Institute (TERI) itself (Spencer et al. 2018). The ETC's mandate mirrors the United Nations' 2015 Sustainable Development Goals of promoting affordable and clean energy and promoting carbon neutrality. The Commission plans to develop a comprehensive policy strategy that will direct investment towards establishing greater flexibility in the energy system in order to support the expanded deployment of renewable energy. Beyond the power sector it also aims to develop a 'credible route to decarbonising the industry sector which cannot be easily electrified' (Mathur et al. 2019; Nelson 2019).

In exploring policy options, the Commission seeks to reconcile a carbon-neutral future with economic growth (Energy Transitions Commission 2016). The transition being envisaged is therefore fully consistent with the global corporate economic liberalisation project advanced by the Modi government (Sartor 2018, 2019; Spencer et al. 2018; Vishwanathan et al. 2018). Indeed, one of the key tasks of the ETC in pursuit of its mission is to promote the use of markets in transitioning from fossil fuels to renewable energy, and to engage more of the corporate world in seeking the economic benefits of abandoning coal as the primary energy source (Energy Transitions Commission 2019). The ETC has co-convened South–South transition partnerships with India, South Africa and Indonesia, reflecting an internationalising focus not unlike the International Solar Alliance which the Modi government envisaged as a springboard for extending and deepening India's renewable energy business ventures in renewable energy technologies into the countries of the Global South. The main preoccupation is with meeting the economic imperatives of transition; issues of social ownership, equity and climate justice are not addressed (Bhushan 2017).

There is now extensive evidence of a rapid slow-down in the the expansion of coal-fired power generation in India. The most recent report from Global Coal Tracker finds that 538 gigawatts of planned coal power was cancelled in India between 2010 and 2019, almost twice the current operating capacity of 229 gigawatts; 37 gigawatts of capacity was under construction, with a further 29 gigawatts planned and approved (Shearer et al. 2020: 25). The Brookings Institution notes that, while it expects coal to remain the dominant fuel electricity generation in India to 2030 and beyond, the growing supply of renewable energy is beginning to displace coal-fired generation, and coal's share of generation is expected to fall (Tongia and Gross 2019). While the pace of the engagement with renewable energy is escalating, serious questions remain about whether this will enable India to meet its Paris commitments (BP 2019; PTI 2018d; The Worrall 2019; Tongia and Gross 2018).

We should, then, be cautious about drawing long-term conclusions about the future of coal in India from these shorter-term trends. Nevertheless, the developments outlined above suggest that the bleak scenario outlined by India's former environment minister, Jairem Ramesh, in the introduction to this book may be less persuasive. The 'cruel coal conundrum' may not be as intractable as Ramesh suggested in 2016 when we interviewed him. India is at least beginning to imagine a future beyond coal; and there is important evidence that coal's dominance is being challenged.

Australia: Post-coal in the Courts

In 2019, the Land and Environment Court in Australia refused to approve a coal mine partly on the basis of the greenhouse gas (GHG) emissions that would result from it. The judgment was hailed as a landmark, as for the first time in Australia the court accepted the argument that climate impacts could be considered in deciding whether or not to approve a mine.

The judgment arose from an unusual set of circumstances. In 2018, the NSW Planning Assessment Commission (PAC) had rejected a proposal from Gloucester Resources Limited (GRL) to open a new coal mine. Its proposed the Rocky Hill mine was to be located near the town of Gloucester, to the north of the Liverpool Plains (EDO 2019; McGrath 2019). In 2019, GRL appealed to the NSW Land and Environment Court and the NSW Department of Planning and Environment opposed GRL, affirming the PAC decision. In addition, the NSW Environmental Defenders Office mounted a case against the mine, acting for Groundswell Gloucester, a long-established, highly active non-profit community group contesting coal and CSG developments in and around Gloucester.

The judgment outlined several grounds for rejecting the mine, encapsulated in the phrase, 'wrong place, wrong time':

> An open-cut coal mine in this part of the Gloucester valley would be in the wrong place at the wrong time . . . Wrong place because an open-cut coal mine in this scenic and cultural landscape, proximate to many people's homes and farms, will cause significant planning, amenity, visual and social impacts. Wrong time because the greenhouse gas emissions of the coal mine and its coal product will increase global total concentrations of greenhouse gas emissions at a time when what is now urgently needed, in order to meet generally

agreed climate targets, is a rapid and deep decrease in greenhouse gas emissions. These dire consequences should be avoided. The project should be refused.

(NSW Land and Environment Court 2019: clause 699)

Local impacts defined the mine as in the 'wrong place', in terms of 'significant planning, amenity, visual and social impacts', and as posing 'extreme social risk' to Aboriginal residents. By recognising these impacts the judgement acknowledged in law the incommensurability between the mine as proposed, and the integrity of the local inhabited places and 'Indigenous social life'. The proposal was also at the 'wrong time', given that the production of increased greenhouse gas emissions from the burning of the mined coal would threaten the capacity to reduce GHG emissions as required under global climate policy. In this way the Rocky Hill judgment for the first time in Australia established a nexus between climate change and coal-mining approvals. With it, regulatory approval for coal mining had to take account of resulting coal emissions, whether or not the coal was burnt in Australia.

Significantly, the proposed mine was relatively small; a large transnational mine would have a much greater impact on climate change. On no less that eight occasions in Australia opponents of coal mines had attempted to persuade courts that GHG emission should be a consideration in mining approvals (EDO 2019). They had failed mainly on the market substitution defence, the so-called drug dealers defence, that if Australia did not supply the coal, then some other country would (McGrath 2019). The Rocky Hill judgement dismissed this defence on the basis of a 2017 precedent from the US Court of Appeals which described it as 'arbitrary and capricious' (2019: clause 543).

The company declined to appeal, no doubt to avoid the risk of a higher court entrenching climate concerns, and the judgement stands as the first of its kind. Significantly, the judgement arose from the efforts of local opponents, challenging the spatial fix that facilitates mining approvals in Australia. It also has significant implications for others in the region, including the Liverpool Plains landowners, who had not sought to challenge the Shenhua mine on the basis of its climate change impacts. By putting climate onto the agenda the judgement essentially re-spatialised the approval process, with potential implications for all fossil fuel developments.

The impact of the judgement was felt in a decision by the NSW PAC later in the same year, when a mine expansion proposed by Glencore and Peabody at the United Wambo project was approved by the PAC on condition that emissions were minimised 'wherever practicable' and that the coal only be exported to countries that had signed the Paris Agreement (Ludlow 2019). As noted, there were parallel developments in Western Australia, where the Environment Protection Authority had proposed to assess development applications in the light of Australia's commitments under the Paris Agreement. The proposed EPA Guidance note explicitly required offsetting for new and expanded projects for emitters with more than 100,000 tonnes annual emissions of carbon dioxide (Garvey and Williams 2019a; Latimer and Hastie 2019).

These developments were contradicted by wider political pressures, especially following the 2019 federal election which reinstalled the pro-coal conservative coalition government. In Western Australia, the Labor Government announced an intention to abandon emissions abatement to maintain competitive advantage for Australia's fossil fuel industries (Thompson 2019). In Queensland, the Labor Government approved the Adani proposal to mine for coal in the Galilee Basin, opening up the region for a succession of proposed coal mines, against strong popular opposition. Labor and the Coalition then supported congratulatory motions in the Queensland parliament, in favour of the mines, and it is widely speculated that other large mines will soon follow in the Basin (Krien 2019).

Germany – A Coal Commission to End Coal

In 2018 the German government established a national commission to set a timeline for an exit from lignite mining, and for closing coal-fired power stations. The Commission on Growth, Structural Change and Employment (CGSCE, colloquially called the Coal Commission) brought together twenty-eight stakeholders from industry, labour unions, *Länder*, ENGOs and key government departments. It was convened in the face of sustained campaigning by *Ende Gelände* and the wider climate movement, and drew on the historical practice of corporatist governance in Germany, of bringing parties together into social dialogue. There were also wider disagreements across the political spectrum over the design of the coal exit strategy, the setting of sectoral emissions reduction targets and the responsibilities to be exercised by the relevant ministries (Wehrmann 2019b). As such the Commission was clearly designed to ameliorate growing political contention over the future of coal, and to do so through a consensus-building planning process for phase-out.

The Commission's Interim Report, issued in January 2019, recommended a staged exit from lignite mining, and from all coal-fired power generation, by 2038. The closures were to be supported by a transition fund of 40 billion Euros to be spent over the ensuing twenty years to assist displaced workers and to develop new industries and employment prospects (Egenter and Wehrmann 2019; Wehrmann 2018). Some *Länder* governments affected by the mining phase-out condemned the proposal, warning of dire economic consequences; trade unions representing workers in the affected industries protested at the planned job losses, and called for 'an energy transition with reason' (Appunn and Wettengel 2018).

There was also controversy over the timing of the phase-out: the 2038 deadline is sufficiently far-off to enable continued expansion of coal mining on the ground, and was locally contested. In a dissenting opinion the four commissioners from environmental NGOs argued a faster phase-out was required, but they ultimately supported the report as a first step (Government of Germany 2019: 120). Only the representative of the Lusatian villagers threatened by continued mining voted against the report. Confirming their concerns, just two weeks after the Commission Report was published the arrangements for relocating the inhabitants of Mühlrose, a village in Lusatia, were finalised (Wehrmann 2019a).

Despite this, there has generally been broad support for the blueprint proposed by the Coal Commission, and in August 2019 the German Cabinet formally adopted the draft legislation – known as the *Strukturstärkungsgesetz*, or Structural Development Act – that is intended to implement the recommendations of the Coal Commission. In its opening sentence, the legislation states that the federal government 'understands structural change in coal regions as an integral part of a comprehensive process of transformation of the economy and society in Germany with the goal of them becoming greenhouse-gas- (carbon) neutral by mid-century' (Deutscher Bundestag 2019). Most importantly for the coal-dependent regions themselves, the draft law allocates up to 14 billion Euros to coal-dependent regions to assist with the process of structural change, aiming to stimulate the economy through spending on public transport, broadband and business infrastructure, and on grants for environmental protection and land management (CEW, Meza 2019). A further 26 billion Euros is promised to support research and development programs and expand federal institutions in coal regions. In addition, the Federal Ministry of Economic Affairs and Energy will set up a new federal and state body to oversee the speedy distribution of grant funding, and a 'Zukunft Revier' or 'Regional Futures Program' to create 'model regions' which will be carbon-neutral, resource-efficient and sustainable (Deutscher Bundestag 2019).

It is significant that the draft law was welcomed by the state premiers of both Brandenburg and Saxony, the two states in Eastern Germany where most coal mines and coal-fired power plants are concentrated. Both Dietmar Woidke, the Social Democrat Premier of Brandenburg, and Michael Kretschmer, Christian Democrat Premier of Saxony, have been strong advocates for the coal industry in the past. Kretschmer told the German Press Agency that the draft law was 'an important milestone for a successful structural transition', while Woidke said 'we have fought hard for this and it has paid off' (CEW, Wettengel 2019). Thus it would appear that a significant political obstacle to a coal exit has been removed.

The phase-out plan is significant because it finally puts into law the closure of lignite mining in Germany, even though the timetable may be revisited in years to come. Some indication of this came from the Minister-President of North Rhine-Westphalia (NRW), Armin Laschet, a long-standing CDU German politician with a record of supporting the coal sector, whose government has immediately halted coal expansion in NRW, and called for funds to enable conversion and secure closures. Further, in a study commissioned by NRW the coal phase-out was found to be sufficient to ensure Germany would meet its proposed timetable for emissions reductions (of 62% below 1990 levels by 2030). In Germany at least the dynamics driving a rapid coal exit, rather than a slow retreat, only appear to be growing stronger.

A Turning Point for Global Energy and Climate Policy?

A confronting warning was issued by the UN's Emission Gap Report in late 2018. To meet the longstanding UN target of keeping global warming below 2°C the world would have to increase its planned emission reductions by 300 per cent (UNEP 2018). The timeline for emission reduction, to meet the commitment to 'net zero' emissions by 2050, has been compressed. At the same time, the widely evident impacts of climate change, in excess of IPCC predictions, have forced a new urgency for more effective climate policy. The focus for that urgency is now on the principal driver of rising global greenhouse emissions – coal.

As the UN has stated, there can be no new coal-fired power stations from 2020 (United Nations 2019). In 2018, the number of coal-fired power plants under development dropped for the third year in a row; the closure of coal-fired power plants continued at a record pace, with more than half occurring in the United States. At the same time, however, Chinese companies resumed work on dozens of suspended projects and the China Electricity Council proposed allowing for 290 gigawatts of new capacity (Shearer, Mathew Shah et al. 2019). As we have outlined in Chapter 7, leading financial and multilateral organisations have responded both to pressure from climate activists and investor campaigns, the increasingly stark scientific evidence of accelerating climate change, and prudential requirements to factor in climate risk, by effectively declaring coal a stranded asset. Yet, according to the latest BP World Energy Outlook, although 'renewables are set to penetrate the global energy system more quickly than any fuel previously in history', without much more aggressive action by governments to curb emissions, known as the 'rapid transition scenario', world demand for coal is not likely to decline for at least twenty years (Macdonald-Smith 2019).

We cannot emphasise strongly enough how sharp this contradiction is, and how irreconcilable the two conflicting 'narratives of coal' which we have outlined in Chapter 1, and traced through this book, still appear to be. At times it is hard to resist the impression that they describe two quite different realities. As we write this conclusion, Australia's Great Barrier Reef Marine Park Authority issued its most recent report downgrading the outlook for the reef from 'poor' to 'very poor'. In unusually strong language, the Authority stated that 'early and effective global and national action on climate change, coupled with local actions to ... facilitate recovery, are imperative over the next 10 years if the region is to have a positive long-term outlook' (Cox and Morton 2019). In the very same week, the Queensland State government, which receives millions of dollars a year in taxation revenue from tourism to the Reef, extinguished indigenous native title over the land on which the proposed Adani coal mine is situated, removing one of the few remaining obstacles to the mine proceeding. For the coal industry in Queensland, the Adani mine is an 'icebreaker' – once final approval is received, a precedent will be set for the opening-up of six further mines in the Galilee Basin. Overall, it is estimated that, if all the coal in the Galilee Basin coal seam were burned, the total emissions would be sufficient to shift the world one-third of the way to a global temperature increase of 2 °C (Krien 2019).

The world's coal phase-out will not happen without a struggle. Asset holders, like the Adani Group and the other companies waiting to follow them into the Galilee Basin, have every incentive to press their case, and re-start the coal boom, recasting the 'peak' as a 'blip'. They are clearly not about to retreat, though they are hedging against the 'risk' of effective climate policy. Some, like BHP Billiton in the case of the proposed Caroona mine, will choose to cut their losses, exiting from this particular project with generous compensation from the state. Others will bide their time, betting that national climate policies will be weakened or circumvented by governments keen to placate the coal–industrial complex or its domestic constituencies, as has happened in Australia. In time the hedge may become the main game, but certainly not by 2020, in time for the UN's declared moratorium on new coal-fired power.

The future of coal, and with it the future of the planet, is now poised at a decisive and historic moment. This book has sought to address this moment, in its making. As we have argued, in order to understand how we arrived here, it is important to understand the shifting dynamics of developmentalist ideology and the centrality of coal, as (hitherto) the primary energy source for industrial capitalism, ubiquitous as the vehicle for development. We have sought to make visible, across a range of national contexts, and encompassing the broad sweep of twentieth-century history, the invisible power of coal. Whilst foundational for development, however, coal is also its own undoing. It has been the principal driver of climate crisis, a force for 'de-development' across large swathes of the planet, substantially negating social advances across a broad front. We have sought to illuminate the ways in which the meaning of coal is now being redefined, not as a source of 'light, strength, power, wealth, and civilization', as Nicolls wrote in the *Coal Catechism* in 1898, but as direct liability for localities in terms of social, health and environmental impacts and resource dependence, and as a threat to planetary climate stability.

The three case studies certainly reveal tensions between local priorities and wider climate concerns, but also suggest closer alignments between them. We have found new and often unexpected political alliances forming in opposition to coal, and explored local, national and transnational strategies for moving to a world beyond coal. In each field site social conflicts over new coal mines resonate across multiple levels of political life and generate new narratives and scripts about coal. These conflicts likely presage major transformations in energy systems, and in associated social relations and power structures. We theorise this as a process of articulation, in which a campaigning against coal mining at the local level opens up a new political space due to climate change and the growing need to do something to address it. This can be a reciprocal process: local anti-coal contestations feed-into and provide grounding for wider pressures for more effective climate policy. A key question is whether such linkages can generate new solutions to the coal conundrum, and offer a means of translating the lived contexts of coal extractivism into effective political agendas, enacting 'ecological solidarity as a political force' (Kunkel 2017).

What is absolutely clear from all three of our case studies is that, whatever the motivations of the actors and the meanings they ascribe to their resistance, whatever scripts inform and animate their persistence in long and often psychologically arduous campaigns, their actions have been effective in keeping coal in the ground. In Germany the people of the Lausitz have halted one major mine expansion altogether, and held the line long enough for national policy to shift decisively in favour of an exit from coal. On the Liverpool Plains, the Caroona coal project has been abandoned by BHP Billiton and the future of the Shenhua mine remains in limbo (despite the $262 million gift to Shenhua from the NSW Government for part of its exploration licence). In the Hasdeo-Arand region in Chhattisgarh, concerted campaigns by Adivasis and a range of allies on the ground and through the courts in defence of '*jal, jangal, jameen*' – 'water, forests, land' – have not halted coal mining altogether, but many of the mines that were proposed when we began our research five years ago are still under legal challenge, while public–private proposals for several new mines and mine expansions have been approved but are still delayed by other means.

If there is one simple but clear lesson from our case studies, it is that local resistance can be highly effective in halting or delaying the extraction of coal over periods of ten years or longer – time in which the political and economic dynamics surrounding coal mining, and the meaning of coal itself, have changed. It is not yet clear whether we have reached the point of no return for coal, a point beyond which its central role in the world's energy mix, and in developmentalist ideology, can only decline. As we have suggested, there are strong signs that the latter is the case; the nascent global climate movement has been remarkably successful in forcing both coal's allies and its opponents to enter what we have called climate time, a zone of uncertainty and possibility in which the dominant economic and political logics of the fossil-fuel era are destabilised. Whether those whose struggles against coal we have documented in this book will be seen in the future as the prophets of a post-coal, post-developmentalist dispensation, or a rear-guard vainly attempting to forestall inevitable climate catastrophe, remains to be seen. The future, as Joe Strummer once said, is as yet unwritten. What is absolutely clear is that we have reached a turning point, either for coal, or for the planet's climate, and with it, life on earth.

References

AAP (2006) 'NSW's Iemma announces new coal mining venture with BHP', *AAP Finance News Wire*.

ABC (2009) 'Watermark farmers, miners reach agreement', *ABC News*, 23 April.

ABC NSW (2015) *Country Hour*, 29 January.

ABC Rural (2010) 'Caroona farmers end long-running blockade', *ABC Rural*, 24 March.

Abraham, J. (2017) 'Just transitions for the miners: Labor environmentalism in the Ruhr and Appalachian coalfields', *New Political Science* 39(2), 218–240.

Abraham. J. (2019) 'Just transitions in a dual labor market: Right wing populism and austerity in the German Energiewende', *Journal of Labor and Society*, 22(6), 679–693.

ABS (2016) *2016 Census*, Canberra: Australian Bureau of Statistics.

Adani (n.d.) 'Government of Rajasthan to set up India's largest solar park', Media Release. www.adani.com, accessed 1 August 2019.

Adani Group (n.d.) 'About Us', website entry. www.adani.com/about-us, accessed 4 April 2019.

AECOM (2012) Watermark Coal Project: Aboriginal Archaeology Impact Assessment, Prepared by AECOM for Hansen Bailey and Shenhua Watermark Coal Pty Ltd.

Agence France-Presse (2017) 'Deutsche Bank pulls out of coal projects to meet Paris climate pledge', *The Guardian*, 1 February.

Aggarwal, M. (2015) '20 gram sabhas in Chhattisgarh pass resolutions against auction of coal mine', *The Mint*, 15 January.

Aggarwal, M. (2017) 'Environment ministry panel eases coal mine expansion rules', *Livemint*, 9 August.

Aggarwal, M. (2019) 'The Hasdeo Arand story: Is coal mining a fait accompli for the pristine forests?', *Mongabay,* 7 March. https://india.mongabay.com/, accessed 14 April 2019.

Agnihotri, G. (2015) 'Germany struggles with too much renewable energy', *Oil Price*, 17 August.

Agora Energiewende (2015) 'New record for power exports', 21 July. www.agora-energiewende.de, accessed 1 August 2019.

Ahmad, N. (2014) 'Colonial Legislation in Postcolonial Times', in Lahiri-Dutt, K. (ed.) *The Coal Nation: Histories, Ecologies and Politics of Coal in India*, Surrey & Burlington: Ashgate, 258–260.

Ahmed, S. (2016) 'India plans to set up solar energy projects in underdeveloped Asian and African countries', *Newscorp VCCircle*, 4 February.

Ahn, S. J. and Graczyk, D. (2012) *Understanding Energy Challenges in India: Policies, Players and Issues*, Paris: International Energy Agency.

Akademie für Raumforschung und Landesplanung (2000) *Arbeitsmaterial: Braunkohlenplanung und Umsiedlungsproblematik in der Raumordnungsplanung Brandenburgs, Nordrhein-Westfalens, Sachsens und Sachsen-Anhalts*, Hannover: ARL.

Aldy, J. (2017) 'Real world headwinds for Trump climate change policy', *Bulletin of Atomic Scientists* 73(6), 376–381.

Allard, T. (2015) 'Why everything you think about the economy in 2015 is probably wrong', *The Sydney Morning Herald,* 16 January.

Allianz (2018) 'Allianz is driving change toward a low-carbon economy with an ambitions climate protection package', Press Release, 4 May.

Alon, I., Wang, H., Shen, J. and Zhang, W. (2014) 'Chinese state-owned enterprises go global', *Journal of Business Strategy* 35(6), 3–18.

Amalgamated Metal Workers and Shipwrights' Union (1979) *Australia Ripped Off*, Sydney: AMWU.

Amir, S. (1977) *Unequal Development: An Essay on the Social Formations of Peripheral Capitalism*, New York: Monthly Review Press.

Amnesty International (2016) *"When Land Is Lost, Do We Eat Coal?": Coal Mining and Violations of Adivasi Rights in India*, Bangalore: Amnesty International.

Anderson, D. and Howe, D. (2019) *Watermark Coal Project Groundwater Model,* Water Research Laboratory, Sydney, University of NSW.

APPEA (2013) *Cutting Green Tape: Streamlining Major Oil and Gas Project Environmental Approvals Processes in Australia*, Canberra: Australian Petroleum Production and Exploration Association Limited.

Applegate, C. (1990) *A Nation of Provincials: The German Idea of Heimat*, Berkeley: University of California Press.

Appunn, K. (2016) 'German federalism: In 16 states of mind over the Energiewende', *Clean Energy Wire,* 10 March.

Appunn, K. (2019) 'Coal in Germany', *Clean Energy Wire*, 7 February.

Appunn, K., Russell, R. and Thalman, E. (2015) 'Controversial Climate Summit Issues – positions in Germany', *Clean Energy Wire,* 20 November.

Appunn, K. and J. Wettengel (2018) 'Taskforce agrees on post-coal strategy for German mining regions', *Clean Energy Wire*, 26 October.

Archiv verschwundener Orte (2009) *Archiv verschwundener Orte*. www.archiv-verschwundene-orte.de, accessed 25 August 2019.

Armstrong, K. (2015) *Coal and Health in the Hunter: Lessons from One Valley for the World*, Clifton Hill: Climate and Health Alliance.

Arnold, A. (2012) 'Two stories beneath climate change induced solidarity', Paper presented at the Annual NSSR Sociology Conference, 31 March.

Aston, H. (2012) 'China drops axe on mine spend after "interference"', *Sydney Morning Herald*, 29 April.

Aston H. (2015) '"Moral" imperative in Australia's biggest coal mine, says Resources Minister Josh Frydenberg', *The Sydney Morning Herald*, 18 October.

Australia Koala Foundation (2014) *Submission to Planning Assessment Commission Review of Proposed Shenhua Watermark Coal Project*, Brisbane: Australia Koala Foundation.

Australian Associated Press (2014) 'Germany's biggest bank pulls funding for Abbot Point coal terminal', *The Guardian*, 23 May.

Australian Broadcasting Corporation (ABC) (2017) 'Digging into Adani', ABC Four Corners Documentary, 2 October 2017. www.abc.net.au/, accessed 4 April 2019.

Baer, H. and Burgmann, V. (2012) *Climate Politics and the Climate Movement in Australia*, Melbourne: Melbourne University Press.

Bagchi, S. (2012) 'Chhattisgarh villages under attack from straying tuskers', *The Hindu*, 6 October.

Bagshaw, E. and Bonyhady, N. (2019) '"Change now or pay later": RBA's stark warning on climate change', *The Sydney Morning Herald*, 12 March.

Bahree, M. (2014) 'Doing Big Business in Modi's Gujarat', *Forbes*, 12 March.

Baily, F. (1897) 'Forestry in India', *Scottish Geographical Magazine* 13(11), 572–590.

Bal, P., Ramachandran, A., Palanivelu, K., Thirumurugan, P., Geetha, R., and Bhaskaran, B. (2016) 'Climate change projections over India by a downscaling approach using PRECIS', *Asia-Pacific Journal of Atmospheric Science* 52(4), 353–369.

Bank Track (2014) *India: Tiger versus Coal*, Nijmegen: Banktrack.

Bank Track (2018) *Banking on Climate Change – 2018 Fossil Fuel Finance Report Card*, Nijmegen: Banktrack.

Bank Track (2018) *Banks and Coal*, Nijmegen: Banktrack.

Barton, G. (2007) *Empire Forestry and the Origins of Environmentalism*, Cambridge: Cambridge University Press.

BDEW (2019) *Erneuerbare decken fast 43% des Stromverbrauchs*, Berlin: Bundesverband der Energie und Wasserwirtschaft e.V.

Beck, U. (2010) 'Climate for change, or how to create a green modernity?', *Theory Culture Society* 27, 254–266.

Bedi, H. P. (2013) 'Environmental mis-assessment, development and mining in Orissa, India', *Development and Change* 44(1), 101–123.

Bell, L. (2013) 'Blood and Gore: Making a killing on anti-carbon investment hype', *Forbes,* 3 November.

Berger, M. (2004) *The Battle for Asia: From Decolonization to Globalization*, Abingdon: Routledge.

Bettany, S. and Kerrane, B. (2011) 'The (post-human) consumer, the (post-avian) chicken and the (post-object) Eglu: Towards a material-semiotics of anti-consumption', *European Journal of Marketing* 45(11/12), 1746–1756.

Bhalla, N. (2016) 'India using funding law to foil dissenting charities – U.N. experts', *Reuters*, 17 June.

Bhushan, R. (2001) 'Godbol committee report and the real story of Dabhol', *Outlook India*, 30 April.

Bickerstaff, K., Walker, G. and Bulkeley, H. (eds) (2013) *Energy Justice in a Changing Climate: Social Equity and Low-Carbon Energy*, London: Zed Books.

Bidwai, P. (2015) 'Modi government cracks down in green NGOs', *Open Democracy*, 17 February.

Bharadwaj, S. (2014) *The Legal Face of Corporate Land Grab in Chhattisgarh,* Bilaspur: Janhit People's Legal Resource Centre.

Bhushan, C, (2017) *India's Energy Transition: Potential and Prospects*, New Delhi: Heinrich Böll Foundation-India & Christian Aid.

Bita, N. (2011) 'Chinese mine giant snaps up 43 NSW farms', *The Australian*, 27 June.

Bloch, M. (2017) 'Australia shuns powering past coal alliance', *Solarquotes blog*, 17 November.

Blondeel, M. and Van der Graaf, T. (2018) 'Toward a global coal mining moratorium? A comparative analysis of coal mining policies in the USA, China, India and Australia', *Climatic Change* 150(1–2), 89–101.

Bloomberg (2019) 'Trump likes fossil fuels but investors don't', *MINING[DOT]COM*, 15 May. www.mining.com/web/trump-likes-fossil-fuels-investors-dont/ Accessed: 1 July 2019.

Bloomberg News (2017) 'World's No. 1 miner sees bigger role for carbon capture systems' *Bloomberg*, 7 December.

Blyton, G., Heitmeyer, D. and Maynaard, J. (2004) *Wannin Thanbarran: A History of Aboriginal and European Contact in Muswellbrook and the Upper Hunter Valley*, Muswellbrook: Muswellbrook Shire Aboriginal Reconciliation Committee.

Bond, P. (2004) 'Water commodification and decommodification narratives: Pricing and policy debates from Johannesburg to Kyoto to Cancun and back', *Capitalism, Nature, Socialism* 15(1), 7–25.

BP (2019) 'India's energy challenge', New Delhi: British Petroleum. http://advertisementfeature.cnn.com/2019/bp-india/, accessed 1 August 2019.

BP Energy Outlook (2018) *BP Energy Outlook 2018 edition* www.bp.com/.../energy-outlook/bp-energy-outlook-2018.pdf, accessed 1 April 2020.

Brändlin, A.-S. (2016) 'Clash in German forest as red line is crossed', *Deutsche Welle*, 1 December.

Breakfree (2016) 'May 3–15, 2016: On six continents, thousands of people took bold action to break free from fossil fuels'. https://breakfree2016.org Accessed 1 August 2019.

Brown, B. and Spiegel, S. (2017) 'Resisting coal: Hydrocarbon politics and assemblages of protest in the UK and Indonesia', *Geoforum* 85, 101–111.

Brown, G. and Sovacool, B. (2017) 'The presidential politics of climate discourse: energy frames, policy, and political tactics from the 2016 primaries in the United States', *Energy Policy* 111, 127–136.

Bryant, G. (2016) 'Creating a level playing field? The concentration and centralisation of emissions in the European Union Emissions Trading System'. *Energy Policy* 99, 308–318.

Bündnis Heimat und Zukunft (n.d.) *Bündnis Heimat und Zukunft*. www.Heimatzukunft.de, accessed 25 August 2019.

Bryant, G. (2019) *Carbon Markets in a Climate Changing Capitalism*, Cambridge: Cambridge University Press.

Buchan, D. (2012) *The Energiewende – Germany's Gamble*, Oxford: Oxford Institute for Energy Studies.

Burke, P., Best, R. and Jotzo, F. (2019) 'Closures of coal-fired power stations in Australia: local unemployment effect', *Australian Journal of Agricultural and Resource Economics* 63(10), 142–165.

Burkett, P. and Foster, J. (2006) 'Metabolism, energy, and entropy in Marx's critique of political economy', *Theory and Society* 53, 109–156.

Burrant, S. R. (ed.) (1987) *East Germany: A Country Study*, Washington, DC: Library of Congress.

Business Standard (2018) 'Budget 2018 to be historical; railway's capital investment to triple: Goyal', *Business Standard*, 21 January.

Cahill, D. and Beder, S. (2005) 'Regulating the power shift: The state, capital and electricity privatisation in Australia', *Journal of Australian Political Economy* 55, 5–22.

Carbon Disclosure Project (2019) *Corporates Step-Up Climate Action: CDP India Annual Report 2018*, New Delhi: CDP.

Carbon Disclosure Report (2016) *Out of the Starting Blocks: Tracking Progress on Corporate Climate Action*, London: CDP.

Carbon Market Watch (2010a) 'Supercritical coal projects violate Kyoto Protocol (Newsletter #7)', *Carbon Market Watch*, 22 March.

Carbon Market Watch (2010b) *CDM Watch Newsletter*, 10 September, Brussels: CMW.

Carl, J. (2015) 'The Causes and Implications of India's Coal Production Shortfall', in Thurber, M. C. and Morse, R. K. (eds) *The Global Coal Market*, Cambridge: Cambridge University Press.

Carle, J. (2015) *Climate Change Seen as Top Global Threat*, London: Pew Research Centre.

Carney, M. (2015) 'Breaking the tragedy of the horizon – climate change and financial stability', Governor of the Bank of England. Speech to Lloyds of London, 29 September.

Carrington, D. (2014a) 'Can Narendra Modi bring the solar revolution to India?', *The Guardian*, 30 September.

Carrington, D. (2014b) 'India will be renewables superpower, says energy minister', *The Guardian*, 1 October.

Carrington, D. and Howard, S. (2015) 'Institutions worth $2.6 trillion have now pulled investments out of fossil fuels', *The Guardian*, 23 September.

Carter, B. and Friemann, G. (2016b) 'Yancoal putting out feelers on Rio's portfolios', *The Australian*, 5 September.

Carter, H. (1974) *The Upper Mooki*, Quirindi: Quirindi and District Historical Society.

Castleden, W. M., Shearman, D., Crisp, G. and Finch, P. (2011) 'The mining and burning of coal: Effects on health and the environment', *Medical Journal of Australia* 195, 333–335.

Catholic University of Leuven (2006) 'Liberalisation, privatisation and regulation in the German electricity sector: Privatisation of public services and the impact on quality, employment and productivity (PIQUE)', Country reports on liberalisation and privatisation processes and forms of regulation, Düsseldorf: Wirtschafts- und Sozialwissenschaftliches Institut (WSI) in der Hans-Böckler-Stiftung.

CCAG (2013) 'RO20/13 Shenhua Watermark Coal Project', Submission to the NSW Planning Assessment Commission, Caroona Coal Action Group. www.ipcn.nsw.gov.au, accessed 1 June 2019.

Centre for Financial Accountability (2018) 'Government-owned banks financed more coal than RE in 2017', 29 June. www.cenfa.org, accessed 1 August 2019.

CFR-LA (2016) *Promise and Performance: Ten Years of the Forest Rights Act in India*, New Delhi: Citizens' Report, Community Forest Rights–Learning and Advocacy.

CFR-LA (2019) *Preliminary Analysis of Parliamentary Constituencies and FRA Potential for 2019 Parliamentary Elections*, New Delhi: Community Forest Resource–Learning and Advocacy.

Chadha, M. (2013) 'India to set up ultra mega solar power plant – 4,000 MW capacity', *Cleantechnica*, 24 September.

Chadha, M. (2014) 'Indian coal producer to invest $80 million in solar, wind energy projects', *Cleantechnica*, 9 October.

Chalmers, S. (2018) 'Rio Tinto completes its exit from coal with the sale of Queensland mine', *ABC News*, 28 March.

Chambers, M. (2016a) 'India's energy chief Piyush Goyal fires up coal hopes', *The Australian*, 11 February.

Chancel, L. et al. (eds) (2016) *World Inequality Report*, Paris: World Inequality Lab.

Chancel, L. and Picketty, T. (2017) 'Indian income inequality, 1922–2014: From British Raj to Billionaire Raj?', WID.world, World Inequality Database Working Paper Series, 2017/11.

Chandrasekaran, K. (2019) 'SoftBank-led energy leads enthusiastic bidding in wind power auction', *Energy World: The Economic Times,* 6 February.

Charis C. and Smith, R. (2018) 'Thousands of students skip school to attend strikes for climate action', *news.com*, 30 November.

Chatterjee, P. (2008) 'Democracy and economic transformation in India', *Economic and Political Weekly* 43(16), 53–62.

Chatterjee, P. (2011) *Lineages of Political Society: Studies in Postcolonial Democracy*, New York: Columbia University Press.

Chazan, G. (2016) 'Eon and RWE sue German government over nuclear shutdown', *The Financial Times*, 16 March.

Chazan, G. and Foy, H. (2016) 'Vattenfall offloads German lignite mines to Czech consortium', *The Financial Times*, 18 April.

Chemmencheri, S. (2013) 'Decentralisation, participation and boundaries of transformation: Forest Rights Act, Wayanad, India', *Commonwealth Journal of Local Governance* 12 (May).

Chemmencheri, S. (2015) 'State, social policy and subaltern citizens in Adivasi India', *Citizenship Studies* 19 (3–4), 436–449.

Chikkatur, A., Sagar, A. and Sankar, T. (2009) 'Sustainable development of the Indian coal sector', *Energy* 34, 942–953.

China Shenhua Energy Company Limited (2014) *Embracing a Green Energy Future Interim Report 2014*, Beijing: Shenhua Group.

Choudhury, C. (2015) 'Not Just a Coal Block', *Peoples Archive of Rural India*, 2 January. https://ruralindiaonline.org/articles/not-just-a-coal-block-hasdeo-arand, accessed 15 May 2017.

Choudhury, C. (2019) 'If we give the Hasdeo forest, where will we go? Jainandan Porte on mining protests in Chhattisgarh', *The Caravan: A Journal of Politics and Culture* 25 February. https://caravanmagazine.in/, accessed 14 April 2019.

Chowdhari, H. (2018) 'BHP wants carbon to be priced: What investors need to know', *Kalkine Media*, 22 October.

Chubb, P. (2014) *Power Failure: The Inside Story of Climate Politics under Rudd and Gillard*, Melbourne: Schwartz Publishing.

Clark, P. (2014) 'German plea to Sweden over threat to coal mines', *The Financial Times*, 25 November.

Clark, P., Crouch, D. and Vasagar, J. (2014) 'German plea to Sweden over threat to coal mines', *The Financial Times*, 25 November.

Clean Energy Finance Corporation (2017) 'CEFC reaches 1GW solar milestone with finance across 20 large scale solar projects', 15 December, Canberra: CEFC.

Clean Energy Wire (2018) 'E.ON CEO says postponing Germany's 2020 climate goal is "appropriate"', 23 January.

Climate Institute (2017) *Climate of the Nation: Australian Attitudes on Climate Change*, Sydney: Climate Institute.

Coghlan, O. (2018) 'Campaigners are taking the government to court on climate change, and they need our support', *Friends of the Earth Ireland*, 7 May. www.foe.ie, accessed 1 August 2019.

Colvin, M. (2008) 'NSW Govt brushes off calls for independent catchment study', *PM*, 19 August.

Comptroller and Auditor General, India (2012) *Performance Audit of Coal Block Allocation*. www.prsindia.org, accessed 1 August 2019.

Connect for Effect (2012) Aboriginal Cultural Heritage Values Assessment Report: Proposed Shenhua Watermark Project NSW, Prepared by Connect for Effect for Hansen Bailey and Shenhua Watermark Coal PTY Ltd.

Connor, L. (2016a) *Climate Change and Anthropos: Planet, People and Places*, Abingdon: Routledge and Earthscan.

Connor, L. (2016b) 'Energy futures, state planning policies and coal mine contests in rural New South Wales', *Energy Policy* 99, 233–241.

Connor, L., Freeman S. and Higginbotham, N. (2009) 'Not just a coalmine: Shifting grounds of community opposition to coal mining in Southeastern Australia', *Ethnos* 74(4), 490–513.

Constable, T. (2019) 'Using Australian coal to power hydrogen's future', *Minerals Council of Australia*, 22 January.

Coorey, P. (2018) 'David Littleproud and the post-Barnaby Joyce evolution of the Nats', *Australian Financial Review*, 7 June.

Corbridge, S. (2002). 'The continuing struggle for India's Jharkhand: Democracy, decentralisation and the politics of names and numbers', *Commonwealth Comparative Politics* 40(3), 55–71.

Cornell, A. (2018) 'The competitive advantage of climate risk awareness' *Bluenotes: ANZ Bank*, 28 October.

Costello, P. (2006) 'Address to the Energy Supply Association of Australia dinner', Parliament House, Canberra, 10 October. www.petercostello.com.au, accessed 1 August 2019.

Cox, L. and Morton, A. (2019) 'Great Barrier Reef outlook now "very poor", Australian government review says', *The Guardian*, 30 August.

Crabtree, J. (2018) 'The staggering rise of India's super-rich', *The Guardian*, 10 July.

Crutzen, P. and Stoermer, E. (2000) 'The "Anthropocene"', *Global Change Newsletter* 41, 17–18.

Cubby, B. and Wilkinson, M. (2009) 'Chinese coalminer to buy up farms', *Sydney Morning Herald*, 22 July.

Daley, M. (2015) 'Traditional owners of our land set to join blockade of shenhua mine if approvals are met', *The Big Smoke*, October 15.

Darby, M. (2016) 'India shelves coal mining target on weak demand', *Climate Home News*, 2 September.

Darby, M. (2019) 'Germany ready to join global phase-out alliance: environment minister', *Climate Change News*, 15 March.

Das, S. R. (2015) 'As India Faces Energy Shortage, Tribal Protests Pose Threat to Fresh Coal Allocations in Chhattisgarh', *NDTV*, 28 January 28. www.ndtv.com/india-news/as-india-faces-energy-shortage-tribal-protests-pose-threat-to-fresh-coal-allocations-in-chhattisgarh-734917, accessed 15 May 2017.

Das Gupta, S. (2009) 'Accessing nature: Agrarian change, forest laws and their impact on an Adivasi economy in colonial India', *Conservation & Society* 7(4), 227–238.

Dave, V. and Jai, S. (2017) 'Gujarat drops 4,000-Mw coal power project', *Business Standard*, 8 May.

DEBRIV – Deutscher Braunkohlen-Industie-Verein (2015) *Braunkohle in Deutschland 2014. Daten und Fakten*. www.braunkohle.de/4-0-Zahlen-und-Fakten.html, accessed 26 November 2015.

Deccan Chronicle (2014) 'Coal is king and extremely important element in developing India: SC', *Deccan Chronicle,* 26 August. www.deccanchronicle.com, accessed 4 April 2019.

Della Bosca, H. and Gillespie, J. (2018) 'The coal story: Generational coal mining communities and strategies of energy transition in Australia', *Energy Policy* 140, 734–740.

DeLuca, M. and Peeples, J. (2002) 'From public sphere to public screen: Democracy, activism, and the "violence" of Seattle'. *Critical Studies in Media Communication* 19(2), 125–151.

Denholm, D. (2001) 'Squatting', in Davison, G., Hirst, J. and Macintyre, S. (eds) *Oxford Companion to Australian History Revised Edition*, Melbourne: Oxford University Press, 610–611.

Denman, E. (2012) 'Strategic Regional Land Use Policy released, but few happy', *ABC News*, 19 September.

Dent, C. (2014) *Renewable Energy in East Asia: Towards a New Developmentalism*, London: Routledge.

Deutsche Bank (2013) 'Deutsche Bank on 7th position of the world's "greenest" banks', Press Release, 2 April.

Deutscher Bundestag (2019) Entwurf eines Strukturstärkungsgesetzes Kohleregionen, (Coal Regions Structural Strengthening Bill), Bill 19/13398, 23 September.

Dhar, A. (2015) 'Adani to develop 10000MW solar parks in Rajasthan', *The Hindu*, 10 September.

DiW Berlin (2018) *Die Beendigung der energetischen Nutzung von Kohle in Deutschland*, Berlin: Deutsches Institut für Wirtschaftsforschung.

Doherty, B. (2012) 'Political indecision strangles India's coal industry', *The Sydney Morning Herald,* 8 May.

Doherty, B. (2018) 'Australia only nation to join US at pro-coal event at COP24 climate talks', *The Guardian*, 11 December.

Donaldson, D. (2014) 'Victorian anti-protest laws passed amid outcries from public gallery', *The Guardian*, 12 March.

Doshi, V. (2016) 'India accused of muzzling NGOs by blocking foreign funding', *The Guardian*, 24 November.

Dostal, J. (2015) 'The Pegida movement and German political culture: Is right-wing populism here to stay?' *The Political Quarterly* 86(4), 523–531.

DPI (2009) *Department of Primary Industry Annual Report.* Sydney: NSW Government.

Dubash, N., Khosla, R., Kelkar, U. and Lele, S. (2019) 'India and climate change: Evolving ideas and increasing policy engagement', *Annual Review of Environment and Resources* 43, 395–424.

Dubash, N. K. and Rajan, S. C. (2001) *The Politics of Power Sector Reform in India*, Washington, DC: World Resources Institute.

Duchêne, F. (1990) 'Less of More Than Europe? European Integration in Retrospect', in Crouch, C. and Marquand, D. (eds) The Politics of 1992: Beyond the Single European Market, Oxford: Basil Blackwell, 9-22.

Duménil, G. and Lévy, D. (2004) *Capital Resurgent: Roots of the Neoliberal Revolution*, Cambridge, MA: Harvard University Press.

Duménil, G. and Lévy, D. (2013) *The Crisis of Neoliberalism*, Cambridge, MA: Harvard University Press.

Dunlap, R. and McCright, A. (2011) 'Organised climate change denial', in Dryzek, J. et al (eds) *The Oxford Handbook of Climate Change and Society*, Oxford: Oxford University Press, 145–162.

Durrant, D. (1990) *Quirindi 1966–1990: Years of Change*, New South Wales: Quirindi Newspaper Company

Durrant, D. (1994) *Quirindi in the Nineteenth Century: How a Town Began*, Quirindi: Quirindi Newspaper Company.

Dutta, R. (2019) '"Govt Cares for Neither Tribals Nor Forests": Lawyer Ritwick Dutta'. www.bloombergquint.com/quint/supreme-court-tribal-forest-land-eviction-order-2019-general-elections, accessed 29 May 2019.

Eckersley, R. (2015) 'Australian democracy and climate politics for the long term', *Meanjin* 74(3), 140–145.

EDGAR (2016a) 'CO_2 time series 1990–2014 per capita for world countries', in *Emissions Database for Global Atmospheric Research*, Brussels: EU Science Hub.

EDGAR (2016b) 'CO2 time series 1990–2014 per region/country', Emissions Database for Global Atmospheric Research, Brussels: EU Science Hub.

Egenter, S. and Wehrmann, B. (2019) 'Germany to quit coal by 2038, under commission proposal', *Climate Home News*, 26 January.

European Environment Agency (2016) *Case Study 3: Germany: Declaration by German Industry and Trade on Global Warming Prevention*, Brussels: EEA.

IEA (2002) *Energy Policies of IEA Countries: Germany – 2002 Review*, Paris: International Energy Agency.

EIA (2019) 'Carbon Dioxide Emission Factors for Coal', US Energy Information Administration. www.eia.gov/ Accessed 1 August 2019.

Ende Gelände (2016) 'Ende Gallende 2016 Mobilisation', Video (English Version): https://vimeo.com/162285020, accessed 1 February 2020.

Energy Australia (n.d.) 'How South Australia is leading the way in renewable energy', Press Release, Adelaide: Energy Australia.

Energy Transitions Commission (2016) *Shaping Energy Transitions*, London: Energy Transitions Commission and SystemIQ.

Energy Transitions Commission (2019) 'Who We Are'. www.energy-transitions.org/who-we-are, accessed 1 August 2019.

Energy World (2016) 'Legal war over, WBPDCL to begin coal mining ops by Dec', *The Economic Times*, 29 July.

Engels, F. (1975/1876) 'The Part Played by Labour in the Transition from Ape to Man', in Marx, K. and Engels, F. *Collected Works*, New York: International Publishers.

Environmental Defenders Office (EDO) (n.d.) *Caroona Coal Action Group Inc v Coal Mines Australia Pty Ltd and Minister for Mineral Resources*, NSW EDO. www.edonsw.org.au/caroona, accessed 13 July 2016.

Environmental Defenders Office (EDO) (2016) *Upper Mooki Landcare Inc v Shenhua Watermark Coal Pty Ltd and NSW Minister for Planning*, NSW EDO, February. www.edonsw.org.au/upper_mooki_landcare_group_v_shenhua_and_the_nsw_minister_for_planning, accessed 13 July 2016.

Environmental Defenders Office (EDO) (2019a) 'Landmark legal win for climate and community', EDO, Sydney. www.edonsw.org.au/gloucester_climate_win, accessed 1 June 2019.

Environmental Defenders Office (EDO) (2019b) *Veronica 'Dolly' Talbott as a member of Gomeroi Traditional Custodians v Minister for the Environment*. NSW EDO. www.edonsw.org.au/gomeroi_shenhua, accessed 27 August 2019.

Escobar, A. 2012. *Encountering Development: The Making and Unmaking of the Third World*. Princeton: Princeton University Press.

ET Bureau (2015) 'Indian coal allocation scam: Congress threatens to hit back at PM Narendra Modi from foreign soil', *The Economic Times*, 18 April.

ET Bureau (2015) 'Congress threatens to hit back at PM Narendra Modi from foreign soil', *Economic Times,* 18 April.

ET Bureau (2017) 'Germany provides support of Euro 200 million for India's Efficient Energy Programme', *The Economic Times*, 10 March.

ET Bureau (2018) 'ET GBS 2018: India will soon leapfrog to cutting-edge rail technology, says Piyush Goyal', *The Economic Times*, 25 February.

ETI (2018) 'Energy Transitions Commission India launched', 15 February. www.teriin.org/sites/default/files/2018-03/ETC-India-launch-15Feb2018.pdf, accessed 1 August 2019.

Euracoal (2015) *Coal Industry across Europe*, Brussels: European Association for Coal and Lignite.

European Commission (2011) 'Emissions trading: Commission welcomes vote to ban certain industrial gas credits', Press Release, 21 January, https://europa.eu/rapid/press-release_IP-11-56_en.htm.

European Environment Agency (2007) *Case study 3: Declaration by German Industry and Trade on Global Warming Prevention (1995) and Updated and Extended Declaration by German Industry and Trade on Global Warming Prevention (1996)*, Brussels: EEA.

Evans, G. (2018) 'Coal remains Australia's energy foundation and has a competitive future', *Australasian Mining Review*, 29 May.

Evershed, N. and Knaus, C. (2019) 'Mining sector met Ministers every week over four years', *The Guardian*, 22 April.

Expert Group (2014) *Final Report; Expert Group on Low-Carbon Strategies for Inclusive Growth*, New Delhi: Planning Commission.

Faber, D. et al. (2017) 'Trump's electoral triumph: Class, race, gender, and the hegemony of the polluter-industrial complex', *Capitalism, Nature, Socialism* 28(1), 1–15.

Fabra, N., Matthes, F., Newberry, D. and Colombier, M. (2015) *The Energy Transition in Europe: Lessons from Germany, France and Spain*, Brussels: Centre on Regulation in Europe.

Fabra, N., Matthes, F. C., Newbery, D., Colombier, M., Mathieu, M. and Rüdinger, R. (2015) *The Energy Transition in Europe: Initial Lessons from Germany, the UK and France: Towards a Low Carbon European Power Sector*, Brussels: Centre on Regulation in Europe (CERRE).

FAO (2019) *The State of Food Security and Nutrition in the World, FAO with IFAD, UNICEF, WFP and WHO*, Rome: Food and Agriculture Organisation.

Feenberg, A. (2002) *Transforming Technology: A Critical Theory Revised*, Oxford: Oxford University Press.

Feenberg, A. (2010) *Between Reason and Experience: Essays in Technology and Modernity*, Cambridge, MA: MIT Press.

Feigenbaum, A., Frenzel, F. and McCurdy, P. (2013) *Protest Camps*, London: Zed Books.

Fickling, D. (2016) 'China's coal cap will bite', *Bloomberg*, 23 September.

Fischer, S. (2016) 'Die deutsche Energiewende in der Europapolitik', in Böttger, K. and Jopp, M. (eds) *Handbuch zur deutschen Europapolitik*, Berlin: Nomos Velag.

Fisher, C. (1983) 'The Joint Coal Board and the Market 1946–1982', Law and Politics of Industrial Relations Project, Monograph Discussion Series, Research School of Social Sciences, Australian National University.

Fitzgerald, A. (2001) *Mining Agreements: Negotiated Frameworks in the Australian Minerals Sector* Chatswood, NSW: Prospect Media.

FMEAE (2015) *The Energy of the Future: Fourth "Energy Transition" Progress Report – Summary*, Berlin: The Federal Ministry for Economic Affairs and Energy.

Focus-Online (2011) 'Energiewende als groβes Experiment', *Focus Online*, 10 June.

Fogarty, D. (2011) 'Carbon credits for India coal power plant stoke criticism', *Reuters Africa*, 12 July.

Forsa. Gesellschaft für Sozialforschung und statistische Analyse mbH (2013) *Die Lausitzer und die Braunkohle. Meinungen und Einstellungen der Bürger*. https://cottbus.igbce.de/vanity/renderDownloadLink/58954/59008, accessed 25 August 2019.

Förster, F. (1968) *Senftenberger Revier 1890–1914. Zur Geschichte der Niederlausitzer Braunkohlenindustrie vom Fall des Sozialistengesetzes bis zum Ausbruch des ersten Weltkrieges*, Bautzen: Domowina-Verlag.

Förster, F. (1990) *Um Lausitzer Braunkohle. 1849–1945*, Bautzen: Domowina-Verlag.

Förster, F. (1996) *Verschwundene Dörfer. Die Ortsabbrüche des Lausitzer Braunkohlenreviers bis 1993*, Bautzen: Domowina-Verlag.

Fossil Free Deutschland (2015) 'In the space of just ten weeks …', 2 December, https://gofossilfree.org/de/in-the-space-of-just-10-weeks/.

Franke, A. (2015) 'German union to protest against coal tax plans on April 25', *S&P Global – Platts*, 17 April.

Franke, S., Hackforth, J. and Hayforth, L. (2017) 'Arbeitsplätze in der ostdeutschen Braunkohle: Strukturwandel im Interesse der Beschäftigten frűhzeitig einleiten', *DIW Wochenbericht* 6(7), 115–122.

Fraune, C. and Knodt, M. (2018) 'Sustainable energy transformations in an age of populism, post-truth politics, and local resistance', *Energy Research and Social Science* 43, 1–7.

Freed, J. (2006) 'BHP up-beat on Gunnedah coal', *The Sydney Morning Herald*, 18 February.

Freese, B. (2005) *Coal: A Human History*, London: William Heinemann.

Friedman, T. (2000) *The Lexus and the Olive Tree*, New York: Harper Collins.

Fuller, K. and Ingall, J. (2012) 'Strategic agricultural land use', *ABC New England North West*, 13 September.

Furlong, C. and Haydar, N. (2018) 'NSW government renews Shenhua Watermark coal mine lease in Liverpool Plains', *ABC News*, 19 July.

Gabriel, K. (1985) *A Coal Basin in Queensland: The Future of the Bowen Basin*, Monograph Series No 13, Townsville: James Cook University.

Gadgil, M. and Guha, R. (1992) *The Fissured Land: An Ecological History of India*, Berkeley: University of California Press.

Galligan, B. (1989) *Utah and Queensland Coal: A Study in the Micro Political Economy of Modern Capitalism and the State*, St Lucia: University of Queensland Press.

Gammage, B. (2011) *The Biggest Estate on Earth: How Aborigines Made Australia*, Sydney: Allen & Unwin.

Garnaut, R. (2008) *The Garnaut Climate Change Review: Final Report*, Cambridge: Cambridge University Press.

Garvey, P. (2019a) 'WA ditches carbon offset rules', *The Australian*, 15 March.

Garvey, P. (2019b) 'EPA backflip shows where the power lies', *The Australian*, 16 March.

Garvey, P. and Williams, P. (2019a) 'Resource chiefs add to backlash over mine ban', *The Australian*, 16 February.

Garvey, P. and Williams, P. (2019b) 'Billions at risk in clamp on carbon', *The Australian*, 8 March.

Ghatak, A. R. (2017) 'Modi and Adani: old friends laying waste to India's environment', *Climate Home News*, 27 June.

Ghosh, D. (2018) 'Risky fieldwork: The problems of ethics in the field', *Energy Research and Social Science* 45, 348–354.

Global Investor Group on Climate Change (2018) 'Climate Initiatives Platform', REF. http://climateinitiativesplatform.org/index.php/Global_Investor_Coalition_on_Climate_Change_(GIC).

Goering, L. (2017) '8 in 10 people now see climate change as "Catastrophic Risk": Survey' *Reuters*, 24 May.

Goldenberg, S. (2013) 'Just 90 companies caused two-thirds of man-made global warming emissions', *The Guardian*, 21 November.

Goodall, H. (1995) 'New South Wales', in McGrath, A. (ed.) *Contested Ground: Australian Aborigines under the British Crown*, Sydney: Allen & Unwin, 55–120.

Goodall, H. (2008) *Invasion to Embassy: Land in Aboriginal Politics in New South Wales, 1770–1972*, Camperdown: Sydney University Press.

Goodman, J. (2008) 'The minerals boom and Australia's "resource curse"', *Journal of Australian Political Economy* 61, 201–220.

Goodman, J. (2009) 'From global justice to climate justice? Justice ecologism under global warming', *New Political Science* 31(2), 499–515.

Goodman, J. (2016) 'The climate dialectic in energy policy: Germany and India compared', *Energy Policy, Special Issue on Coal, Climate and Development* 99, 184–193.

Goodman, J. and Rosewarne, S. (2015) 'Slowing Uranium in Australia: Lessons for Urgent Transition beyond Coal, Gas and Oil.' in Princen, T., Manno, J. and Martin, P. (eds), *Ending the Fossil Fuel Era*, Cambridge, MA: The MIT Press, 193–222.

Government of Chhattisgarh (2017) *A Treasure Trove for Minerals*, Raipur: Mineral Resources Department.

Government of Chhattisgarh (2019) 'Coal Deposits in Chhattisgarh', Mineral Resources Department. http://chhattisgarhmines.gov.in/en/coal, accessed 1 June 2019.

Government of Germany (2019) 'Final Report, Commission on Growth, Structural Change and Employment, Federal Ministry for Economic Affairs and Energy', Berlin.

Government of India (2008) 'National Action Plan on Climate Change', New Delhi.

Government of India (2012) 'Twelfth Five-Year Plan 2012–2017: Faster, More Inclusive and Sustainable Growth', New Delhi.

Government of India (2015) 'India's Intended Nationally-Determined Contribution', New Delhi.

Gramsci, A. (1971) *Selections from the Prison Notebooks*, London: Lawrence and Wishart.

Gray, D. (2019) 'BHP joins Bill Gates in CO_2 war', *The Sydney Morning Herald*, 6 March.

Green, F. (2018) 'Anti-fossil fuel norms', *Climatic Change* 150, 103–116

Greenpeace (2016) 'EPH - Braunkohledeal. Spekulative Wette auf die ungewisse Zukunft der Braunkohle'. www.greenpeace.de/sites/www.greenpeace.de/files/publications/eph-braunkohledeal-layout.pdf, accessed 25 August 2019.

Greenpeace India (2011) *Elephant in the Room: A Case Study on Human-Elephant Conflict in the Hasdeo-Arand and Mandraigarh Coalfields in Chhattisgarh*, New Delhi: Greenpeace.

Greenpeace India (2012) *How Coal Mining Is Trashing Tigerland*, New Delhi: Greenpeace.

Griffiths, L. (2017) 'Adani's $200m, 140MW Whyalla solar project gets the go ahead', *news.com.au*, 27 September.

Groll, S. (ed) (2017) 'Protests: A broad alliance with staying power', in *Coal: Facts and Figures on a Fossil Fuel*, Second Edition, Berlin: Heinrich Böll Stiftung.

GroundXero (2018) 'In Conversation with Adivasi Poet Jacinta Kerketta', *GroundXero, Adivasi Resurgence*, 18 January. www.adivasiresurgence.com/conversation-adivasi-poet-jacinta-kerketta/, accessed 4 April 2019.

Gruenspecht, H. (2019) *The US Energy Sector: recent and continuing challenges*, Washington, DC: Brookings Institute.

Grüne Liga (n.d.) 'Lausitzer Braunkohle'. www.lausitzer-braunkohle.de, accessed 25 August 2019.

Gupta, A. and Ferguson, J. (eds) (1997) *Culture Power Place: Explorations in Critical Anthropology*, Durham and London: Duke University Press.

Gupta, D. and Paul, B. (2018) 'Chhattisgarh's "No-Go Area" for Coal Mining Faces the Prospect of Being Opened Up', *The Wire*, 5 October. https://thewire.in, accessed: 14 April 2019.

Gupta, S. (2003) 'India, CDM and Kyoto Protocol', *Economic and Political Weekly*, 11 October.

Hager, C. and Steffe, C. (eds) (2016) *Germany's Energy Transition: A Comparative Perspective*, London: Palgrave Macmillan.

Hannan P. (2015a) 'Climate change: NSW Farmers Association changes policy, calls for fossil fuels transition', *Sydney Morning Herald*, 16 July.

Hannam, P. (2015b) 'Big coal accused of land grab', *The Sydney Morning Herald*, 17–18 January.

Hannam, P. (2015c) 'Giant Shenhua Watermark coal mine wins federal approval from Environment Minister Greg Hunt', *Sydney Morning Herald*, 8 July.

Hannam, P. (2018) 'Land-clearing codes remade', *The Sun Herald*, 11 March.

Hannam, P. (2019) 'Emissions keep rising off back of pollution', *The Sydney Morning Herald*, 1 March.

Hannam, P. and Latimer, C. (2018) '"Solar tsunami" coming to Australia as NSW accelerates approvals', *The Sydney Morning Herald*, 7 February.

Hanrieder, W. F. (1989) *Germany, America, Europe: Forty Years of German Foreign Policy*, New Haven: Yale University Press.

Harlan, S., Pello, D., Timmons Roberts, J., Bell, S., Holt, W. and Nagel, J. (2015) 'Climate Justice and Inequality', in Dunlap, R. and Brulle, R. (eds) *Climate Change and Society: Sociological Perspectives*, Oxford: Oxford University Press, 127–163.

Harraway, D. (2015) 'Anthropocene, capitalocene, plantationocene, chthulucene: Making kin', *Environmental Humanities* 6, 159–165.

Harvey, D. (2004) The 'new' imperialism: Accumulation by dispossession', *Socialist Register* 40, 63–87.

Harvey, D. (2005) *A Brief History of Neoliberalism*, Oxford: Oxford University Press.

Harvey, F. (2017) 'US switches focus of its Bonn event from clean energy to fossil fuels', *The Guardian*, 11 November.

Hastie, H. and Latimer, C. (2019) 'EPA buckles under pressure from WA govt, oil and gas sector', *WAToday*, 15 March.

Hayden, M. E. (2015) 'India seeks to balance development with need for clean energy'. www.latimes.com/world/asia/la-fg-india-modiclimate-20151202-story.html, accessed 30th April 2016

Heed, R. (2014) 'Tracing anthropogenic carbon dioxide and methane emissions to fossil fuel and cement producers 1854–2010', *Climatic Change* 122, 229–241.

Henkel, G. (2014) *Das Dorf. Landleben in Deutschland – gestern und heute*, Bonn: Bundeszentrale für politische Bildung.

Hewett, J. (2019) 'How the EPA was brought to heel', *The Australian Financial Review*, 15 March, 2.

Higginbotham, N., Freeman, S., Connor, L. and Albrecht, G. (2010) 'Environmental injustice and air pollution in coal affected communities, Hunter Valley, Australia', *Health & Place* 16, 259–266.

Hildyard, N. (2016) *Licensed Larceny: Infrastructure, Financial Extraction and The Global South*, Manchester: Manchester University Press.

Hillebrand, R. (2013) 'Climate protection, energy security, and Germany's policy of ecological modernisation', *Environmental Politics* 22(4), 664–682.

Hirschman, A. (1965) 'Obstacles to development: A classification and a quasi-vanishing act', *Economic Development and Cultural Change* 13(4), 385–393.

Hirschman, A. (1981) 'The Rise and Decline of Development Economics', in *Essays in Trespassing – Economics to Politics and Beyond*, Cambridge: Cambridge University Press, 1–24.

Hobson, J. (1902) *Imperialism: A Study*, New York: James Pott & Co.

Hockenos, P. (2015) 'The history of the *Energiewende', Clean Energy Wire*, 22 June.

Hoffmann V. H. (2007) 'EU ETS and investment decisions: the case of the German electricity industry', *European Management Journal* 25(6), 464–474.

Hogan, B. (2015) *The Life Saving Potential of Coal. How Australian Coal Could Help 82 Million Indians Access Electricity*, Melbourne: Institute of Public Affairs.

Hospers, G.-J. (2004) 'Restructuring Europe's rust-belt: The case of the German Ruhrgebeit', *Intereconomics* 39(3), 147–156.

Howard, E. (2015) 'Hague climate change judgement could inspire a global civil movement', *The Guardian,* 25 June.

Human Rights Watch (1999) *The Enron Corporation: Corporate Complicity in Human Rights Violations*, New York: Human Rights Watch.

Hutton, D. (2013) *Mining the Queensland Way*, Brisbane: At A Glance Pty Ltd.

Iannucci, E. (2019) 'Santos eyes solar power in South Australia', *Mining Weekly*, 19 June.

IANS bc/vd (2018) 'India's excess power capacity an aberration, should export: Minister', *Web India*, 13 February.

Iannucci, E. (2019) 'BHP invests in Canadian firm removing CO_2 from air', *Mining Weekly,* 5 March.

IEA (2012) *Coal Information 2012*, Paris: International Energy Agency.

IEA (2018) *Coal Information 2018*, Paris: International Energy Agency.

IEA Clean Coal Centre (2018) *Annual Review 2018*, Paris: International Energy Agency.

IMF Survey (2016) *Evolution Not Revolution: Rethinking Policy at the IMF*, Washington, DC: International Monetary Fund.

Inamdar, N. (2014) '7 things you wanted to know about "Coalgate"', *Business Standard*, 16 October.

India Brand Equity Foundation (2016) 'Power sector in India – solar, renewable and wind energy sectors'. www.ibef.org, accessed 1 June 2019.

India Infoline News Service (2015) 'Government opens a new chapter in coal sector', 1 January. www.indiainfoline.com, accessed 1 June 2019.

Indian Express (2014) 'Adani to resume mining after pact with Chhattisgarh villagers', *Express News Service,* 3 September. https://indianexpress.com, accessed 1 June 2019.

Institute of Rural Management Anand (2009) *State of the Panchayati Raj Report 2008-09*, New Delhi: Ministry of Panchayati Raj.

International Directory of Company Histories (1992) *Directory: Vol. 5*, Detroit: St. James Press and Gale Pubishing.

International Energy Agency (2011) *World Energy Outlook*, Paris: IEA.

International Energy Agency (2012a) *CO_2 Emissions from Fuel Combustion*, Paris: IEA.

International Energy Agency (2012b) *World Energy Outlook*, Paris: IEA.

International Energy Agency (2012c) *Trace Element Emissions from Coal*, Paris: IEA.

International Energy Agency (2015) *Global Energy Outlook*, Paris: IEA.

International Energy Agency (2017) *Global Energy Outlook*, Paris: IEA.

International Energy Agency (2018a) *Global Energy Outlook*, Paris: IEA.

International Energy Agency (2018b) *Coal Information Overview*, Paris: IEA.

Incropera, F. (2016) *Climate Change: A Wicked Problem: Complexity and Uncertainty at the Intersection of Science, Economics, Politics, and Human Behavior*, New York: Cambridge University Press.

Insurance Journal (2018) 'Swiss Re no longer offers Re/Insurance with more than 30% coal exposure', *Insurance Journal,* 3 July.

Intergovernmental Panel on Climate Change (IPCC) (2018) *Global Warming of 1.5DegC*, Geneva: Intergovernmental Panel on Climate Change.
International Energy Agency (1982) *Coal Prospects and Policies in IEA Countries: 1981 Review*, Paris: IEA.
International Energy Agency Governing Board Meeting (1979) 'Principles for IEA Action on Coal', 21–22 May, in IEA (1982) *Coal Prospects and Policies in IEA Countries: 1981 Review*, Paris: IEA.
International Energy Agency (2012) *Coal Information (2012 edition)*, Paris: IEA.
International Energy Agency (2014) *Coal Information (2014 edition)*, Paris: IEA.
International Energy Agency (2015) *Coal Information (2015 edition)*, Paris: IEA.
International Finance Corporation (2019) 'Across India, solar brings more than light', Photo Essay, January. www.ifc.org, accessed 1 June 2019.
IPCC (2014) *Climate Change 2014: Synthesis Report*, Geneva: Intergovernmental Panel on Climate Change.
Irfan, U. (2014) 'History of lignite mining in Germany: How East Germany cleaned up dirty power', *Climate Wire*, 3 November.
Jafry, T. (ed.) (2014) *Routledge Handbook of Climate Justice*, London: Routledge.
Jafry T. (ed.) (2018) *Routledge Handbook of Climate Justice*, London: Routledge.
Jai, S. (2016) 'Govt opens up coal sector beyond Coal India monopoly', *Business Standard*, 17 March.
Jain, A. (2018) 'Indian coal power faces long-term headwinds', *Bloomberg NEF*, 11 December.
Jamasmie, C. (2019) 'BHP injects $6 million into emissions reduction company', *Mining.com*, 4 March.
Janda, M. (2017) 'BHP set to leave World Coal Association, threatens Minerals Council withdrawal', *ABC News*, 19 December.
Jänicke, M. and Jacob, K. (2004) 'Lead markets for environmental innovations: A new role for the nation state', *Global Environmental Politics* 4(1), 29–46.
Jayakumar, P. B. (2018) 'Solar investments pouring into India', *Business Today*, 13 March.
Jingjing, H., Nelson, M. and Stephens, J. D. (2008) 'Decommodification and activation in social democratic policy: Resolving the paradox', *Journal of European Social Policy* 18(1), 5–20.
Joseph, K. L. (2010) 'The politics of power: Electricity reform in India', *Energy Policy* 38 (1), 503–511.
Karp, P. (2018) 'Coalition backbenchers unite to lobby for coal under the banner of Monash Forum', *The Guardian*, 3 April.
Karp, P. and Evershed, N. (2018) 'Coal lobby ads biggest third party political expenditure in Australia', *The Guardian*, 1 February.
Kelly, M. (2019) 'Call to revoke approval for Shenhua Watermark's proposed mine on the Liverpool Plains', *Sydney Morning Herald,* 1 May.
Kemfert, C. (2017) 'Germany must go back to its low-carbon future', *Nature* 549, 26–27.
Kennedy, A. (2017) *Environmental Justice and Land Use Conflict: The Governance of Mineral and Gas Resource Development*, Abingdon: Routledge.
Ker, P. (2016a) 'Coking coal deal frenzy has further to go, says new Foxleigh mine owner', *The Australian Financial Review*, 5 September.
Ker, P. (2016b) 'New coal faces look familiar', *The Australian Financial Review*, 15 October.
Ker, P. (2017) 'Shenhua to continue with Liverpool Plains coal project despite $262m NSW buyback', *Australian Financial Review*, 12 July.
Kerketta, J. (2016) *Angor, Poems in Hindi and English*, Kolkata: Adivaaani.

KfW (n.d.) 'India. Finding ways for socially responsible, climate friendly growth', Press Release, New Delhi: KfW Development Bank. www.kfw-entwicklungsbank.de, accessed 1 June 2019.

King, E. (2014) 'India PM Modi targets "saffron" revolution for solar energy', *Climate Change News,* 9 June.

Kirkwood, I. (2008) 'Chinese giant's $600m coal bid', *Newcastle Herald,* 28 July.

Kiro (2018) 'The State's Violent Response to Tribal Discontent Is Fuelling the Pathalgadi Movement', *The Wire,* 29 June. https://thewire.in/, accessed 14 April 2019.

Kleiner, J. P. (2013) 'Old Comrade Coal: Lignite Mining in the GDR', *The GDR Objectified,* Blog, 13 April. https://gdrobjectified.wordpress.com/, accessed 1 June 2019.

Kohli, A. (2007) 'State, business, and economic growth in India', *Studies in Comparative International Development* 42(1), 87–114.

Kohli, K. (2012) *Countering Coal: Community Forest Rights and Coal Mining Regions in India*, Bengaluru: Kalpvriksh and Greenpeace.

Kohli, K. (2019) *Historical Injustice and 'Bogus' Claims: Large Infrastructure, Conservation and Forest Rights in India*, New Delhi: Heinrich-Böll-Stiftung.

Kohli, K. and Gupta, D. (2017) *Mapping Dilutions in a Central Law (2017): A Comparative Analysis of Rules Made under the Right to Fair Compensation and Transparency in Land Acquisition, Rehabilitation and Resettlement (RFCTLARR) Act, 2013* (Occasional Paper), New Delhi: Centre for Policy Research.

Kohli, K. and Shukla, A. (2016) 'Burying the Law to Make Way for a Coal Mine', *The Wire*, 19 February.

Kopp, R. E., Shwom, R., Wagner, G. and Yuan, J. (2016) 'Tipping elements and climate-economic shocks: Pathways toward integrated assessment', *Earth's Future* 4(8), 346–372.

Kopstein, J. (1997) *The Politics of Economic Decline in East Germany 1945–1989,* Chappel Hill: The University of North Carolina Press.

Koshy, J. (2017) 'Sarguja Mine Expansion Stalled', *The Hindu*, 16 February.

Koshy, J. (2019) 'Aliens in their own lands: when Chhattisgarh's tribals were turned into encroachers', *The Hindu,* 6 April. .

Kössler, G. (2013) 'Die Klimabewegung in Deutschland', in Dietz, M. and Garrelts, H. (eds) *Die internationale Klimabewegung*, Wiesbaden: Springer Fachmedien, 185–204.

Kothari, A., Salleh, S., Escobar, A., Demaria, F. and Acosta, A. (eds) (2019) *Pluriverse: A Post-Development Dictionary*, New York: Columbia University Press.

KPMG (2012) *Yancoal Australia Ltd. China's First Coal Mine in New South Wales and Australia*, Sydney: China Studies Centre, The University of Sydney.

Kremer, E. and Neuhaus, P. (2001) *Bergrecht*, Stuttgart: Kohlhammer.

Krien, A. (2019) 'Part one: Inside the Adani blockade', *The Saturday Paper*, 31 August.

Krishnan, D. S. (2015) 'India's Supreme Court Reinforces Renewable Energy Target for Industry', *WRI India*, 25 June.

Krümmelbein, J., Bens, O., Raab, T. and Anne Naeth, M. (2012) 'A history of lignite coal mining and reclamation practices in Lusatia, Eastern Germany', *Canadian Journal of Soil Science* 92(1), 53–66.

Kuruvilla, C. (2018) '19th-century German church is demolished to make way for coal mining", *Huffington Post*, 10 January.

Lahiri-Dutt, K. (2014) 'Introduction to Coal in India: Energising the Nation', in Lahiri-Dutt, K. (ed.) *The Coal Nation Histories, Ecologies and the Politics of Coal in India*, Farnham, Surrey: Ashgate, 1–36.

Lahiri-Dutt, K. (2017) 'Resources and the politics of sovereignty: The moral and immoral economies of coal mining in India', *South Asia: Journal of South Asian Studies* 40(4), 792–809.

Lahiri-Dutt, K., Krishnan, R. and Ahmad, N. (2012) 'Land acquisition and dispossession: Private coal companies in Jharkhand', *Economic and Political Weekly* 47(6), 39–45.

Lahiri-Dutt, K., Williams, D. and Imam, J. (2014) *Revisiting Coal Cycles in Eastern India: Report of a 2012 Survey*, Canberra: Australian National University Crawford School of Public Policy.

Latimer, C. (2016) 'BHP develop Carbon Capture Knowledge Centre', *Australian Mining*, 8 February.

Latimer, C. and Hastie, H. (2019) 'Big polluters face tough guidelines', *The Sydney Morning Herald*, 8 March.

Lazarus, M. and Van Asselt, H. (2018) 'Fossil fuel supply and climate policy: Exploring the road less taken', *Climatic Change* 150, 1–15.

Lee, M. and Draper, S. (1988) 'The coal industry: The current crisis and the campaign for a National Coal Authority', *The Journal of Australian Political Economy* 23, 45–60.

Lee, T., Markowitz, E., Howe, P., Ko, C. and Leiserowitz, A. (2015) 'Predictors of public climate change awareness and risk perception around the world', *Nature Climate Change*, 5, 1014–1020.

Lenin, V. I. (1916) 'Imperialism, the Highest Stage of Capitalism', in *Selected Works*, Moscow: Progress Publishers.

Lenin, V. I. (1920a) Our Foreign and Domestic Position and Party Tasks, www.marxists .org/archive/lenin/works/1920/nov/21.htm

Lenin, V. I. (1920b) Speech Delivered at the First All-Russia Congress of Mineworkers, www.marxists.org/archive/lenin/works/1920/apr/01.htm

Liverpool Plains Youth (2016) 'Mine your food bowl?' Four Online Videos. www .liverpoolplainsyouth.com/videos, accessed 3 May 2019.

Lloyd, G. (2013) 'Burke's water safeguards to stifle investment: business', *The Australian*, 13 March.

Lock the Gate Alliance (2019) 'About Us'. www.lockthegate.org.au/about_us, accessed 1 August 2019.

Lockwood, A. H., Welker-Hood, K., Rauch, M. and Gottlieb, B. (2009) *Coal's Assault on Human Health*, Washington, DC: Physicians for Social Responsibility.

Lockwood, M. (2014) 'Right-wing populism and the climate change agenda: Exploring the linkages', *Environmental Politics* 27(4), 712–732.

Lockwood, M. (2018) 'Right-wing populism and the climate change agenda: exploring the linkages', *Environmental Politics* 27(4), 712–732.

Lowrey, T. (2017) 'Federal government could finance coal-fired power stations with clean energy funding', *ABC News*, 30 May.

Lucarelli, B. (2015) *Australia's Black Coal Industry: Past Achievements and Future Challenges'*, Working Paper 101, Stanford: Program on Energy and Sustainable Development.

Ludlow, M. (2017) 'Indian energy giant to build $100 million solar plant in Australia', *The Australian Financial Review*, 13 September.

Ludlow, M. (2019) 'Approval restricts coal from new mine to carbon-cutting countries', *The Australian Financial Review,* 30 August.

Luxemberg, R. (1951) *The Accumulation of Capital*, London: Routledge & Kegan Paul.

Macdonald, G. (2010) 'Colonizing processes, the reach of the state and ontological violence: Historizing Australian aboriginal experience', *Anthropologica* 52(1), 49–66.

Macdonald, G. (2017) 'Focussing on creeks: Wiradjuri ecology, sociality and cosmology', *Journal of the Anthropological Society of South Australia* 41, 63–92.

Macdonald-Smith, A. (2016) 'BHP Billiton funds carbon capture research for Chinese steel sector', *The Sydney Morning Herald*, 6 June.

Macdonald-Smith, A. (2019a) 'Carbon rule threatens WA projects', *The Australian Financial Review*, 8 March.

Macdonald-Smith, A. (2019b) 'WA resources projects "face endless court"', *The Australian Financial Review*, 13 March.

Macdonald-Smith, A. (2019c) 'Woodside seeks foreign offsets', *The Australian Financial Review*, 4 May.

Macdonald-Smith, A. (2019d) 'BP says coal demand is stuborly resistant in the face of surging renewables', *Australian Financial Review*, 15 February.

Major, P. (2010) *Behind the Berlin Wall: East Germany and the Frontiers of Power*, Oxford: Oxford University Press.

McCarthy, J. (2019) 'Expansion of Hunter coal mine conditional on Paris agreement', *The Sydney Morning Herald,* 30 August.

McGrath, C. (2019) 'NSW Gloucester Resources Case', *Environmental Law Australia Weblog*. http://envlaw.com.au/gloucester-resources-case/, accessed 1 August 2019.

Macdonald-Smith, A. and Thompson, B. (2019) 'Western Australian to pull zero-carbon ruling', *The Australian Financial Review*, 15 March.

Madhavan, V. (2015) 'Controversy Over Land Acquisition Bill: All You Need to Know', *The Indian Express,* 7 March.

Maier, H. (2002) '"Lauchhammer", "Döbern" und "Ragow". Imaginäre und reale Verknotungen der Niederlausitzer Landschaft in die Elektrizitätswirtschaft des 20. Jahrhunderts', in Bayerl, G. and Maier, D. (eds) *Die Niederlausitz vom 18. Jahrhundert bis heute. Eine gestörte Kulturlandschaft?*, Münster: Waxmann, 149–195.

Malik, A. (2013) 'Coal block controversy: A new round,' *LiveMint,* 18 October.

Malm, A. (2016) *Fossil Capital*, London: Verso.

Manoharan, S. (1974) *The Oil Crisis: the End of an Era*, New Delhi: S. Chand and Co.

Market Forces (2019) *Lending to Coal Mines*, Melbourne: Market Forces.

Marshall, J. (2016) 'Disordering fantasies of coal and technology: Carbon capture and storage in Australia', *Energy Policy* 99, 288–298.

Marx, E. (2015) 'German Greens and moderates mount campaign to end coal use', *E&E News/Climatewire* 7 May.

Massola, J. (2017) 'Minerals Council steps up coal lobbying as AGL calls for end to political gridlock', *The Sydney Morning Herald*, 19 June.

Mathieson, K. (2018) 'Australia asked to join pro-Trump coal alliance', *Renew Economy*, 13 December.

Mathur, A., Turner, A., Leprince-Ringuet, N. (eds) (2018) *Green, Reliable and Viable: Perspectives on India's Shift towards Low-Carbon Energy*, Energy Transitions Commission and The Energy Resources Institute (TERI), New Delhi: CRC Press.

McDonald, M. (2016) 'Bordieu, environmental NGOs and Australian climate politics', *Environmental Politics* 25(6), 1058–1078.

McDonald, M. (2016) 'India to ramp up solar investment in 2017', *Oil Price*, 22 October.

McDuie-Ra, D. and Kikon, D. (2016) 'Tribal communities and coal in Northeast India: The politics of imposing and resisting mining bans', *Energy Policy* 99, 261–269.

McGlade, C. and Ekins, P. (2015) 'The geographical distribution of fossil fuels unused when limiting global warming to 2°C', *Nature* 517, 187–190.

McManus, P. and Connor, L. (2013) 'What's mine is mine(d): Contests over marginalisation of rural life in the Upper Hunter, NSW', *Rural Society* 22(2), 166–183.

McOwan, J. and Thomas, K. (2015) 'Environment minister "stops the clock" on Shenhua assessment, seeks more information on water', *ABC News*, 28 February.

Mehrotra, K. and Witzig, J. (2015) 'Gutam Adani, the millionaire who trots the globe with Narendra Modi', *LiveMint*, 29 May.

Menzies, R. G. (1961) 'Speeches', 15 November, Museum of Australian Democracy, Canberra.

Merritt, J. (2001) 'Wool', in Davison, G., Hirst, J. and Macintyre, S. (eds) *Oxford Companion to Australian History*, Revised Edition. Melbourne: Oxford University Press, 690–691.

Merzian, R. (2018) 'Australia lies low at Katowice as UN scrapes together rules for climate deal', *Renew Economy*, 17 December.

Mez, L. (2012) 'Germany's merger of energy and climate policy', *Bulletin of the Atomic Scientists* 68(8), 22–29.

Meza, E. (2019) 'German cabinet adopts draft law to strengthen mining regions during coal exit', *Clean Energy Wire,* 28 August.

Milman, O. (2015) 'Josh Frydenberg puts "strong moral case" for coal exports to prevent deaths', *The Guardian*, 18 October.

Milman, O. (2018) 'Trump administration scraps Obama-era regulation on coal emissions', *The Guardian,* 22 August.

Milman, O. and Jericho, G. (2016) 'For Tony Abbott, it's full steam ahead on coal, "the foundation of prosperity"', *The Guardian*, 17 July.

Mining Act (NSW) (1992) New South Wales Government, No 29. www.legislation.nsw.gov.au, accessed 1 June 2019.

Mining Regulations (NSW) (2010), New South Wales Government, No 619. www.legislation.nsw.gov.au, accessed 1 June 2019.

Ministry of Rural Development (n.d.) 'About the Ministry', website. https://rural.nic.in/about-us/about-ministry, accessed 4 April 2019.

Ministry of Tribal Affairs (2006) *The Scheduled Tribes and Other Traditional Forest Dwellers (Recognition of Forest Rights) Act 2006 (No.2 of 2007)*, New Delhi: Government of India.

Ministry of Tribal Affairs (2012) *The Scheduled Tribes and Other Traditional Forest Dwellers (Recognition of Forest Rights) Amendment Rules 2012 (GS.R. 669(E))*, New Delhi: Government of India.

Ministry of Tribal Affairs (2013) *Statistical Profile of Scheduled Tribes in India*, New Delhi: Government of India.

Ministry of Tribal Affairs (2018) *Statewise implementation of the Scheduled Tribes and other Traditional Forest Dwellers Rights (Forest Rights Act 2002), as on 31 December 2018*, New Delhi: Ministry of Tribal Affairs.

Mitchell, T. (2011) *Carbon Democracy: Political Power in the Age of Oil*, London: Verso.

Mitchell, G. (2015) 'Greg Hunt makes Shenhua promise after fiery Alan Jones interview', *Sydney Morning Herald*, 16 July.

Mitscherlich, A. (Ed.) (1971) *Hauptworte, Hauptsachen*, München: Piper.

Mohan, V. (2015) 'India calls for a paradigm shift in global attitudes towards climate change', *The Times of India,* 19 January.

Moore, J. (2014a) *The Capitalocene, Part I: On the Nature & Origins of Our Ecological Crisis*, London: Verso.

Moore, J. (2014b) *The Capitalocene, Part II: Abstract Social Nature and the Limits to Capital*, London: Verso.

Moore, J. W. (2015) *Capitalism in the Web of Life: Ecology and the Accumulation of Capital*, London: Verso.

Moore, J. (2016) *Capitalism in the Web of Life: Ecology and the Accumulation of Capital*, London: Verso.

Morrice, E. and Colagiuri, R. (2013) 'Coal mining, social injustice and health: A universal conflict of power and priorities', *Health & Place* 19, 74–79.

Morris, C. and Pehnt, M. (2015) *Energy Transition: The German Energiewende*, Berlin: Henrich Böll Stiftung.

Morton, T. (2014) 'Thousands protest against coal mining, forming 8km human chain in river neisse along German–Polish border', *ABC International Online*, 27 August.

Morton, T. and Müller, K. (2016) 'Lusatia and the coal conundrum: The lived experience of the German Energiewende', *Energy Policy* 99, 277–287.

Moss, T., Becker, S. and Naumann, M. (2015) 'Whose energy transition is it, anyway? Organisation and ownership of the *Energiewende* in villages, cities and regions', *Local Environment* 20(12), 1547–1563.

Ms, N. (2018) 'Coalgate 2.0: The Adani Group reaps benefits worth thousands of crores of rupees as the coal scam continues under the Modi government', *The Caravan: A Journal of Politics and Culture*, 1 March.

Muecke, S. (2013) 'The composition and decomposition of commodities: The colonial careers of coal and ivory', *TEXT Special Issue* 20.

Murphy, J. (2015) 'Hundreds at Harvest anti-mine event', *Northern Daily Leader*, 6 November.

Murphy, J. (2017) 'Shenhua says Watermark mine will go ahead despite buy back', *Northern Daily Leader,* 12 July.

Murphy, K. (2018a) 'Energy guarantee protects coal sector from competition – analysis', *The Guardian*, 2 February.

Murphy, K. (2018b) 'Nationals to debate building of high-efficiency coal plants at federal council', *The Guardian*, 18 August.

Myers, P (2010) 'Coal brings cold comfort on the farm', *Sydney Morning Herald*, 17 April.

Nagarajan, G. (2015) 'Reliance to build 6 gigawatts of solar projects in India', *Renewable Energy World*, 13 February.

Nandi, J. (2018) 'Centre's nod for mining in 170,000 hectares of forest in Chhattisgarh', *Hindustan Times*, 21 March. www.hindustantimes.com/, accessed 14 April 2019.

Napier-Raman, K. (2019) 'Is Queensland returning to the reign of Sir Joh?', *Crikey*, 22 August.

National Green Tribunal (2014) 'Judgement in Sudiep Srivastava v/s Union of India and Ors in Appeal no. 73/2012', 24 March, New Delhi: National Green Tribunal.

National Greenhouse Advisory Panel (1996) *Report on the National Greenhouse Response Strategy*, Canberra: NGAP.

National Institute for Transforming India (NITI) (2017) 'Draft National Energy Policy, National Institution for Transforming India', June, New Delhi: NITI

Navroz, K. Dubash, N., Khosla, R., Kelkar, U. and Lele, S. (2018) 'India and climate change: Evolving ideas and increasing policy engagement', *Annual Review of Environment and Resources* 43, 395–424.

Nawrocki, J. (1981) 'Wenn Braunkohle zu Eis wird', *Die Zeit* 13(3), available online at www.zeit.de/1981/12/wenn-braunkohle-zu-eis-wird, accessed 25 August 2019.

NCCNSW (2016) 'Shenhua court judgment: Liverpool Plains koalas left vulnerable', *New South Wales Nature Conservation Council*, Media Release, 19 February.

Needham, K. (2019) 'Coal industry fears US-China deal', *Sydney Morning Herald,* 22 March.

Nelson, D. (2019) 'India's shift towards low carbon economy'. www.energy-transitions .org/content/indias-shift-towards-low-carbon-energy, accessed 1 August 2019.

Neslen, A. (2014) 'Dutch government ordered to cut carbon emissions in landmark ruling', *The Guardian,* 24 June.

NFF (2016) Climate Policy, National Farmers Federation, November, Canberra. www.nff.org.au/policy/nrm.html, accessed 1 June 2019.

Ng, E. (2016) 'Shenhua Energy raises coal-fired power plant construction budget by 7.5 billion yuan', *South China Morning Post*, 29 August.

Nicholls, W. (1906) *Coal Catechism*, Philadelphia: George W. Jacobs.

Nitzan, J. and Bichler, S. (2009) *Capital as Power: A Study of Order and Creorder*, Oxford: Routledge.

Norgaard, R. B. (1994) *Development Betrayed: The End of Progress and a Coevolutionary Revisioning of the Future*, London: Routledge.

Norman, H. (2015) *'What Do We Want?': A Political History of Aboriginal Land Rights in New South Wales*, Canberra: Aboriginal Studies Press.

NSW DPI (2009) *Annual Report 2008–2009*, Sydney: NSW Department of Planning and Infrastructure.

NSW DPI (2012) *New England North West Strategic Regional Land Use Plan*, Sydney: NSW Department of Planning and Infrastructure.

NSW Government (2007) State Environmental Planning Policy (Mining, Petroleum Production and Extractive Industries), Sydney: New South Wales Government, 29 September.

NSW Government (2015a) 'NSW Planning Assessment Commission Determination Report: Watermark Coal Project', Sydney: Planning Assessment Commission. www.ipcn.nsw.gov.au, accessed 1 June 2019.

NSW Government (2015b) 'Development Consent: Shenhua Watermark', Sydney: Planning Assessment Commission, January 28. www.ipcn.nsw.gov.au, accessed 1 June 2019.

NSW Land and Environment Court (2019) 'Gloucester Resources Limited v Minister for Planning [2019] NSWLEC 7', NSW Case Law, Sydney. www.caselaw.nsw.gov.au/, accessed 1 June 2019.

NSW Minerals Council (2012) *Submission: Draft Strategic Land Use Plans NSW*, Sydney: NSWMC.

O'Connor, J. (1998a) *Natural Causes: Essays in Ecological Marxism*. New York: Guilford Press.

O'Connor, J. (1998b) 'Second Contradiction of Capitalism', in *Natural Causes: Essays in Ecological Marxism*, New York: Guilford Press, 158–177.

O'Connor, M. (1992) 'The system of capitalized nature', *Capitalism Nature Socialism* 3 (3), 94–99.

O'Connor, M. (1994a) 'On the Misadventures of Capitalist Nature', in O'Connor, M. (ed.) *Is Capitalism Sustainable? Political Economy and the Politics of Ecology*, New York: The Guilford Press, 125–151.

O'Connor, M. (1994b) 'The second contradiction of capitalism', *Capitalism Nature Socialism* 5(4), 105–114.

Ong, T. (2015) 'Australian companies sign on for climate change action ahead of the Paris conference', *ABC News*, 5 November.

O'Rourke, M. (1997) *The Kamilaroi Lands: North-Central NSW in the Early 19th Century*, Griffith: Self-published.

Oskarsson, P. (2013) 'Dispossession by confusion from mineral-rich lands in central India', *South Asia: Journal of South Asian Studies* 36(2), 199–212.

Ostry, J. D., Loungani, P. and Furceri, D. (2016) 'Neoliberalism Oversold?', *Finance & Development* (June), 38–41.

Packard, V. (1960) *The Waste Makers*, New York: David Mckay.

Pai, S. and Handoo, B. (2017) 'Coal India raises doubts about its future', *Nikkei Asian Review*, 31 January.

Parajuli, P. (1996) 'Ecological ethnicity in the making: Developmentalist hegemonies and emergent identities in India', *Identities* 3(1–2), 14–59.

Pargal, S. and Banerjee, S. G. (2014) More Power to India: The Challenge of Electricity Distribution, New York: The World Bank.

Parker, L. (2019) 'Kids suing governments about climate: It's a global trend', *National Geographic,* 26 June.

Parkin, B. (2016) 'Daimler's home divests from oil, coal in growing German movement', 18 August.

Parkinson, G. (2018a) 'AGL seeking big wind projects to help replace Liddell', *Renew Economy*, 13 February.

Parkinson, G. (2018b) 'Xenophon's SA Best says 90% renewables by 2030 feasible, but not a target', *Reneweconomy*, 28 February.

Parks, B. and Roberts, J. (2008) 'Inequality and the global climate regime: Breaking the north-south impasse', *Cambridge Review of International Affairs* 21(4), 621–648.

Pascoe, B. (2014) *Dark Emu. Black Seeds: Agriculture or Accident*, Broome: Magabala Books.

Pathak, M. (2015) 'Adani Enterprises, Rajasthan sign deal for 10,000 MW solar project', *LiveMint*, 9 February.

Peace, A., Connor, L. and Trigger, D. (2012) 'Environmentalism, culture, ethnography', *Oceania* 82(3), 217–227.

Pearse, G., McKnight, D. and Burton, B. (2013) *Big Coal: Australia's Dirtiest Habit*, Sydney: NewSouth Publishing.

Pearse, R. (2016) 'Moving targets: Carbon pricing, energy markets and social movements in Australia', *Environmental Politics* 25(6), 1079–1101.

Pearse, R. (2018) *Pricing Carbon in Australia: Contestation, the State and Market Failure*, Oxon: Routledge.

Peiterse, J. (1998) 'My paradigm or yours? Alternative development, post-development, reflexive development', *Development and Change* 2(2), 343–371.

Penney, K. and Cronshaw, I. (2015) *Coal in India*, Canberra: Department of Industry and Science.

Phukan, S. (2015) 'Bills to Auction Mines, Cancelled Coal Blocks Passed in Rajya Sabha', *NDTV*, 20 March. www.ndtv.com/india-news/bill-to-auction-mines-passed-in-rajya-sabha-748223, accessed 13 November 2015.

Pinjarkar, V. (2016) 'What renewables? 16,372MW thermal capacity gets eco nod', *Times of India*, 27 August.

Planning Commission (2008) *Development Challenges in Extremist Affected Areas*, New Delhi: Government of India.

Productivity Commission (1998) *The Australian Black Coal Industry,* Canberra: Productivity Commission.

Plehwe, D. (2014) 'Think tank networks and the knowledge-interest nexus: The case of climate change', *Critical Policy Studies* 8(1), 101–115.

Potter, B. (2019) 'Australian companies urged to disclose climate change risks, ASX says', *The Australian Financial Review*, 7 March.

Prasad, R. (2015) 'Adani Group in pact for 10,000 MW in power park in JV with Rajasthan government', *The Economic Times*, 16 June.

Princen, T., Manno, J. and Martin, P. (2015) *Ending the Fossil Fuel Era*, Cambridge, MA: MIT Press.

Pro Lausitzer Braunkohle e.V. (n.d.) *Pro Lausitz*. www.pro-lausitz.de, accessed 25 August 2019.

PTI (2010) 'Coal India issue price fixed at Rs.245 per share', *The Hindu*, 25 October.

PTI (2012) 'ICVL looking to acquire overseas coal asset by March', *Zee News*, 8 November.

PTI (2016) 'Coal India to set up 600MW solar plants in four states', *Zeebiz*, 4 September.

PTI (2018a) 'Coal India annual production target 630 MT in FY'19: Government', *The Economic Times*, 5 January.

PTI (2018b) 'India should aim for 50 per cent renewable energy by 2030, Piyush Goyal', *Energy World The Economic Times*, 3 February.

PTI (2018c) 'Govt approves opening of coal mining to private sector', *India TV News*, 20 February.

PTI (2018d) 'India needs to make smooth, viable transition from coal: IPCC', *DNA India*, 14 October.

PTI (2019) 'Tata Power Solar launches residential rooftop solution in Kolkata', *Energy World The Economic Times*, 20 March.

Quartz Media (2018) 'Nearly 40% of all new power capacity in India this year is solar'. https://qz.com/, accessed 1 June 2019.

Rangarajan, S., Palaniyappan, D. and Ramachandran, P. (2018) 'National Green Tribunal of India – an observation from environmental judgements', *Environmental and Pollution Research* 25(2), 11313–11318.

Razaghi, A., Fuller, K. and Thomas, K. (2017) 'Investigation into Aboriginal heritage on proposed Shenhua mine site launched', *ABC New England*, 18 January.

Renn, O. (2011) 'The social amplification/attenuation of risk framework: Application to climate change', *Wiley Interdisciplinary Reviews Climate Change* 2 (2), 154–169.

Reserve Bank of Australia (RBA) (2009) *Australia and the Global market for Bulk* Commodities, January Bulletin, Canberra: Reserve Bank of Australia.

Reuters (2016a) 'China's Shanxi gives $142 million for capacity cuts', 6 September.

Reuters (2016b) 'China to cap coal at 55 percent of total power output by 2020: NEA', 7 November.

Reuters (2019) 'Australia's solar, wind boom to power past grid woes in 2019', *Investing.com*, 20 January.

Reynolds, H. (2006) *The Other Side of the Frontier: Aboriginal Resistance to the European Invasion of Australia*, Sydney: UNSW Press.

Richardson, J. (2015) 'Germany could make $2 billion by exporting electricity', *Clean Technia*, 10 November.

Ritchie, H. and Roser, M. (2019) 'CO_2 and Greenhouse Emissions', *Our World in Data*, Online Database. https://ourworldindata.org/co2-and-other-greenhouse-gas-emissions, accessed 1 August 2019.

Robertson, J. (2017) 'Big four banks distance themselves from Adani mines as Westpac rules out loan', *The Guardian*, 28 April.

Rockström, J. and Klum, M. (2015) *Big World, Small Planet: Abundance within Planetary Boundaries*, Stockholm: Max Ström.

Roddan, M. (2019) 'Finance sector fears climate change: APRA', *The Australian*, 21 March.

Rosewarne, S. (1992) 'The Green Accord in Australia', *Capitalism Nature Socialism* 3(1), 11–17.

Rosewarne, S. (1997) 'Marxism, the *Second Contradiction* and socialist ecology', *Capitalism Nature Socialism* 8(2), 99–120.

Rosewarne, S. (2010) 'Meeting the challenge of climate change: The poverty of the economic narrative and market solutions as subterfuge', *Journal of Australian Political Economy* 66, 17–50.

Rosewarne, S. (2016) 'The transnationalisation of the Indian coal economy and the Australian political economy: The fusion of regimes of accumulation?' *Energy Policy* 99, 214–223.

Rostow, W. (1960) *The Stages of Economic Growth: A Non-Communist Manifesto*, Cambridge: Cambridge University Press.

Roy, S. (2002a) 'Enron in India – the Giant's first fall', *Outlook Pacific*, 7 February.

Roy, A. (2002b) 'Shall we leave it to the experts: Enron's power project in India demonstrates who benefits from globalization', *The Nation,* 18 February.

Ryan, L. et al. (2019) 'Colonial Frontier Massacres in Central and Eastern Australia 1788–1930', Website interactive resource, University of Newcastle. https://c21ch.newcastle.edu.au/colonialmassacres/, accessed 1 June 2019.

Ryan, V. (2008) 'Shenhua Moves on NSW', *Australia's Mining Monthly*, 15 August.

Sachs, W. (Ed.). (1992) 'Development: a guide to the ruins', *New Internationalist* June, 1–3.

Said, E. (1994) *Culture and Imperialism*, New York: Vintage.

Saldanha, A. (2018) 'As India's Poor, Tribal Heartland Votes Today, Widespread Unrest over BJP Failure to Settle Land and Forest Claims', *Sabrang,* 20 November. https://sabrangindia.in/, accessed 14 April 2019.

Sale, K. (1996) *Rebels against the Future: The Luddites and Their War on the Industrial Revolution*, New York: Addison-Wesley.

Salleh, A. and Goodman, J. (2013) 'The "green economy": Hegemony and counter-hegemony', *Globalisations* 10(3), 411–424.

Sampson, N. (2015) 'Shenhua Watermark – Gomeroi Traditional Custodians', Submission, PAC, Sydney. www.ipcn.nsw.gov.au, accessed 1 June 2019.

Sant, G. and Gambhir, A. (2015) 'Energy Development and Climate Change', in N. K. Dubash (ed.) *Handbook of Climate Change and India: Development, Politics and Governance*, New York: Routledge, 289–303.

Sarker, D. (2011) 'The implementation of the Forest Rights Act in India: Critical issues', *Economic Affairs* 31(2), 25–29.

Sartor, O. (2018) *Implementing Coal Transitions: Insights from Case Studies of Major Coal-Consuming Economies*, Ahmedabad: IDDRI.

Sartor, O. (2019) *Just Transitions for the Coal Sector Are Going Mainstream, but Policies Also Need to Be Strengthened*, Ahmedabad: IDDRI.

Saurabh (2016) 'Coal India announces 600 MW solar power projects', *Clean Technica*, 12 September.

Saurabh (2018) 'Indian coal mining companies plan $1.6bn solar investment', *Clean Technica*, 17 October.

Schneider, J., Schwarze, S., Bsumek, P. and Peeples, J. (2016) *Under Pressure: Coal Industry Rhetoric and Neoliberalism*, London: Palgrave Macmillan.

Schreurs, M. (2003) 'Divergent paths: Environment policy in Germany, the United States, and Japan', *Environment Science and Policy for Sustainable Development* 45(8), 8–17.

Schwartz, B. (1974) 'Waiting, exchange, and power: The distribution of time in social systems', *American Journal of Sociology* 79(4), 841–871.

Scott, M. (2014) 'Coal to be hardest hit by fossil fuel divestment campaign', *Forbes*, 26 August.

Scott, S., Fruendt, M. and Schöning, S. (2018) 'The citizen-led movement that divested Berlin', *CleanTechnica*, 21 September.

Seetharaman, G. (2015) 'How community rights under the Forest Rights Act could transform the lives of millions of forest dwellers', *The Economic Times*, 9 August. https://economictimes.indiatimes.com, accessed 14 April 2019.

Selby, J. (2019) 'The Trump presidency, climate change, and the prospect of a disorderly energy transition', *Review of International Studies* 45(3), 471–490.

Sengupta, N. (2010) 'Natural resources in indian legal system', *History and Sociology of South Asia* 4(1), 25–39.

Sethi, A. (2011) 'If villagers won't go to town, town will come to villagers', *The Hindu*, 17 January. www.thehindu.com/news/national/other-states/If-villagers-wont-go-to-town-town-will-come-to-villagers/article15521065.ece, accessed 24 June 2019.

Setton, D., Matuschke, I. and Renn, O. (2017) *Social Sustainability Barometer for the German Energiewende 2017: Core Statements and Summary of the Key Findings*, Potsdam.

Sharma, S. (2011) 'Chhattisgarh govt scraps elephant reserve plan for coal mine', *Times of India*, 16 January. https://timesofindia.indiatimes.com, accessed 14 April 2019.

Shearer, C. et al. (2019) 'Global slowdown in coal power investment continues', *Global Energy Monitor*, 27 March. https://endcoal.org/2019/03/, accessed 1 June 2019.

Shearer, C., Mathew-Shah, N., Myllyvirta, L., Yu, A. and Nace, T. (2019) 'Boom and bust 2019: Tracking the global coal plant pipeline,' *Global Coal Plant Tracker*. https://endcoal.org/global-coal-plant-tracker/reports/boom-and-bust-2019/, accessed 1 July 2019.

Shearer, C., Myllyvirta, L., Yu, A., Aitken, G., Mathew-Shah, N., Dallos, G. and Nace, T. (2020) *Boom and Bust 2020: Tracking The Global Coal Plant Pipeline*, New York: Global Coal Tracker.

Shen, L. (2016) 'Here's another big sign the coal industry is burning out', *Fortune*, 21 March. https://fortune.com/2016/03/21/coal-losing-lending-credit/, accessed 1 June 2019.

Shenhua (2013), *Shenhua Watermark Coal Project: Corporate Social Responsibility Report*, Gunnedah: Shenhua.

Sherval, M., Askland, H., Askew, M., Hanley, J., Farrugia, D., Threadgold, S. and Coffey, J. (2017) 'Farmers as modern-day stewards and the rise of new rural citizenship', *Local Environment* 23(1), 100–116.

Shiva, V. (1988) *Staying Alive: Women, Ecology and Development.* London: Zed Books.

Shrestha, P. (2013) 'Indian coal sector needs "urgent" deregulation', *Energy Live News*, 31 May.

Shrivastava, K. S. (2015) 'New Rules to Make FRA Effective', *Down to Earth.* www.downtoearth.org.in/news/new-rules-to-make-fra-effective-38706, accessed 1 June 2015.

Slezak, M. (2016a) 'NSW anti-protest laws an attack on democracy, say legal experts', *The Guardian*, 15 March.

Slezak, M. (2017b) 'Bob Brown wins high court challenge to Tasmania's anti-protest laws', *The Guardian*, 18 October.

Smith, M. (2019) 'China state investment giant quits coal', *The Australian Financial Review*, 20 March.

Smith, P. and Howe, N. (2015) *Climate Change as Social Drama: Global Warming in the Public Sphere*, Cambridge: Cambridge University Press.

Smith-Spark, L. (2018) 'Hambach forest clearance halted by German court', *CNN*, 5 October.

Smyth, J. and Mundy, S. (2017) 'Adani bets on Australian solar as coal battle looms', *The Financial Times*, 4 April.

Sourcewatch (2011) Clean Development Mechanism. www.sourcewatch.org/index.php/Clean_Development_Mechanism, accessed 1 June 2019.

Spegele, B. (2016) 'World news: Beijing to beef up its coal capacity', *The Wall Street Journal*, 8 November.

Spencer, T., Pachouri, R., Renjith, G. and Vorah, S. (2018) *Coal Transition in India*, New Delhi: TERI.

State Investment Promotion Board (2015) Government of Chhattisgarh, List of MOUS. http://industries.cg.gov.in/sipb/pdf/MOU_List_English%20-%202015.pdf, accessed 12 November 2015.

Statistische Ämter des Bundes und der Länder (2014) *Sozialversicherungspflichtig Beschäftigte. Beschäftigte am Arbeitsort nach Geschlecht, Nationalität und Wirtschaftszweigen.* www.destatis.de, accessed 1 June 2019.

Steger, M., Goodman, J. and Wilson, E. (2013) *Justice Globalism: Ideology, Crises, Policy*, London: Sage.

Stern, N. (2007) *The Economics of Climate Change: The Stern Review*, Cambridge: Cambridge University Press.

Stiftung für das sorbische Volk (Ed.) (2009) *Die Sorben in Deutschland*, Bautzen: Lausitzer Druck und Verlagshaus.

Talberg, A., Hui, S. and Loynes, K. (2015) 'Australian climate change policy to 2015: A chronology', Parliamentary Library, Parliament of Australia.

Talukdar, R. (2017) 'Hiding neoliberal coal behind the Indian poor', *Journal of Australian Political Economy* 28, 132–158.

Talukdar, R. (2018) 'Sparking a debate on coal: Case study on the Indian Government's crackdown on Greenpeace', *Cosmopolitan Civil Societies: An Interdisciplinary Journal* 10(1), 47–62.

Tata Power (2018) 'Renewables to power growth', Sustainability Report. www.tatapower.com/pdf/sustainability/sustainability_report-2018.pdf, accessed 1 June 2019.

Taylor, M., Laville, S., Walker, A., Noor, P. and Henley, J. (2019) 'School pupils call for radical climate action in UK-wide strike', *The Guardian,* 16 February.

TERI (2005) *CDM Implementation in India*, New Delhi: The Energy and Resources Institute.

Teske, S. (ed.) (2019) *Achieving the Paris Climate Agreement Goals: Global and Regional 100% Renewable Energy Scenarios*, New York: Springer.

Thaker, J. and Leiserowitz, A. (2014) Shifting discourses of climate change in India', *Climatic Change* 123(2), 107–119.

Thaker, J., Maiker, E. and Leisowitz, A. (2016) 'The role of collective efficacy in climate adaptation in India', *Weather, Climate and Society* 8, 21–34.

Thaker, J., Zhao, X. and Leieserowitz, A. (2017) 'Media use and public perception of global warming in India', *Environmental Communication* 11(3), 353–369.

The Economist (2001) 'Enron's Maharashtra power project continues to spark controversy', The Economist, 11 January.

The Economist (2015) 'Divestment campaigns', *The Economist,* 25 June.

The Energy Resources Institute (TERI) (2018)*'Accelerating India's transition to renewables: Key findings from Energy Transitions Commission India,* 13 February, New Delhi: TERI.

The Land (2013) 'Grassroots farmers have welcomed a move', *The Land*, 14 March.

Thomas, S. (2003) 'The seven brothers', *Energy Policy* 31, 393–403.

Thompson, A. (2019) 'Ex-NSW Labor minister Ian Macdonald and union friend John Maitland's convictions thrown out', *Sydney Morning Herald*, 25 February.

Thompson, B. (2019) 'Butler hits back over WA emissions rules', *The Australian Financial Review,* 30 August.

Thompson, B. and Macdonald-Smith, A. (2019b) 'Scene set for renewed clash over emissions' *The Australian Financial Review* 16 March.

Thompson, F. (2006) 'Handout aims for approval on mine', *Herald,* 13 May.

Thompson, F. (2008) 'Surface tension', *Newcastle Herald,* 30 August.

Thurber, M. and Morse, R. (eds) (2015) *The Global Coal Market: Supplying the Major Fuel for Emerging Economies*, Cambridge: Cambridge University Press.

Timsit, A. (2018) '1.7 million peoples have signed a petition in favour of suing France over climate change inaction,' *Quartz*, 27 December.

Tongia, R. (2003) 'The political economy of Indian power sector reforms', *Program on Energy and Sustainable Development* Working Paper 4, Stanford: Stanford University.

Tongia, R. and Gross, S. (2018) 'Working to turn ambition into reality: The politics and economics of India's turn to renewable power', The Brookings Institute Paper 4, September.

Topping, N. (2019) 'Zero-carbon power: 5 signs that a 100% clean power system is already in sight', We Mean Business Coalition, 11 March.

Türcke, C. (2006) *Heimat. Eine Rehabilitierung*, Springe: Klampen.

Tyfield, D. (2014) '"King coal is dead! Long live the king!": The paradoxes of coal's resurgence in the emergence of global low-carbon societies', *Theory, Culture, Society* 31(5), 59–81.

Tyson, R. (2018) 'Its not over yet, action group warns', *Northern Daily Leader*, 6 September.

United Nations (2019) 'Climate action: 4 shifts the UN chief encourages Governments to make', *UN News*, 12 May.

United Nations Environment Program (UNEP) (2018) *Emissions Gap Report*, New York: UNEP.

United News of India (2018) 'Indian chapter of Energy Transitions Commission launched', *United News of India,* 15 February.

Upadhyay, A. (2016) 'PM Narendra Modi said to plan $3.1 billion for India's solar factories', *The Economic Times*, 18 October.

Urry, J. (2014) 'The problem of energy', *Theory, Culture & Society*, 31(5), 3–20.

Validakis, V. (2013) 'Coal India to acquire $4 billion worth of Australian assets', *Australian Mining*, 16 June.

Vanclay, F. and Endicott, G. (2011). 'The role and functioning of cultural scripts in farming and agriculture', *Sociologia Ruralis* 51(3), 256–271.

Vattenfall Europe Mining AG (2005) Aus Braunkohle wird Energie. Tagebaue Jänschwalde und Cottbus-Nord. Cottbus.

Verghese, G. (2013) 'A Temple of Modern India', *Business Standard News,* 26 February. www.business-standard.com/article/beyond-business/a-temple-of-modern-india-106080701046_1.html, accessed 14 April 2019.

Vidal, J. (2010) 'Rich countries to pay energy giants to build new coal-fired power plants', *The Guardian*, 14 July.

Vincent, E. and Neale, T. (2017) 'Unstable relations: a critical appraisal of indigeneity and environmentalism in contemporary Australia', *The Australian Journal of Anthropology* 28(3), 301–323.

Vishwanathan, S., Garg, A. and Tiwari, V. (2018) *Coal Transition in India: Assessing India's Transition Options*, Ahmedabad: IDDRI.

Vittal, H. and Karmakar, S. (2019) 'A Comprehensive Social Vulnerability Analysis at a National Scale', in Venkataraman, C., Mishra, T., Ghosh, S. and Karmakar, S. (eds) *Climate Change Signals and Response: A Strategic Knowledge Compendium for India*, Singapore: Springer, 162–176.

Von Bismarck, F. (2010) 'Land in Motion – Opencast Restoration and Recultivation in Lusatia', in Kuhn, R. and Scholz, B. (eds) *Bergbaufolgelandschaft. Post-Mining Landscape*, Jovis: Berlin.

Vorrath, S. (2017) 'Adani gets to work on 170MW solar farm in Queensland coal country', *Reneweconomy*, 12 September.

Walker, B. (2016) 'China stokes global coal growth', *China Dialogue*, 23 September.

Wallerstein, I. M. 2005. 'After developmentalism and globalization, what?' *Social Forces*, 83(3), 1263–1278.

Watts, J. (2017) 'Germany's dirty coal mines become the focus for a new wave of direct action', *The Guardian*, 9 November.

Wehrmann, B. (2017) 'Sino-German tandem: Export champions promote global energy transition', *Clean Energy Wire*, 6 July.

Wehrmann, B. (2018) 'Germany's coal exit commission', *Clean Energy Wire*, 13 December.

Wehrmann, B. (2019a) 'German village to be demolished for lignite mine despite coal exit', *Clean Energy Wire*, 15 February.

Wehrmann, B. (2019b) 'German climate law put off as disagreements weigh on governing coalition', *Clean Energy Wire*, 18 February.

Wehrmann, B. (2019c) 'Renewables over take fossil fuels in Germany's annual production for first time', *Clean Energy Wire,* 2 December.

Weibe, K. and Yamano, N. (2016) *Estimating CO_2 Emissions Embodied in Final Demand and Trade*, Paris: OECD.

Wen, P. (2013) 'China mine boss vents concerns', *Sydney Morning Herald*, 24 April.

Wettengel, J. (2019) 'Eastern German coal states welcome proposal phase-out support', *Clean Energy Wire,* 22 August.

Wheelwright, E. L. and Crough, G. (1982) Australia: A Client State, Ringwood: Penguin Books.

Whitbourn, M. (2017) 'Former NSW Labor minister Ian Macdonald found guilty of misconduct in public office', *Sydney Morning Herald,* 7 March.

Wild, F. (2017a) 'Carbon capture and storage – keeping our eyes on the target', *BHP*, 7 February.

Wild, F. (2017b) 'Could China take the lead in CCS', *BHP*, 12 October.

Williamson, J. 2003. 'From reform agenda to damaged brand name: A short history of the Washington Consensus', *Finance & Development* (September), 10–13.

Winestock, G (2015) 'Shenhua Watermark bets on nature to pass next hurdle', *Australian Financial Review*, 18 July.

Wittig, H. (1998) 'Braunkohlen- und Sanierungsplanung im Land Brandenburg', in Pflug, W. (ed.) *Braunkohlentagebau und Rekultivierung. Landschaftsökologie – Folgenutzung – Naturschutz*, Berlin: Springer, 475–486.

Wolf, K. and Kuhn, R. (eds) (2011) *IBA Lausitz 2010. Landschaft erobern, zum Mars reisen, Paradies 2 inszenieren. Internationale Bauausstellung Fürst-Pückler-Land*, Großräschen: IBA Fürst-Pückler-Land.

World Coal Association (2019) 'Reducing CO_2 Emissions'. www.worldcoal.org, accessed 1 August 2019.

World Wildlife Fund (WWF) (2011) 'State Bank of India become signatory to the Carbon Disclosure Project', 21 February.

Worrall, L., Roberts, L., Viswanathan, B. and C. Beaton (2019) *India's Energy Transition: Stranded Coal Power Assets, Workers and Energy Subsidies*, Manitoba: International Institute for Sustainable Development.

Wynn, G. (2016) 'In coal giveaway to Czech energy group, a public-relations problem for a Swedish utility', *IEEFA*, 2 June.

Yeates, C. (2019) 'BHP commits to coal and climate action', *The Sydney Morning Herald*, 6 March, 22.

Ylä-Anttila, T. and Swarnakar, P. (2017) 'Crowding in: How Indian civil society organizations began mobilizing around climate change', *British Journal of Sociology* 68(2), 273–292.

Index

Lightning Source UK Ltd.
Milton Keynes UK
UKHW031056250321
380951UK00008B/266